LOVELESS

THICKER THAN BLACKWATER

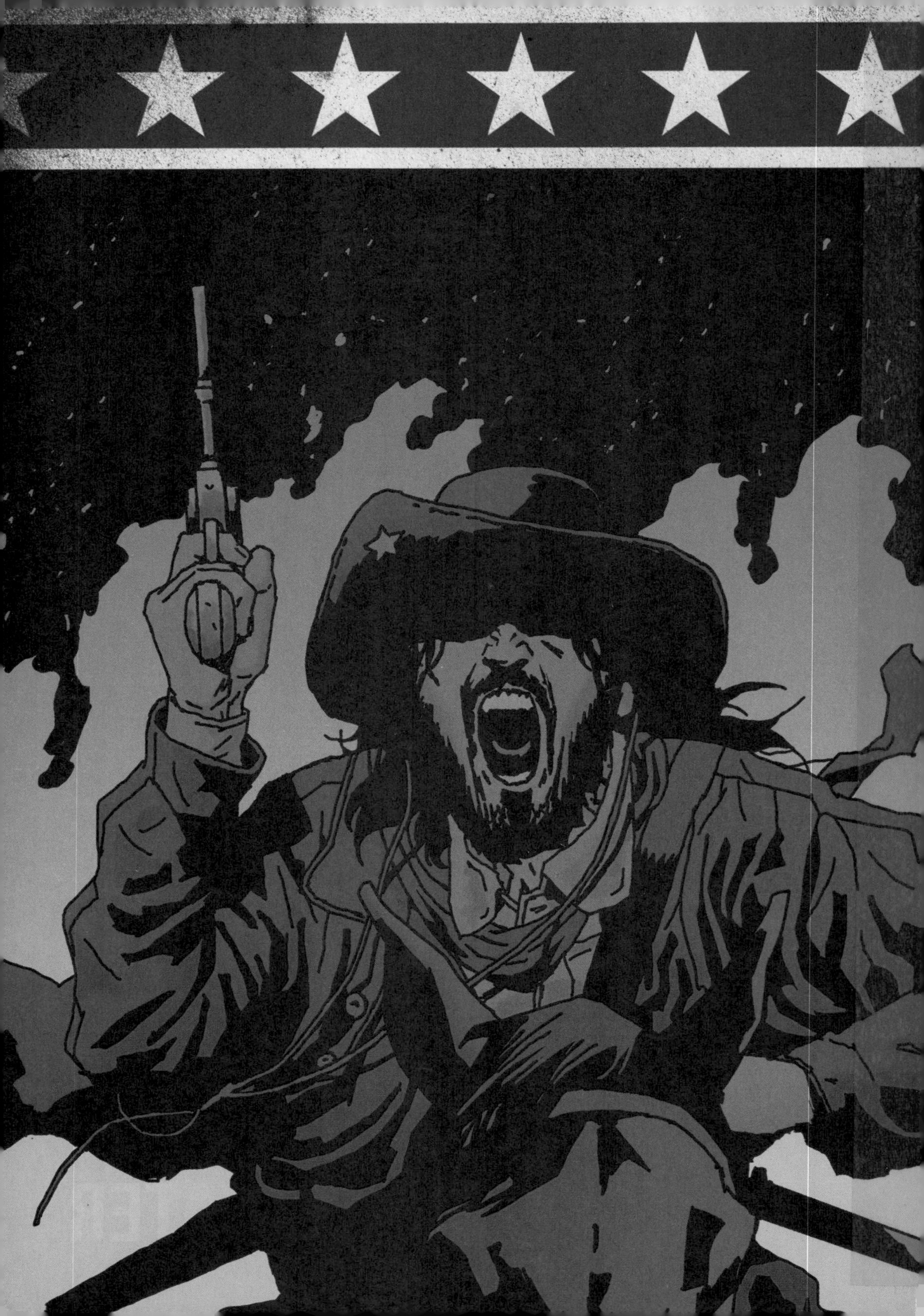

THICKER THAN BLACKWATER

BRIAN AZZARELLO
writer

A PEACE OF IRON   A TICKLE OF BLOOD   WARN DOWN

DANIJEL ZEZELJ
art

THICKER THAN BLACKWATER

MARCELO FRUSIN
art – parts 1 & 2

WERTHER DELL'EDERA
art – parts 3 & 4

PATRICIA MULVIHILL and **MARTIN BRECCIA** colorists
CLEM ROBINS letterer

Original series covers by
MARCELO FRUSIN

Loveless created by
BRIAN AZZARELLO and **MARCELO FRUSIN**

KAREN BERGER
Senior VP-Executive Editor

JOHN CUNNINGHAM
VP-Marketing

WILL DENNIS
Editor-original series

TERRI CUNNINGHAM
VP-Managing Editor

CASEY SEIJAS
Assistant Editor-original series

STEPHANIE FIERMAN
Senior VP-Sales & Marketing

BOB HARRAS
Editor-collected edition

ALISON GILL
VP-Manufacturing

ROBBIN BROSTERMAN
Senior Art Director

HANK KANALZ
VP-General Manager,
WildStorm

PAUL LEVITZ
President & Publisher

JIM LEE
Editorial Director-WildStorm

GEORG BREWER
VP-Design &
DC Direct Creative

PAULA LOWITT
Senior VP-Business &
Legal Affairs

RICHARD BRUNING
Senior VP-Creative Director

MARYELLEN MCLAUGHLIN
VP-Advertising &
Custom Publishing

PATRICK CALDON
Executive VP-Finance
& Operations

JOHN NEE
VP-Business Development

CHRIS CARAMALIS
VP-Finance

GREGORY NOVECK
Senior VP-Creative Affairs

CHERYL RUBIN
Senior VP-Brand Management

JEFF TROJAN
VP-Business Development,
DC Direct

BOB WAYNE
VP-Sales

Cover illustration by Marcelo Frusin.
Logo design by Ken Lopez
Publication design by Brainchild Studios/NYC.

LOVELESS: THICKER THAN BLACKWATER
Published by DC Comics. Cover and compilation
copyright © 2007 DC Comics. All Rights Reserved.

DC Comics, 1700 Broadway, New York, NY 10019
A Warner Bros. Entertainment Company.
Printed in Canada. First Printing.
ISBN: 1-4012-1250-6
ISBN 13: 978-1-4012-1250-6

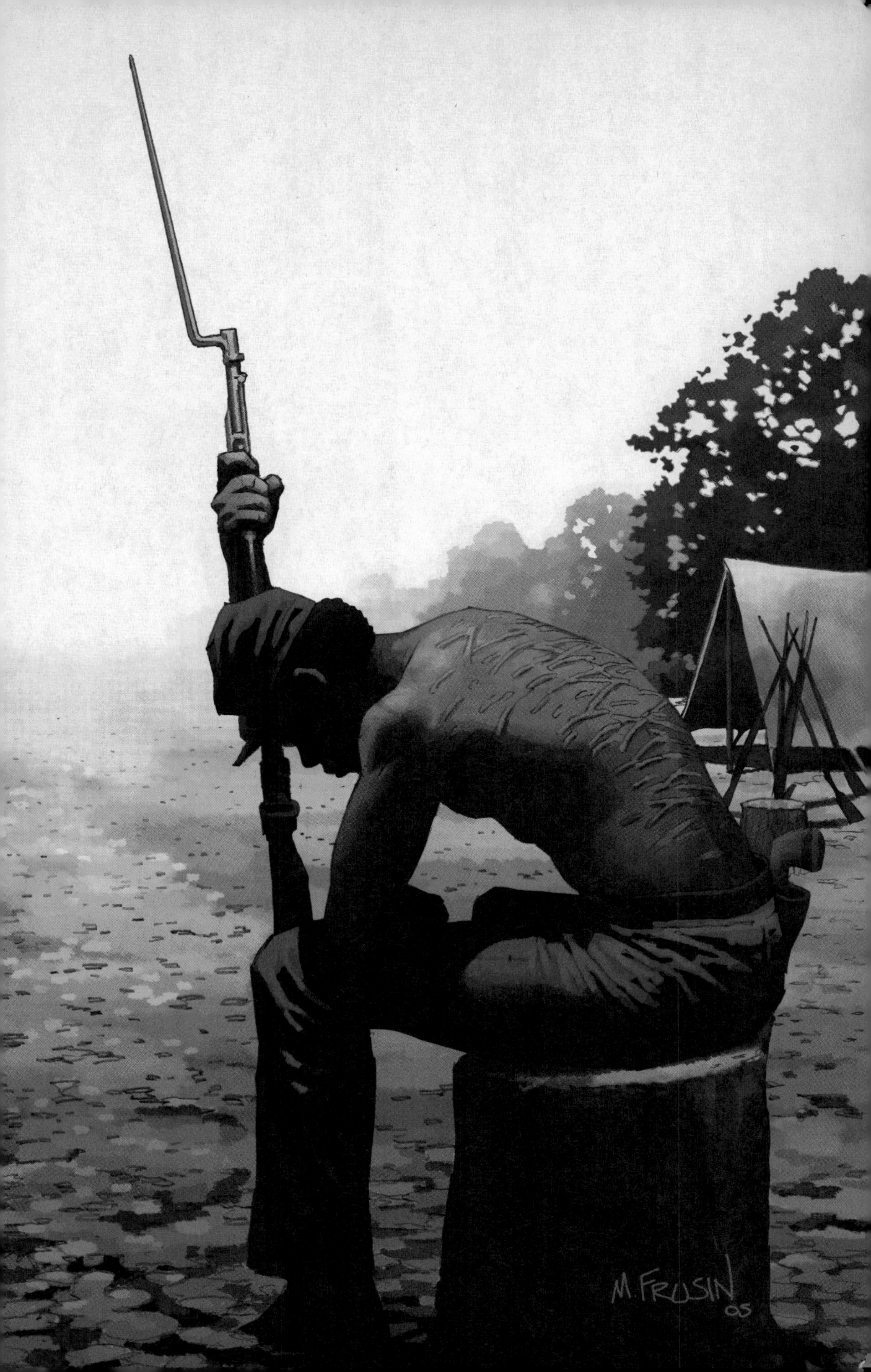
M. FRUSIN
05

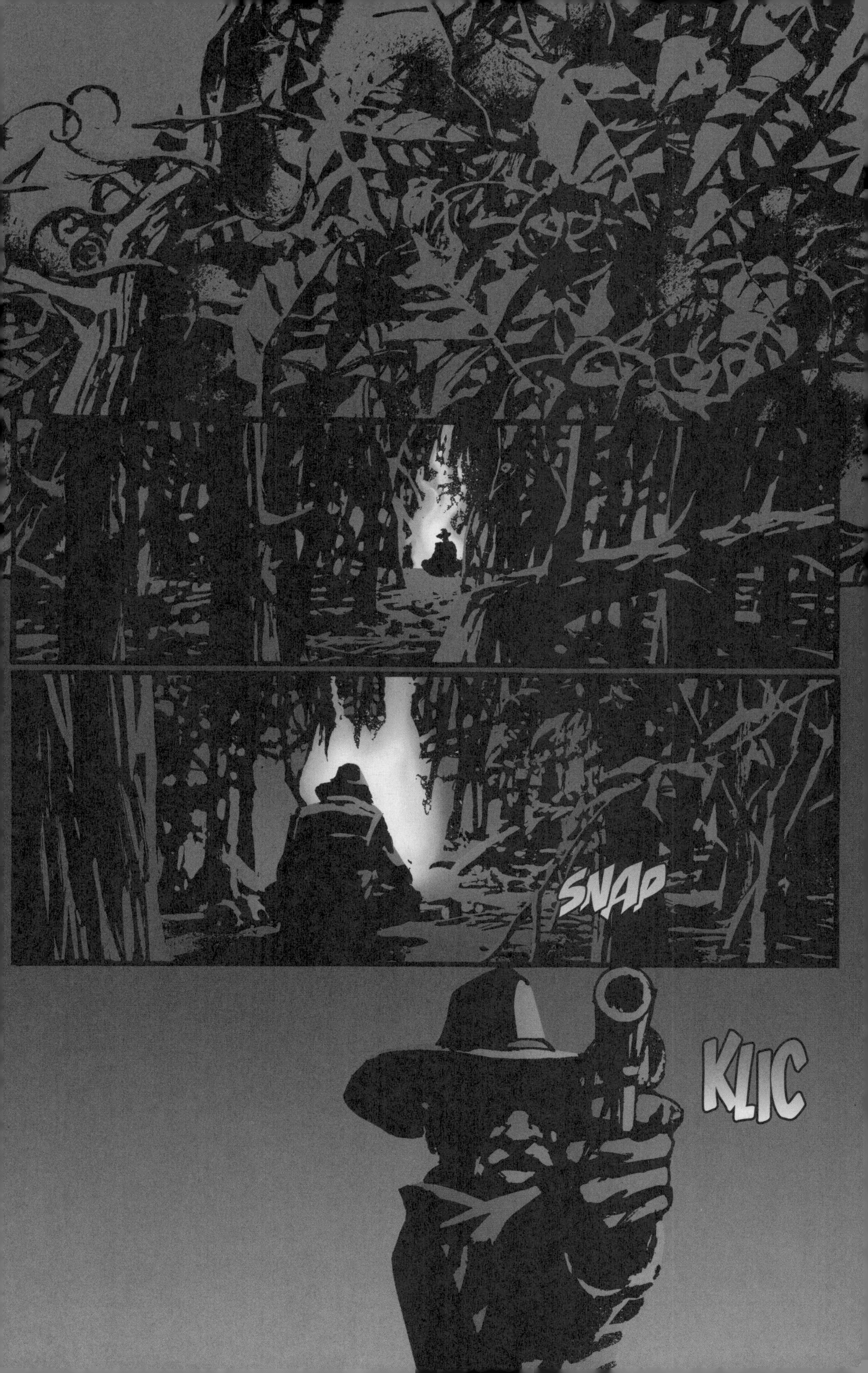
SNAP
KLIC

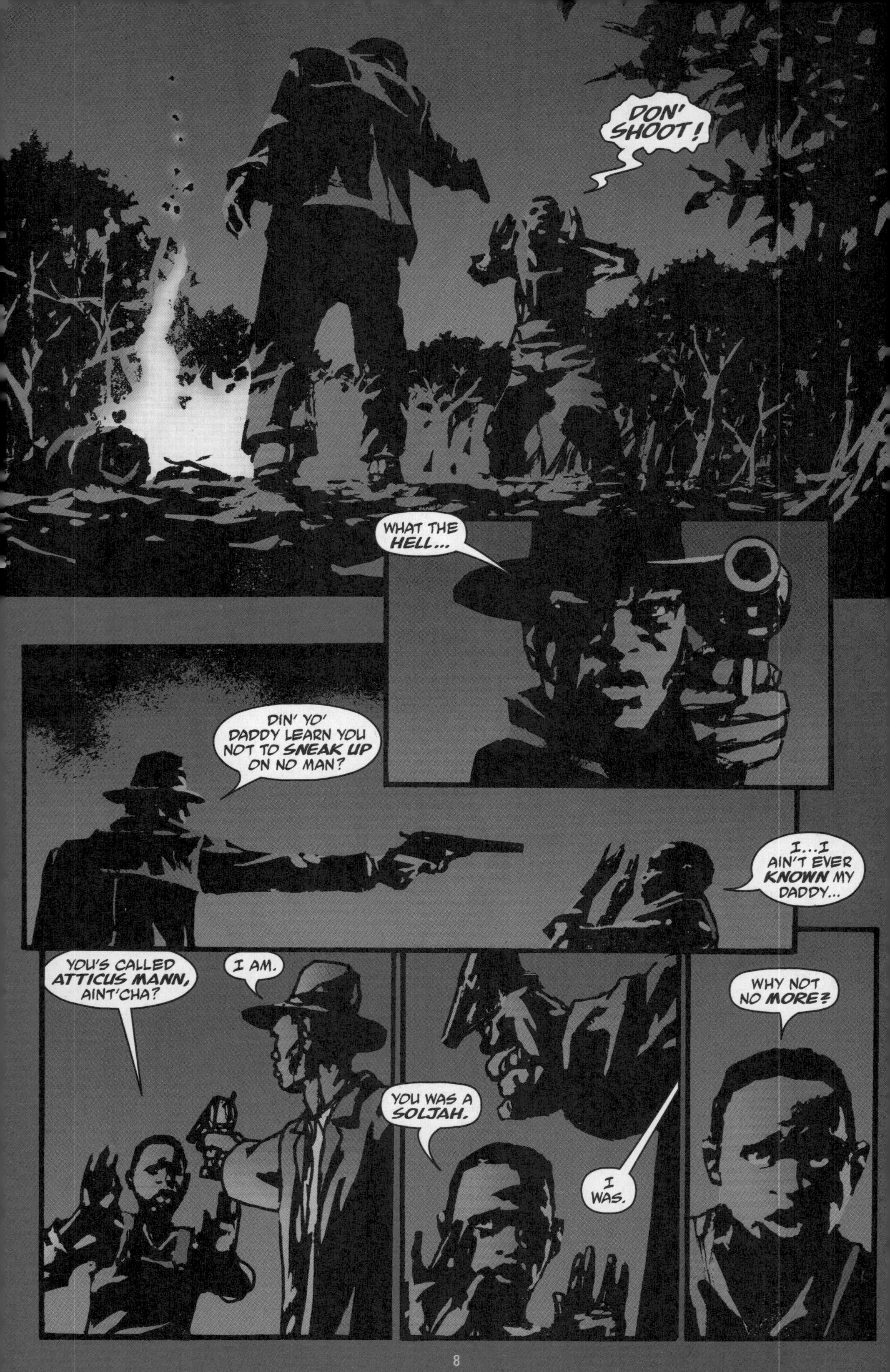
DON' SHOOT!
WHAT THE HELL...
DIN' YO' DADDY LEARN YOU NOT TO SNEAK UP ON NO MAN?
I...I AIN'T EVER KNOWN MY DADDY...
YOU'S CALLED ATTICUS MANN, AINT'CHA?
I AM.
YOU WAS A SOLJAH.
I WAS.
WHY NOT NO MORE?

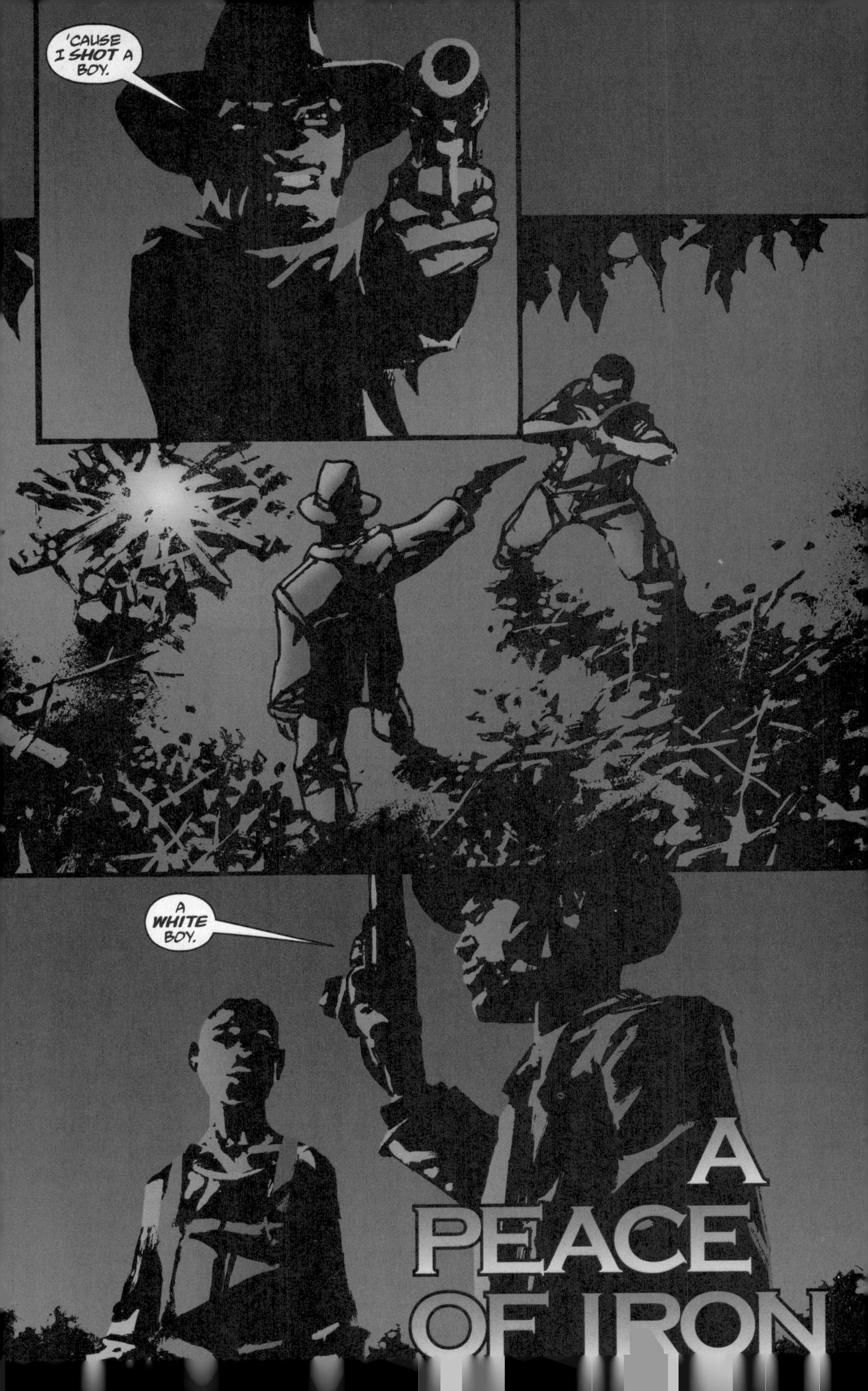
'CAUSE I SHOT A BOY.
A WHITE BOY.
A PEACE OF IRON

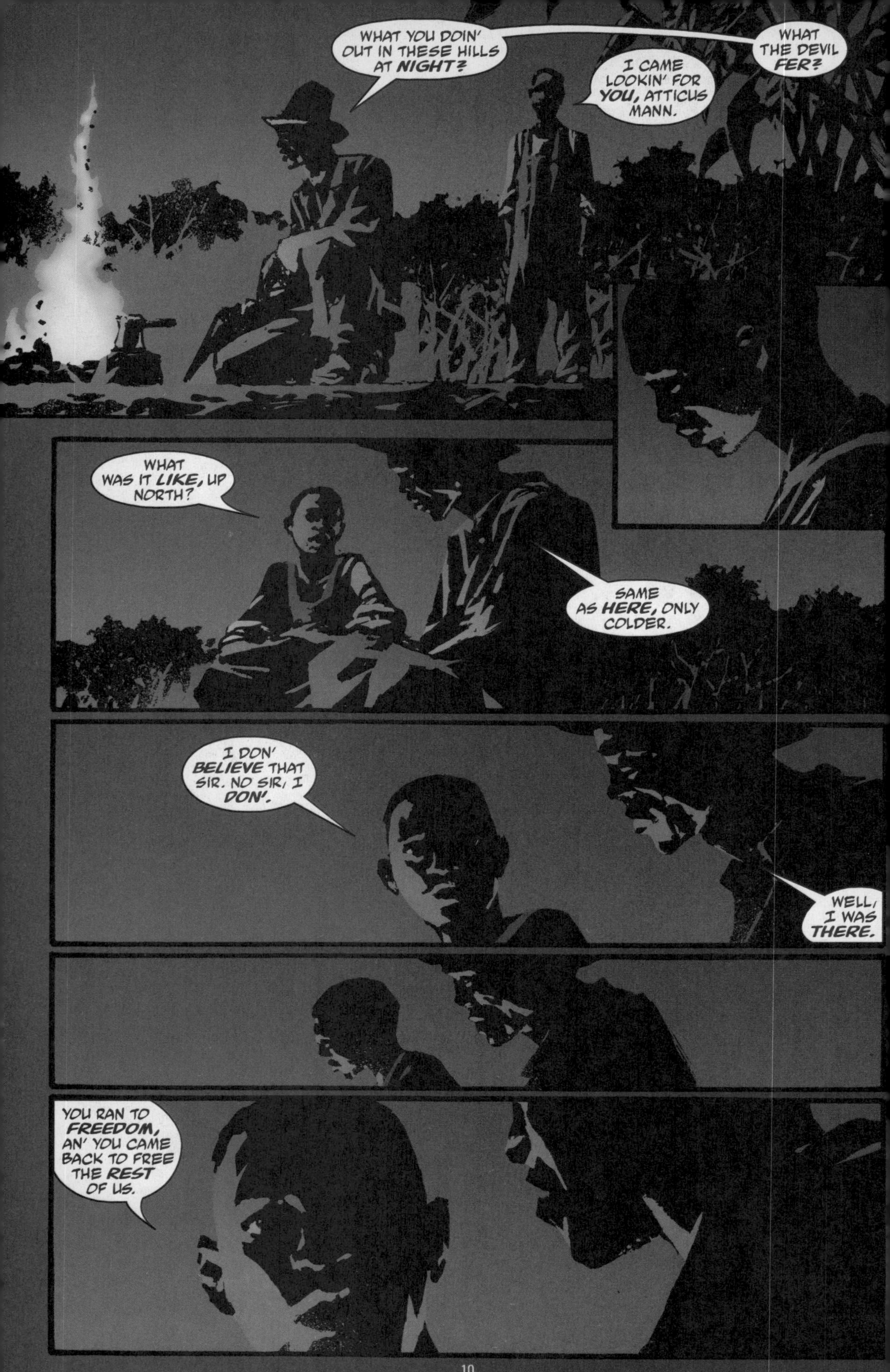
WHAT YOU DOIN' OUT IN THESE HILLS AT NIGHT?
I CAME LOOKIN' FOR YOU, ATTICUS MANN.
WHAT THE DEVIL FER?
WHAT WAS IT LIKE, UP NORTH?
SAME AS HERE, ONLY COLDER.
I DON' BELIEVE THAT SIR. NO SIR, I DON'.
WELL, I WAS THERE.
YOU RAN TO FREEDOM, AN' YOU CAME BACK TO FREE THE REST OF US.

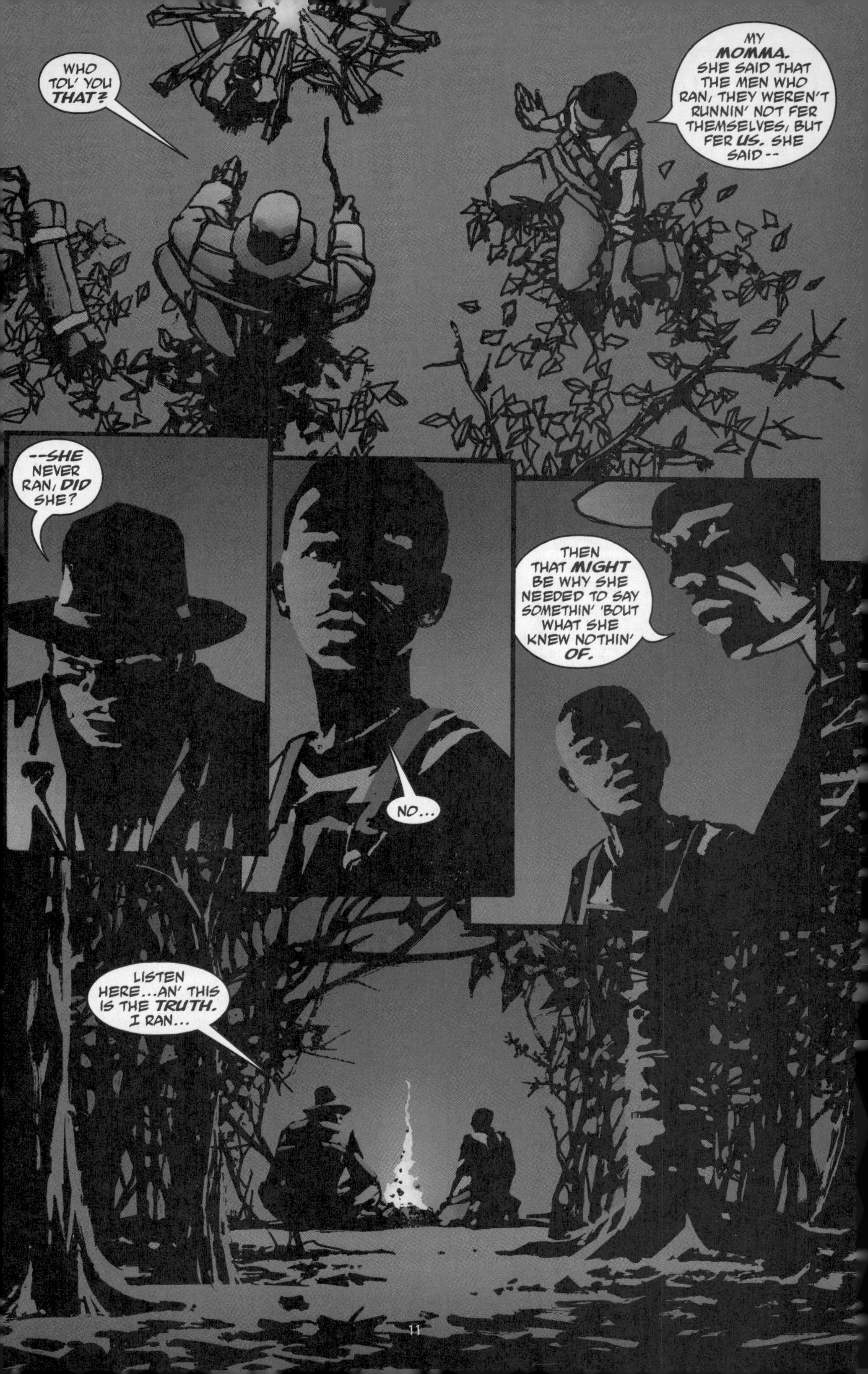
WHO TOL' YOU THAT?
MY MOMMA. SHE SAID THAT THE MEN WHO RAN, THEY WEREN'T RUNNIN' NOT FER THEMSELVES, BUT FER US. SHE SAID--
--SHE NEVER RAN, DID SHE?
NO...
THEN THAT MIGHT BE WHY SHE NEEDED TO SAY SOMETHIN' 'BOUT WHAT SHE KNEW NOTHIN' OF.
LISTEN HERE...AN' THIS IS THE TRUTH. I RAN...

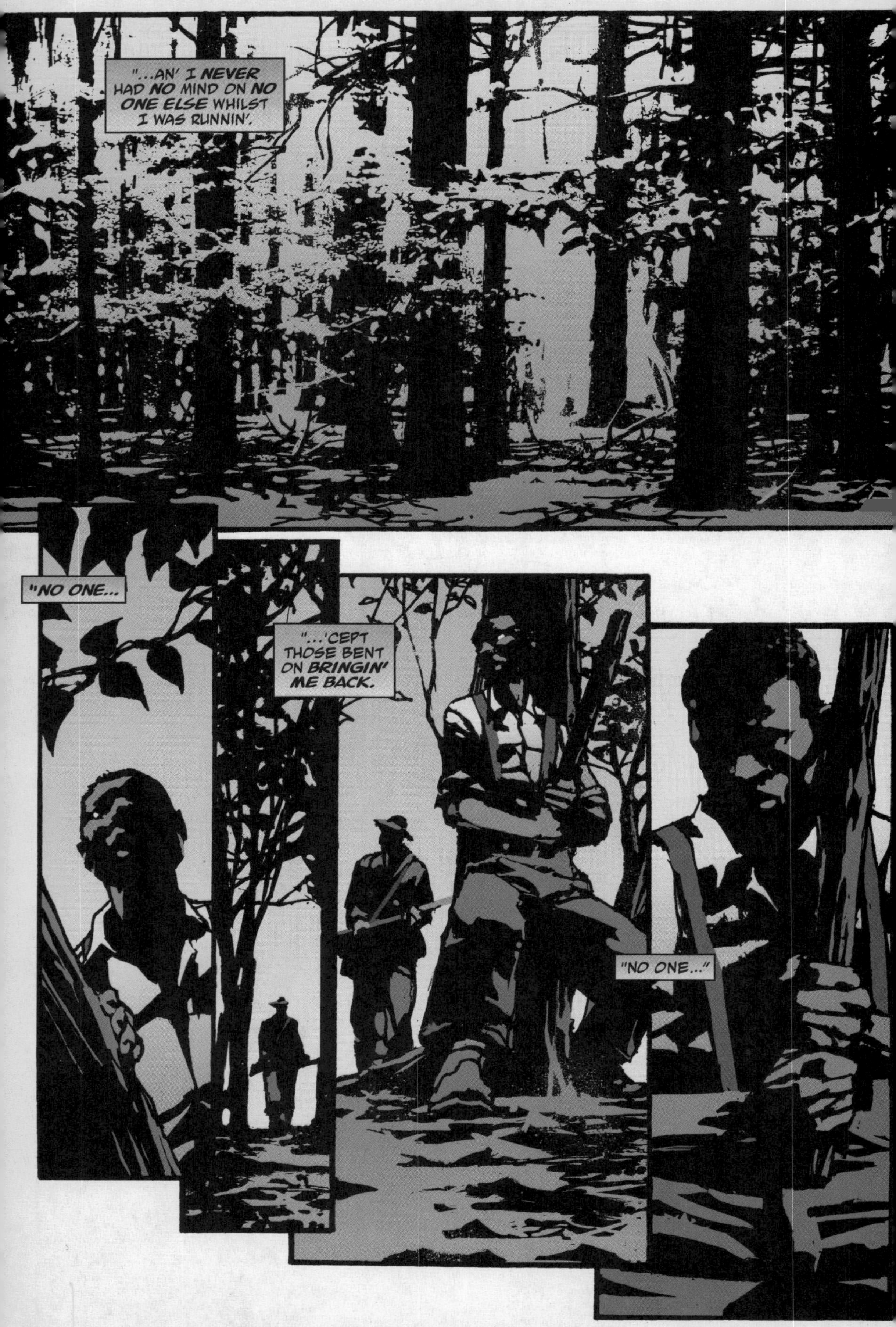
"...AN' I NEVER HAD NO MIND ON NO ONE ELSE WHILST I WAS RUNNIN'.
"NO ONE...
"...'CEPT THOSE BENT ON BRINGIN' ME BACK.
"NO ONE..."

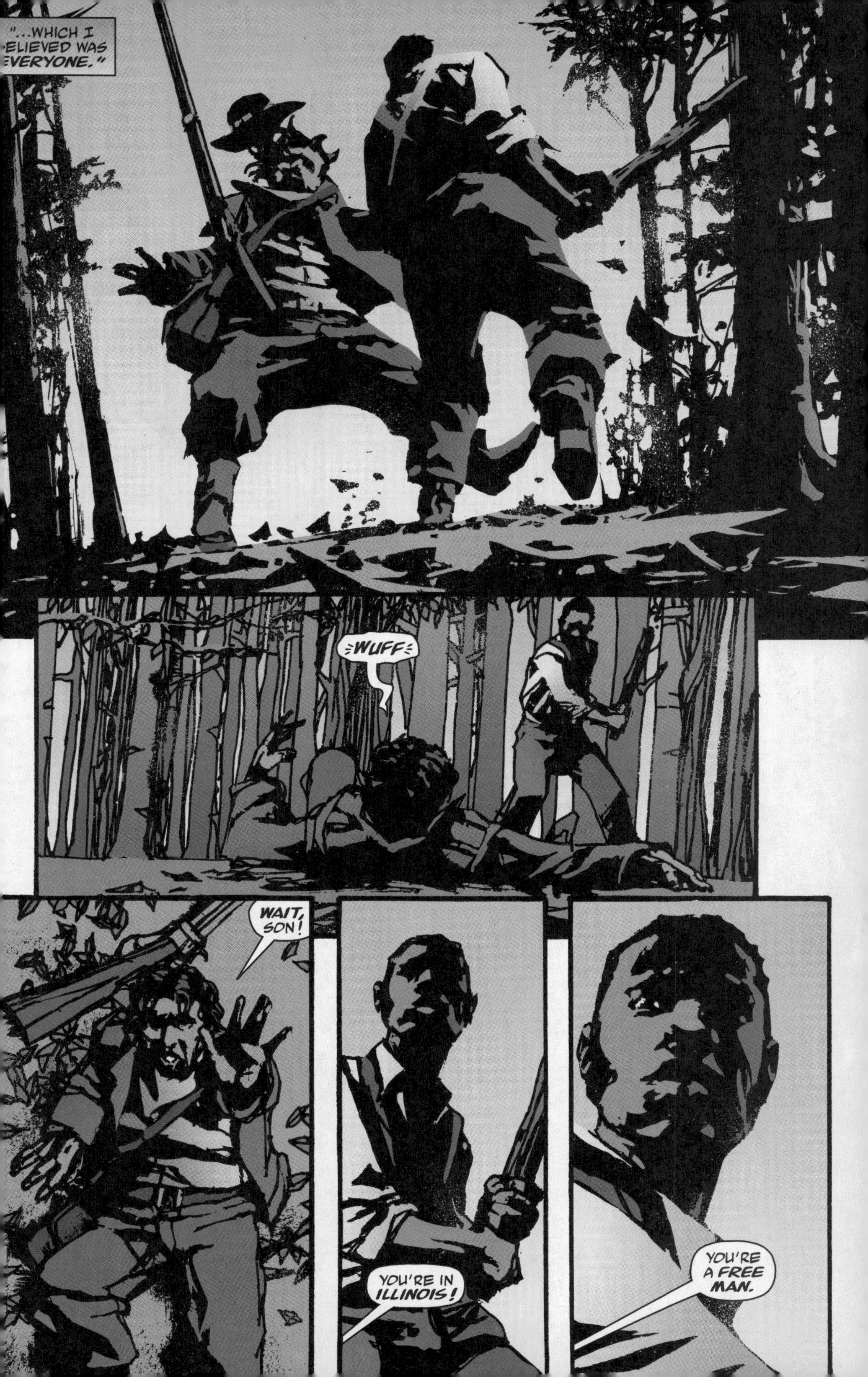
"...WHICH I
BELIEVED WAS
EVERYONE."
WUFF
WAIT, SON!
YOU'RE IN ILLINOIS!
YOU'RE A FREE MAN.

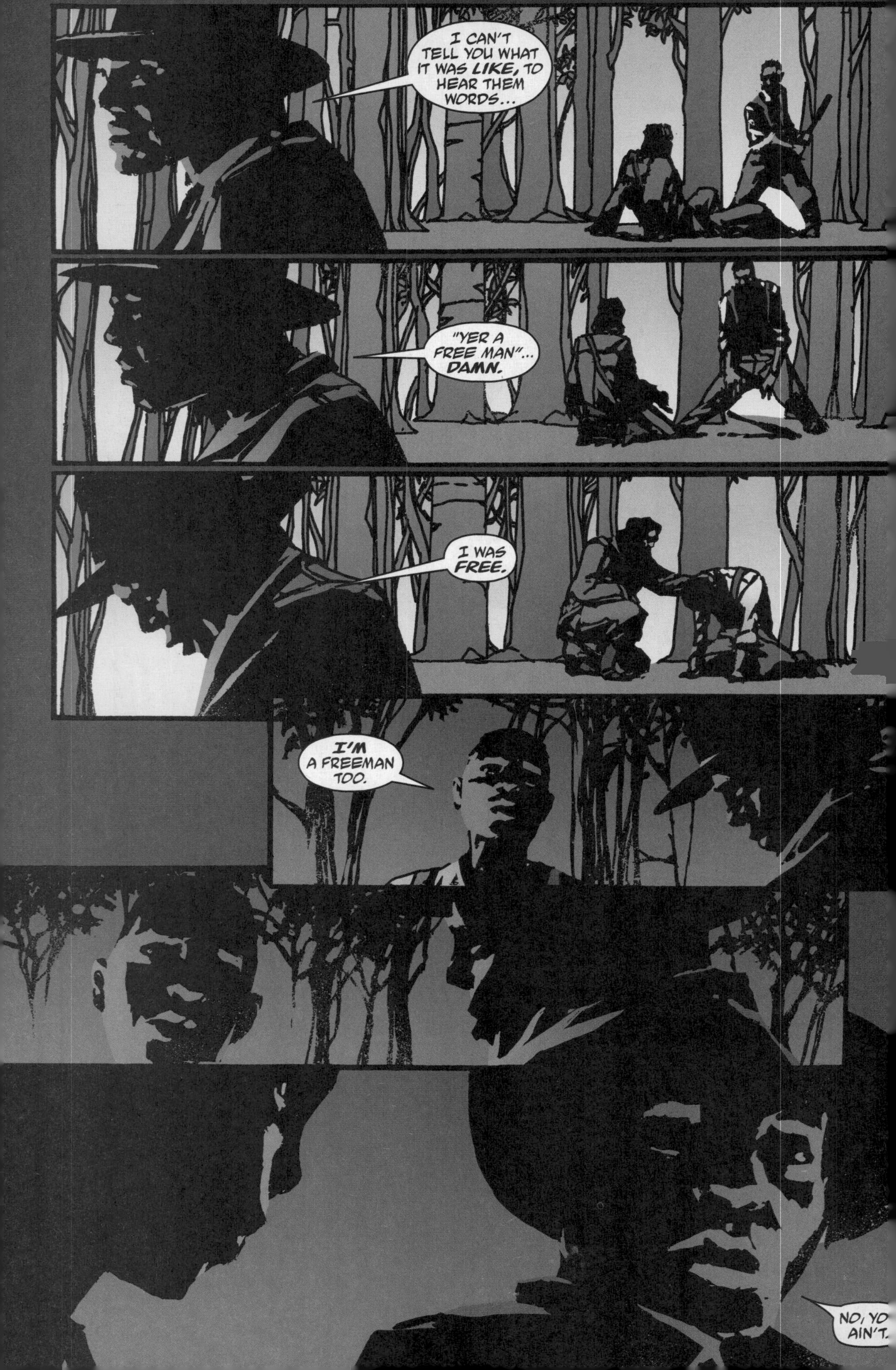
I CAN'T TELL YOU WHAT IT WAS LIKE, TO HEAR THEM WORDS...
"YER A FREE MAN"... DAMN.
I WAS FREE.
I'M A FREEMAN TOO.
NO, YO AIN'T.

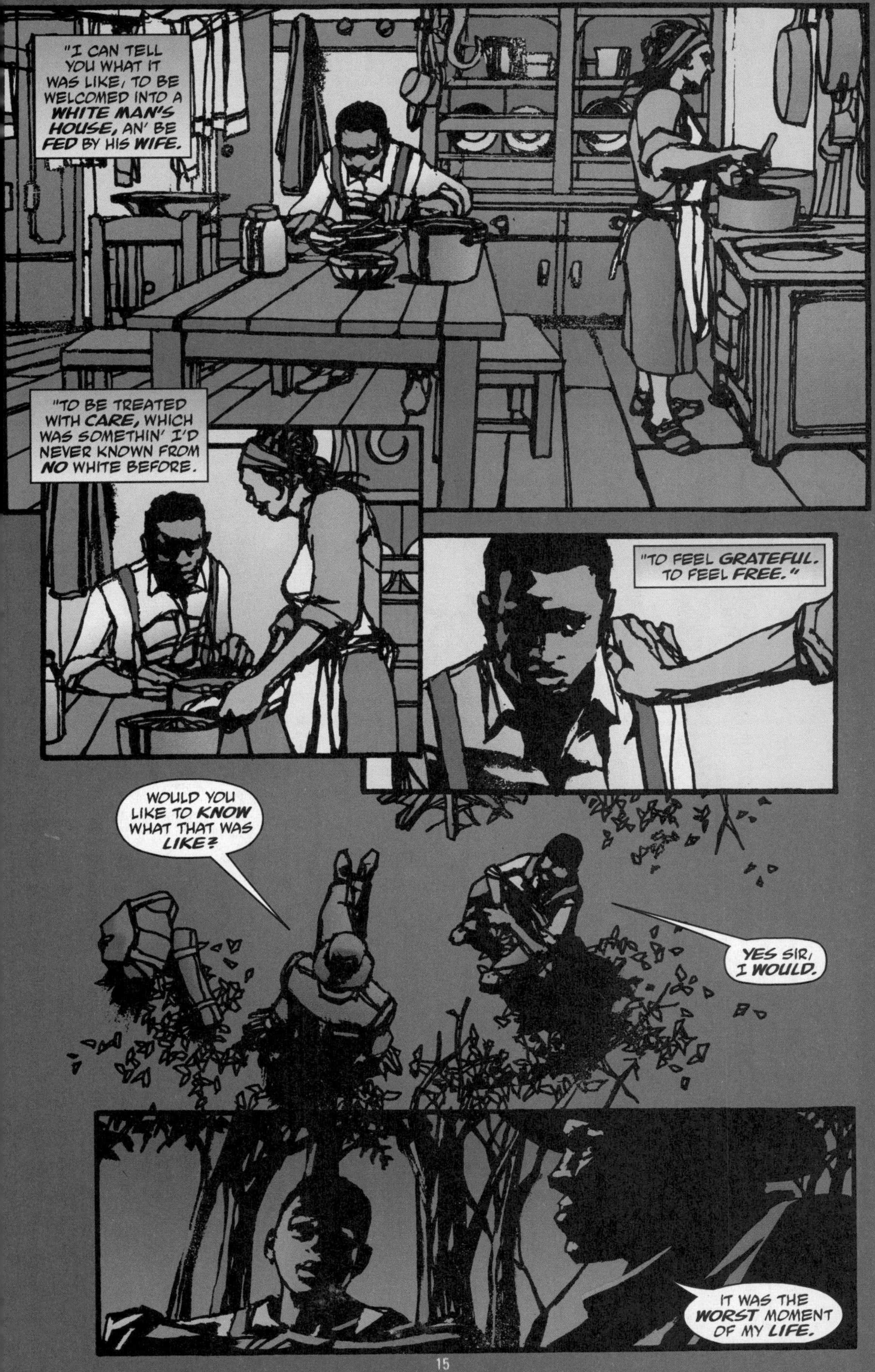
"I CAN TELL YOU WHAT IT WAS LIKE, TO BE WELCOMED INTO A WHITE MAN'S HOUSE, AN' BE FED BY HIS WIFE.
"TO BE TREATED WITH CARE, WHICH WAS SOMETHIN' I'D NEVER KNOWN FROM NO WHITE BEFORE.
"TO FEEL GRATEFUL. TO FEEL FREE."
WOULD YOU LIKE TO KNOW WHAT THAT WAS LIKE?
YES SIR, I WOULD.
IT WAS THE WORST MOMENT OF MY LIFE.

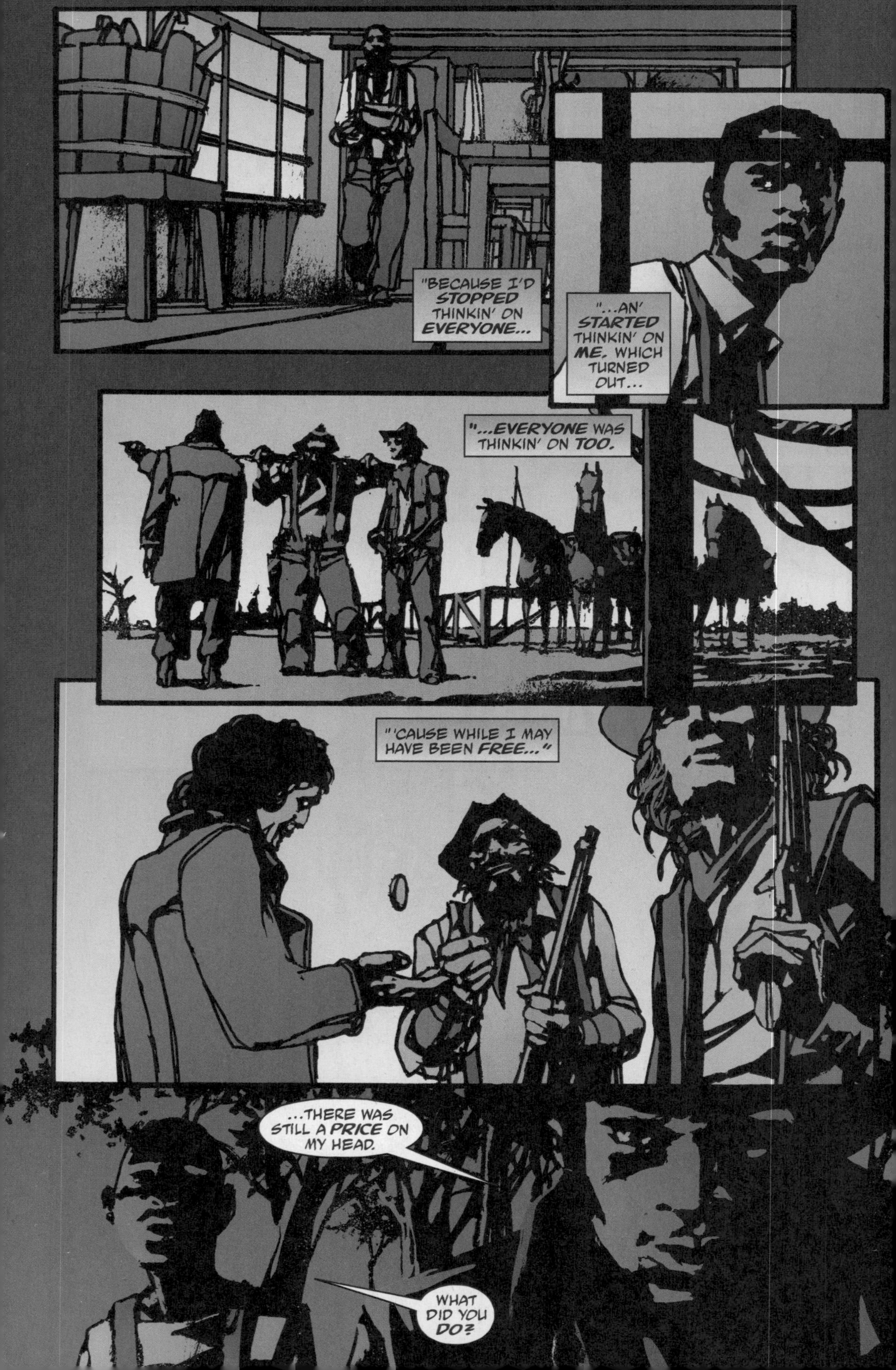
"BECAUSE I'D STOPPED THINKIN' ON EVERYONE...
"...AN' STARTED THINKIN' ON ME. WHICH TURNED OUT...
"...EVERYONE WAS THINKIN' ON TOO.
"'CAUSE WHILE I MAY HAVE BEEN FREE..."
...THERE WAS STILL A PRICE ON MY HEAD.
WHAT DID YOU DO?

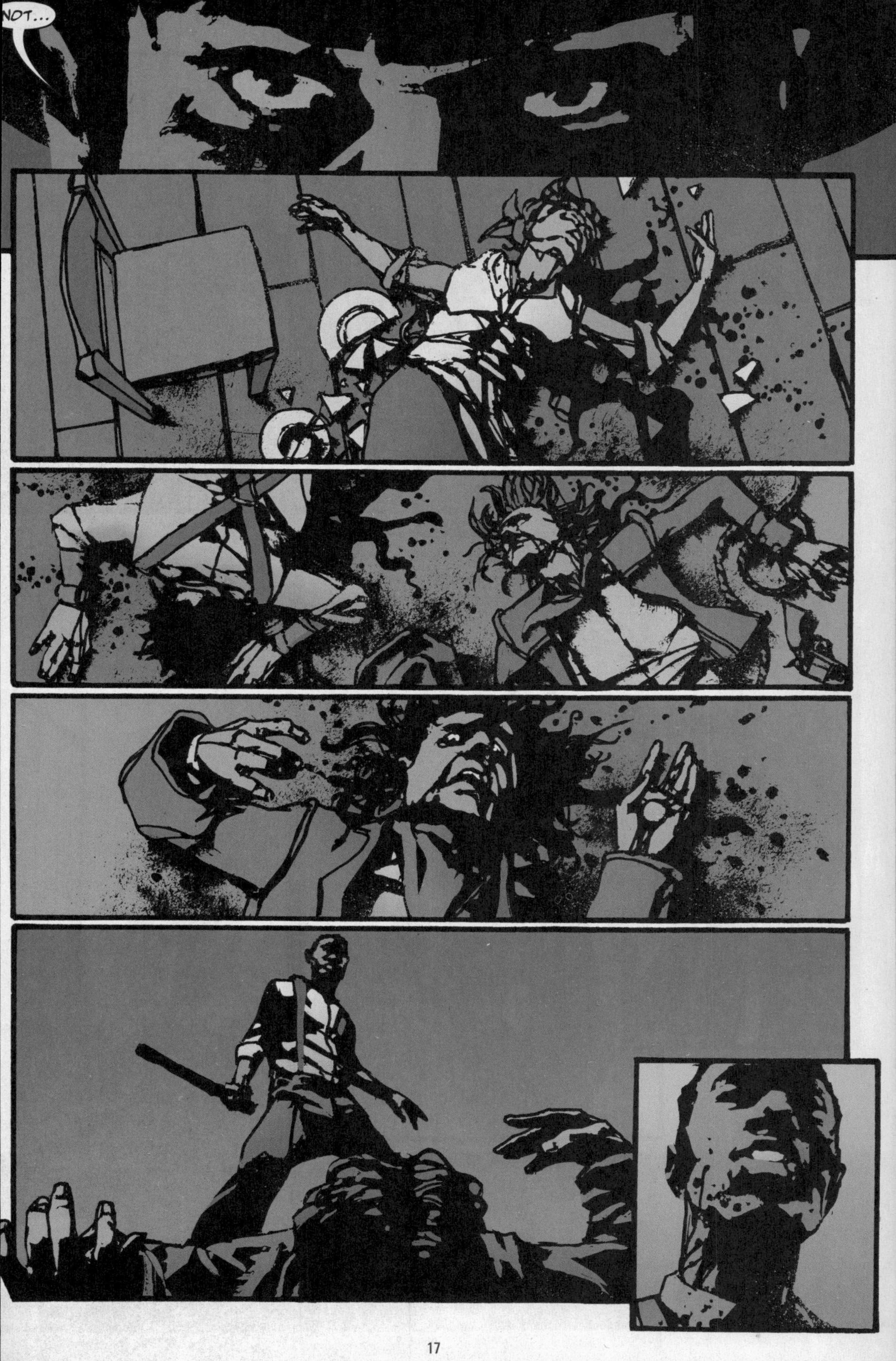
NOT...

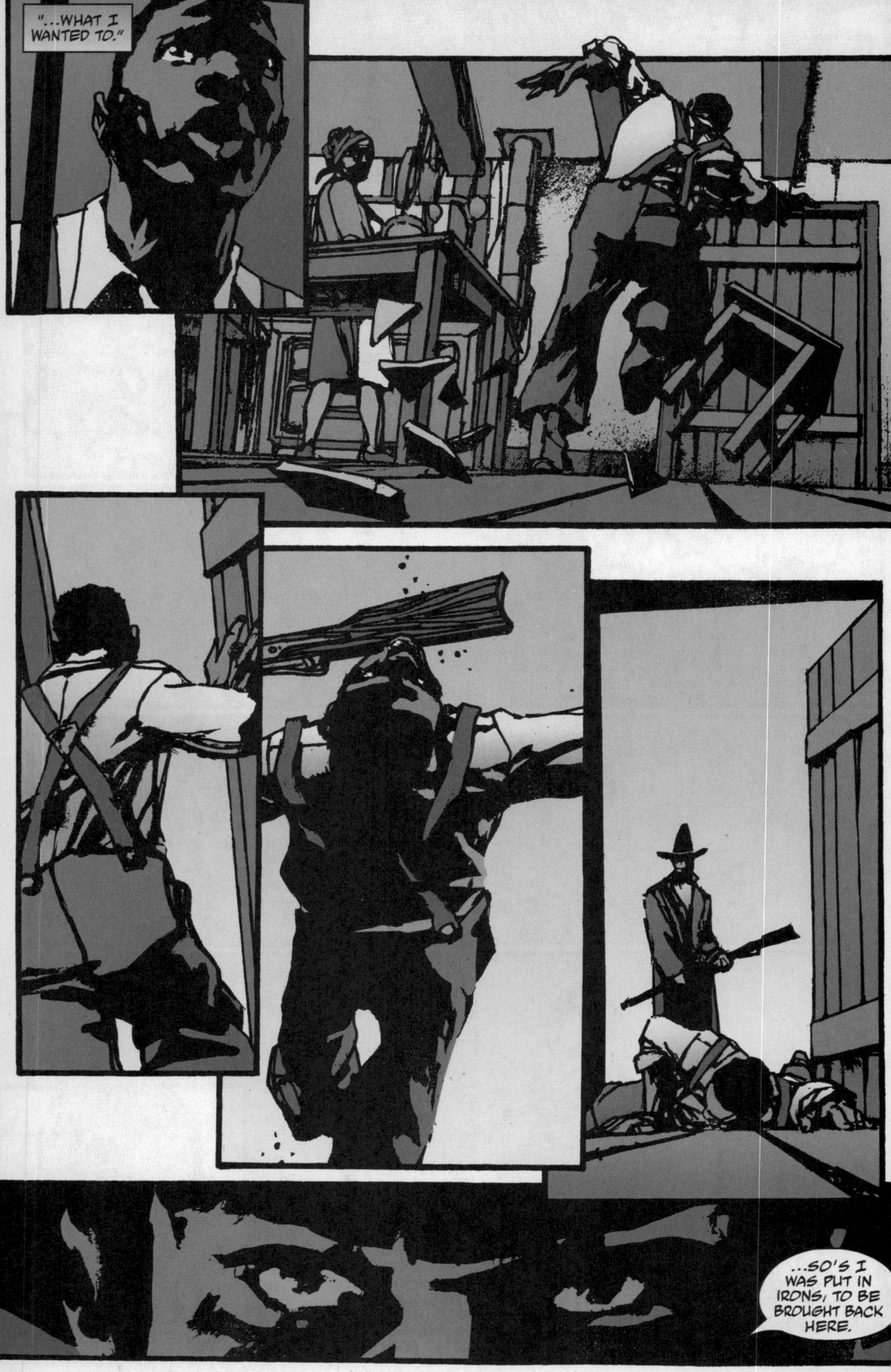
"...WHAT I WANTED TO."
...SO'S I WAS PUT IN IRONS, TO BE BROUGHT BACK HERE.

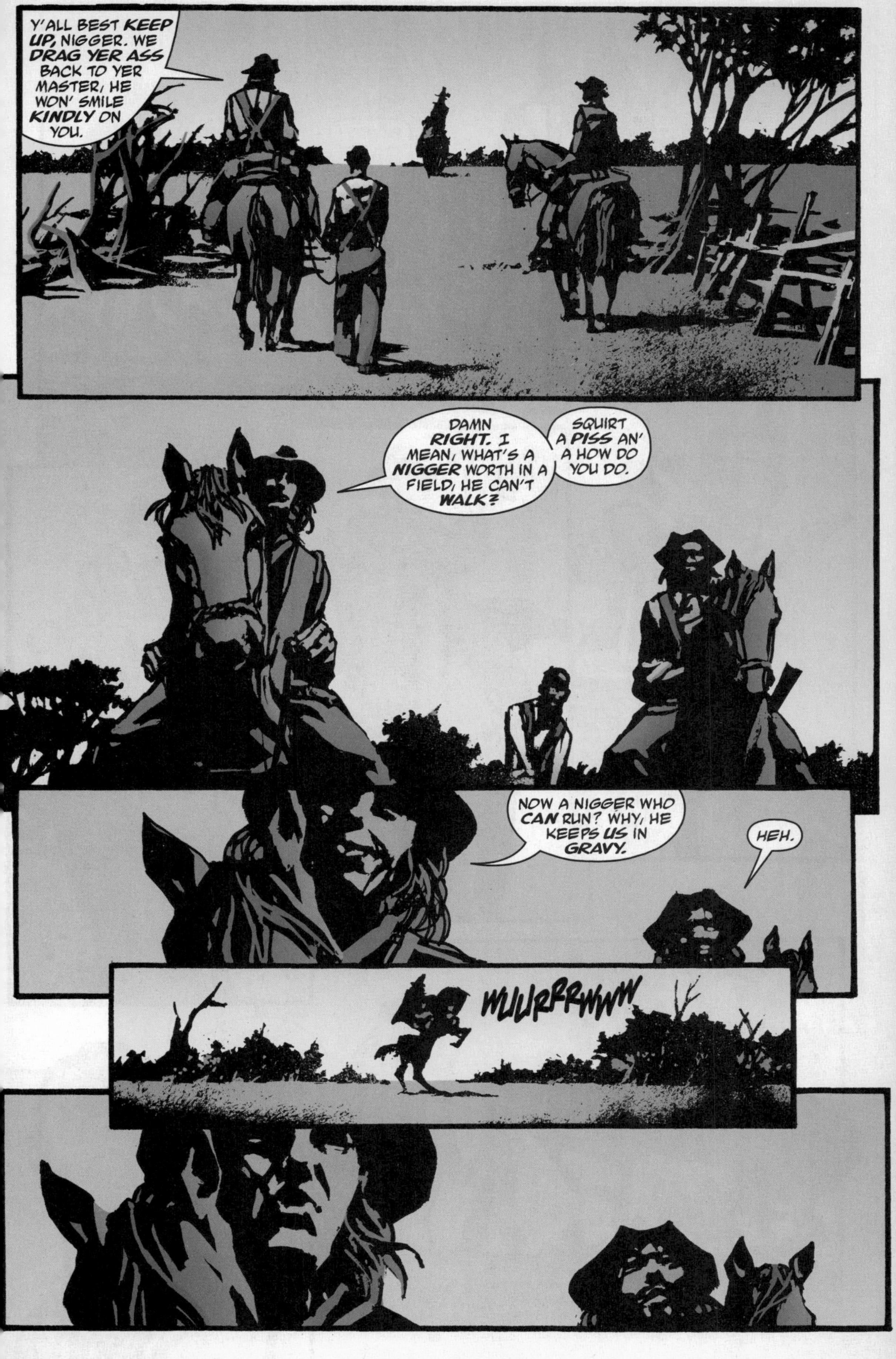
Y'ALL BEST KEEP UP, NIGGER. WE DRAG YER ASS BACK TO YER MASTER, HE WON' SMILE KINDLY ON YOU.
DAMN RIGHT. I MEAN, WHAT'S A NIGGER WORTH IN A FIELD, HE CAN'T WALK?
SQUIRT A PISS AN' A HOW DO YOU DO.
NOW A NIGGER WHO CAN RUN? WHY, HE KEEPS US IN GRAVY.
HEH.
WUURRRWWW

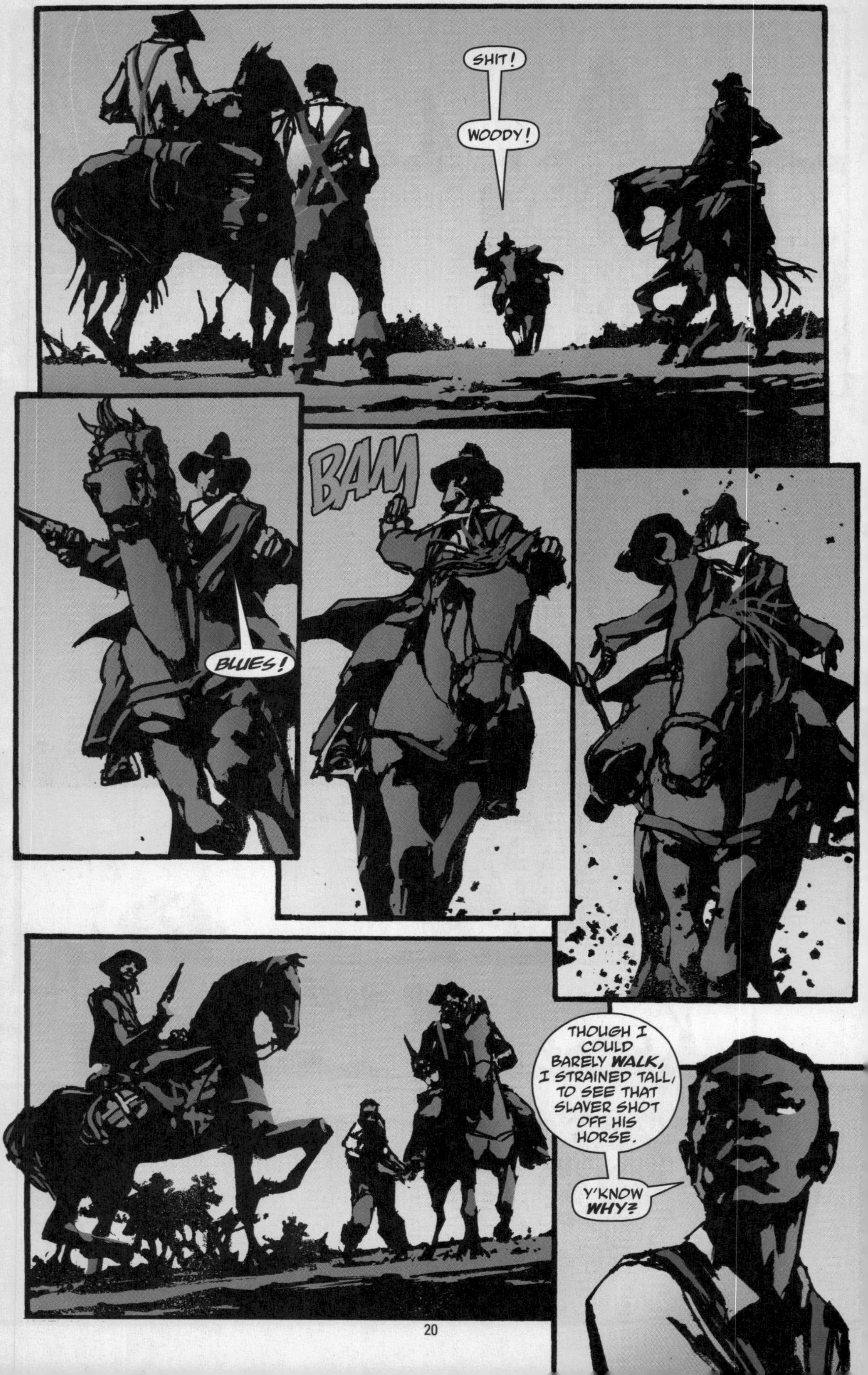
SHIT!
WOODY!
BLUES!
BAM
THOUGH I COULD BARELY WALK, I STRAINED TALL, TO SEE THAT SLAVER SHOT OFF HIS HORSE.
Y'KNOW WHY?

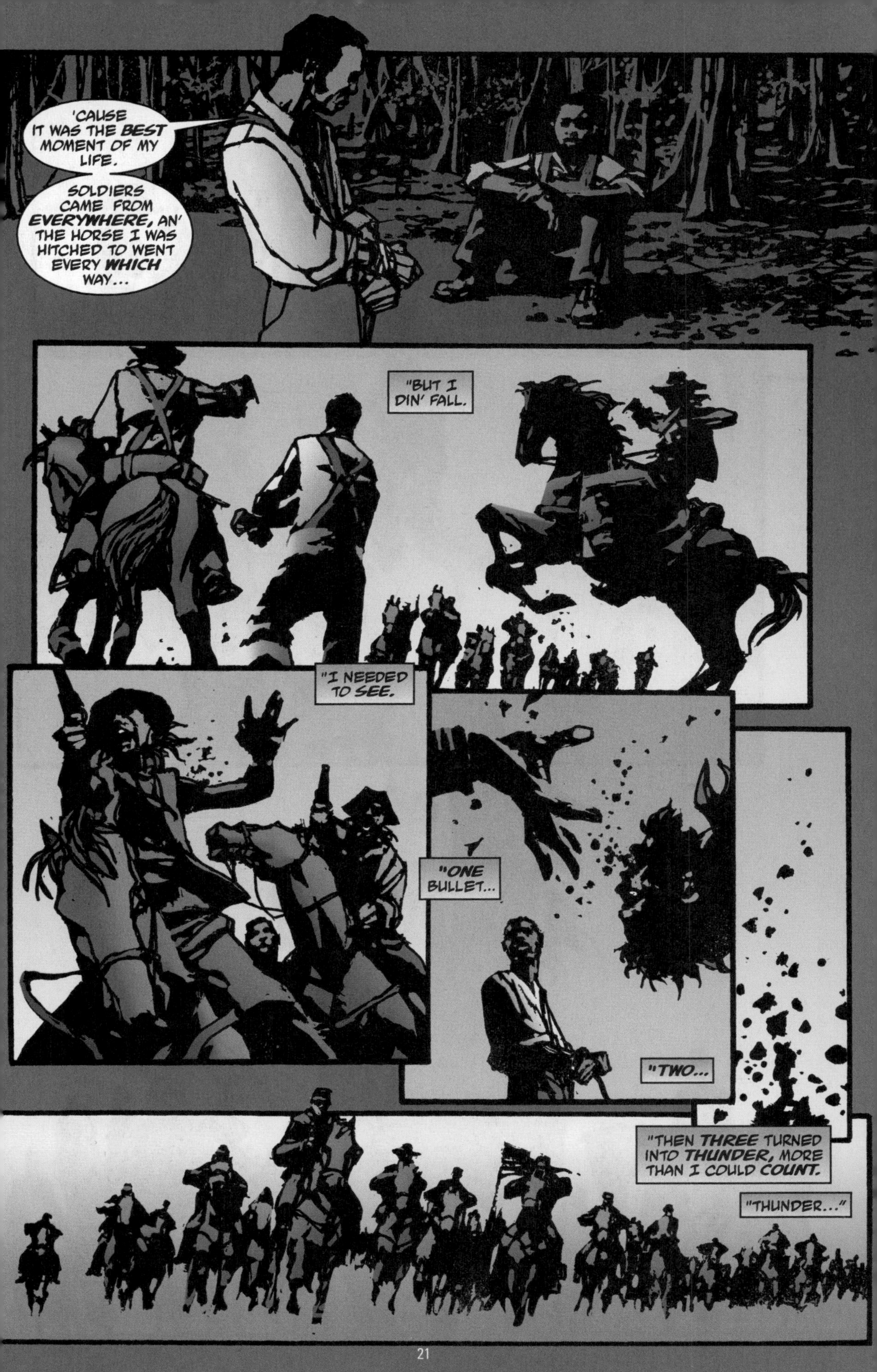
'CAUSE IT WAS THE BEST MOMENT OF MY LIFE.
SOLDIERS CAME FROM EVERYWHERE, AN' THE HORSE I WAS HITCHED TO WENT EVERY WHICH WAY...
"BUT I DIN' FALL.
"I NEEDED TO SEE.
"ONE BULLET...
"TWO...
"THEN THREE TURNED INTO THUNDER, MORE THAN I COULD COUNT.
"THUNDER..."

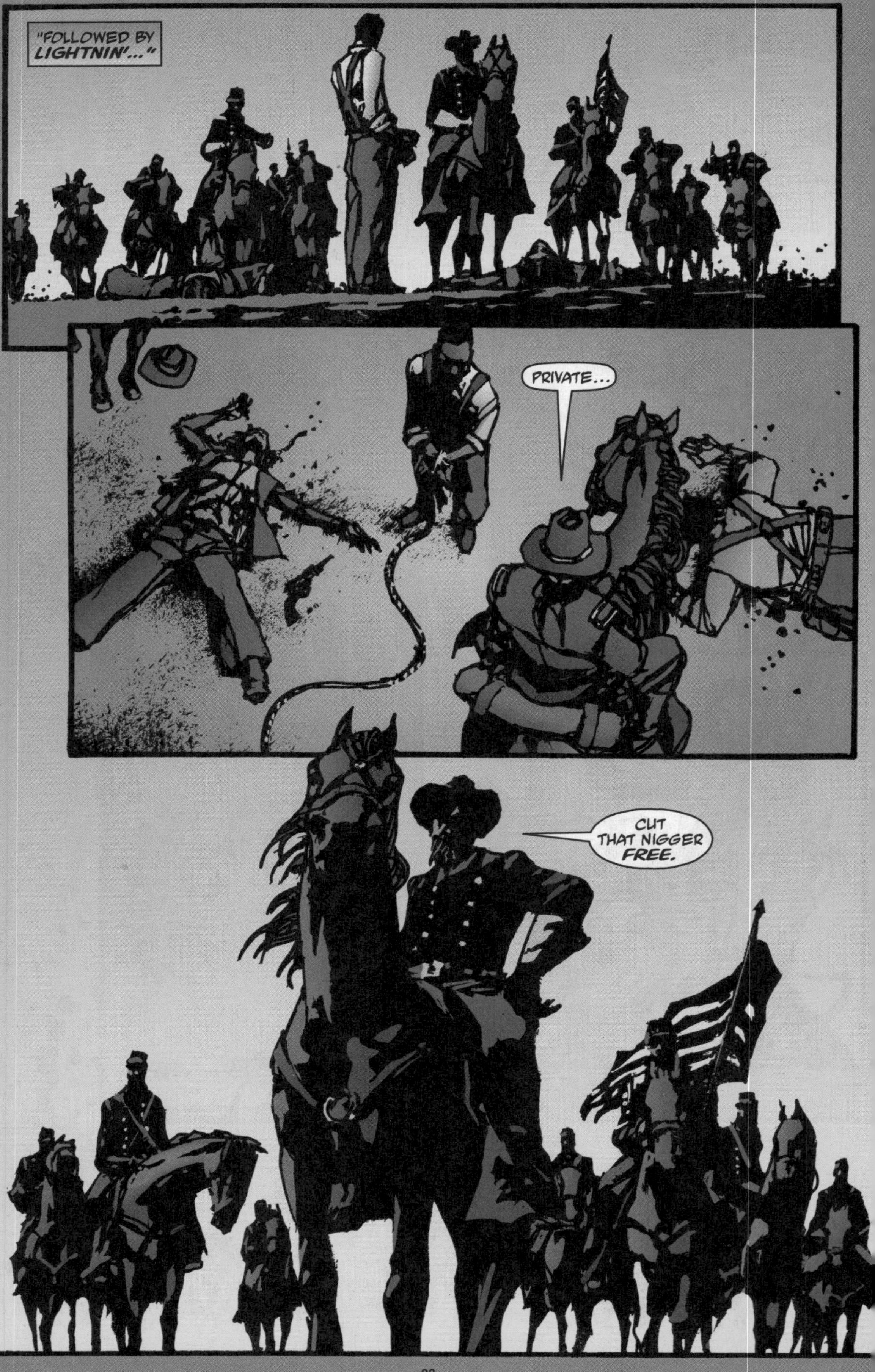
"FOLLOWED BY LIGHTNIN'..."
PRIVATE...
CUT THAT NIGGER FREE.

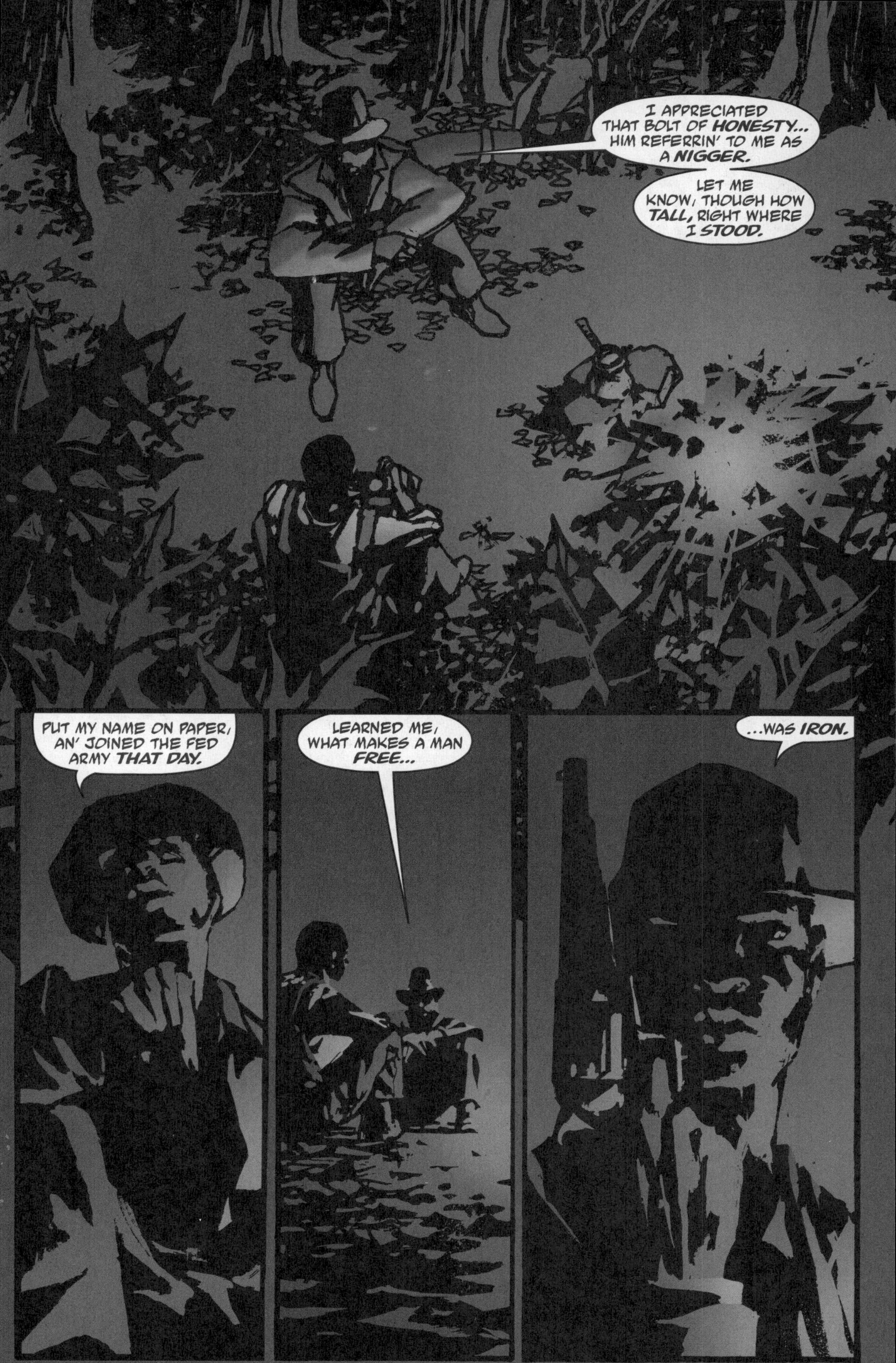

I APPRECIATED THAT BOLT OF HONESTY... HIM REFERRIN' TO ME AS A NIGGER.
LET ME KNOW, THOUGH HOW TALL, RIGHT WHERE I STOOD.
PUT MY NAME ON PAPER, AN' JOINED THE FED ARMY THAT DAY.
LEARNED ME, WHAT MAKES A MAN FREE...
...WAS IRON.

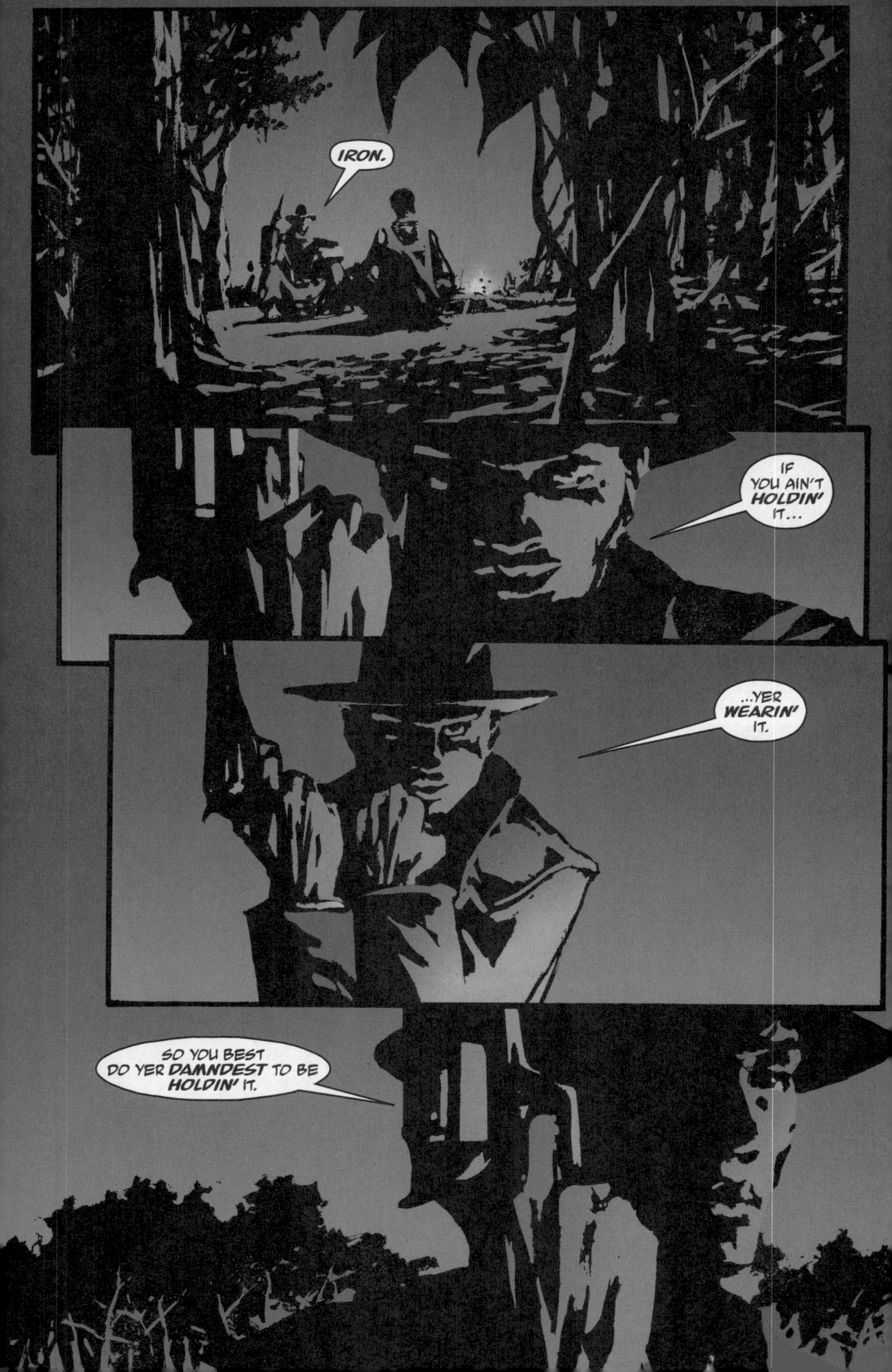
IRON.
IF YOU AIN'T HOLDIN' IT...
...YER WEARIN' IT.
SO YOU BEST DO YER DAMNDEST TO BE HOLDIN' IT.

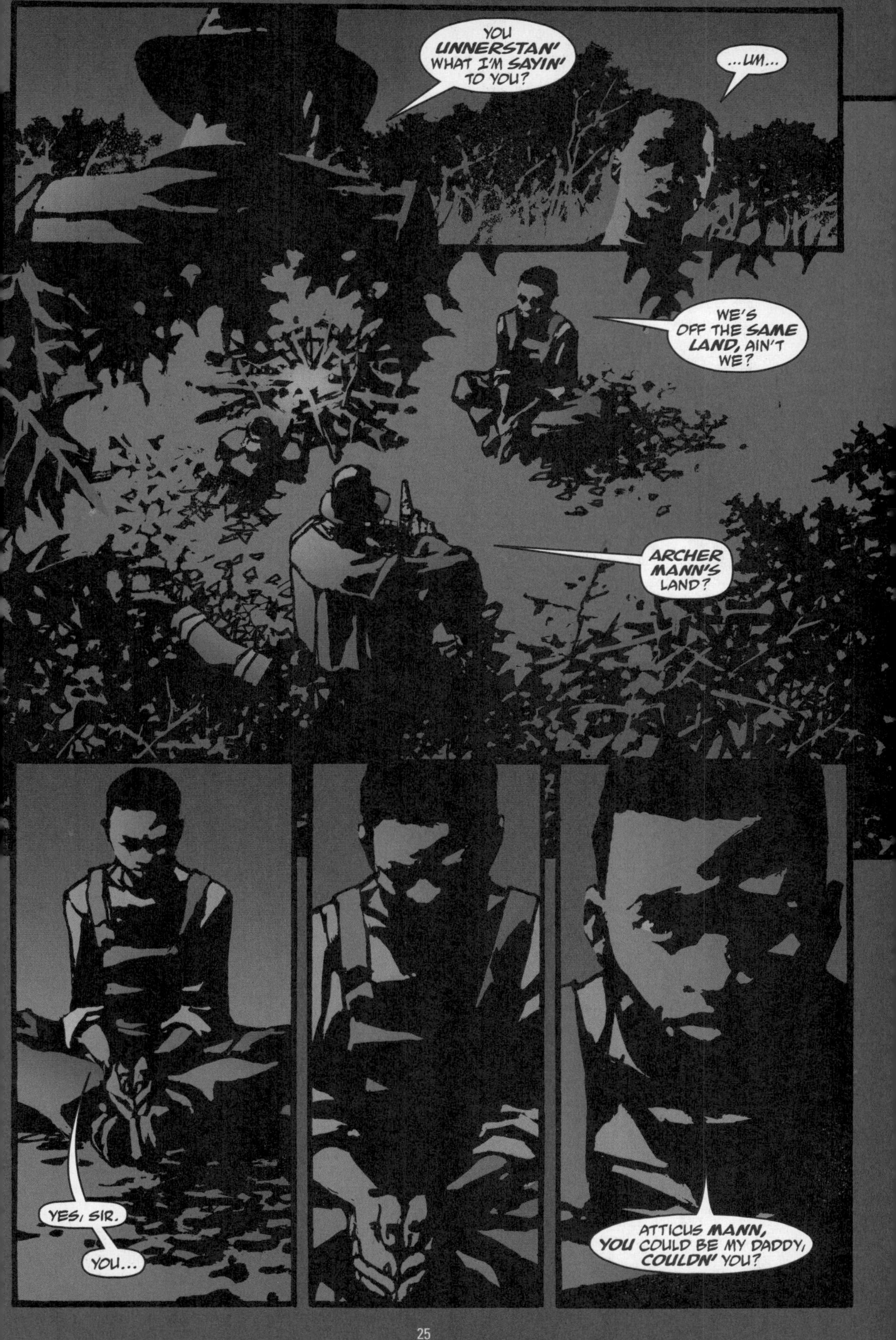
YOU UNNERSTAN' WHAT I'M SAYIN' TO YOU?
...UM...
WE'S OFF THE SAME LAND, AIN'T WE?
ARCHER MANN'S LAND?
YES, SIR.
YOU...
ATTICUS MANN, YOU COULD BE MY DADDY, COULDN' YOU?

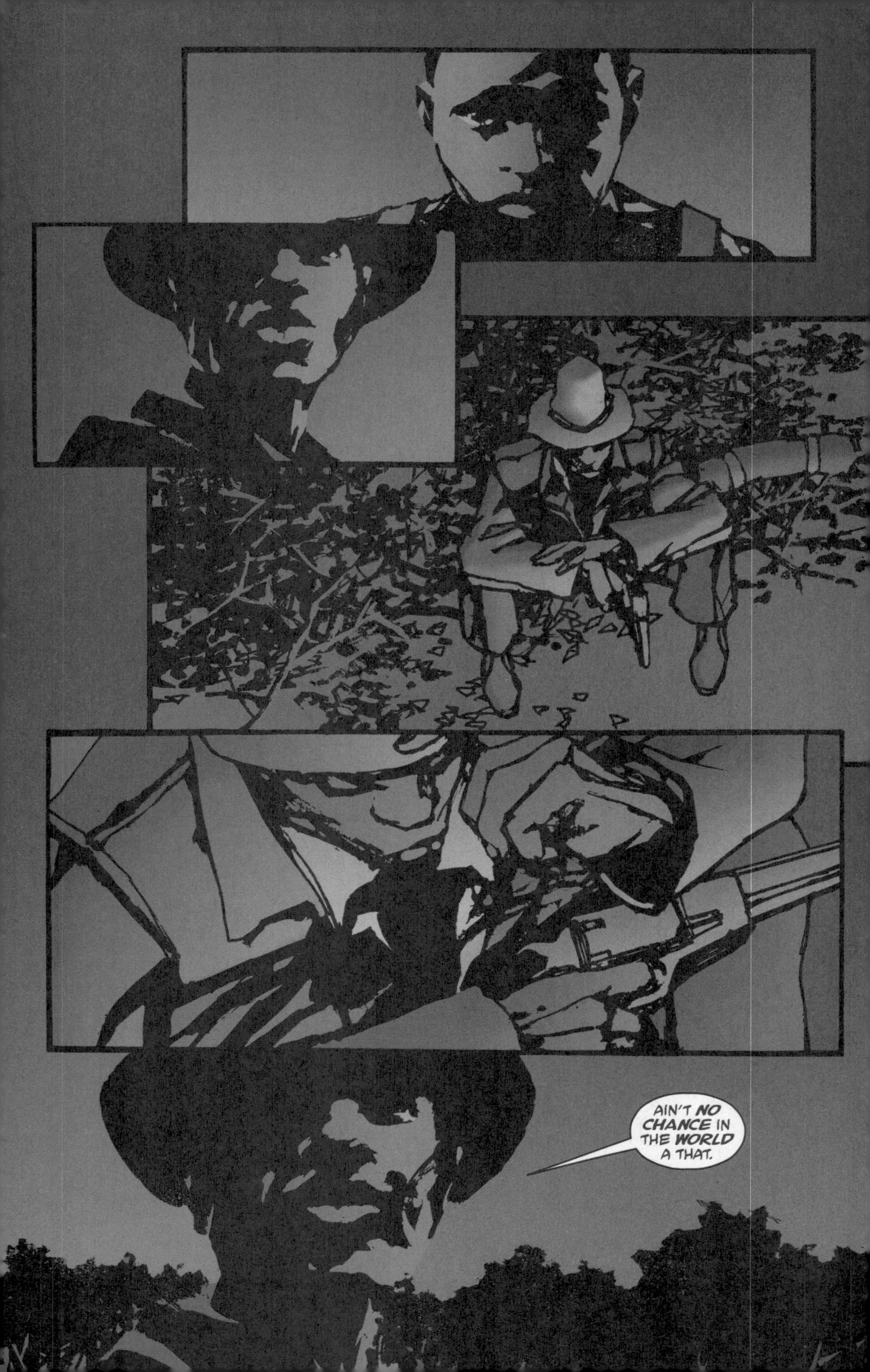
AIN'T **NO** **CHANCE** IN THE **WORLD** A THAT.

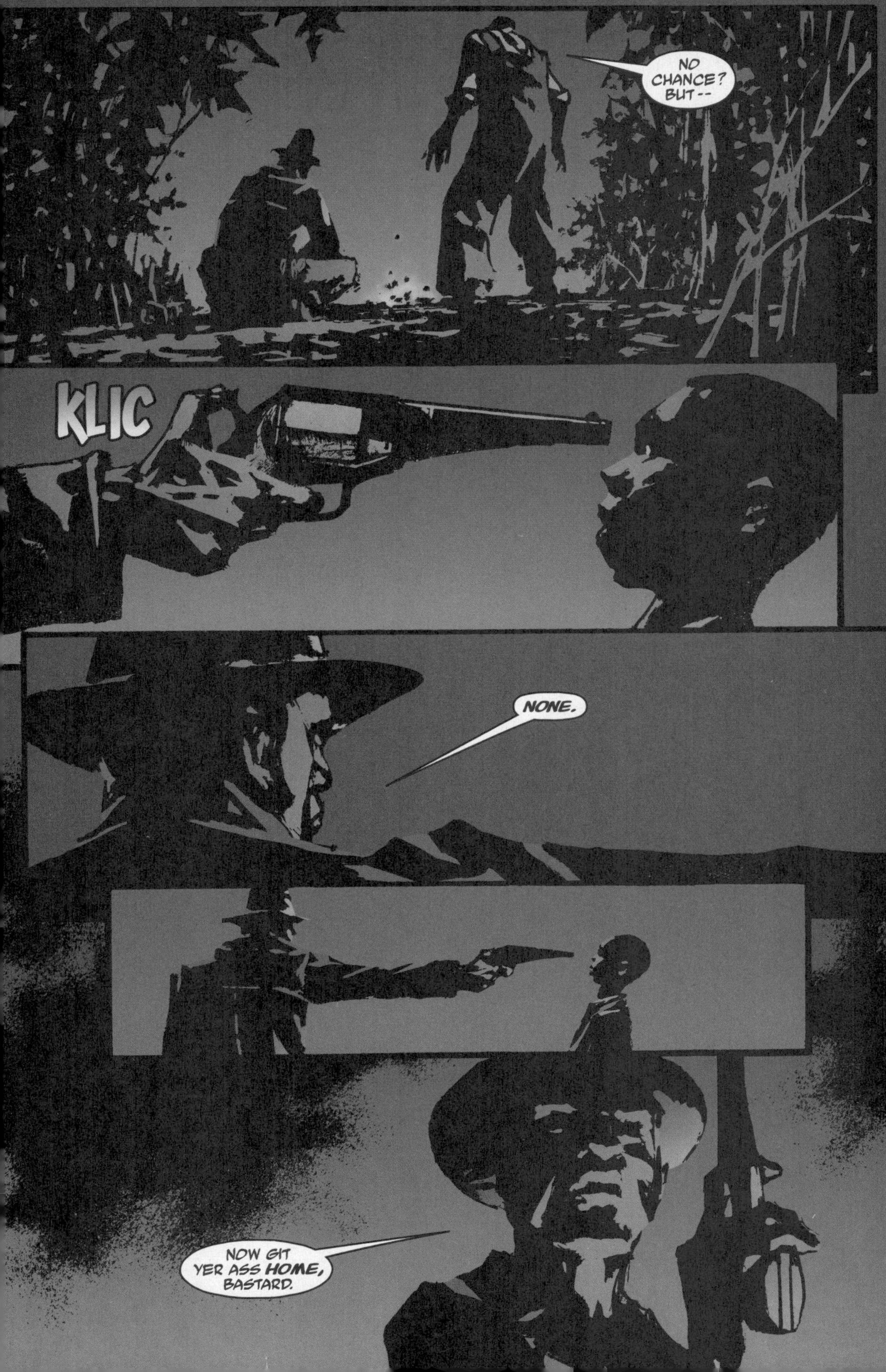
NO CHANCE? BUT --
KLIC
NONE.
NOW GIT YER ASS HOME, BASTARD.

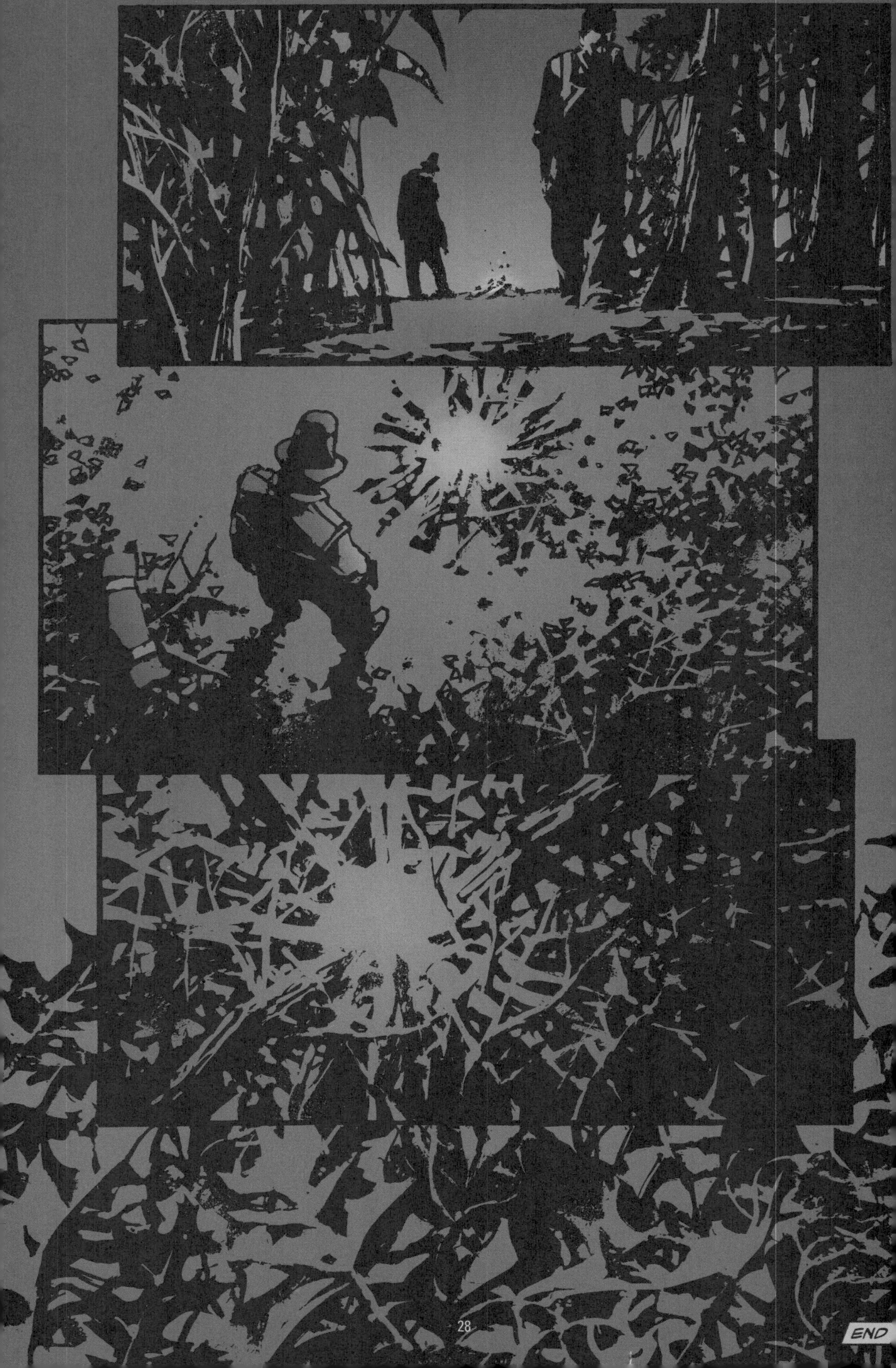
END

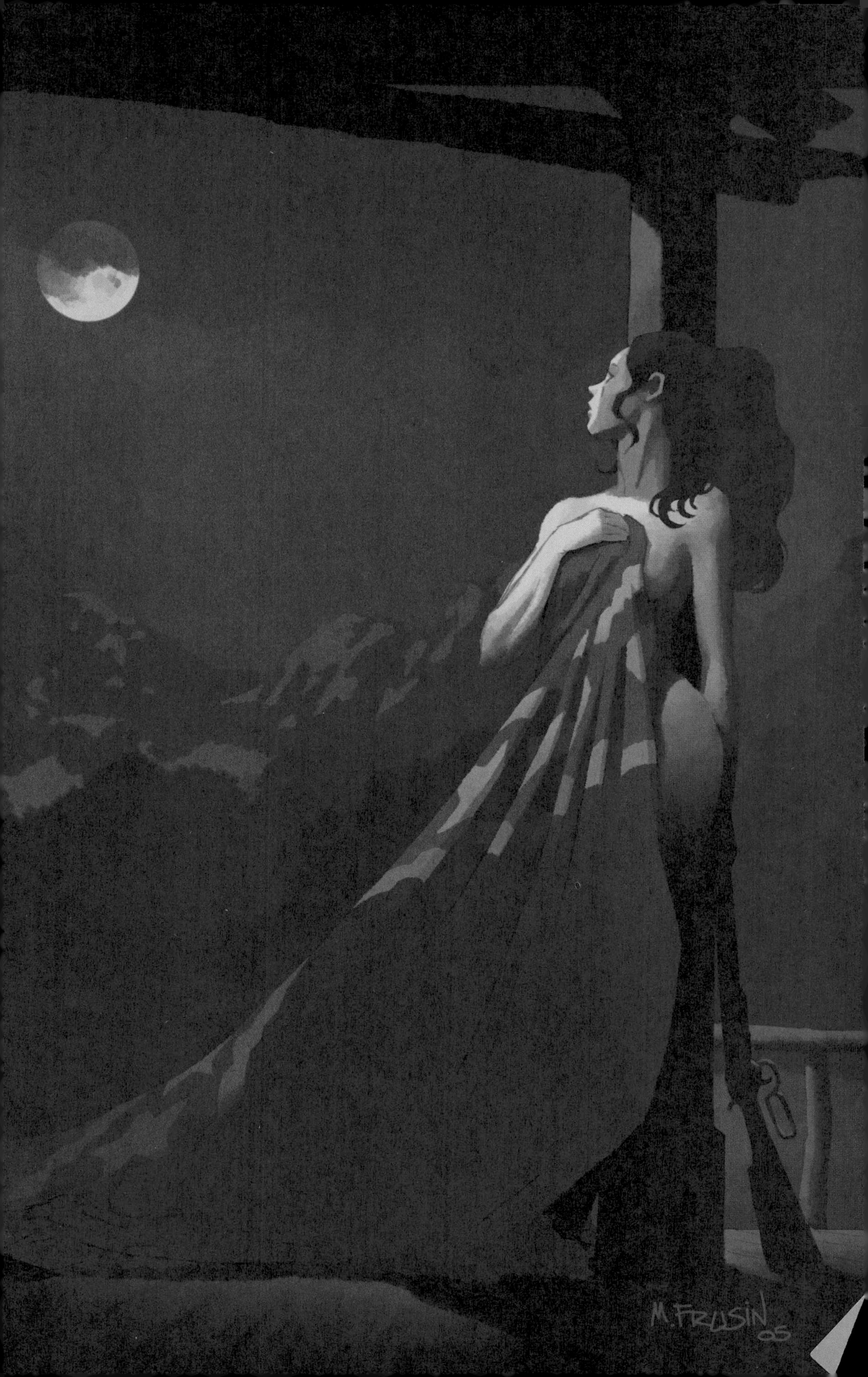
M. FRUSIN 05

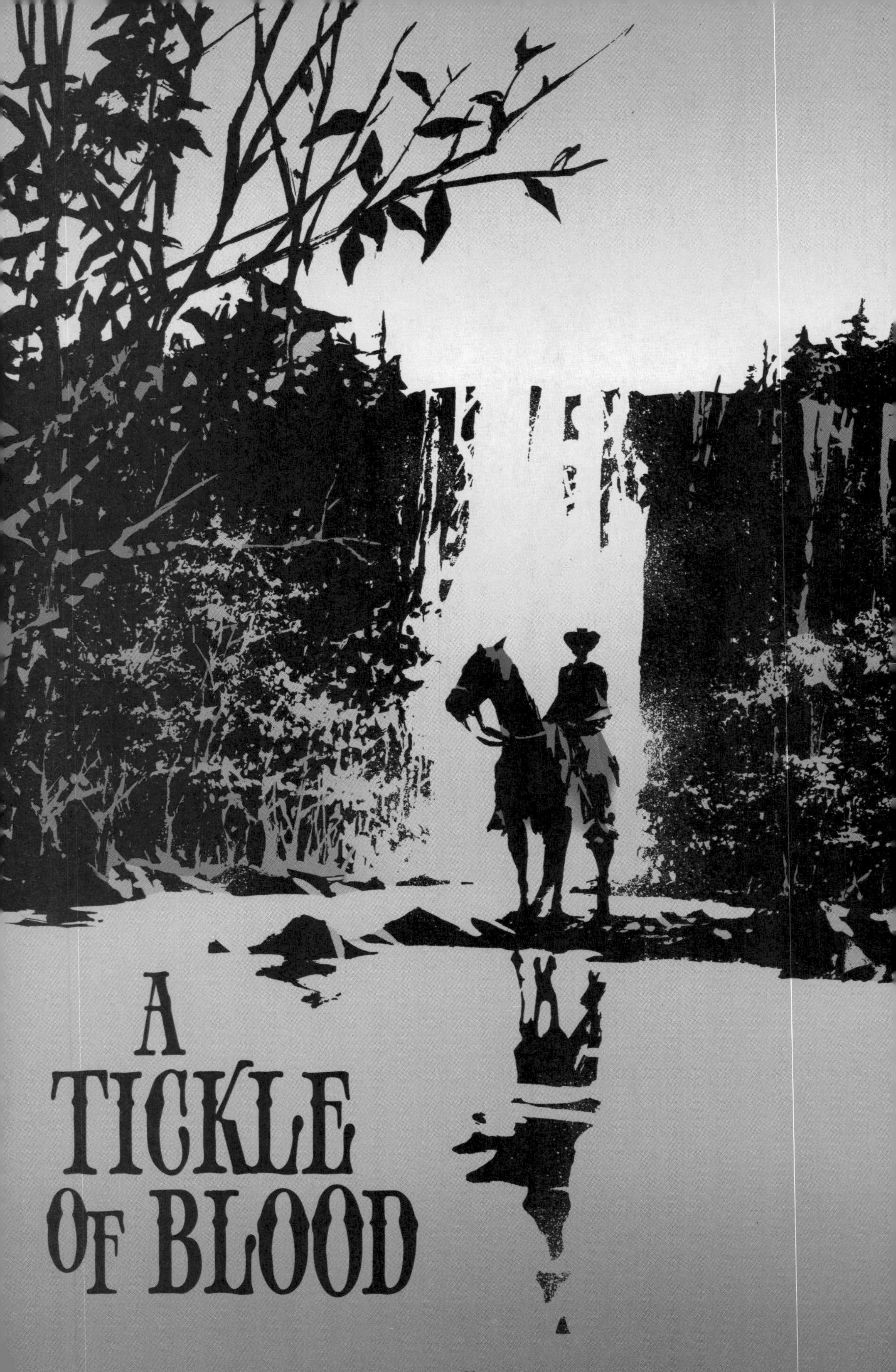

A TICKLE OF BLOOD

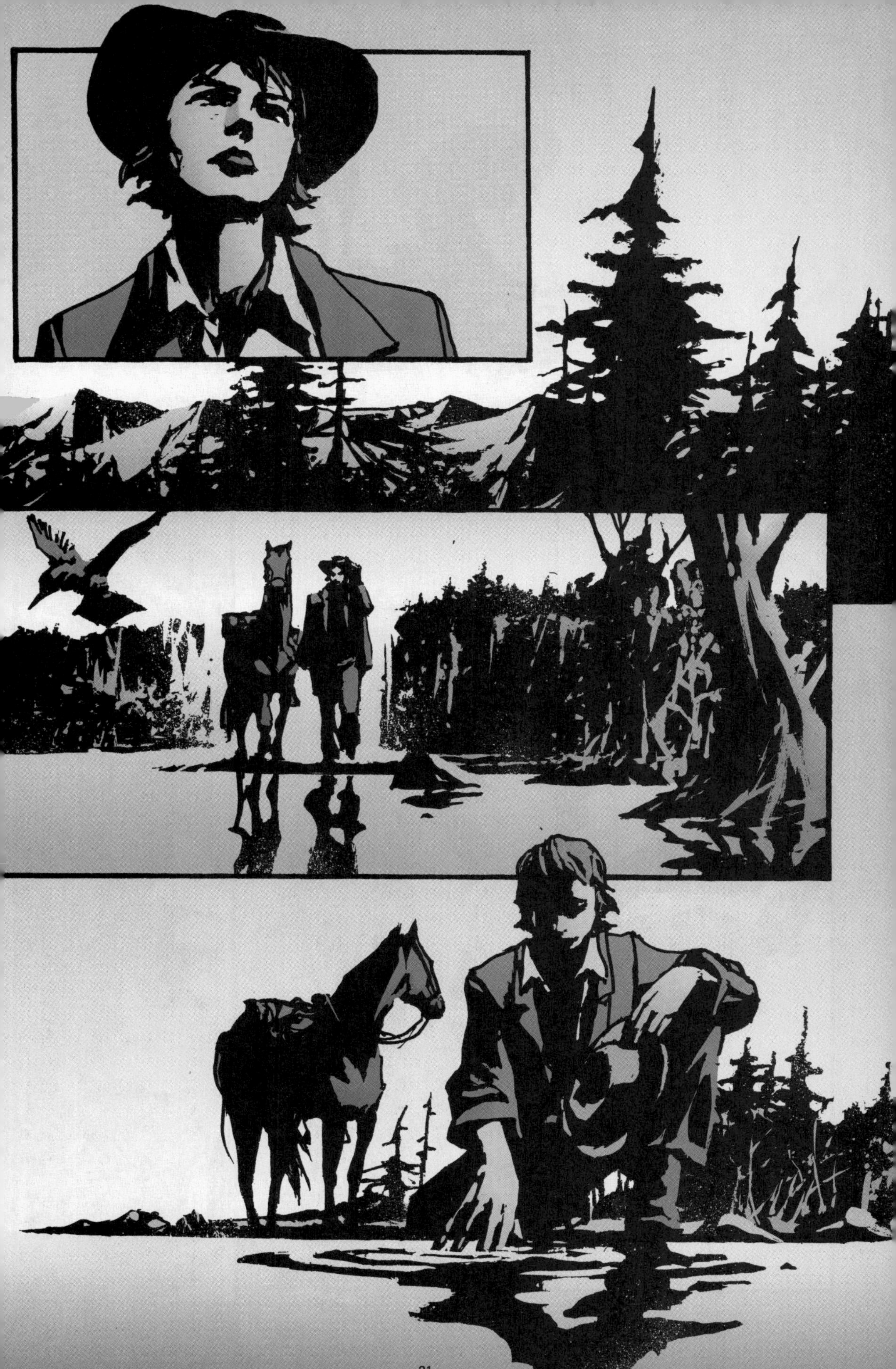

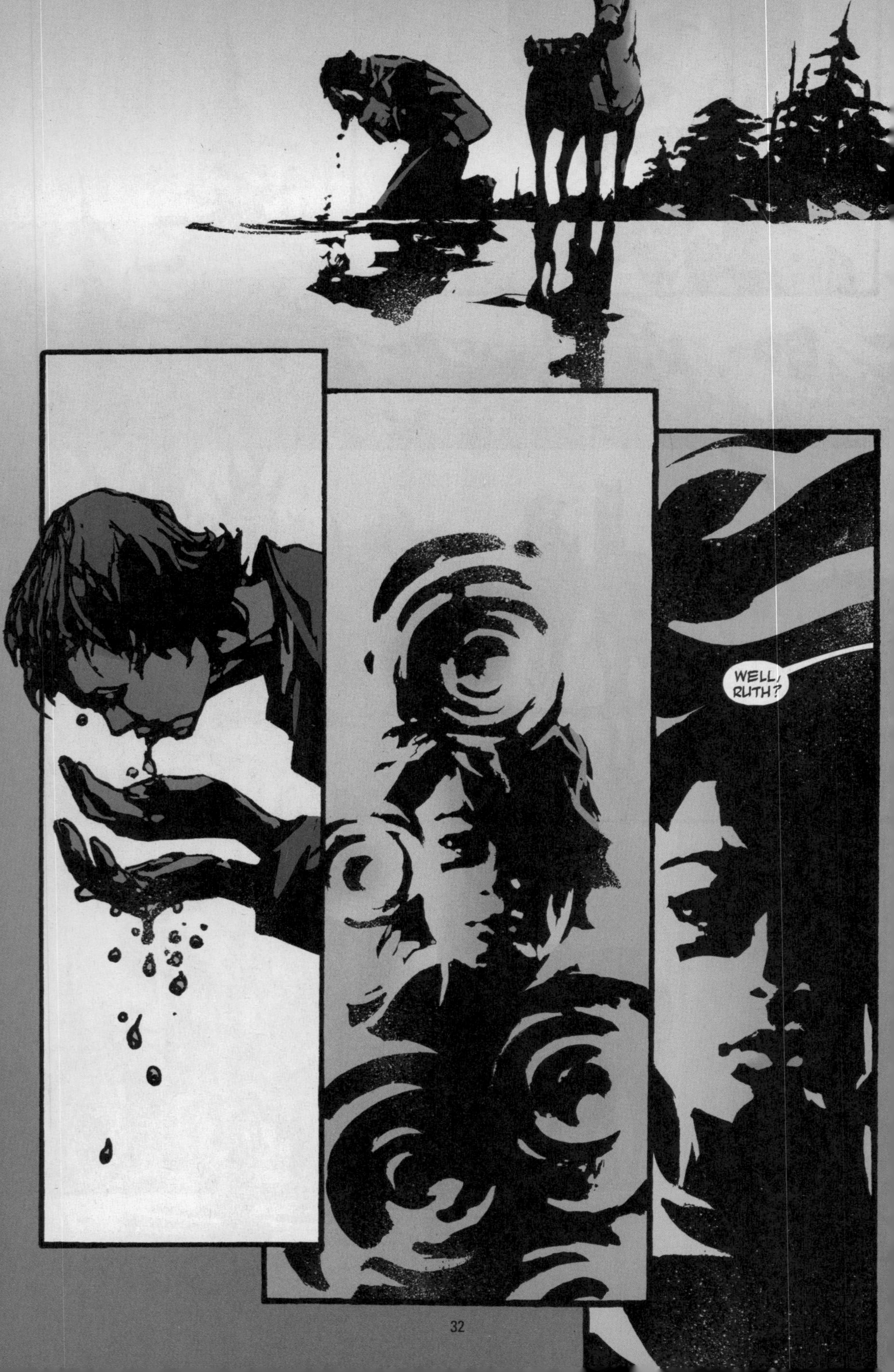
WELL, RUTH?

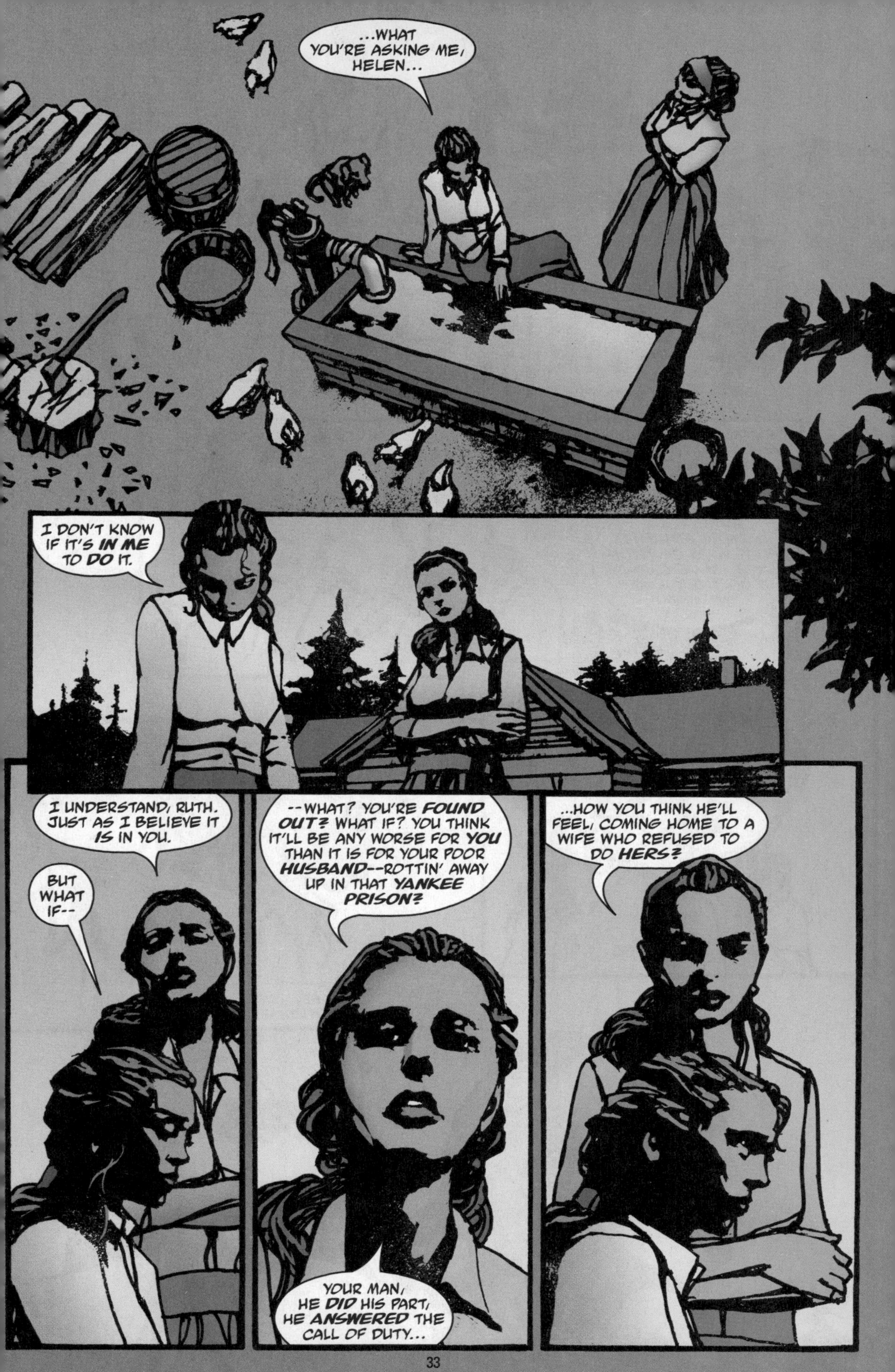
...WHAT YOU'RE ASKING ME, HELEN...
I DON'T KNOW IF IT'S IN ME TO DO IT.
I UNDERSTAND, RUTH. JUST AS I BELIEVE IT IS IN YOU.
BUT WHAT IF--
--WHAT? YOU'RE FOUND OUT? WHAT IF? YOU THINK IT'LL BE ANY WORSE FOR YOU THAN IT IS FOR YOUR POOR HUSBAND--ROTTIN' AWAY UP IN THAT YANKEE PRISON?
YOUR MAN, HE DID HIS PART, HE ANSWERED THE CALL OF DUTY...
...HOW YOU THINK HE'LL FEEL, COMING HOME TO A WIFE WHO REFUSED TO DO HERS?

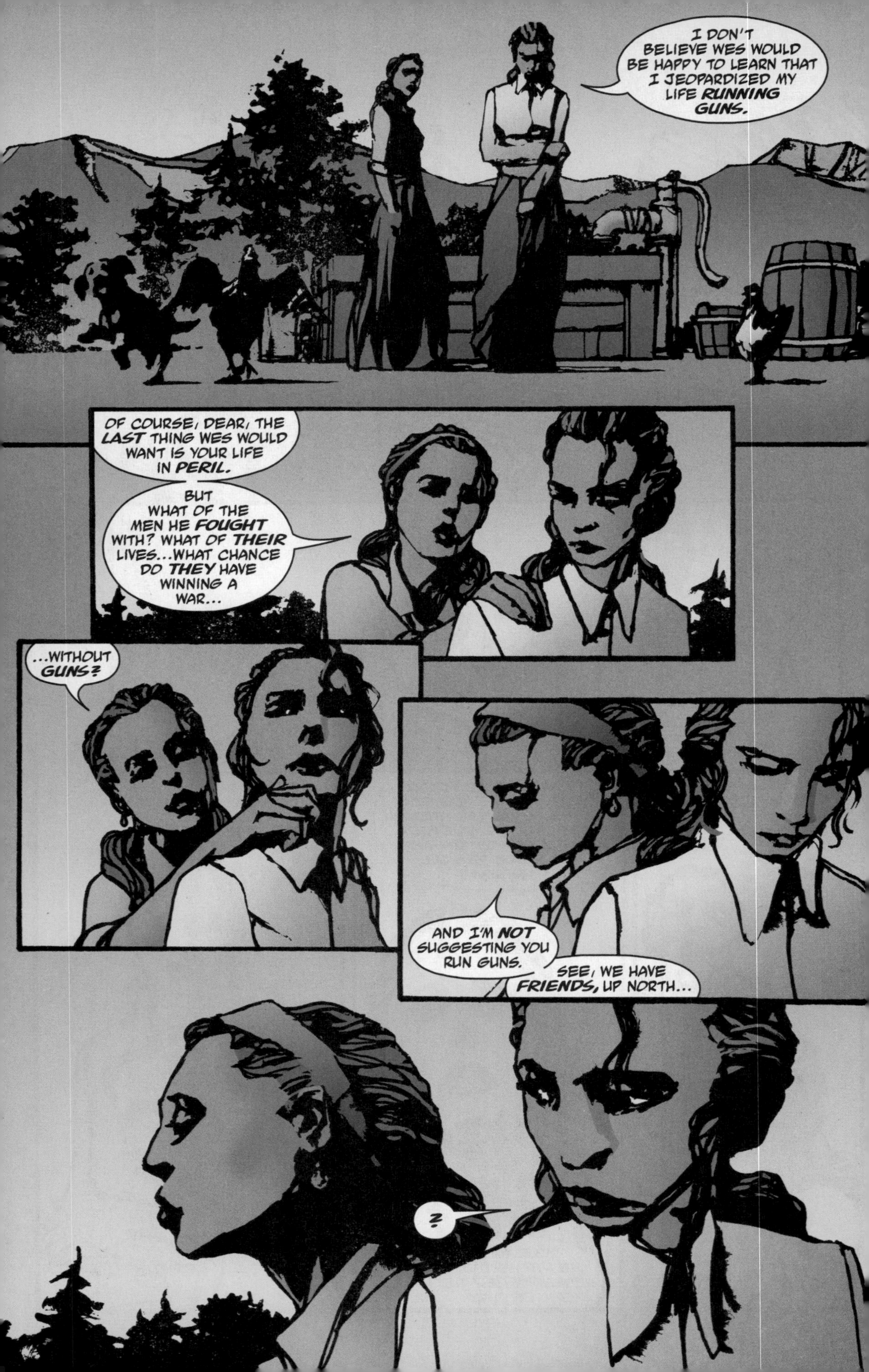
I DON'T BELIEVE WES WOULD BE HAPPY TO LEARN THAT I JEOPARDIZED MY LIFE **RUNNING GUNS.**
OF COURSE, DEAR, THE **LAST** THING WES WOULD WANT IS YOUR LIFE IN **PERIL.**
BUT WHAT OF THE MEN HE **FOUGHT** WITH? WHAT OF **THEIR** LIVES...WHAT CHANCE DO **THEY** HAVE WINNING A WAR...
...WITHOUT **GUNS?**
AND I'M **NOT** SUGGESTING YOU RUN GUNS.
SEE, WE HAVE **FRIENDS,** UP NORTH...
?

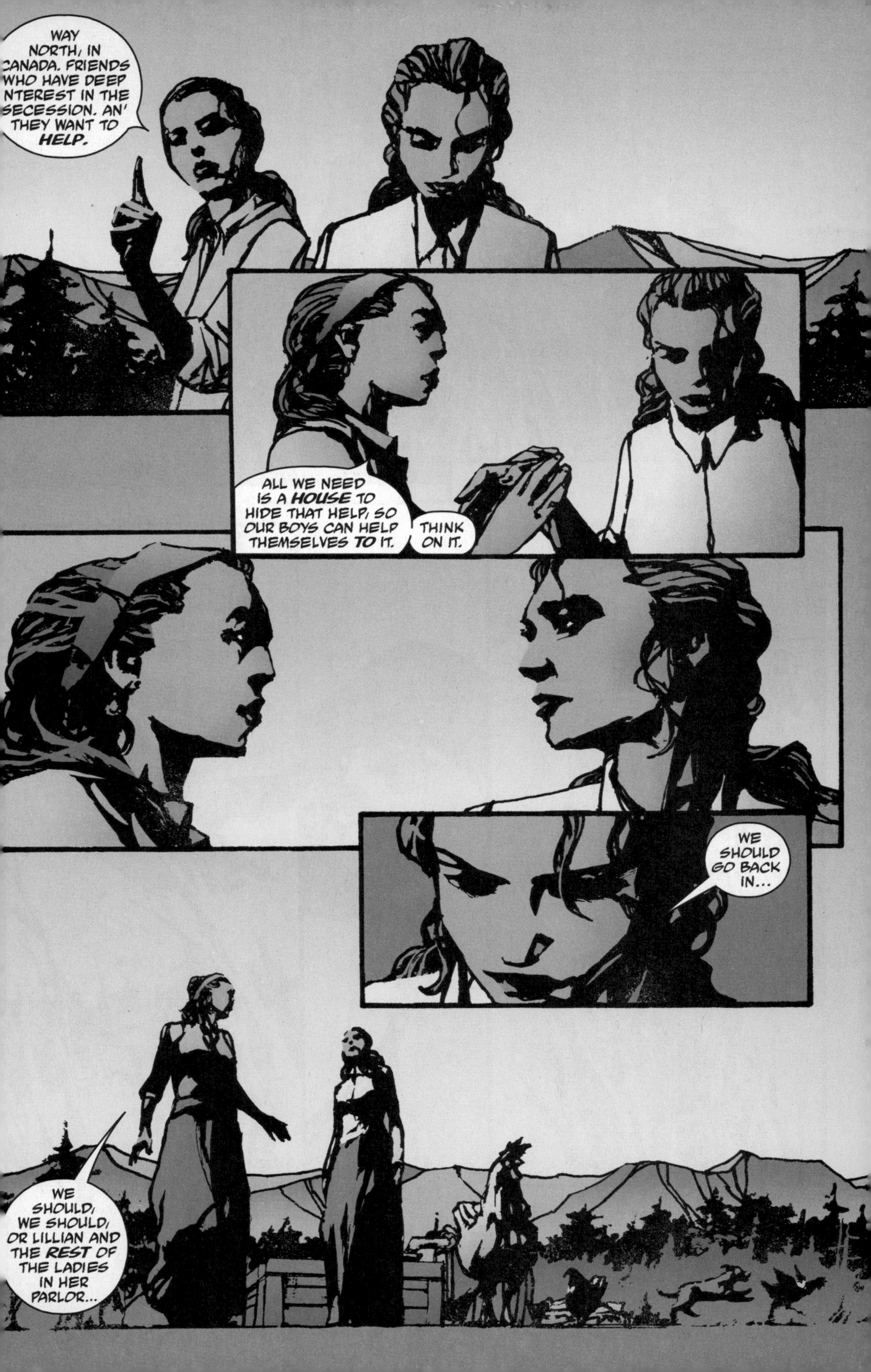
WAY NORTH, IN CANADA. FRIENDS WHO HAVE DEEP INTEREST IN THE SECESSION. AN' THEY WANT TO HELP.
ALL WE NEED IS A HOUSE TO HIDE THAT HELP, SO OUR BOYS CAN HELP THEMSELVES TO IT.
THINK ON IT.
WE SHOULD GO BACK IN...
WE SHOULD, WE SHOULD, OR LILLIAN AND THE REST OF THE LADIES IN HER PARLOR...

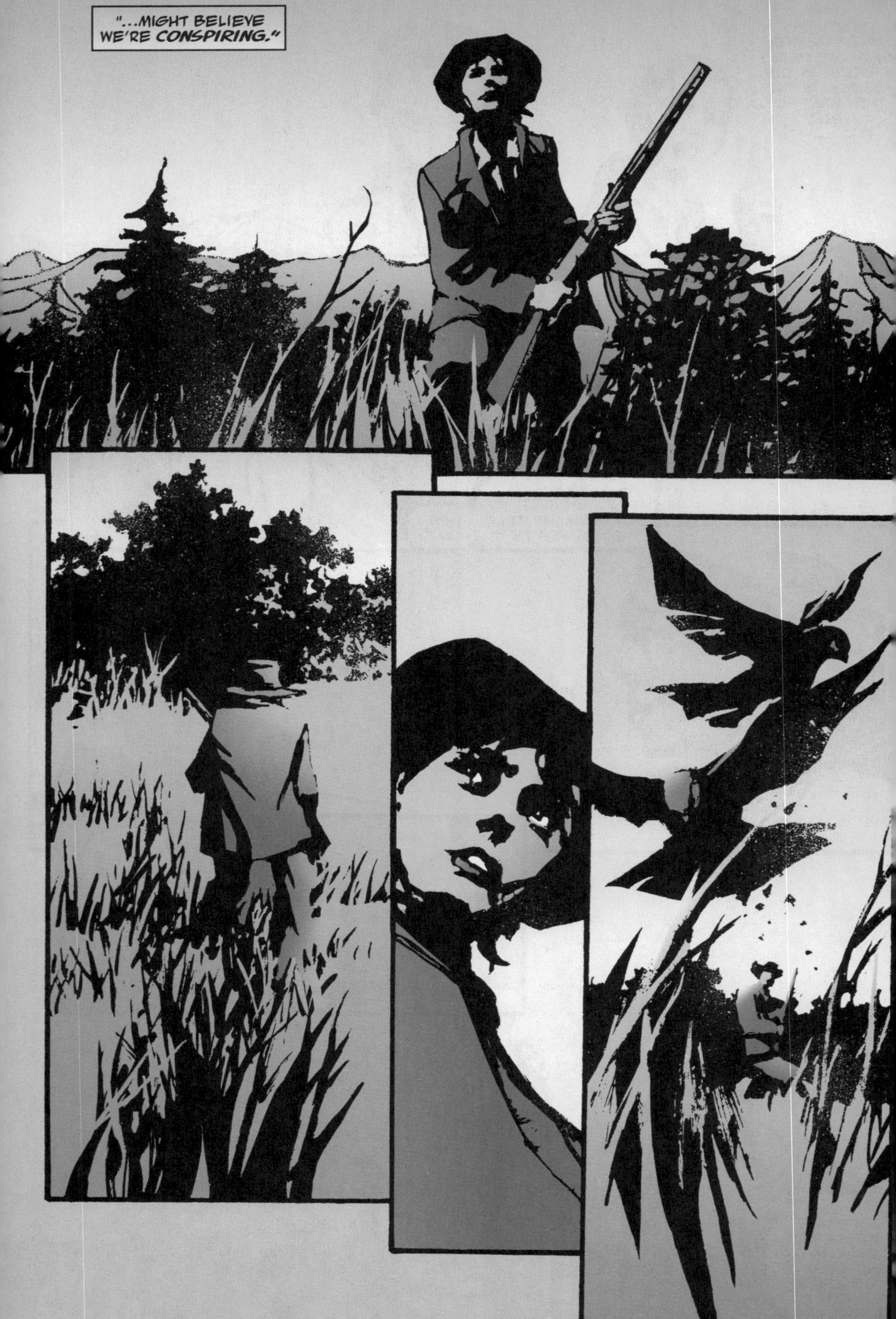
"...MIGHT BELIEVE WE'RE CONSPIRING."

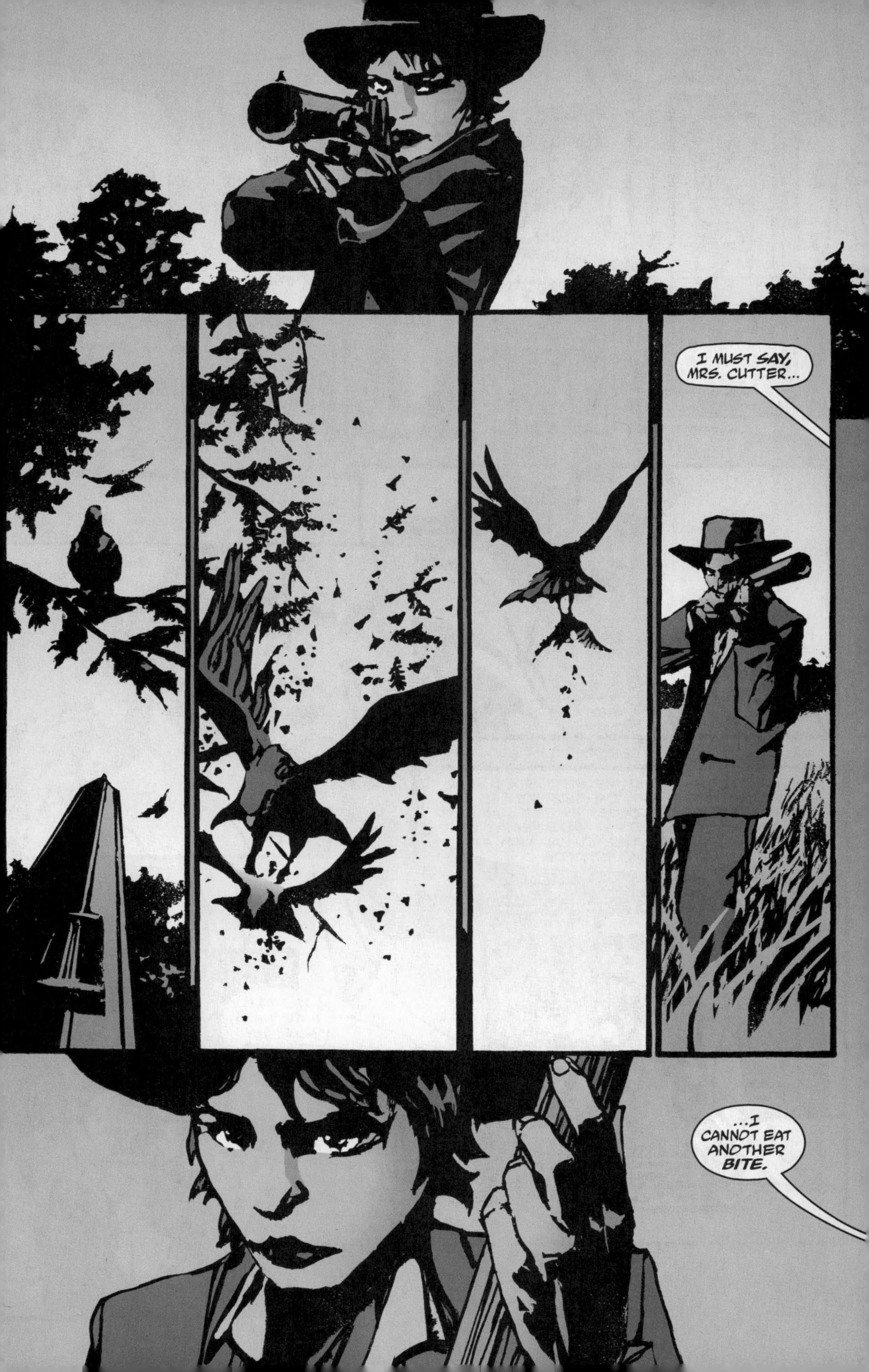
I MUST SAY, MRS. CUTTER...
...I CANNOT EAT ANOTHER BITE.

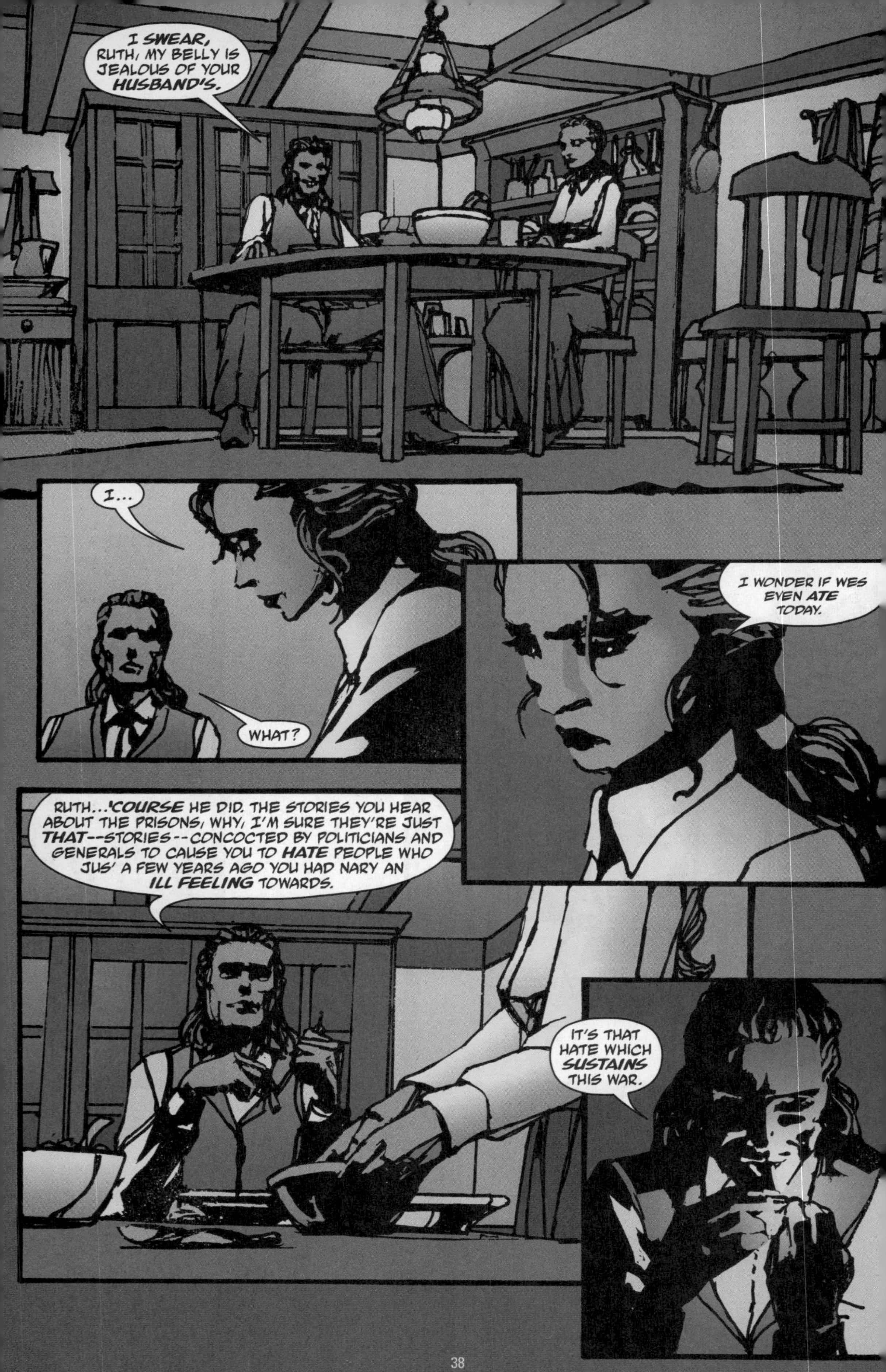
I SWEAR, RUTH, MY BELLY IS JEALOUS OF YOUR HUSBAND'S.
I...
WHAT?
I WONDER IF WES EVEN ATE TODAY.
RUTH...'COURSE HE DID. THE STORIES YOU HEAR ABOUT THE PRISONS, WHY, I'M SURE THEY'RE JUST THAT--STORIES--CONCOCTED BY POLITICIANS AND GENERALS TO CAUSE YOU TO HATE PEOPLE WHO JUS' A FEW YEARS AGO YOU HAD NARY AN ILL FEELING TOWARDS.
IT'S THAT HATE WHICH SUSTAINS THIS WAR.

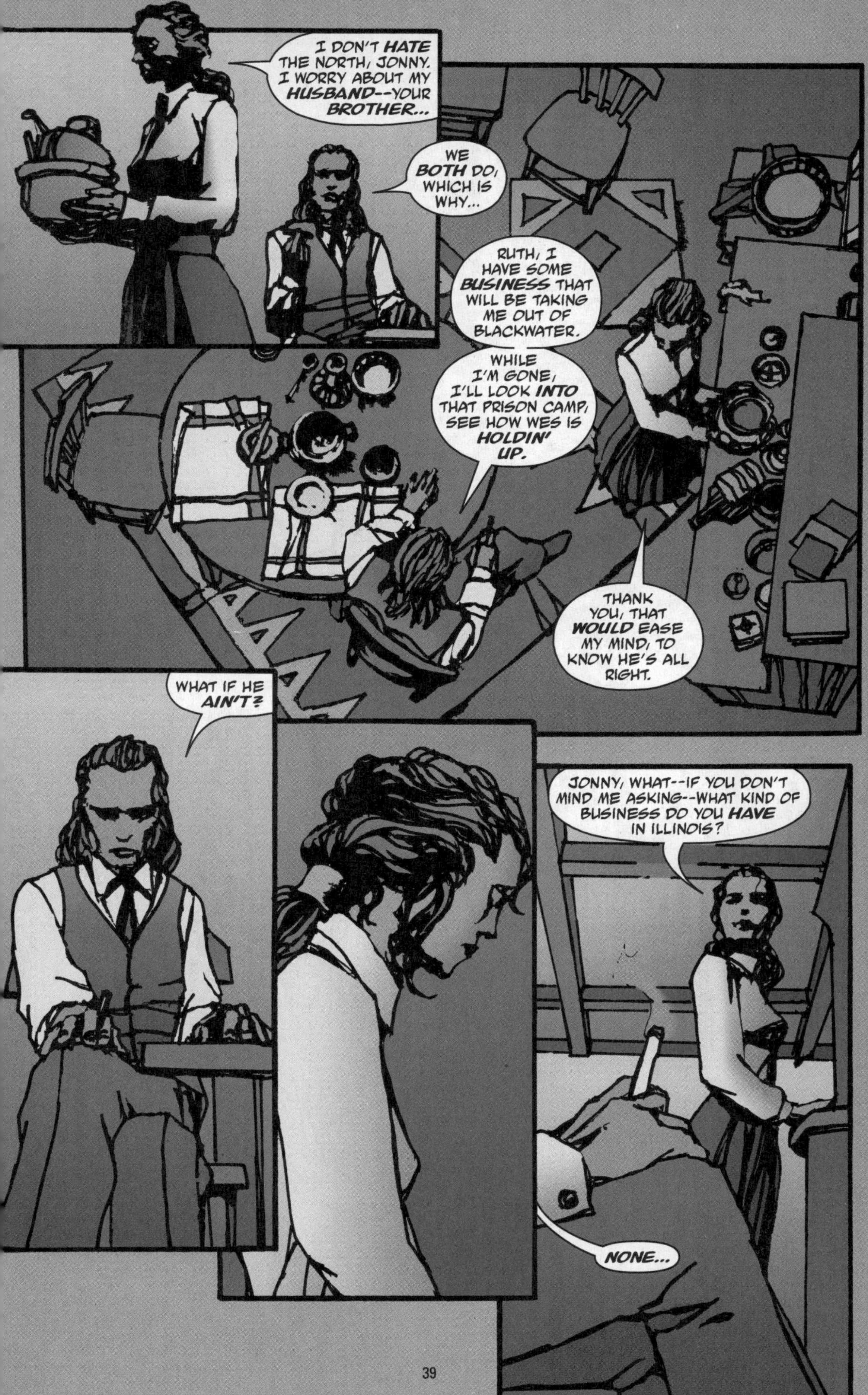
I DON'T HATE THE NORTH, JONNY. I WORRY ABOUT MY HUSBAND--YOUR BROTHER...
WE BOTH DO, WHICH IS WHY...
RUTH, I HAVE SOME BUSINESS THAT WILL BE TAKING ME OUT OF BLACKWATER.
WHILE I'M GONE, I'LL LOOK INTO THAT PRISON CAMP, SEE HOW WES IS HOLDIN' UP.
THANK YOU, THAT WOULD EASE MY MIND, TO KNOW HE'S ALL RIGHT.
WHAT IF HE AIN'T?
JONNY, WHAT--IF YOU DON'T MIND ME ASKING--WHAT KIND OF BUSINESS DO YOU HAVE IN ILLINOIS?
NONE...

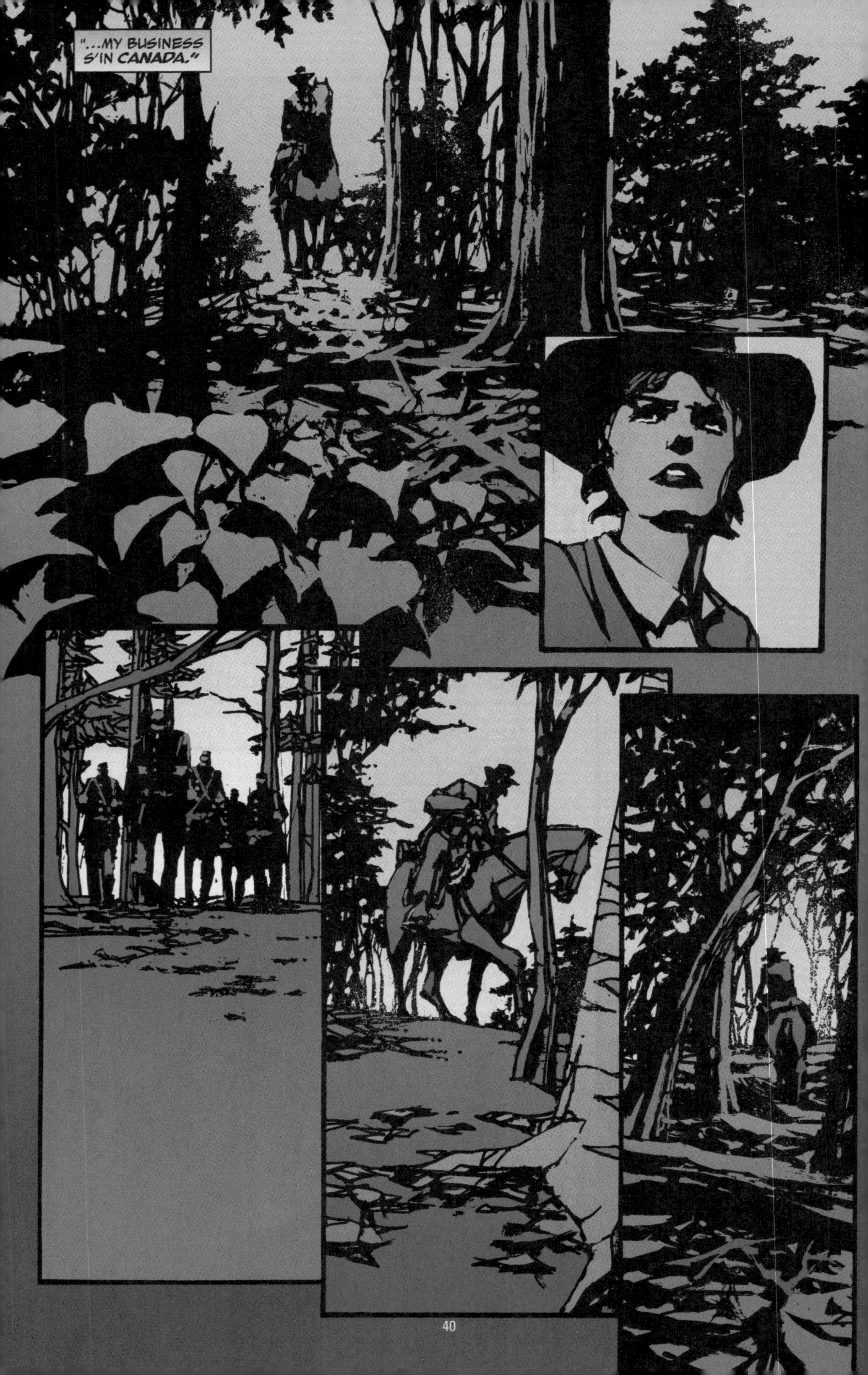
"...MY BUSINESS S'IN CANADA."

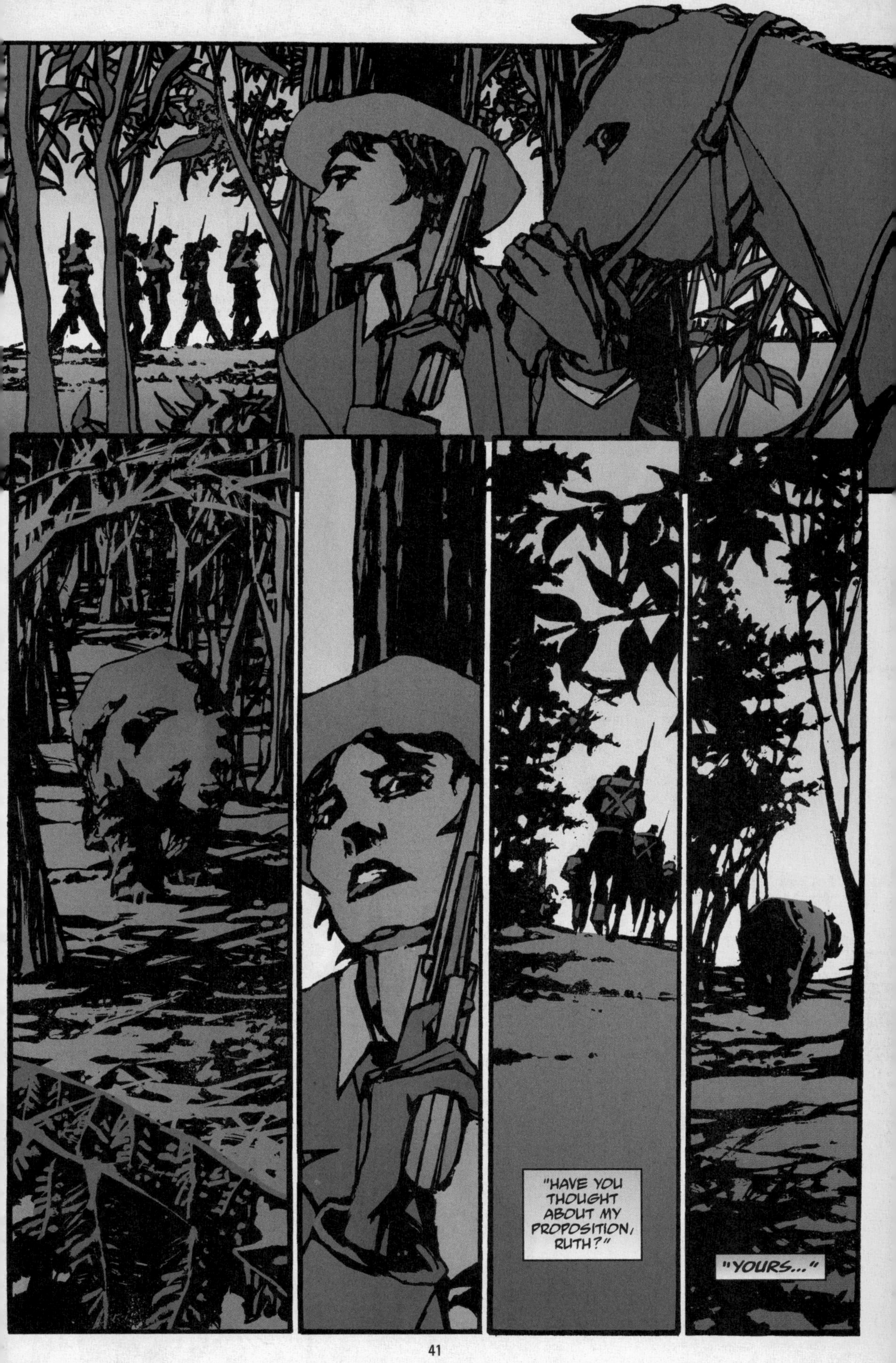
"HAVE YOU THOUGHT ABOUT MY PROPOSITION, RUTH?"
"YOURS..."

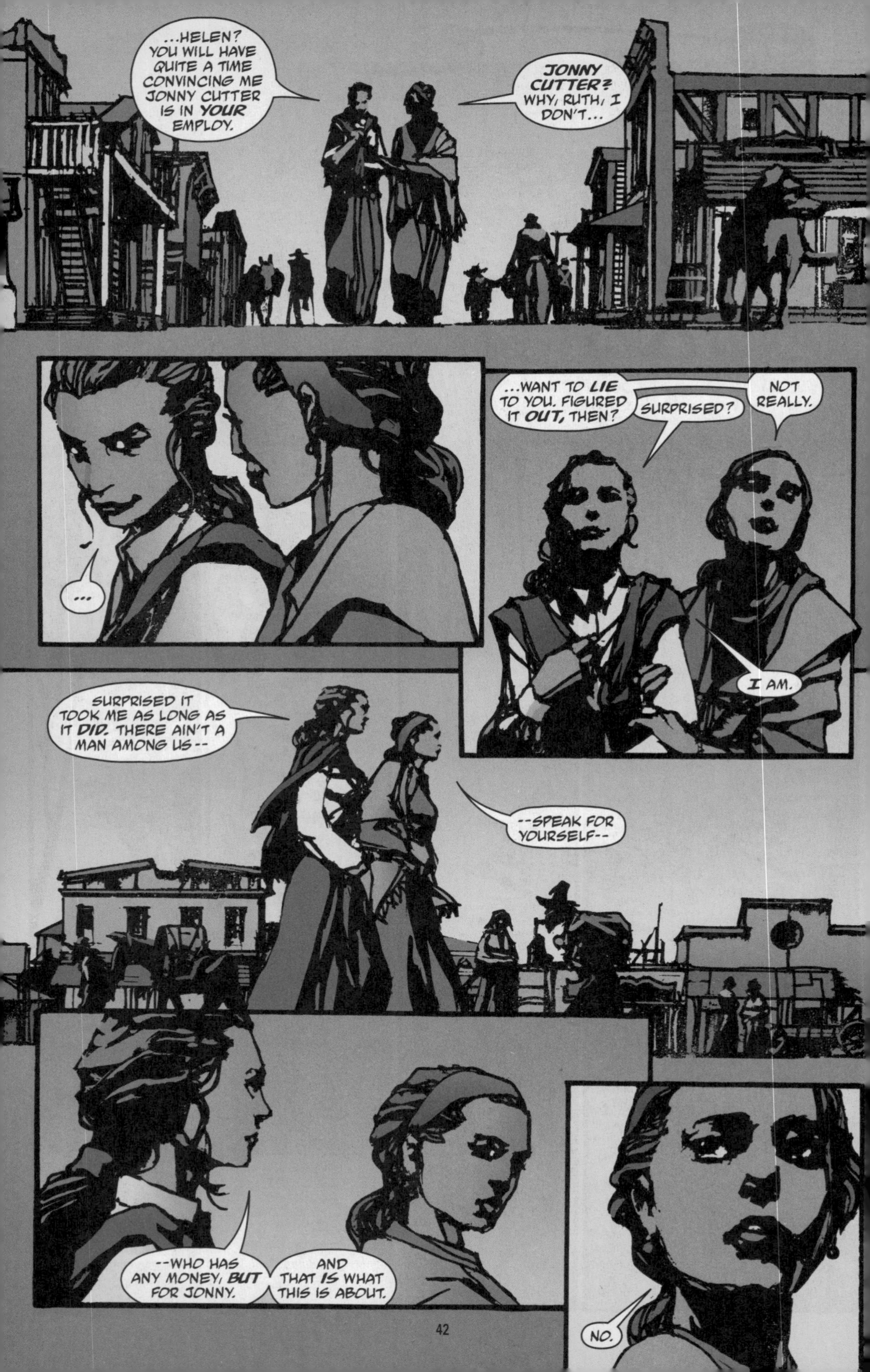
...HELEN? YOU WILL HAVE QUITE A TIME CONVINCING ME JONNY CUTTER IS IN YOUR EMPLOY.
JONNY CUTTER? WHY, RUTH, I DON'T...
...
...WANT TO LIE TO YOU. FIGURED IT OUT, THEN?
SURPRISED?
NOT REALLY.
I AM.
SURPRISED IT TOOK ME AS LONG AS IT DID. THERE AIN'T A MAN AMONG US--
--SPEAK FOR YOURSELF--
--WHO HAS ANY MONEY, BUT FOR JONNY.
AND THAT IS WHAT THIS IS ABOUT.
NO.

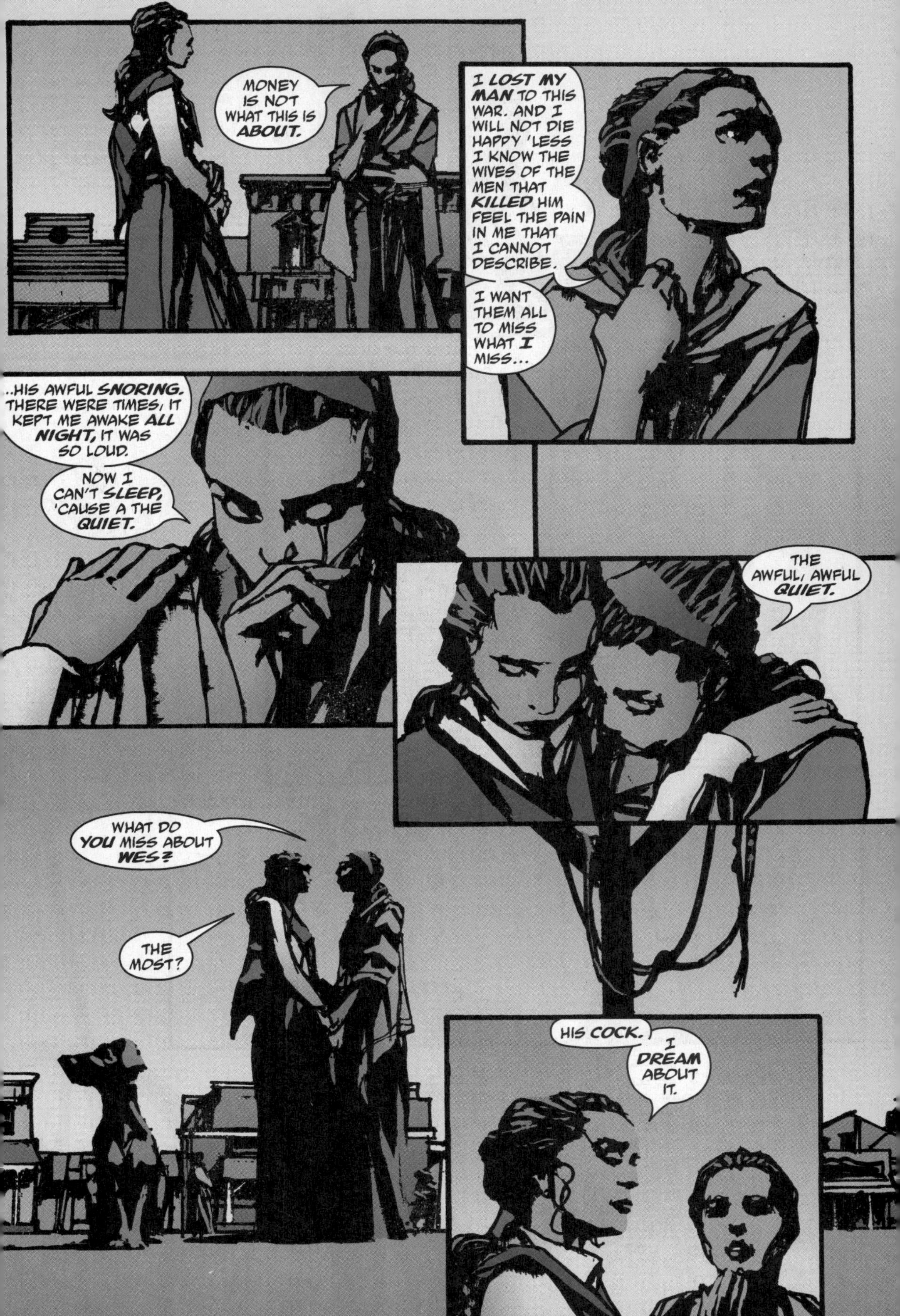
MONEY IS NOT WHAT THIS IS ABOUT.
I LOST MY MAN TO THIS WAR. AND I WILL NOT DIE HAPPY 'LESS I KNOW THE WIVES OF THE MEN THAT KILLED HIM FEEL THE PAIN IN ME THAT I CANNOT DESCRIBE.
I WANT THEM ALL TO MISS WHAT I MISS...
...HIS AWFUL SNORING. THERE WERE TIMES, IT KEPT ME AWAKE ALL NIGHT, IT WAS SO LOUD.
NOW I CAN'T SLEEP, 'CAUSE A THE QUIET.
THE AWFUL, AWFUL QUIET.
WHAT DO YOU MISS ABOUT WES?
THE MOST?
HIS COCK.
I DREAM ABOUT IT.

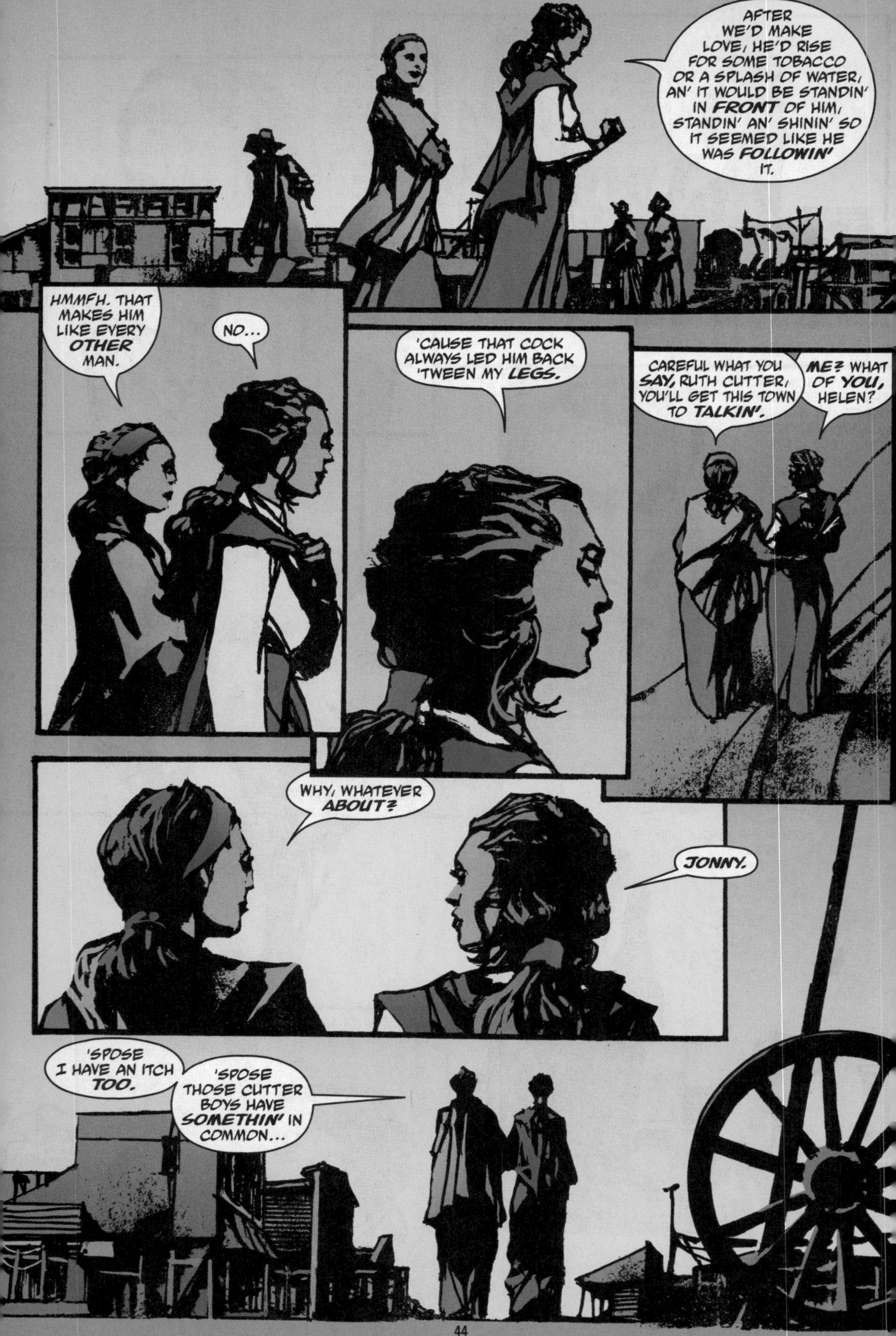
AFTER WE'D MAKE LOVE, HE'D RISE FOR SOME TOBACCO OR A SPLASH OF WATER, AN' IT WOULD BE STANDIN' IN FRONT OF HIM, STANDIN' AN' SHININ' SO IT SEEMED LIKE HE WAS FOLLOWIN' IT.
HMMFH. THAT MAKES HIM LIKE EVERY OTHER MAN.
NO...
'CAUSE THAT COCK ALWAYS LED HIM BACK 'TWEEN MY LEGS.
CAREFUL WHAT YOU SAY, RUTH CUTTER, YOU'LL GET THIS TOWN TO TALKIN'.
ME? WHAT OF YOU, HELEN?
WHY, WHATEVER ABOUT?
JONNY.
'SPOSE I HAVE AN ITCH TOO.
'SPOSE THOSE CUTTER BOYS HAVE SOMETHIN' IN COMMON...

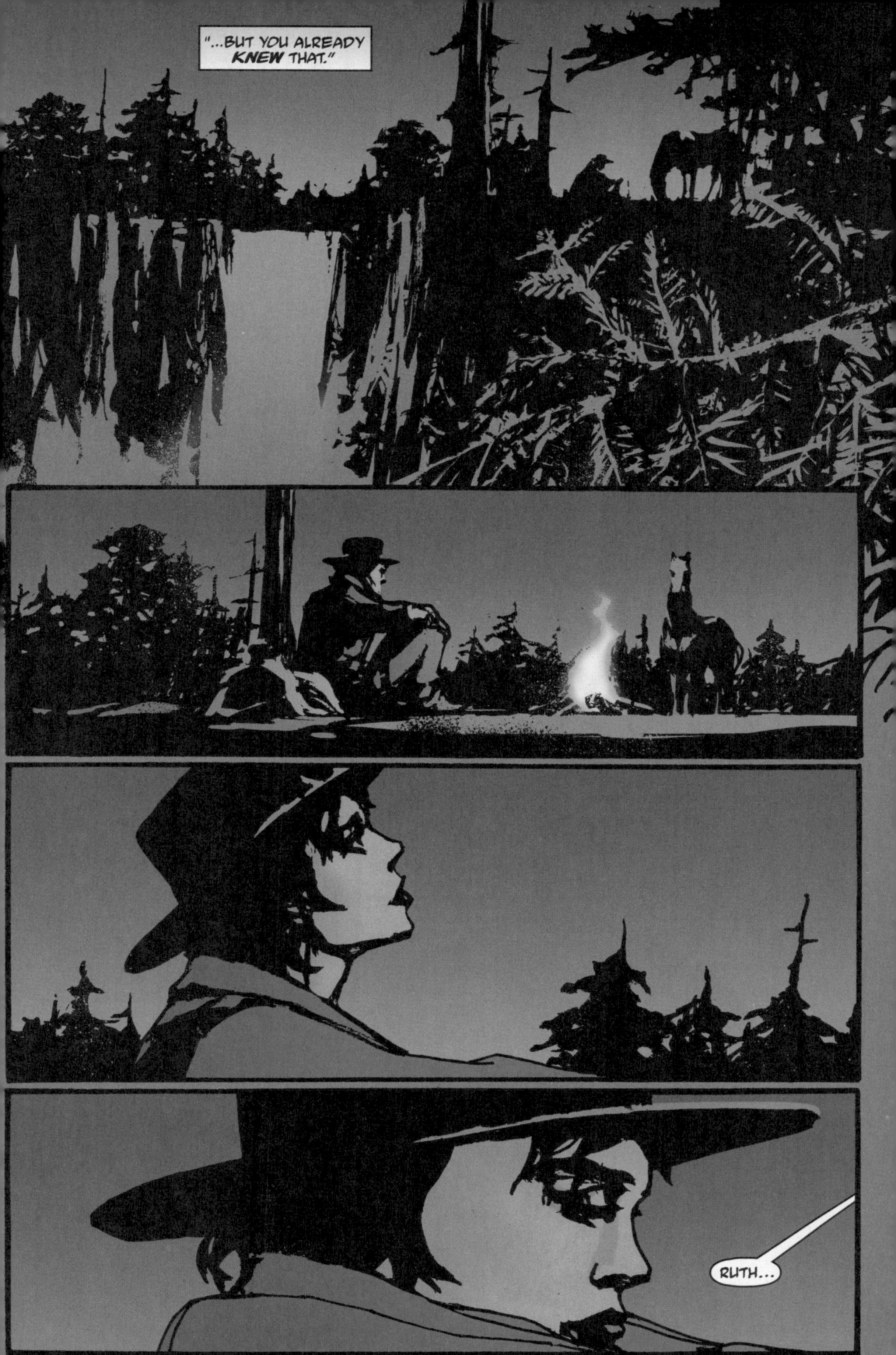
"...BUT YOU ALREADY KNEW THAT."
RUTH...

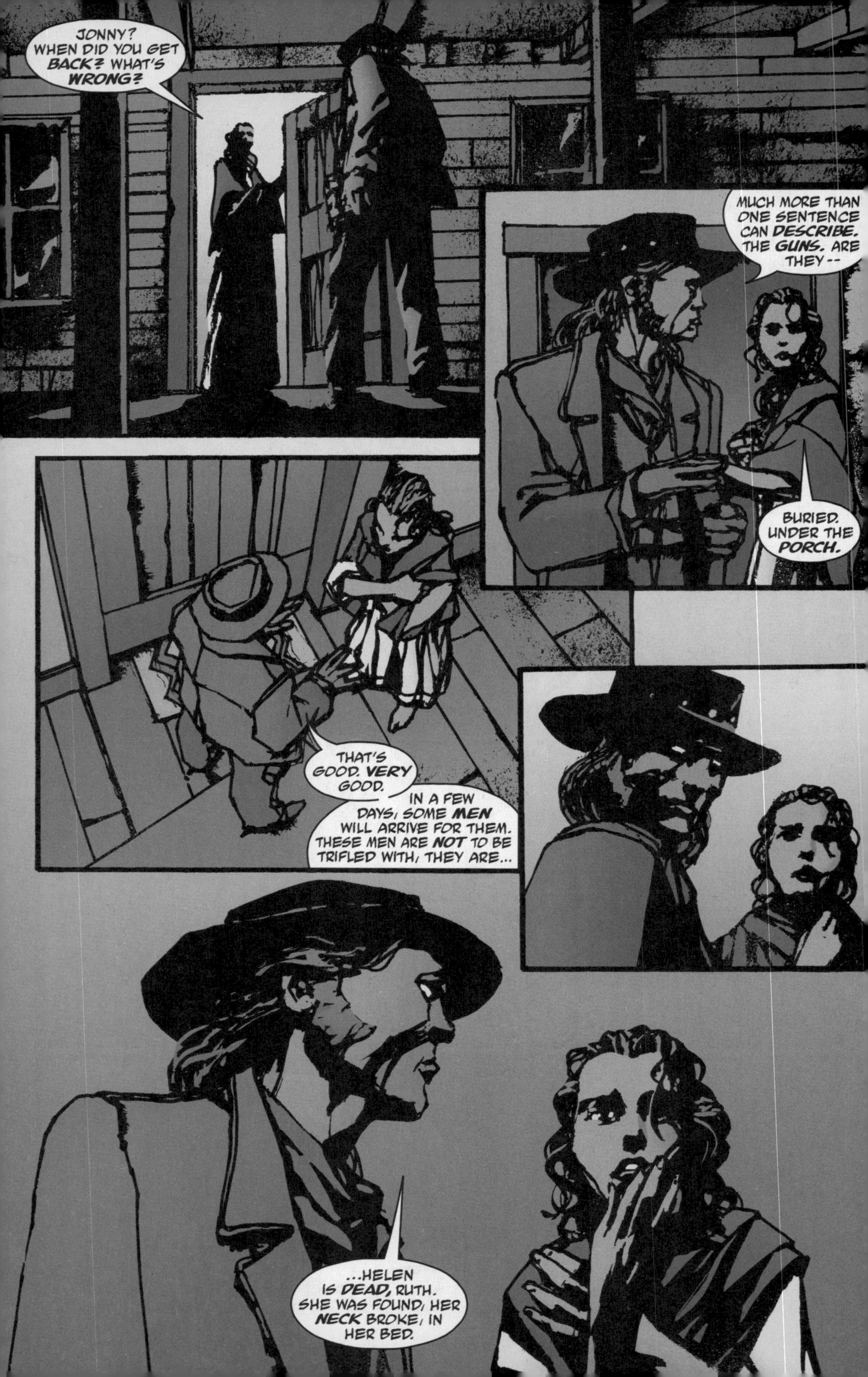
JONNY? WHEN DID YOU GET BACK? WHAT'S WRONG?
MUCH MORE THAN ONE SENTENCE CAN DESCRIBE. THE GUNS. ARE THEY --
BURIED. UNDER THE PORCH.
THAT'S GOOD. VERY GOOD.
IN A FEW DAYS, SOME MEN WILL ARRIVE FOR THEM. THESE MEN ARE NOT TO BE TRIFLED WITH, THEY ARE...
...HELEN IS DEAD, RUTH. SHE WAS FOUND, HER NECK BROKE, IN HER BED.

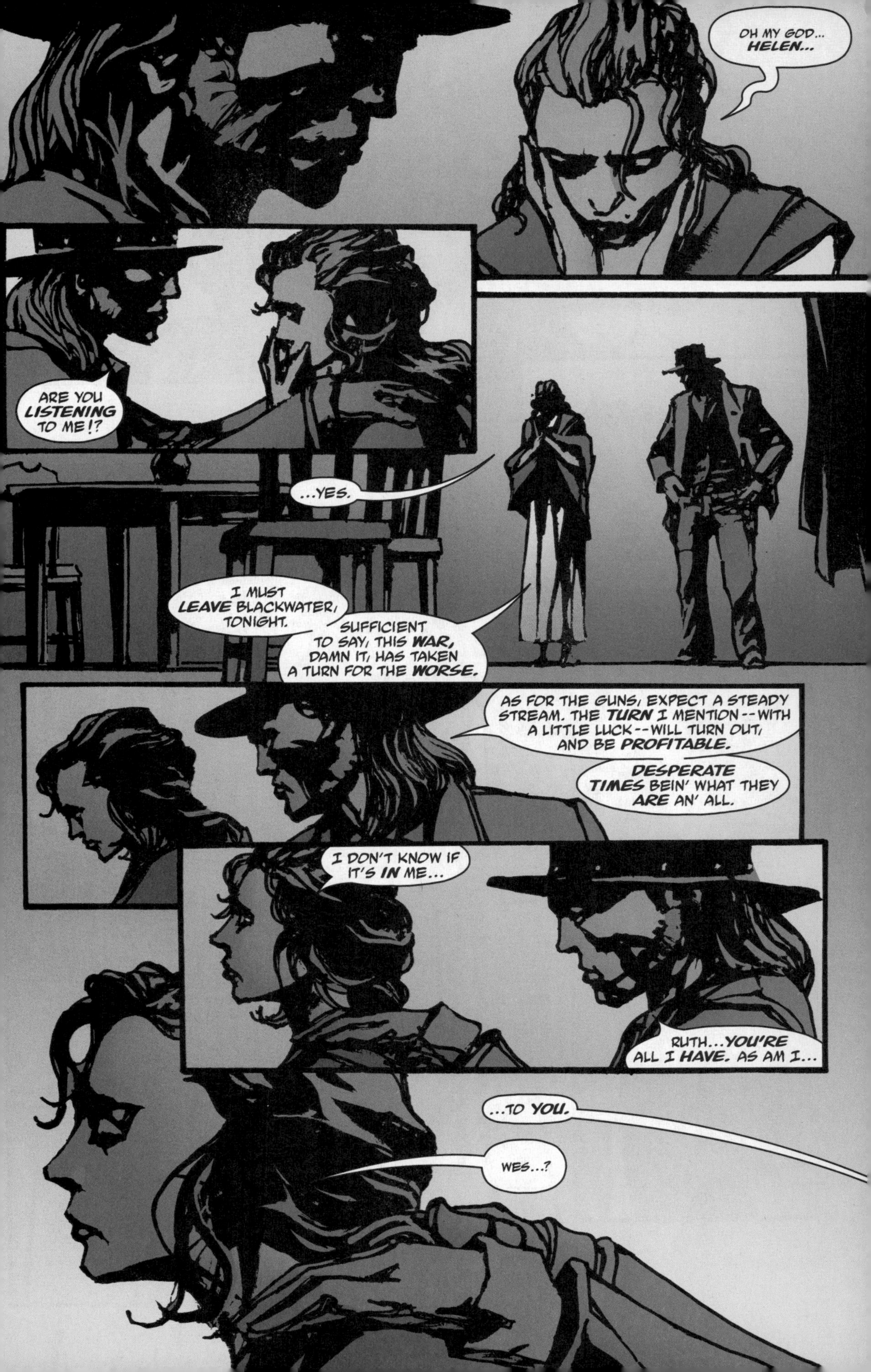
OH MY GOD... HELEN...
ARE YOU LISTENING TO ME!?
...YES.
I MUST LEAVE BLACKWATER, TONIGHT.
SUFFICIENT TO SAY, THIS WAR, DAMN IT, HAS TAKEN A TURN FOR THE WORSE.
AS FOR THE GUNS, EXPECT A STEADY STREAM. THE TURN I MENTION--WITH A LITTLE LUCK--WILL TURN OUT, AND BE PROFITABLE.
DESPERATE TIMES BEIN' WHAT THEY ARE AN' ALL.
I DON'T KNOW IF IT'S IN ME...
RUTH...YOU'RE ALL I HAVE. AS AM I...
...TO YOU.
WES...?

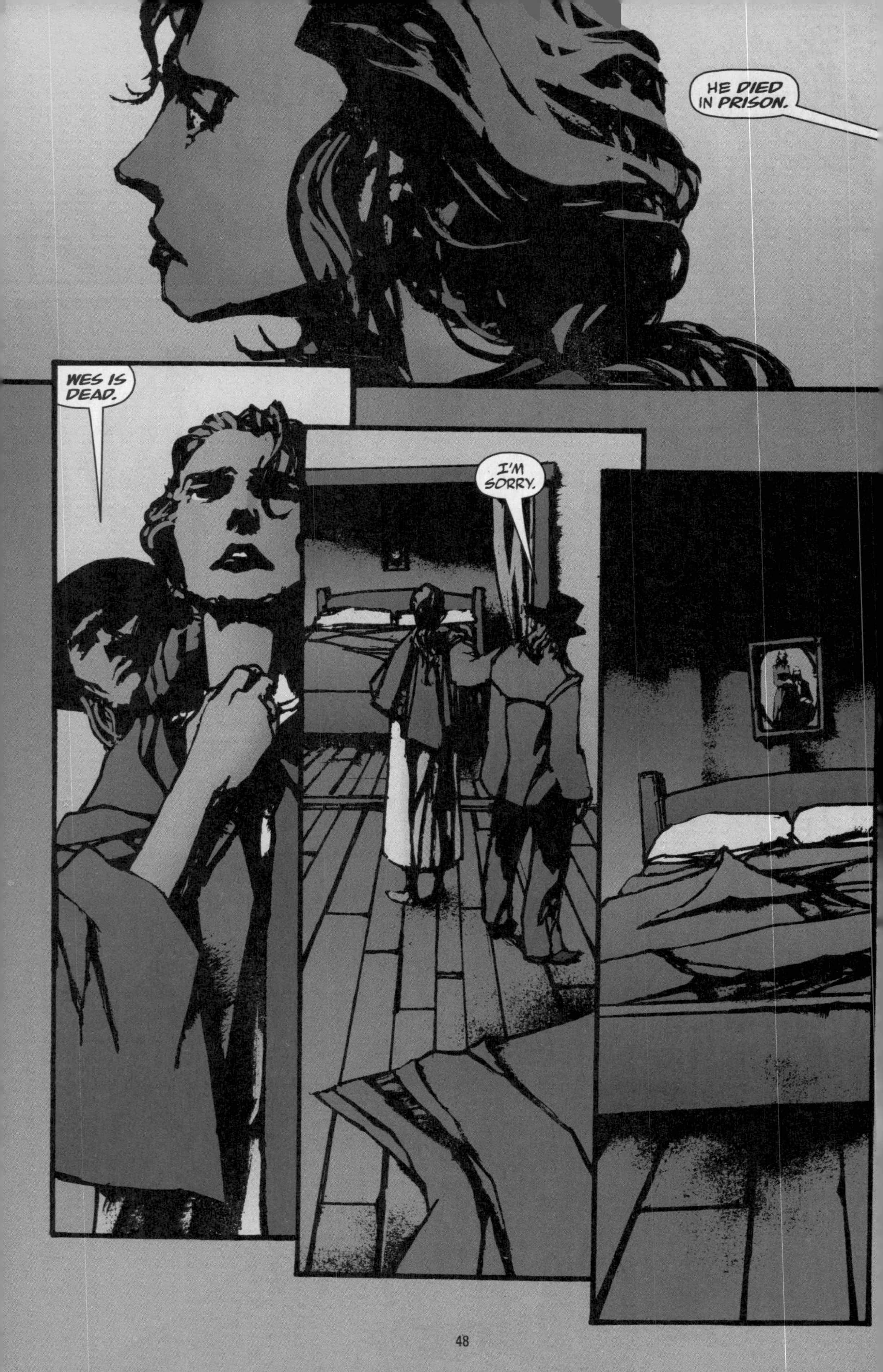
HE DIED IN PRISON.
WES IS DEAD.
I'M SORRY.

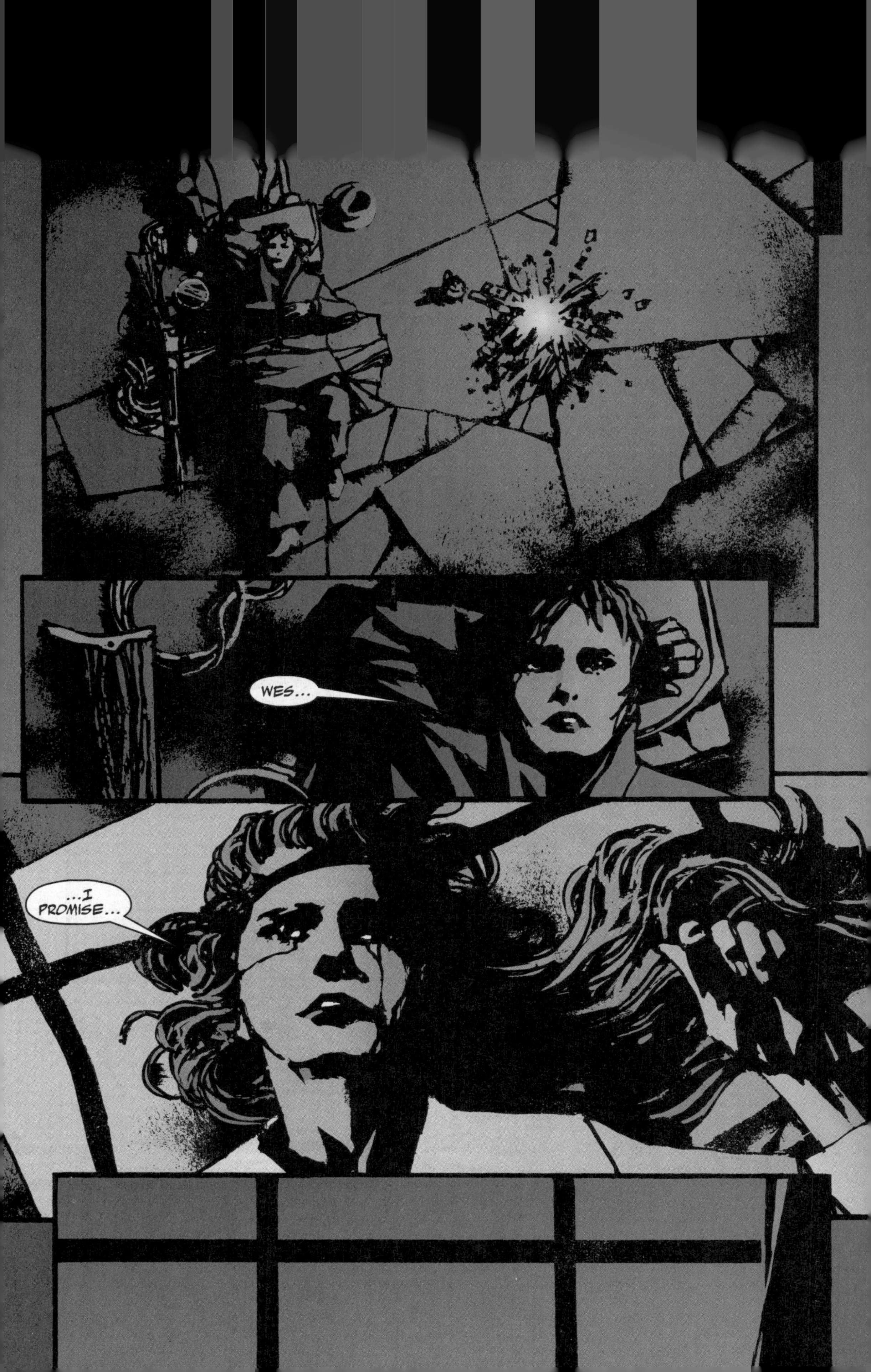
WES...
...I PROMISE...

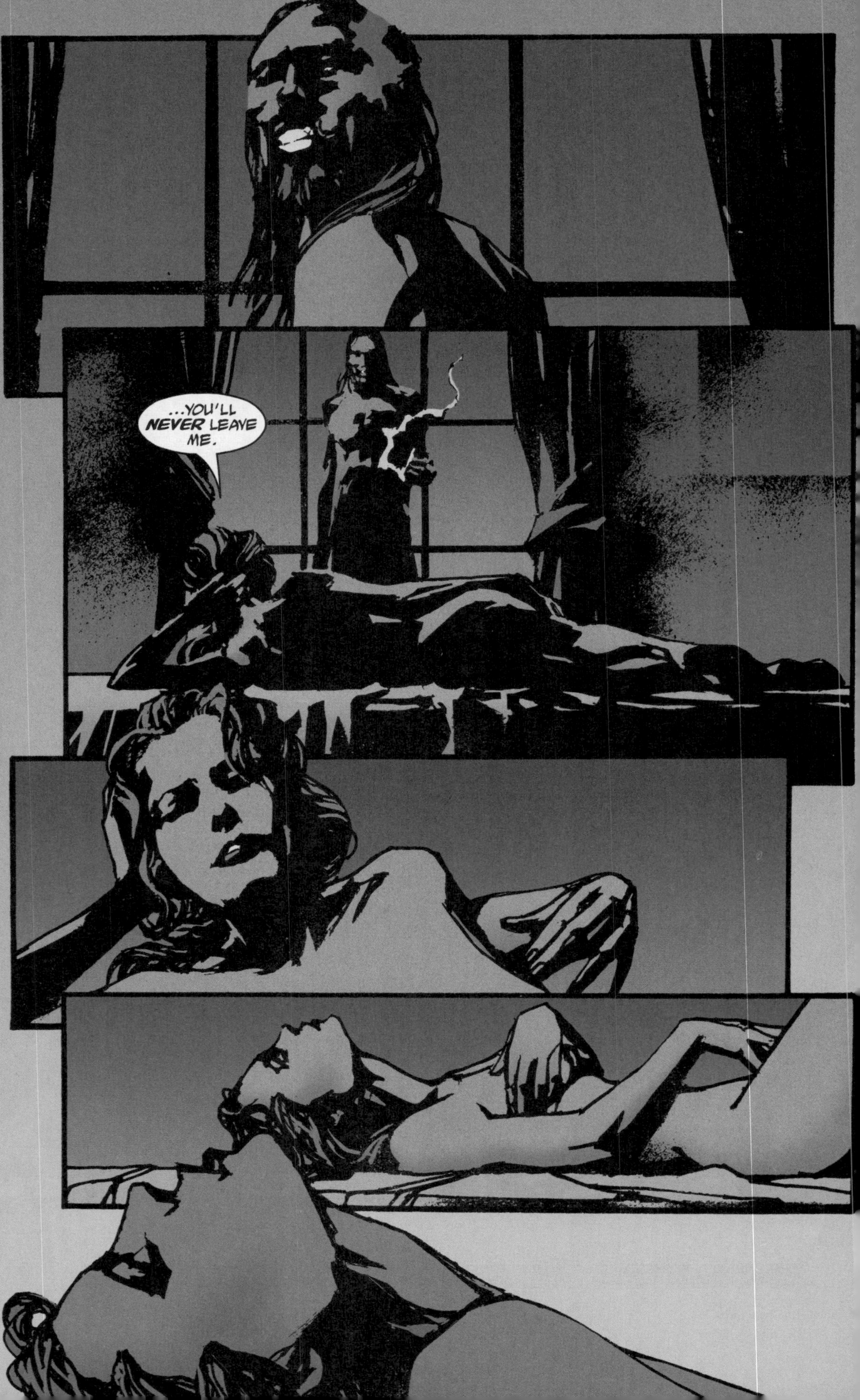
...YOU'LL NEVER LEAVE ME.

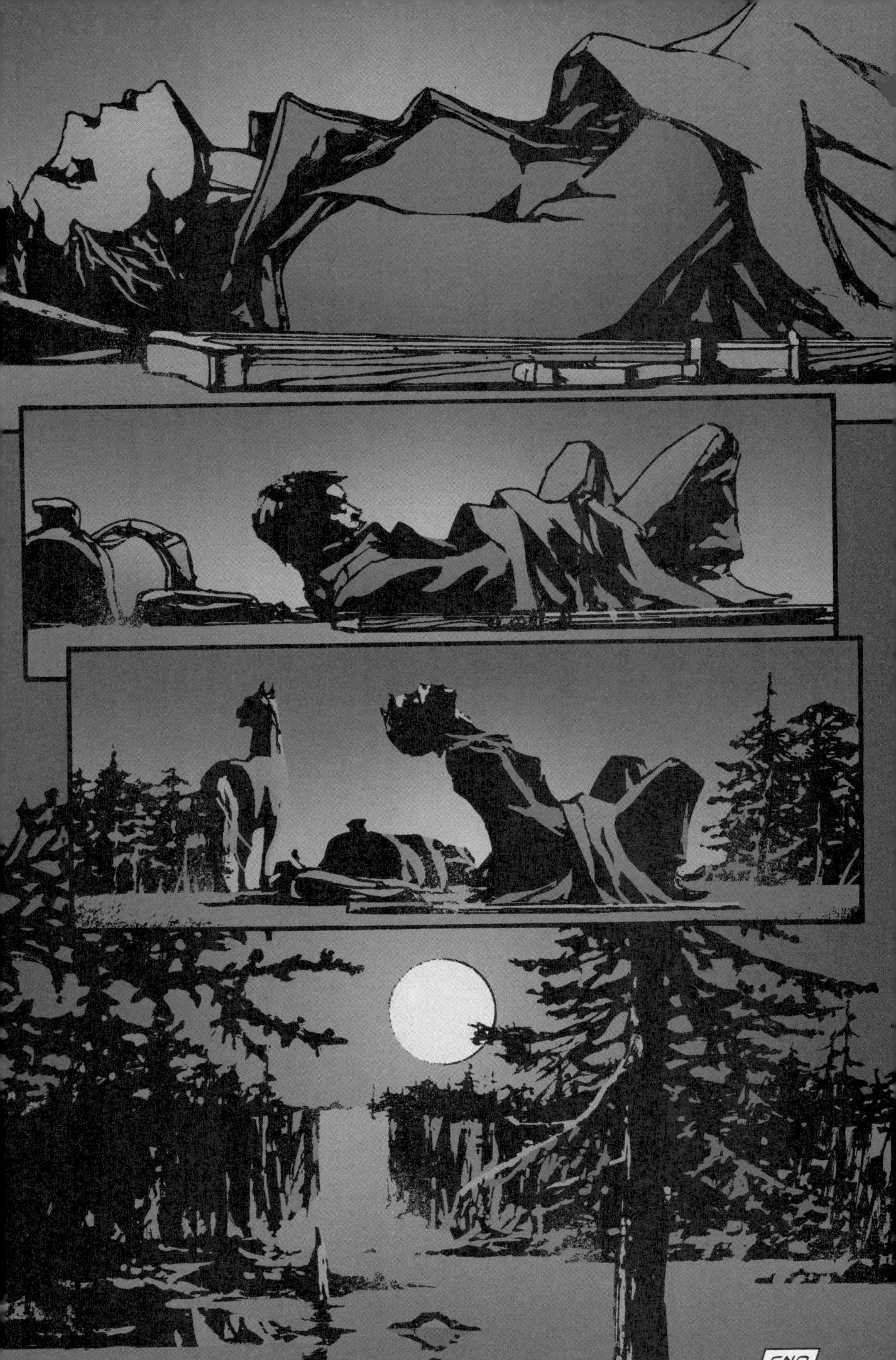
END

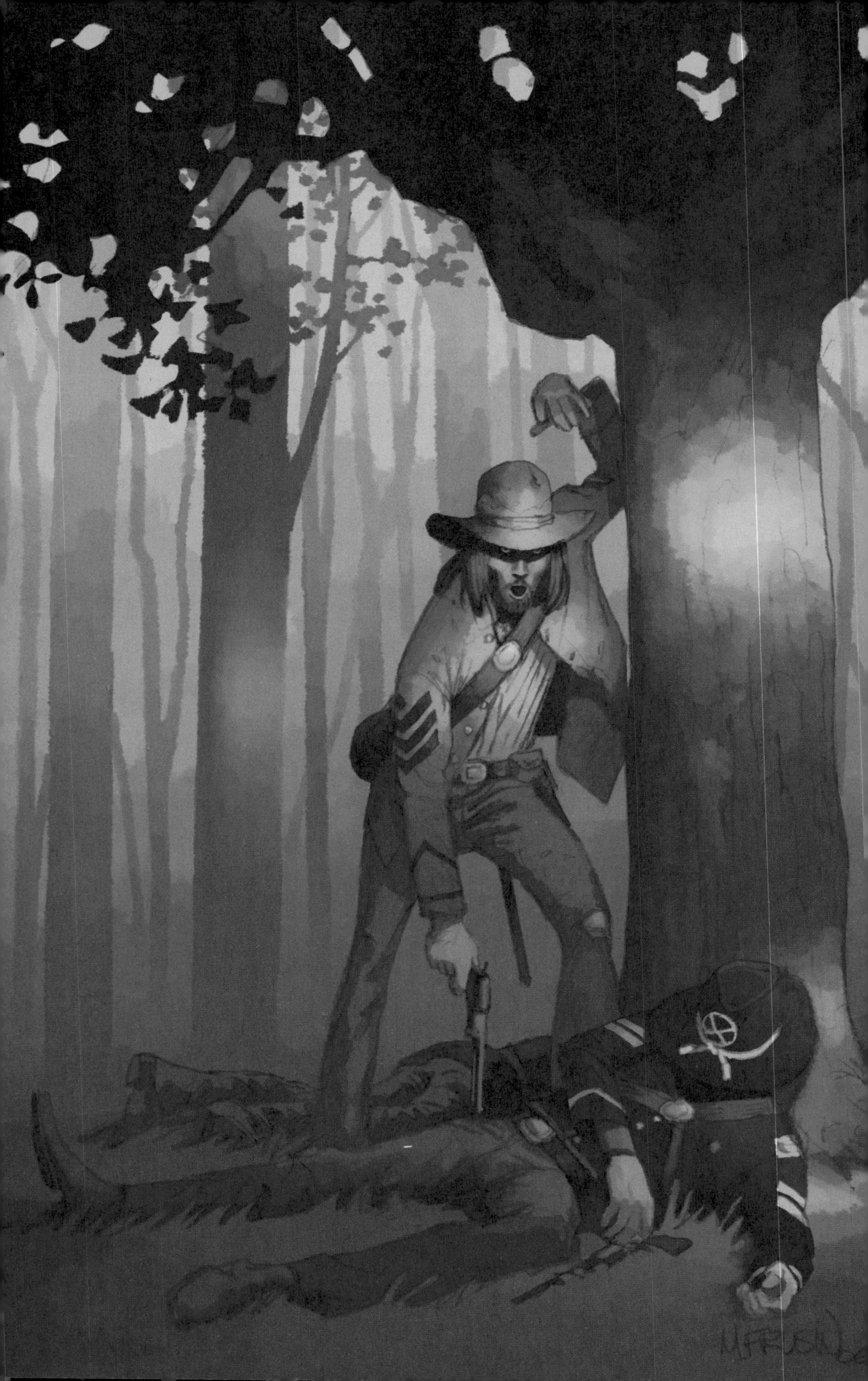

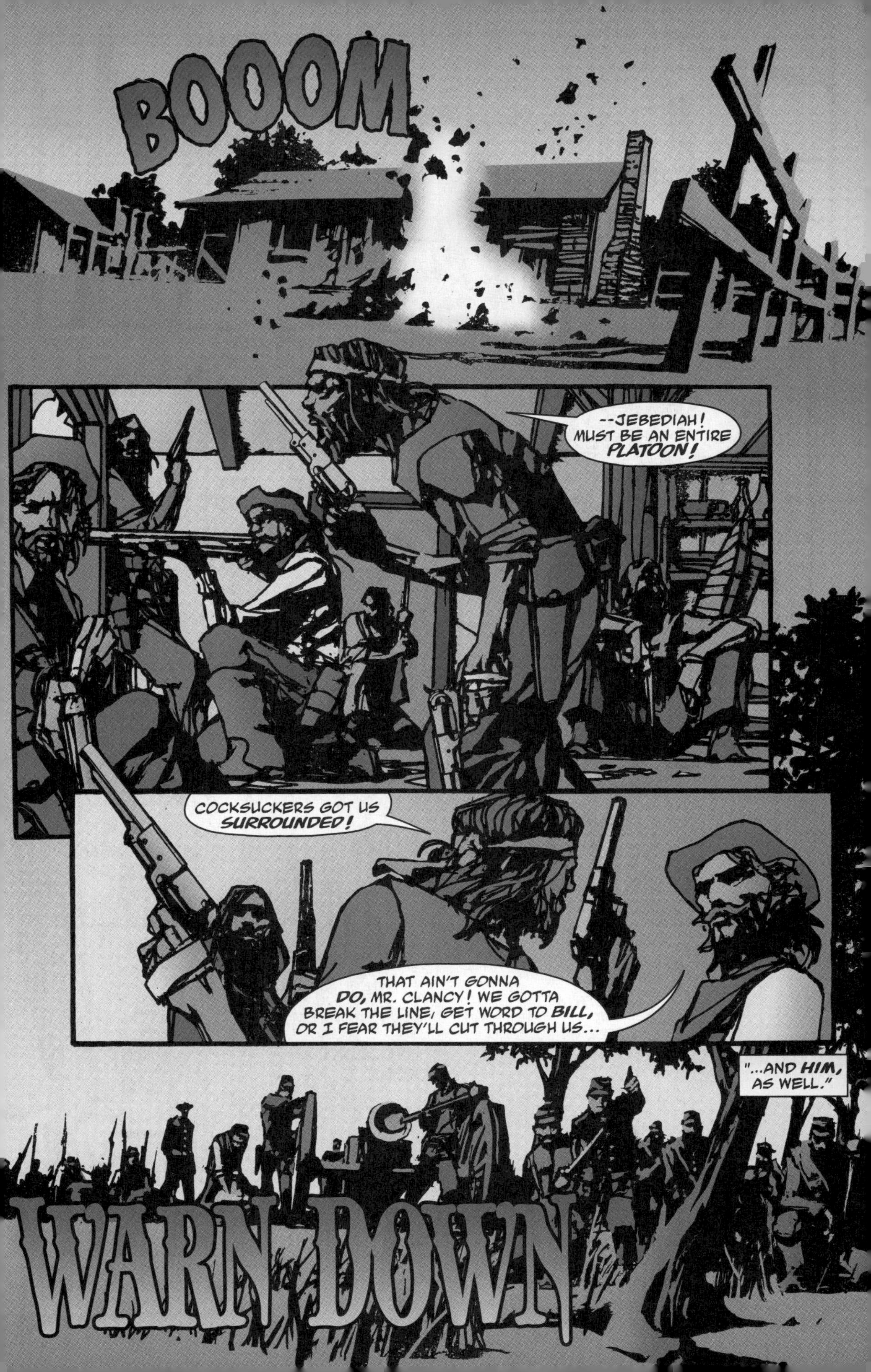
BOOOM
--JEBEDIAH! MUST BE AN ENTIRE PLATOON!
COCKSUCKERS GOT US SURROUNDED!
THAT AIN'T GONNA DO, MR. CLANCY! WE GOTTA BREAK THE LINE, GET WORD TO BILL, OR I FEAR THEY'LL CUT THROUGH US...
"...AND HIM, AS WELL."
WARN DOWN

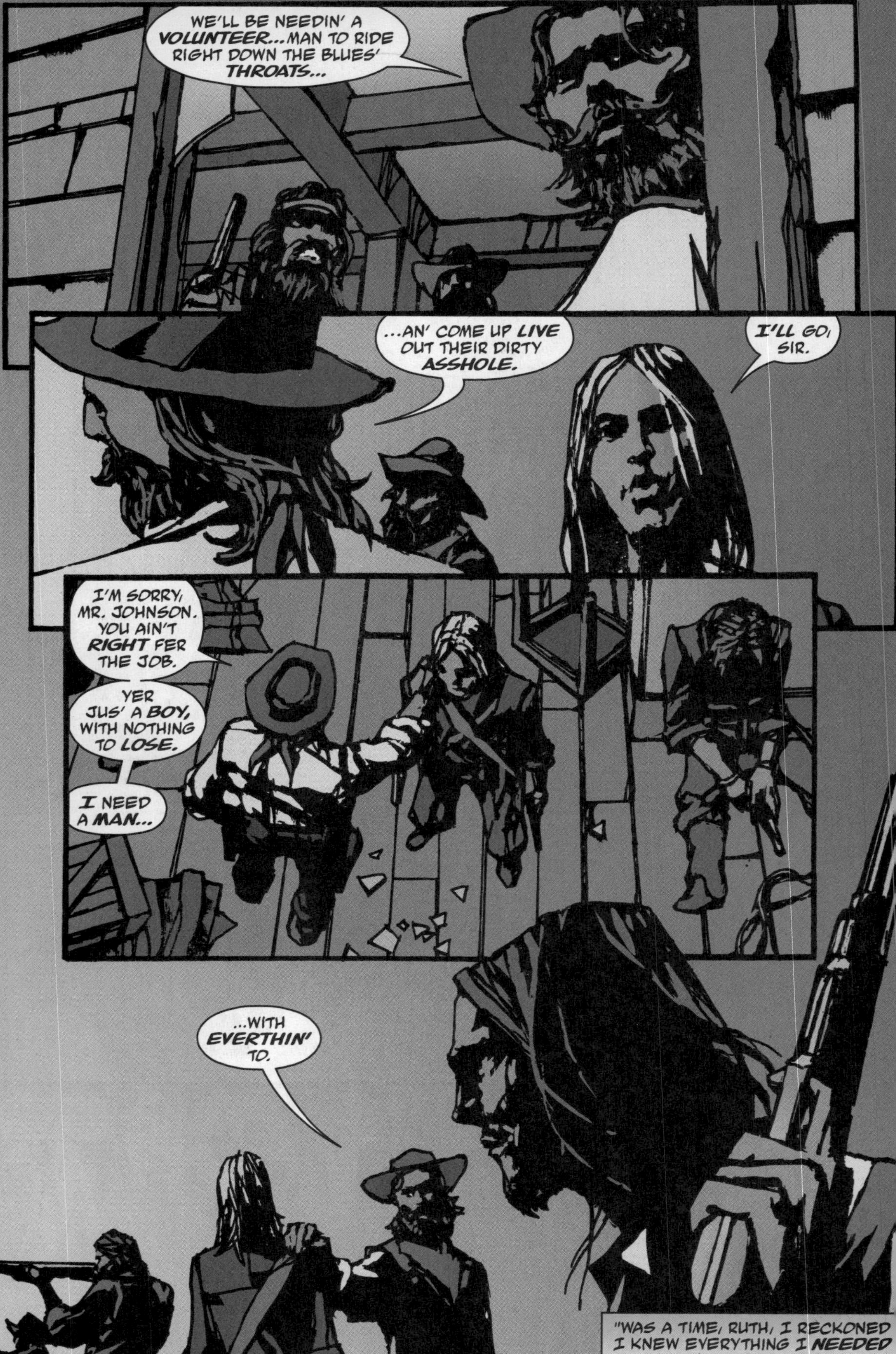

WE'LL BE NEEDIN' A VOLUNTEER... MAN TO RIDE RIGHT DOWN THE BLUES' THROATS...
...AN' COME UP LIVE OUT THEIR DIRTY ASSHOLE.
I'LL GO, SIR.
I'M SORRY, MR. JOHNSON. YOU AIN'T RIGHT FER THE JOB.
YER JUS' A BOY, WITH NOTHING TO LOSE.
I NEED A MAN...
...WITH EVERTHIN' TO.
"WAS A TIME, RUTH, I RECKONED I KNEW EVERYTHING I NEEDED TO KNOW ABOUT YOU..."

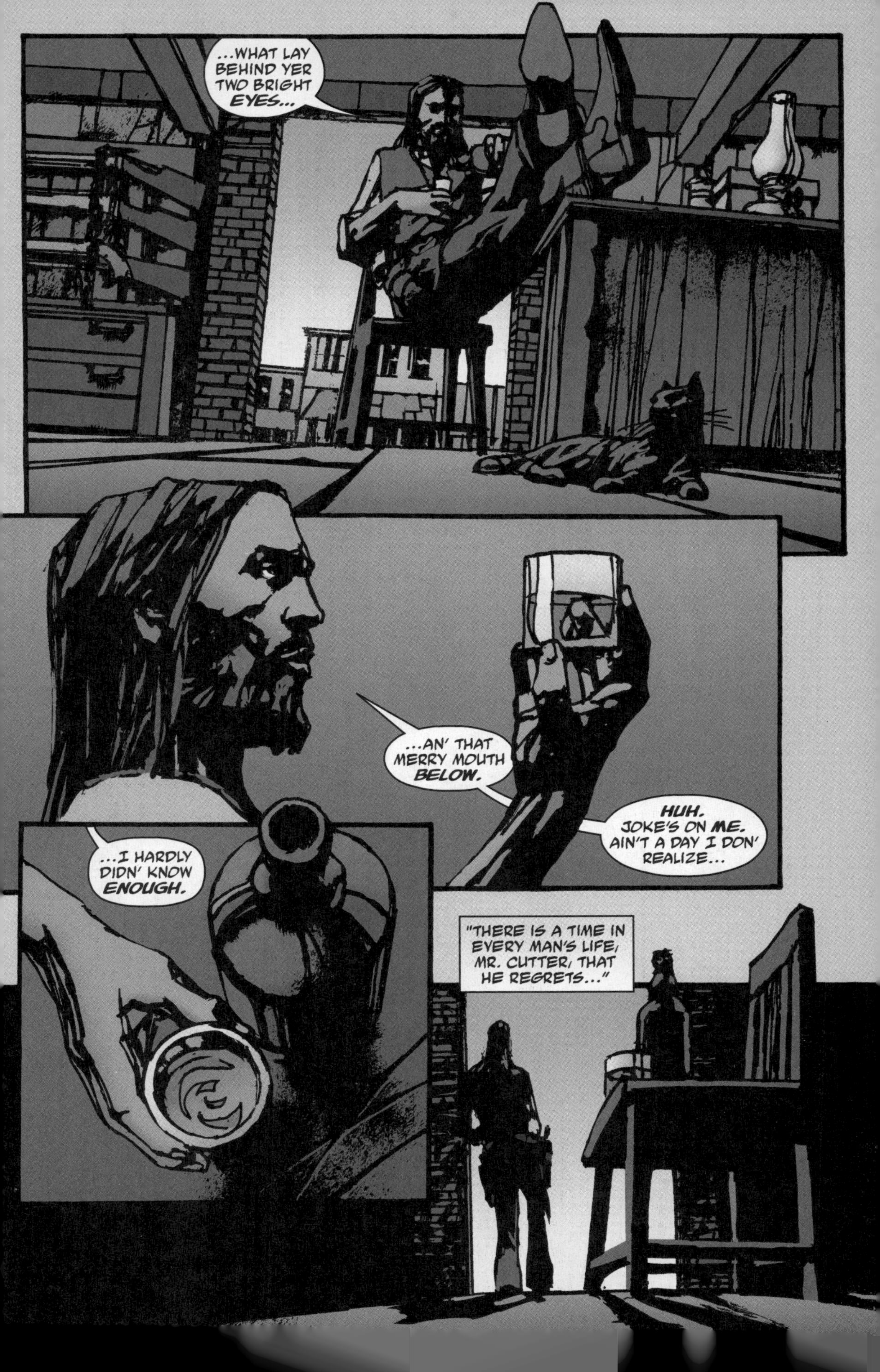
...WHAT LAY BEHIND YER TWO BRIGHT EYES...
...AN' THAT MERRY MOUTH BELOW.
HUH. JOKE'S ON ME. AIN'T A DAY I DON' REALIZE...
...I HARDLY DIDN' KNOW ENOUGH.
"THERE IS A TIME IN EVERY MAN'S LIFE, MR. CUTTER, THAT HE REGRETS..."

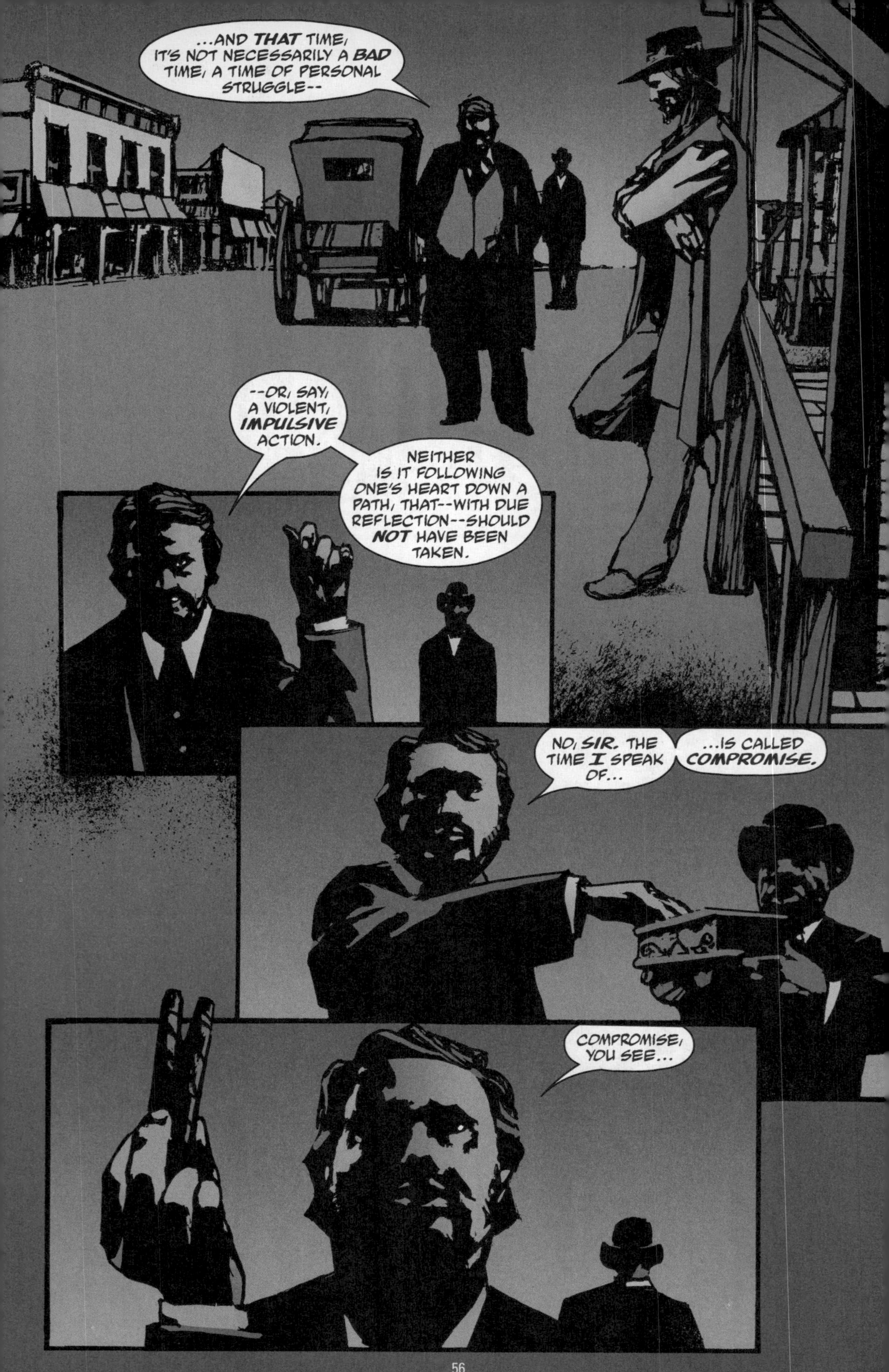
...AND THAT TIME, IT'S NOT NECESSARILY A BAD TIME, A TIME OF PERSONAL STRUGGLE--
--OR, SAY, A VIOLENT, IMPULSIVE ACTION.
NEITHER IS IT FOLLOWING ONE'S HEART DOWN A PATH, THAT--WITH DUE REFLECTION--SHOULD NOT HAVE BEEN TAKEN.
NO, SIR. THE TIME I SPEAK OF...
...IS CALLED COMPROMISE.
COMPROMISE, YOU SEE...

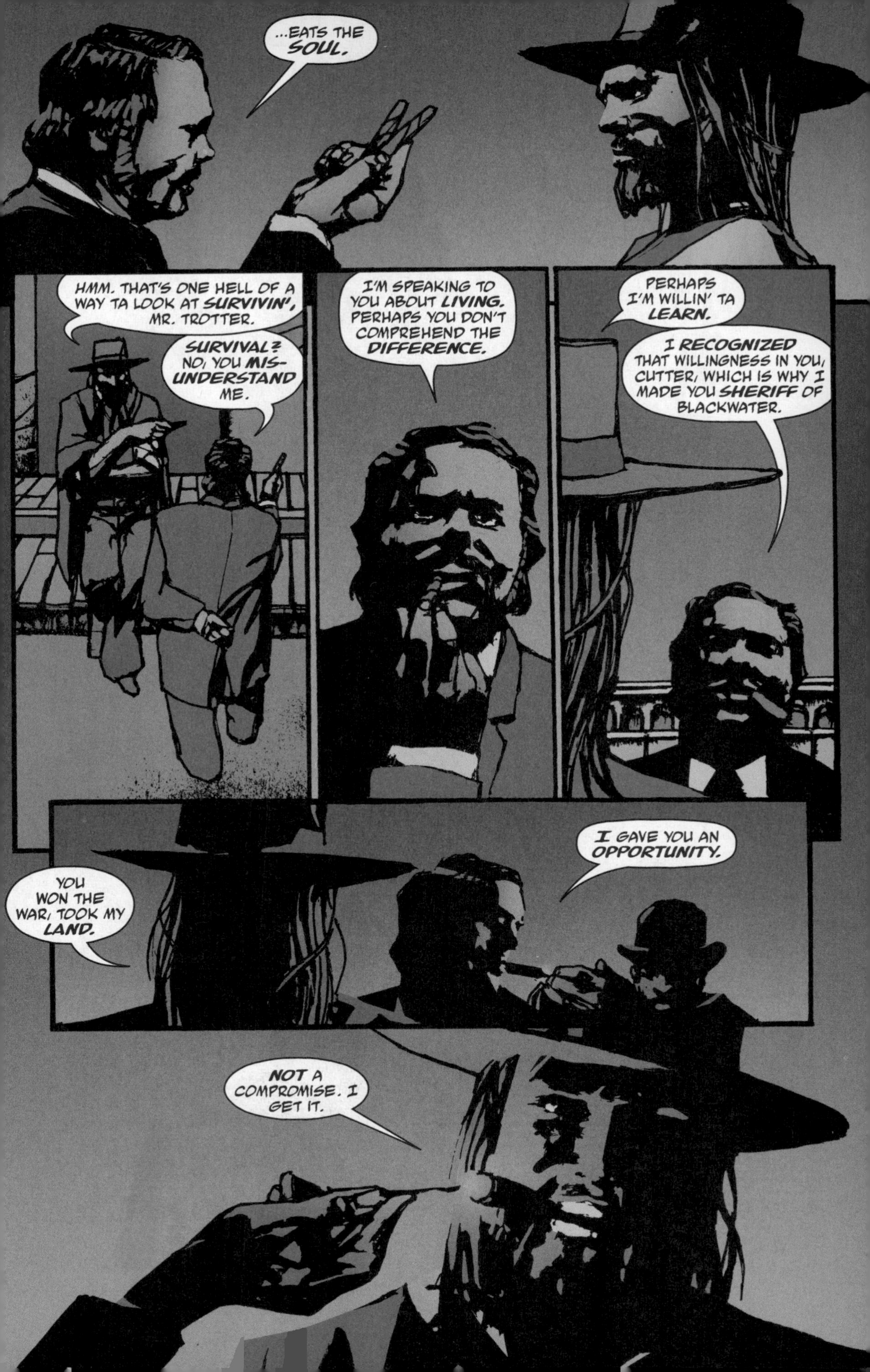
...EATS THE SOUL.
HMM. THAT'S ONE HELL OF A WAY TA LOOK AT SURVIVIN', MR. TROTTER.
SURVIVAL? NO, YOU MIS-UNDERSTAND ME.
I'M SPEAKING TO YOU ABOUT LIVING. PERHAPS YOU DON'T COMPREHEND THE DIFFERENCE.
PERHAPS I'M WILLIN' TA LEARN.
I RECOGNIZED THAT WILLINGNESS IN YOU, CUTTER, WHICH IS WHY I MADE YOU SHERIFF OF BLACKWATER.
YOU WON THE WAR, TOOK MY LAND.
I GAVE YOU AN OPPORTUNITY.
NOT A COMPROMISE. I GET IT.

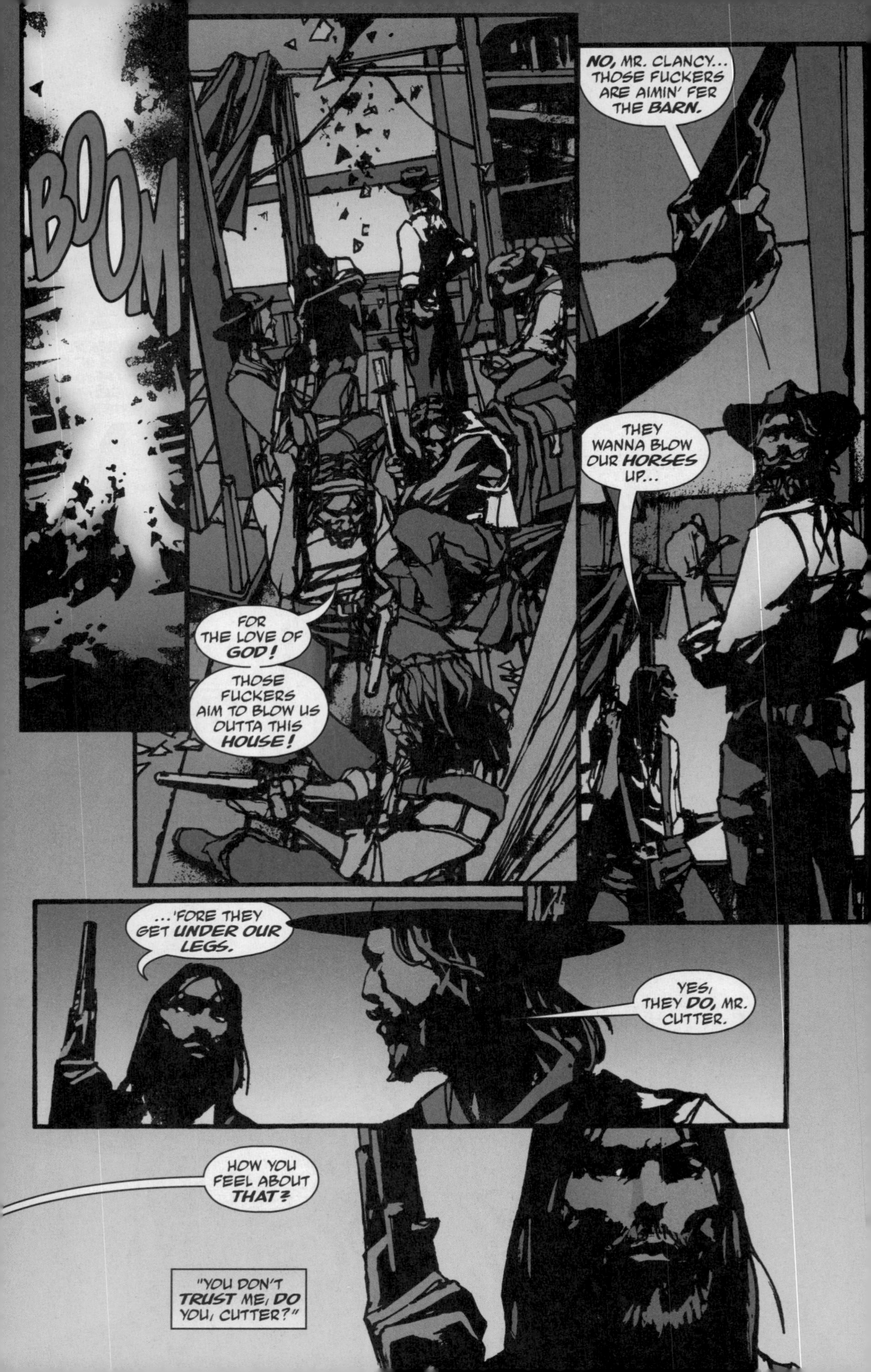
BOOM
FOR THE LOVE OF GOD! THOSE FUCKERS AIM TO BLOW US OUTTA THIS HOUSE!
NO, MR. CLANCY... THOSE FUCKERS ARE AIMIN' FER THE BARN.
THEY WANNA BLOW OUR HORSES UP...
...'FORE THEY GET UNDER OUR LEGS.
YES, THEY DO, MR. CUTTER.
HOW YOU FEEL ABOUT THAT?
"YOU DON'T TRUST ME, DO YOU, CUTTER?"

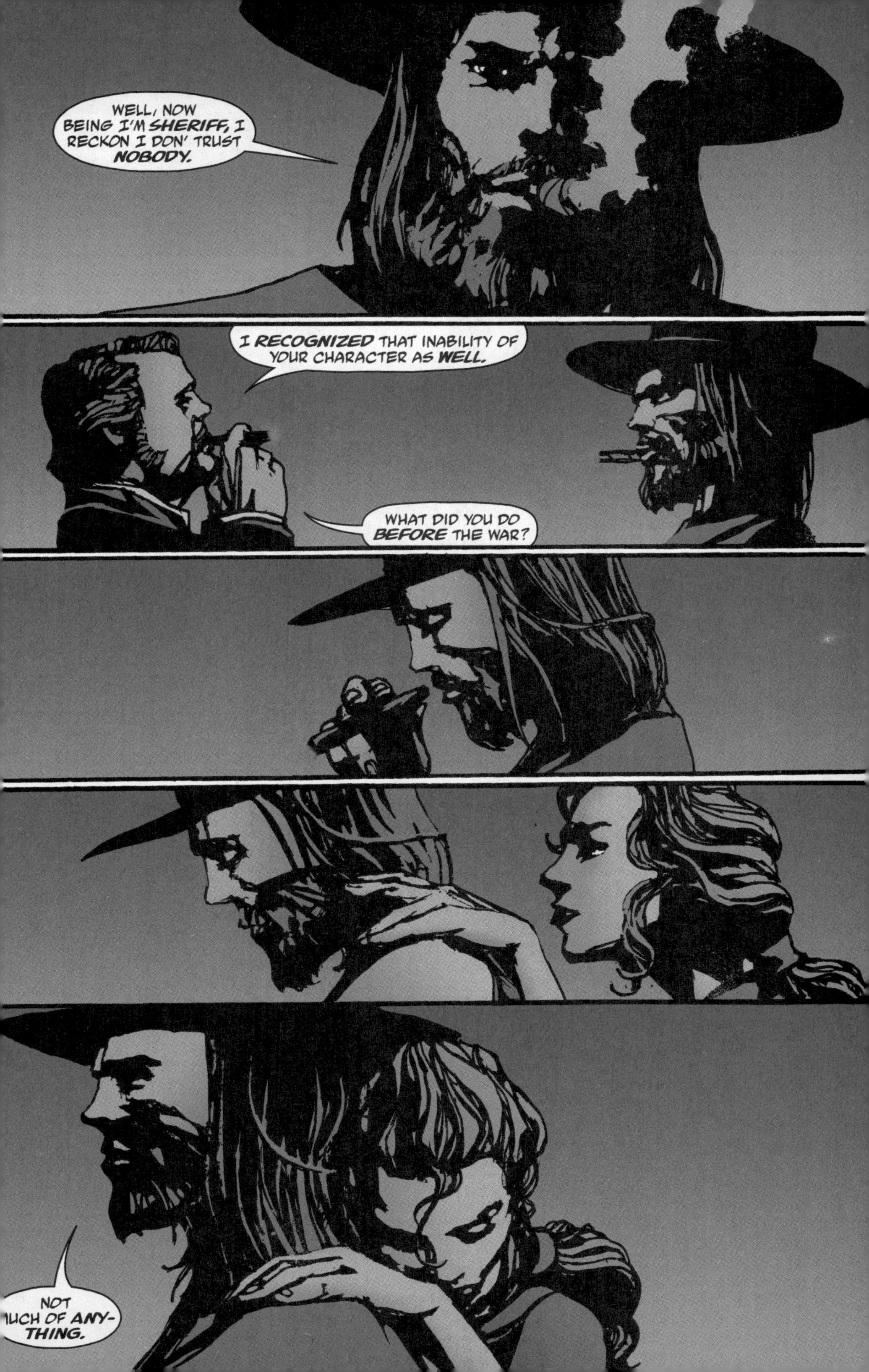
WELL, NOW BEING I'M SHERIFF, I RECKON I DON' TRUST NOBODY.
I RECOGNIZED THAT INABILITY OF YOUR CHARACTER AS WELL.
WHAT DID YOU DO BEFORE THE WAR?
NOT MUCH OF ANY-THING.

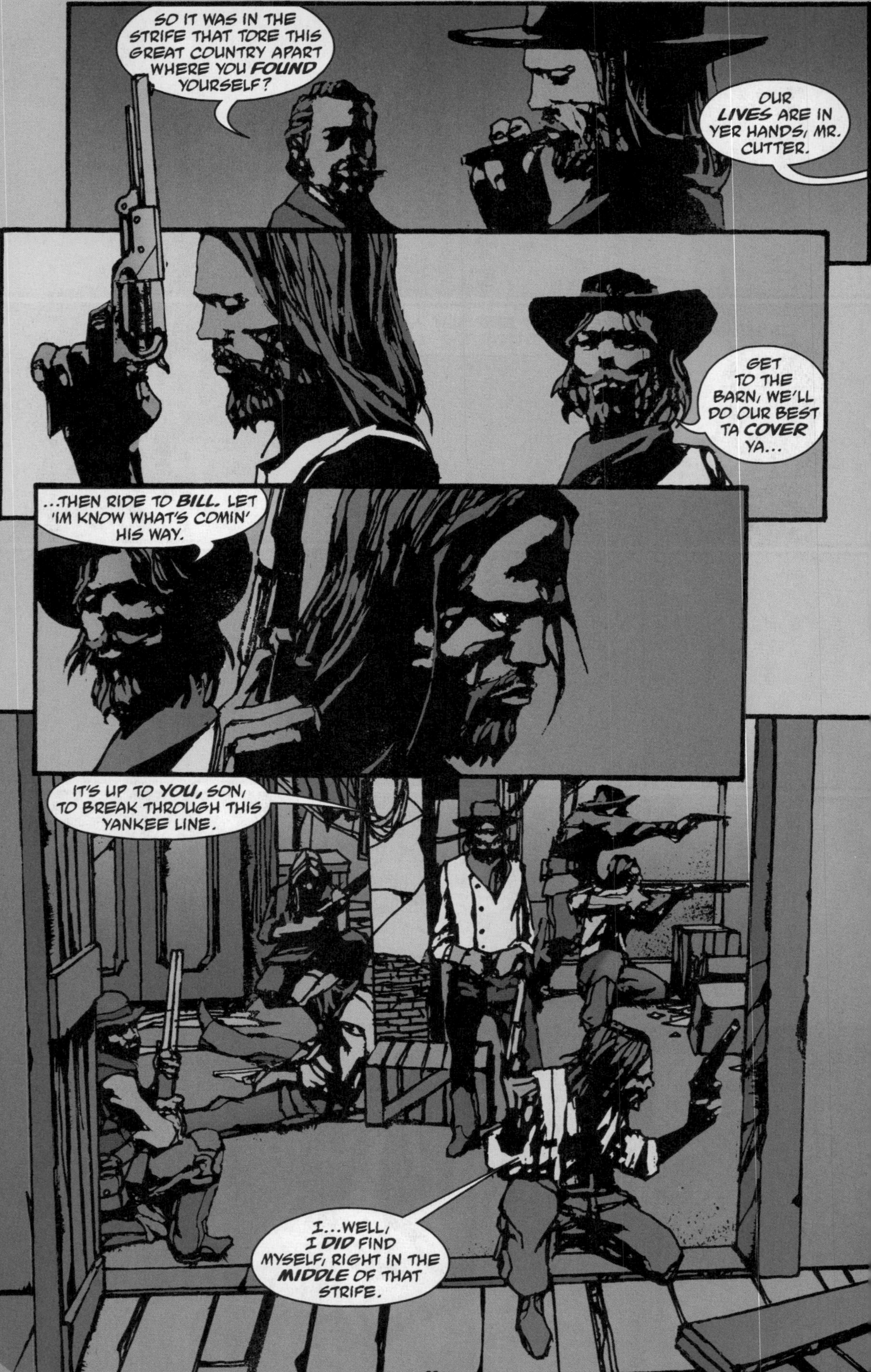
SO IT WAS IN THE STRIFE THAT TORE THIS GREAT COUNTRY APART WHERE YOU FOUND YOURSELF?
OUR LIVES ARE IN YER HANDS, MR. CUTTER.
GET TO THE BARN, WE'LL DO OUR BEST TA COVER YA...
...THEN RIDE TO BILL. LET 'IM KNOW WHAT'S COMIN' HIS WAY.
IT'S UP TO YOU, SON, TO BREAK THROUGH THIS YANKEE LINE.
I...WELL, I DID FIND MYSELF, RIGHT IN THE MIDDLE OF THAT STRIFE.

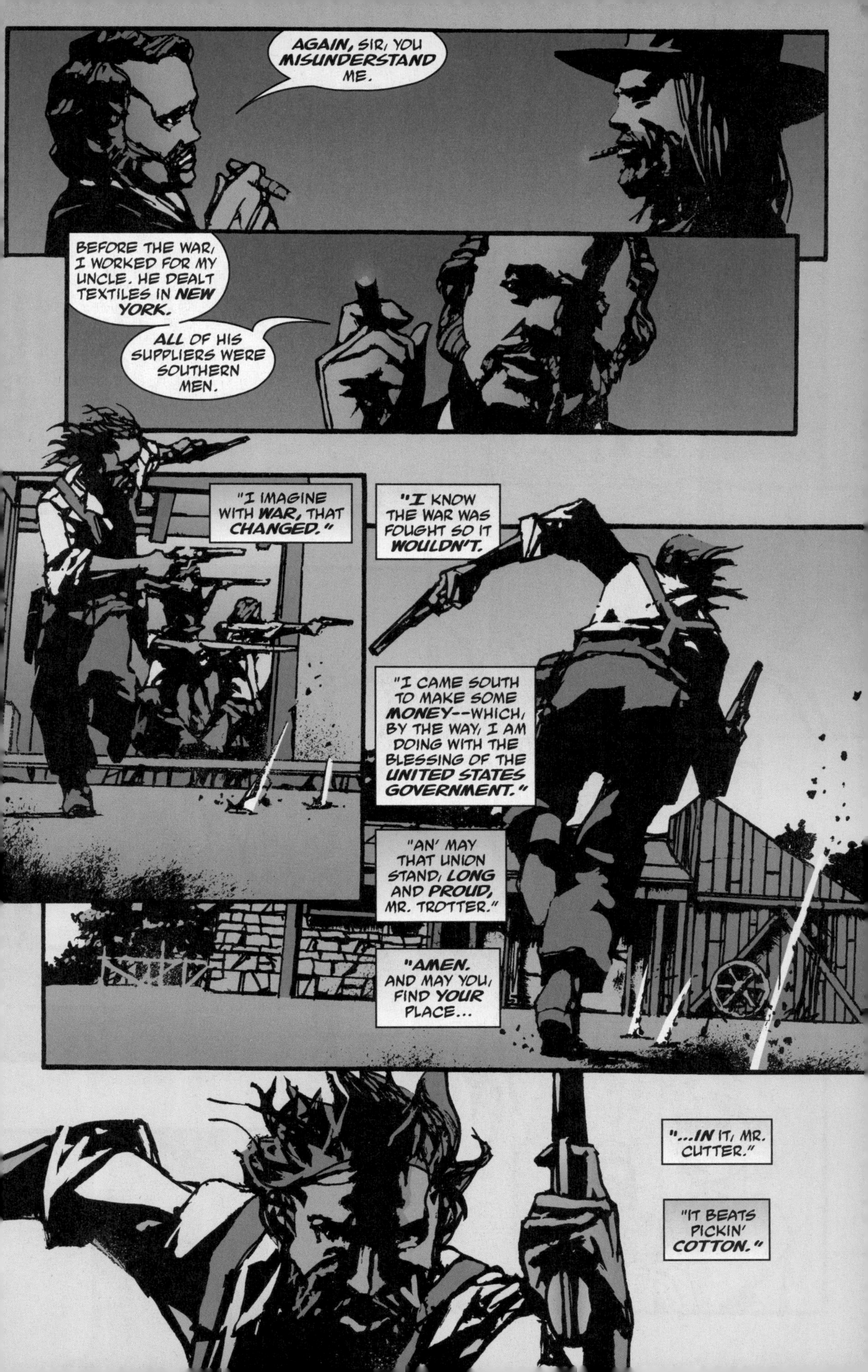
AGAIN, SIR, YOU MISUNDERSTAND ME.
BEFORE THE WAR, I WORKED FOR MY UNCLE. HE DEALT TEXTILES IN NEW YORK.
ALL OF HIS SUPPLIERS WERE SOUTHERN MEN.
"I IMAGINE WITH WAR, THAT CHANGED."
"I KNOW THE WAR WAS FOUGHT SO IT WOULDN'T.
"I CAME SOUTH TO MAKE SOME MONEY--WHICH, BY THE WAY, I AM DOING WITH THE BLESSING OF THE UNITED STATES GOVERNMENT."
"AN' MAY THAT UNION STAND, LONG AND PROUD, MR. TROTTER."
"AMEN. AND MAY YOU, FIND YOUR PLACE...
"...IN IT, MR. CUTTER."
"IT BEATS PICKIN' COTTON."

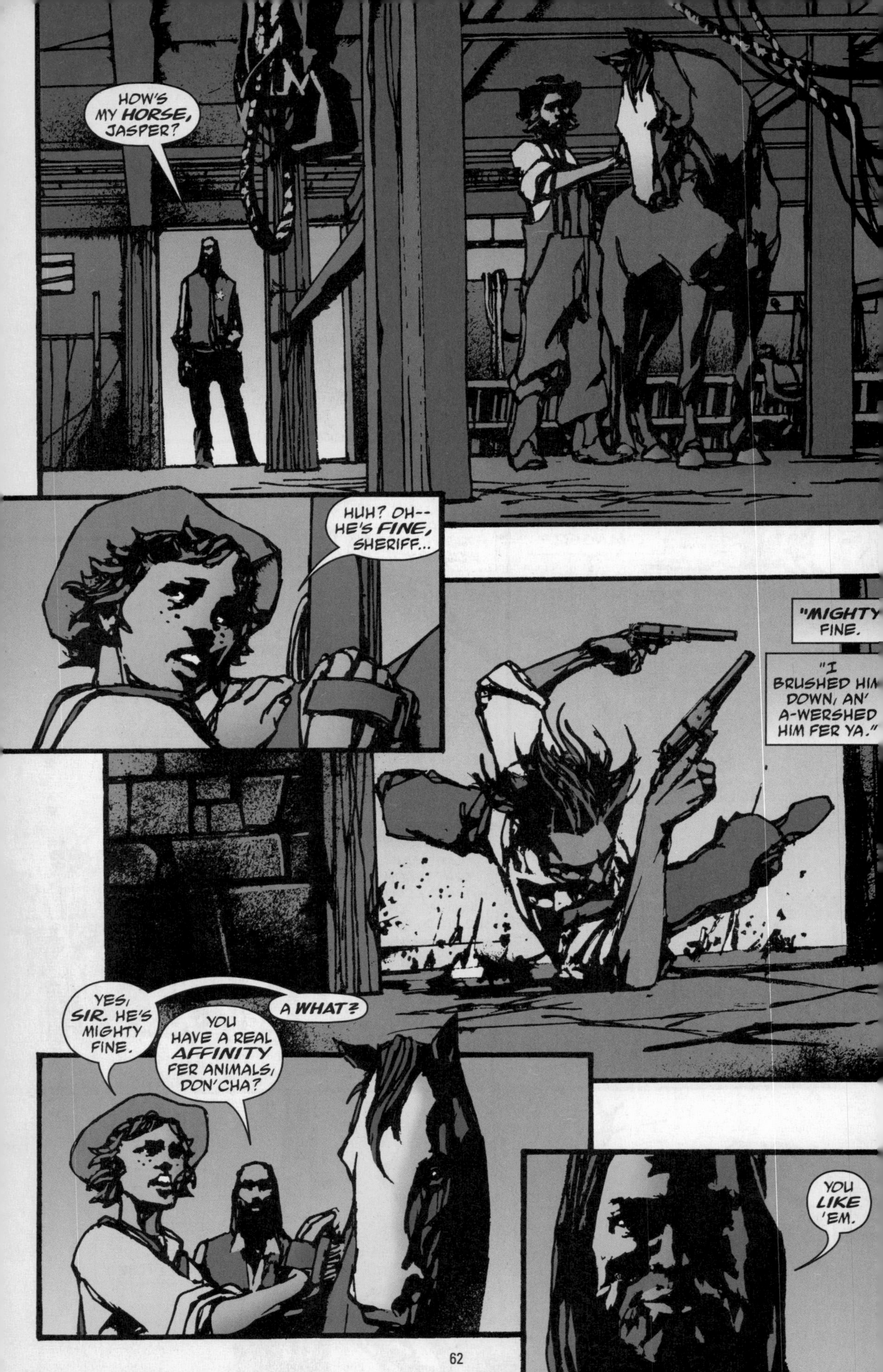

HOW'S MY HORSE, JASPER?
HUH? OH-- HE'S FINE, SHERIFF...
"MIGHTY FINE.
"I BRUSHED HIM DOWN, AN' A-WERSHED HIM FER YA."
YES, SIR. HE'S MIGHTY FINE.
YOU HAVE A REAL AFFINITY FER ANIMALS, DON'CHA?
A WHAT?
YOU LIKE 'EM.

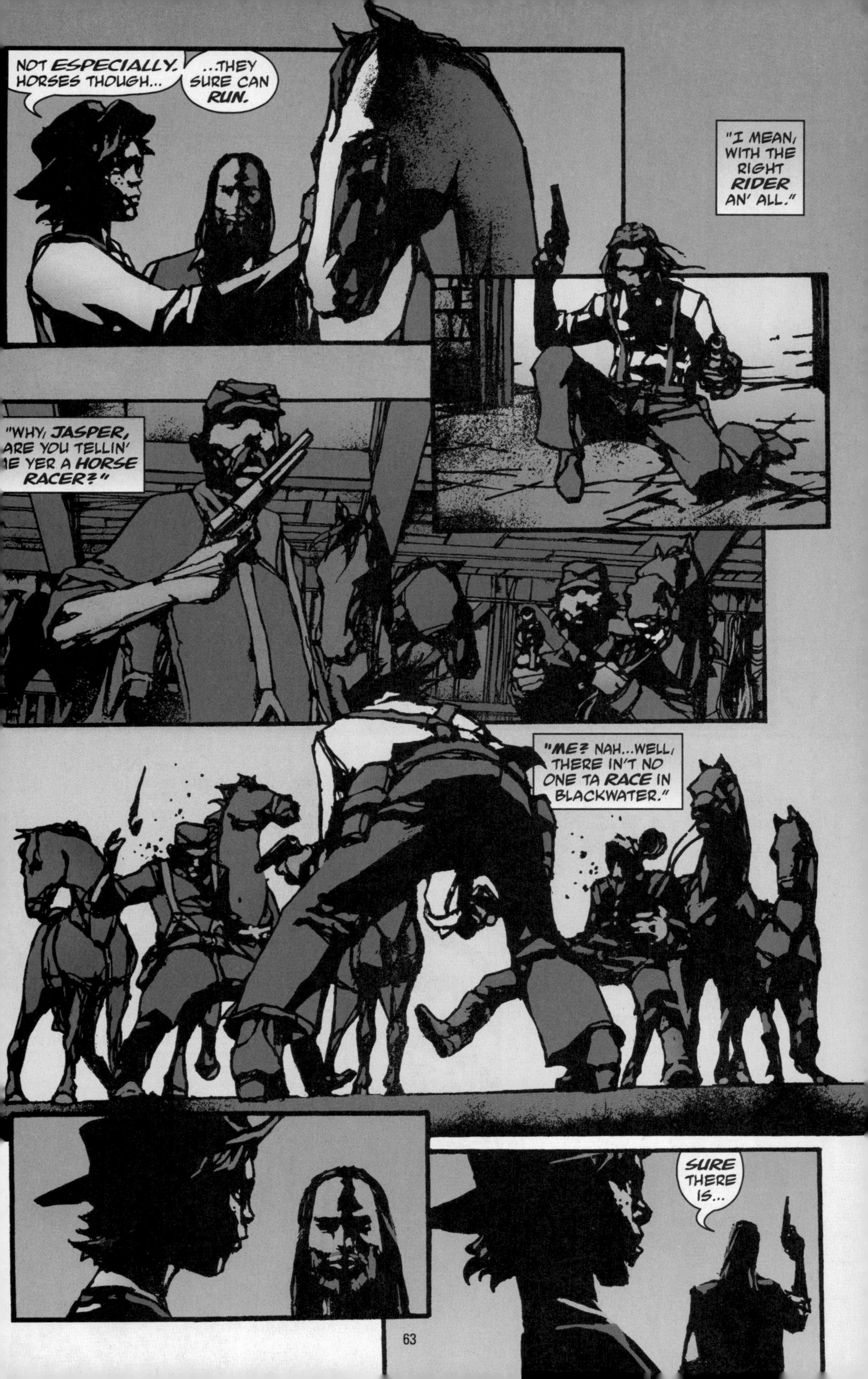

NOT ESPECIALLY. HORSES THOUGH...
...THEY SURE CAN RUN.
"I MEAN, WITH THE RIGHT RIDER AN' ALL."
"WHY, JASPER, ARE YOU TELLIN' ME YER A HORSE RACER?"
"ME? NAH...WELL, THERE IN'T NO ONE TA RACE IN BLACKWATER."
SURE THERE IS...

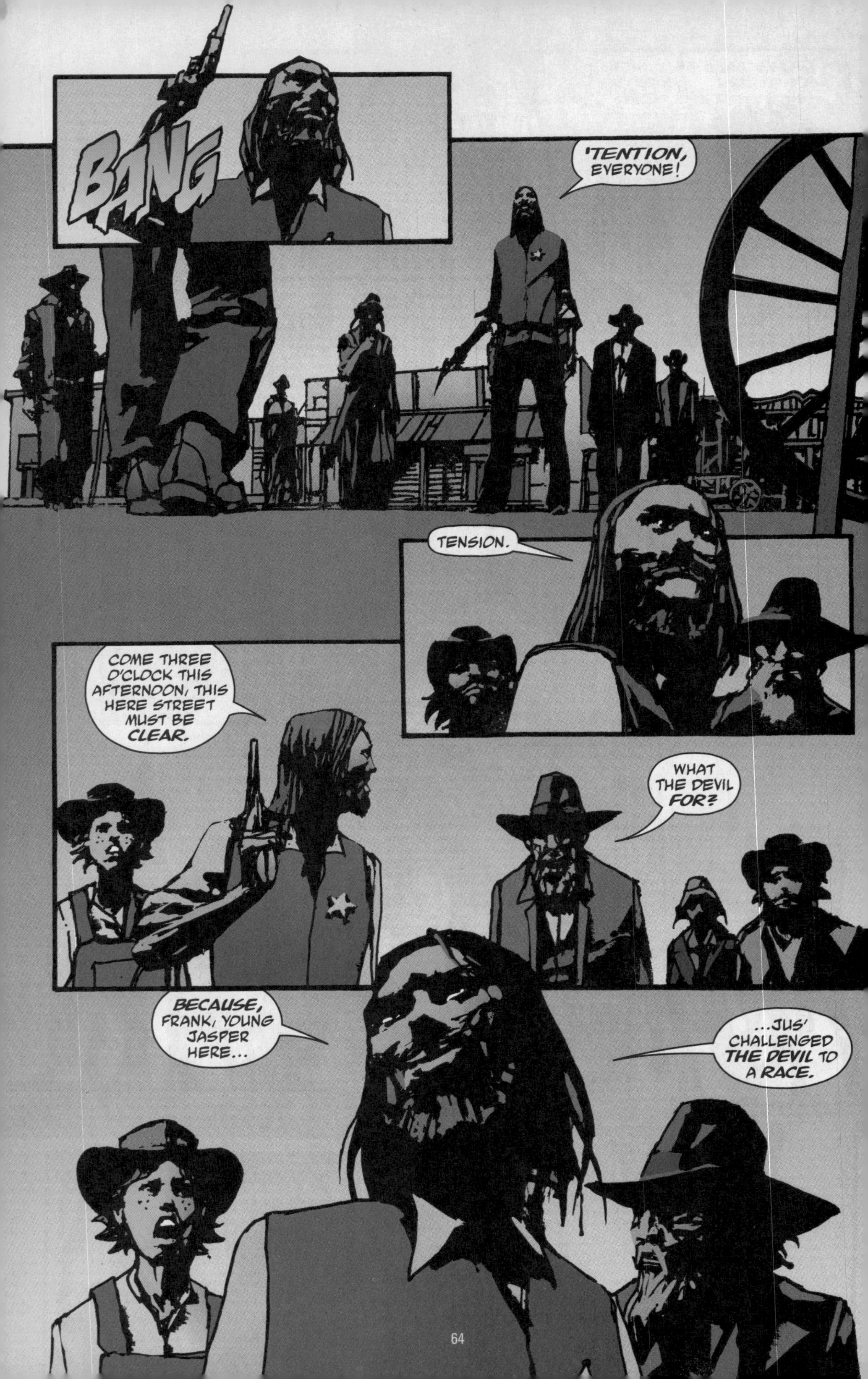
BANG
'TENTION, EVERYONE!
TENSION.
COME THREE O'CLOCK THIS AFTERNOON, THIS HERE STREET MUST BE CLEAR.
WHAT THE DEVIL FOR?
BECAUSE, FRANK, YOUNG JASPER HERE...
...JUS' CHALLENGED THE DEVIL TO A RACE.

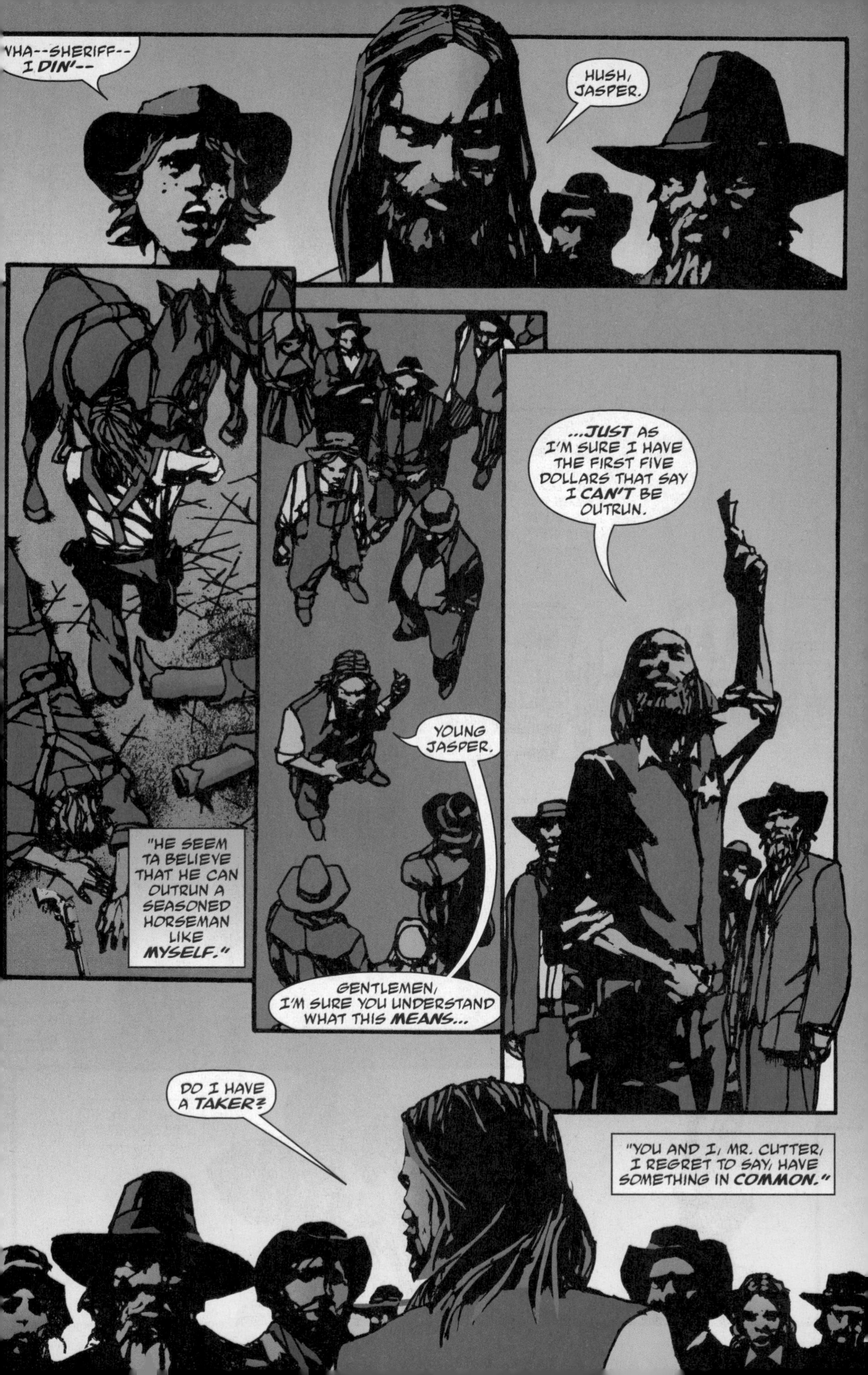
WHA--SHERIFF-- I DIN'--
HUSH, JASPER.
"HE SEEM TA BELIEVE THAT HE CAN OUTRUN A SEASONED HORSEMAN LIKE MYSELF."
YOUNG JASPER.
GENTLEMEN, I'M SURE YOU UNDERSTAND WHAT THIS MEANS...
...JUST AS I'M SURE I HAVE THE FIRST FIVE DOLLARS THAT SAY I CAN'T BE OUTRUN.
DO I HAVE A TAKER?
"YOU AND I, MR. CUTTER, I REGRET TO SAY, HAVE SOMETHING IN COMMON."

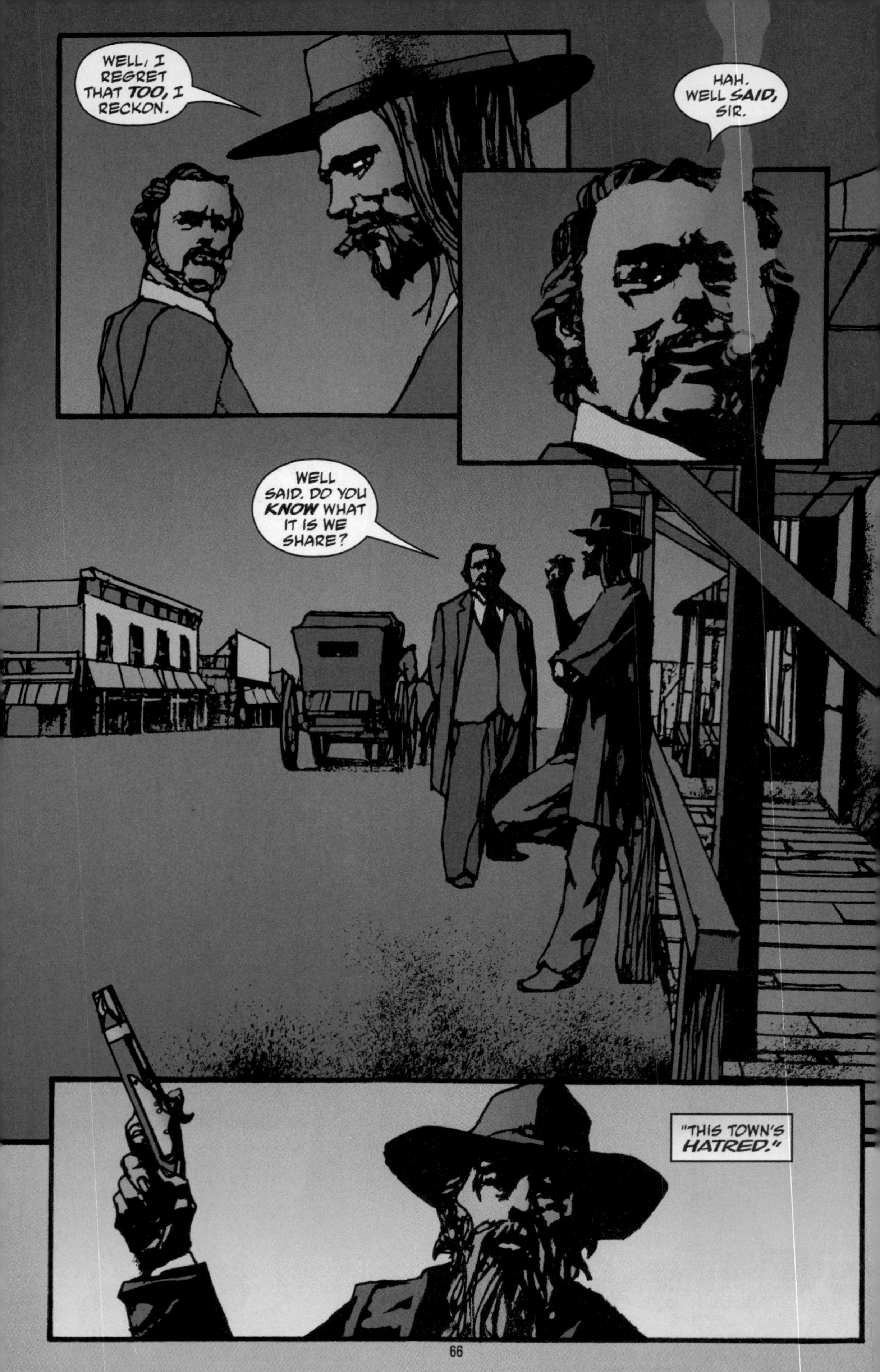
WELL, I REGRET THAT **TOO,** I RECKON.
HAH. WELL **SAID,** SIR.
WELL SAID. DO YOU **KNOW** WHAT IT IS WE SHARE?
"THIS TOWN'S **HATRED.**"

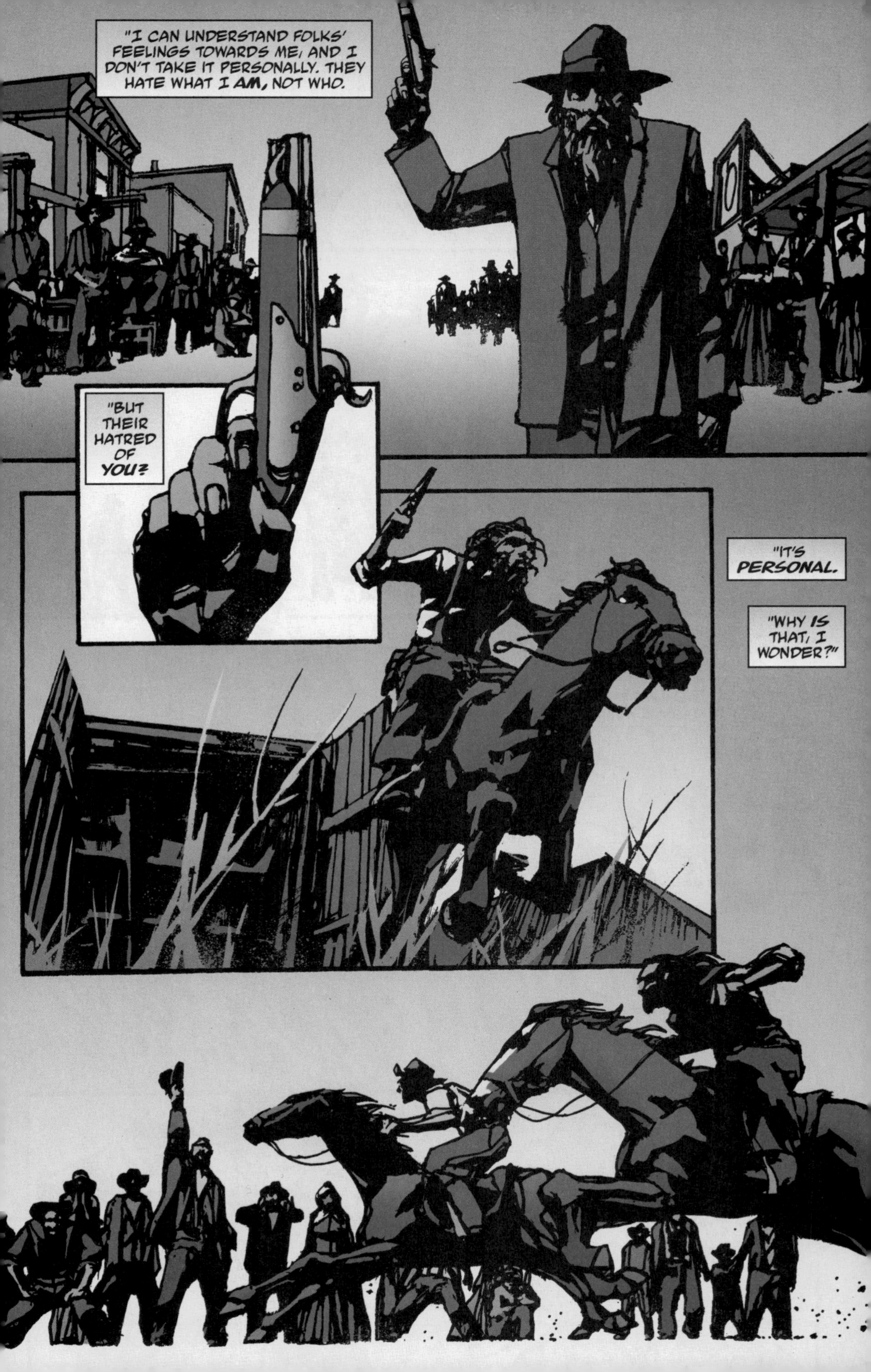
"I CAN UNDERSTAND FOLKS' FEELINGS TOWARDS ME; AND I DON'T TAKE IT PERSONALLY. THEY HATE WHAT I **AM**, NOT WHO.
"BUT THEIR HATRED OF ***YOU***?
"IT'S ***PERSONAL.***
"WHY ***IS*** THAT, I WONDER?"

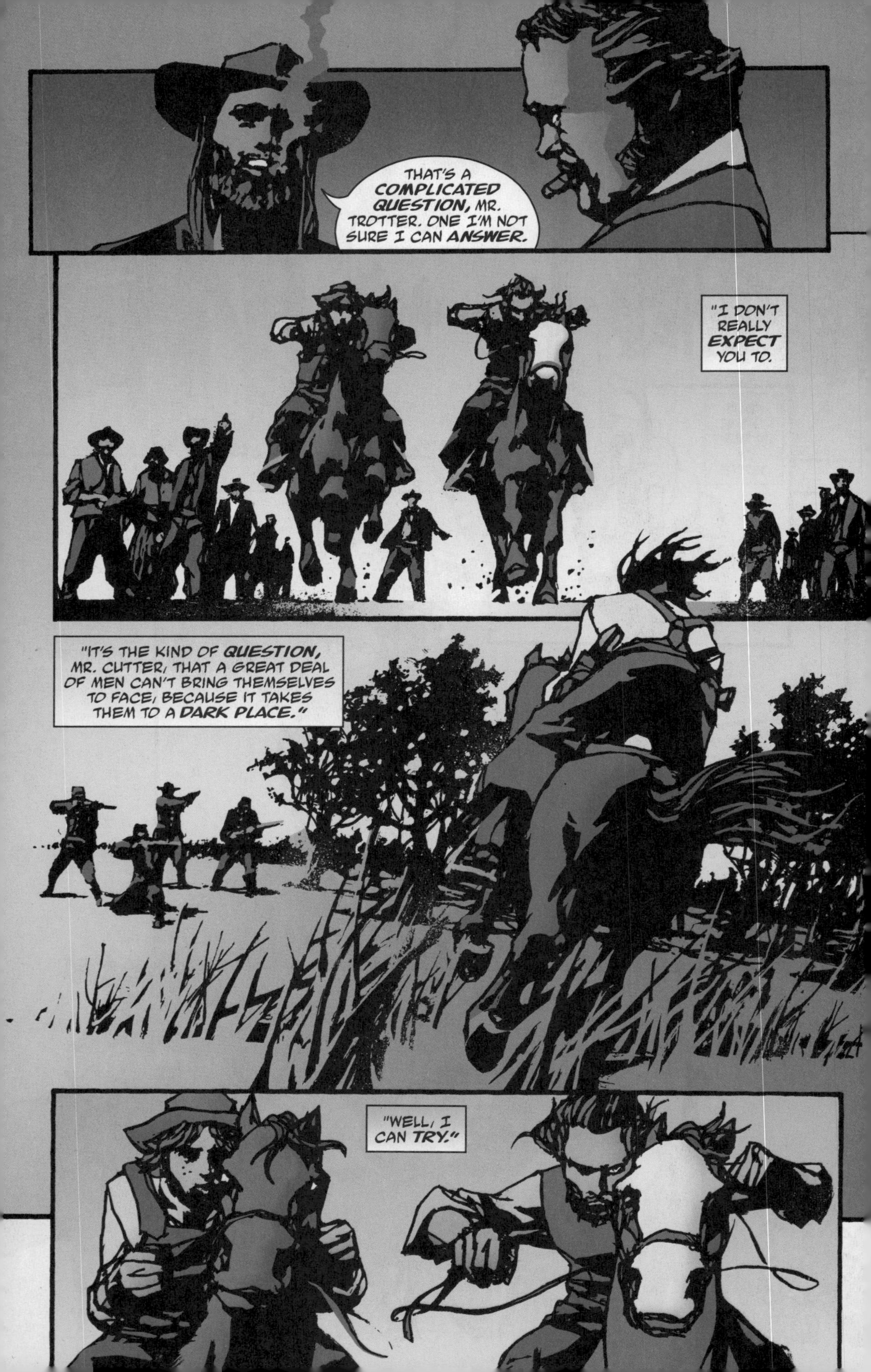
THAT'S A COMPLICATED QUESTION, MR. TROTTER. ONE I'M NOT SURE I CAN ANSWER.
"I DON'T REALLY EXPECT YOU TO.
"IT'S THE KIND OF QUESTION, MR. CUTTER, THAT A GREAT DEAL OF MEN CAN'T BRING THEMSELVES TO FACE, BECAUSE IT TAKES THEM TO A DARK PLACE."
"WELL, I CAN TRY."

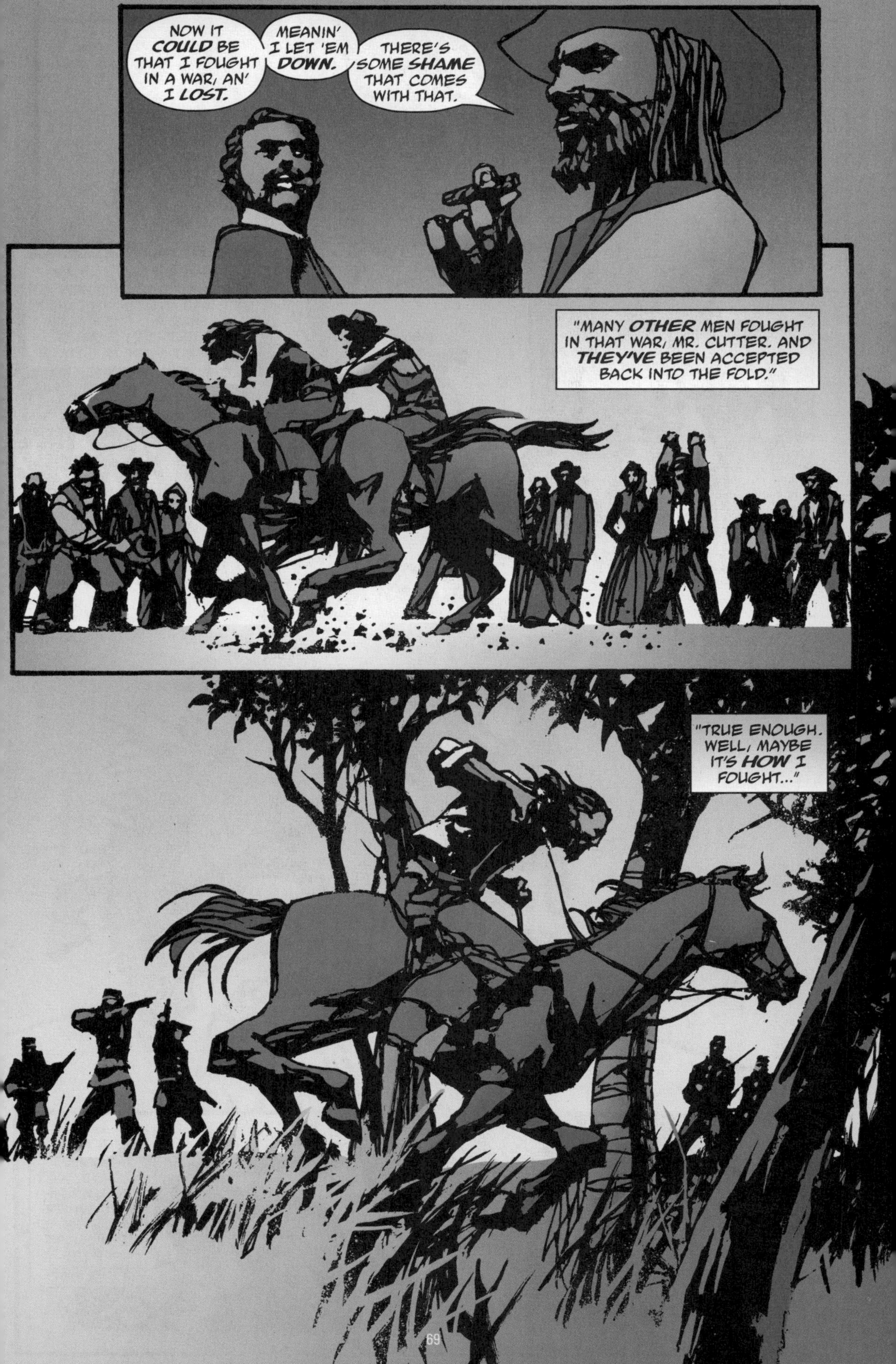
NOW IT COULD BE THAT I FOUGHT IN A WAR, AN' I LOST.
MEANIN' I LET 'EM DOWN.
THERE'S SOME SHAME THAT COMES WITH THAT.
"MANY OTHER MEN FOUGHT IN THAT WAR, MR. CUTTER. AND THEY'VE BEEN ACCEPTED BACK INTO THE FOLD."
"TRUE ENOUGH. WELL, MAYBE IT'S HOW I FOUGHT..."

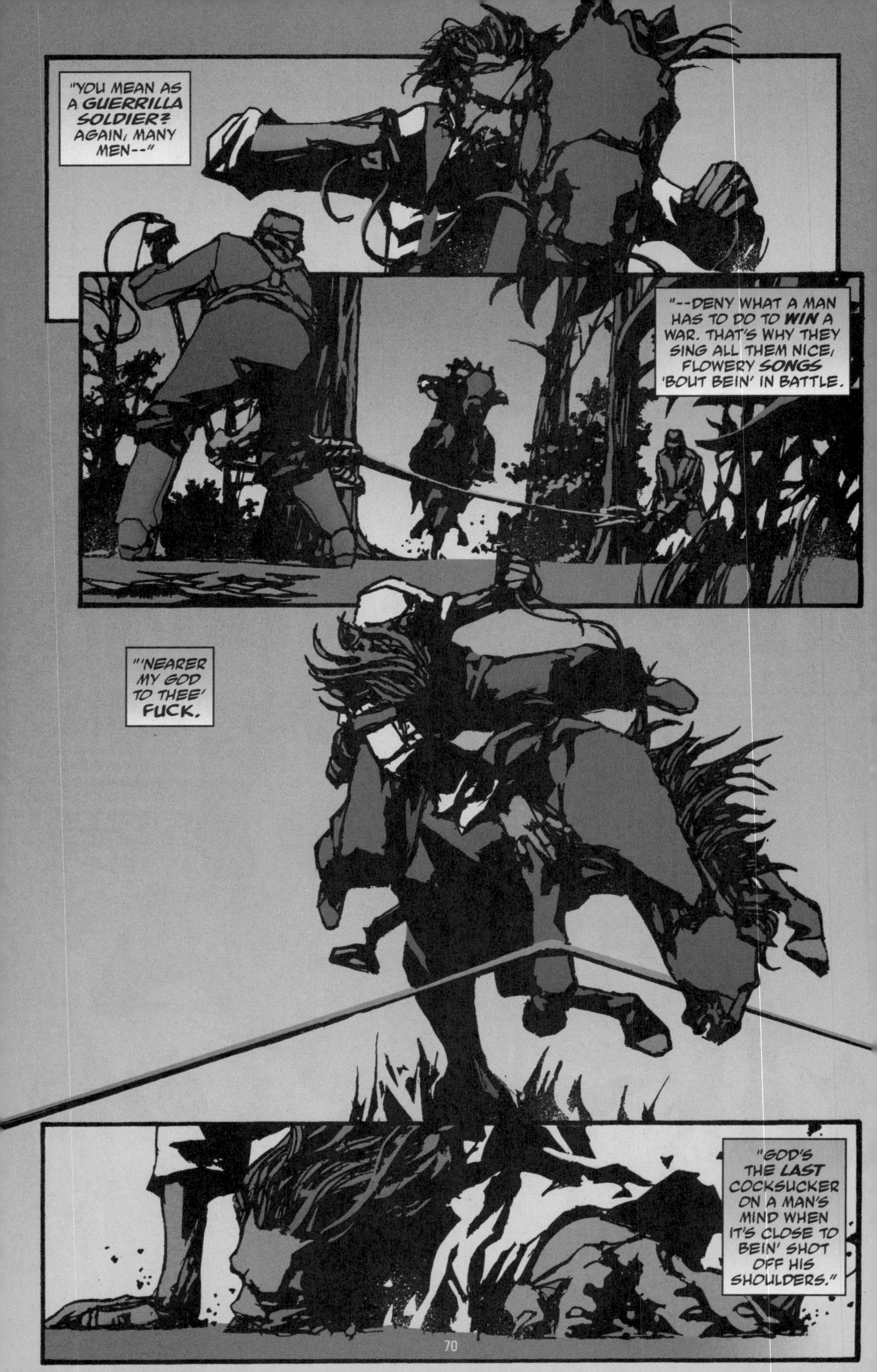
"YOU MEAN AS A GUERRILLA SOLDIER? AGAIN, MANY MEN--"
"--DENY WHAT A MAN HAS TO DO TO WIN A WAR. THAT'S WHY THEY SING ALL THEM NICE, FLOWERY SONGS 'BOUT BEIN' IN BATTLE.
"'NEARER MY GOD TO THEE' FUCK.
"GOD'S THE LAST COCKSUCKER ON A MAN'S MIND WHEN IT'S CLOSE TO BEIN' SHOT OFF HIS SHOULDERS."

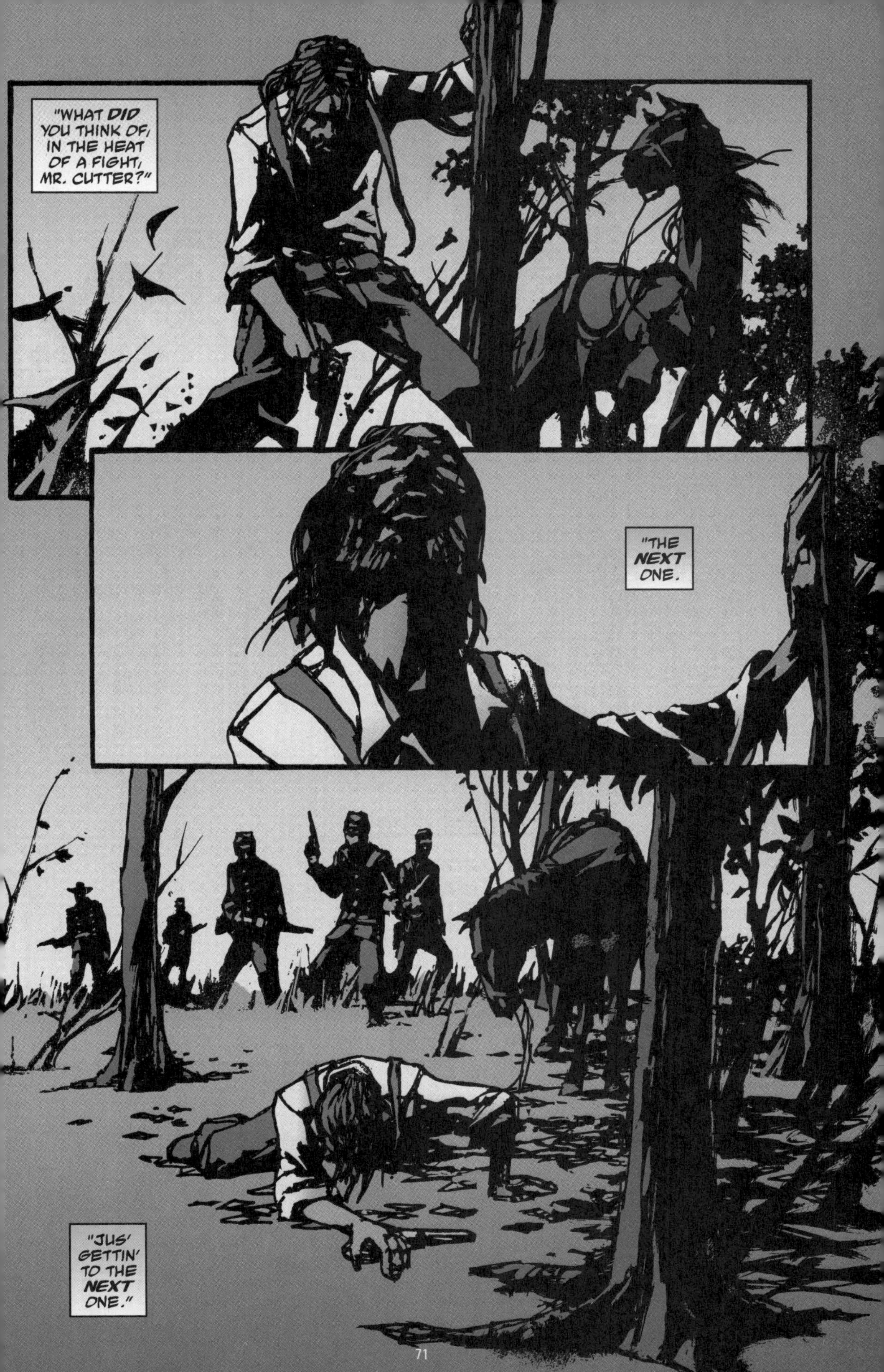
"WHAT DID YOU THINK OF, IN THE HEAT OF A FIGHT, MR. CUTTER?"
"THE NEXT ONE.
"JUS' GETTIN' TO THE NEXT ONE."

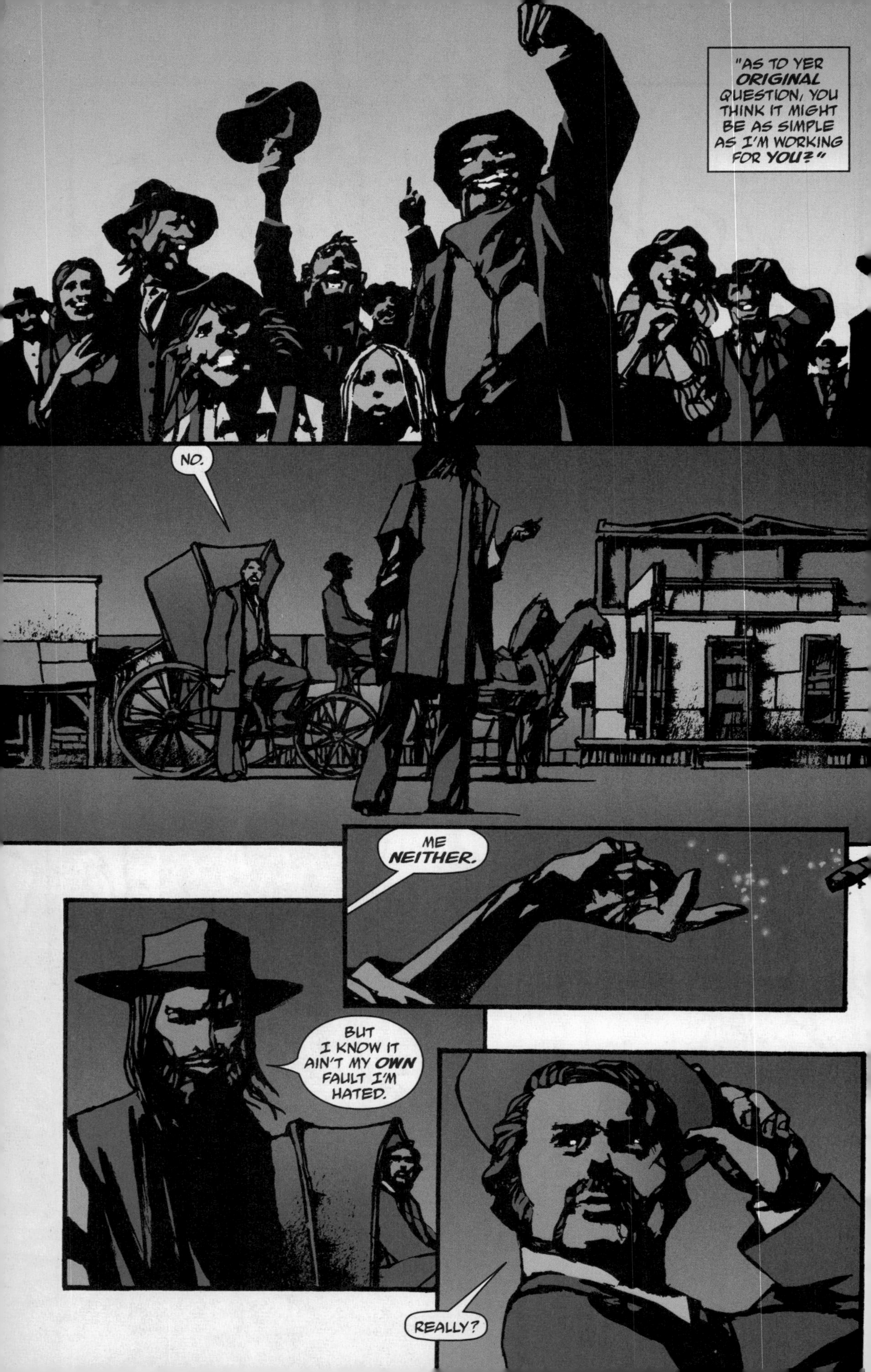
"AS TO YER ORIGINAL QUESTION, YOU THINK IT MIGHT BE AS SIMPLE AS I'M WORKING FOR YOU?"
NO.
ME NEITHER.
BUT I KNOW IT AIN'T MY OWN FAULT I'M HATED.
REALLY?

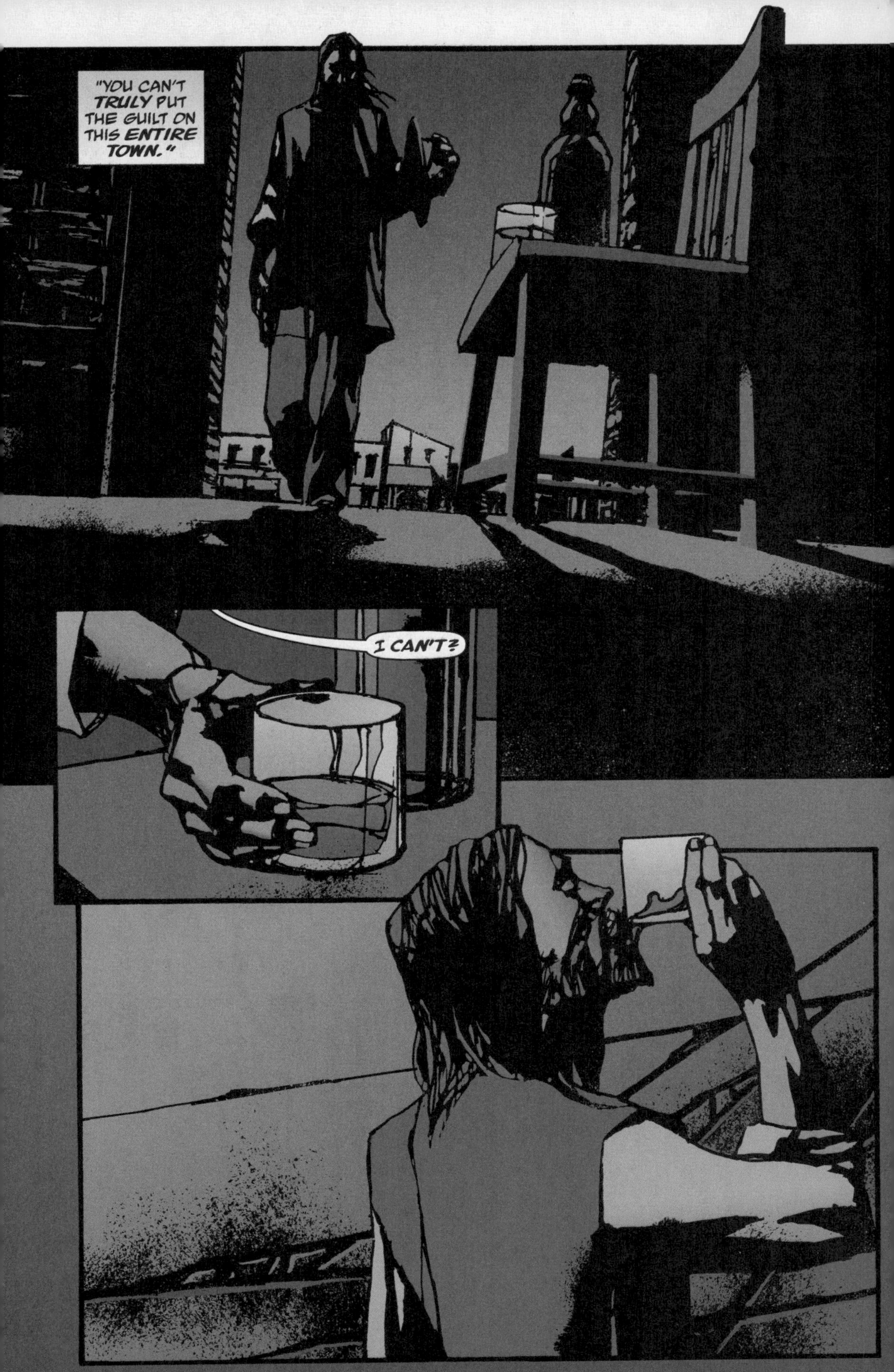
"YOU CAN'T TRULY PUT THE GUILT ON THIS ENTIRE TOWN."
I CAN'T?

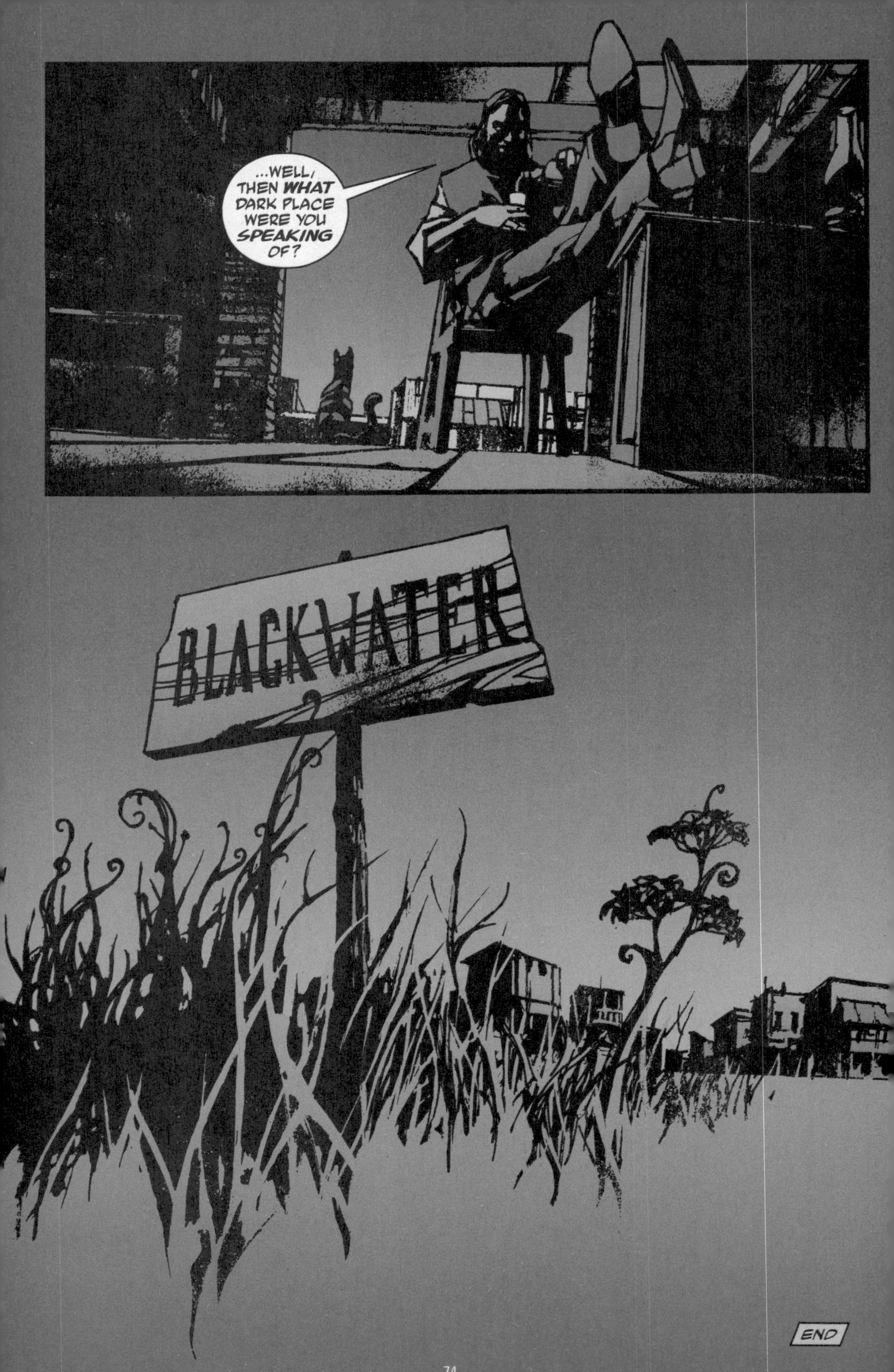
...WELL, THEN WHAT DARK PLACE WERE YOU SPEAKING OF?
BLACKWATER
END

M. FRUSIN
06

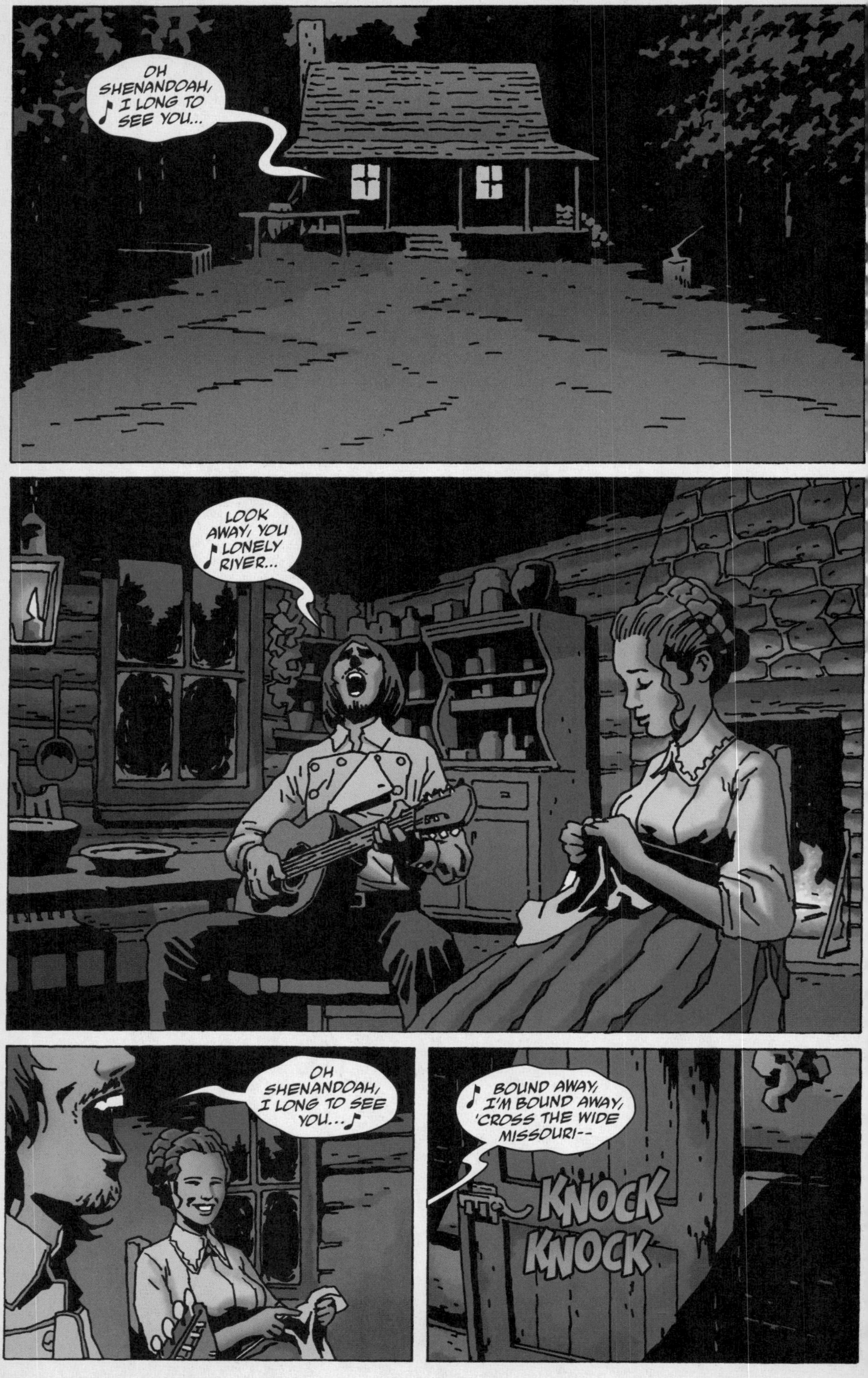
OH SHENANDOAH, ♪ I LONG TO SEE YOU...
LOOK AWAY, YOU ♪ LONELY RIVER...
OH SHENANDOAH, I LONG TO SEE YOU...♪
♪ BOUND AWAY, I'M BOUND AWAY, 'CROSS THE WIDE MISSOURI--
KNOCK
KNOCK

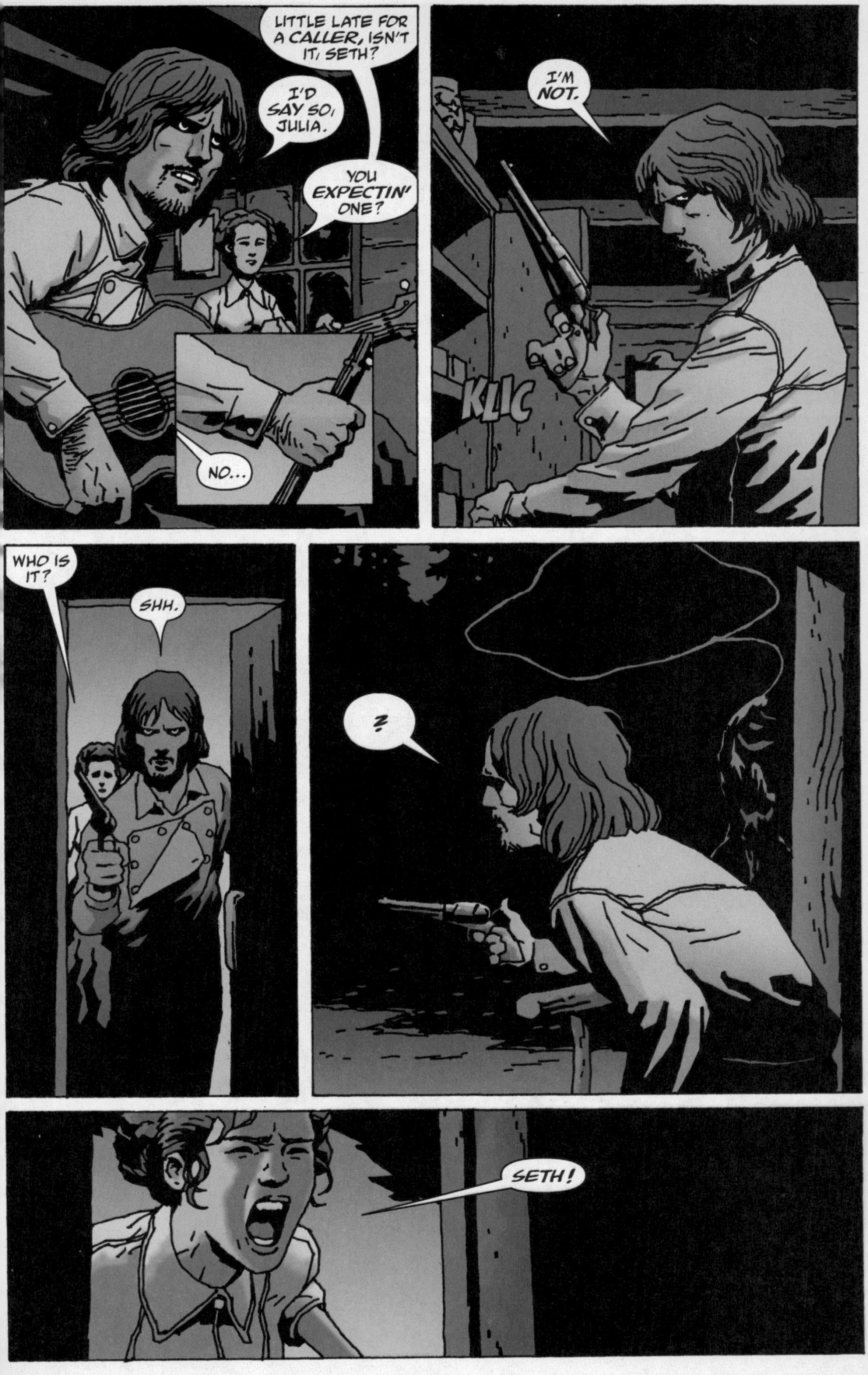

LITTLE LATE FOR A CALLER, ISN'T IT, SETH?
I'D SAY SO, JULIA.
YOU EXPECTIN' ONE?
NO...
I'M NOT.
KLIC
WHO IS IT?
SHH.
?
SETH!

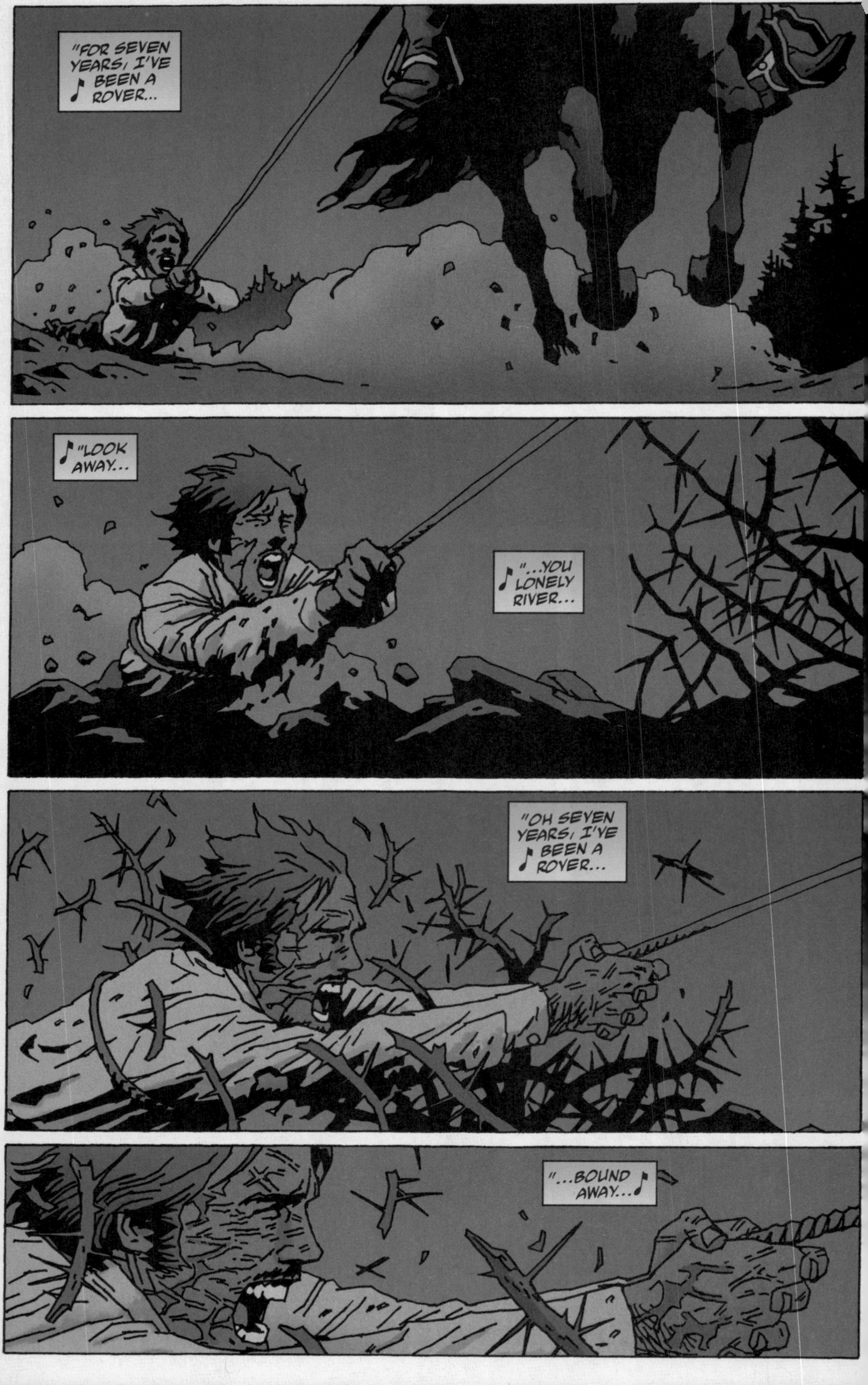
"FOR SEVEN YEARS, I'VE ♪ BEEN A ROVER...
♪ "LOOK AWAY...
♪ "...YOU LONELY RIVER...
"OH SEVEN YEARS, I'VE ♪ BEEN A ROVER...
"...BOUND AWAY...♪

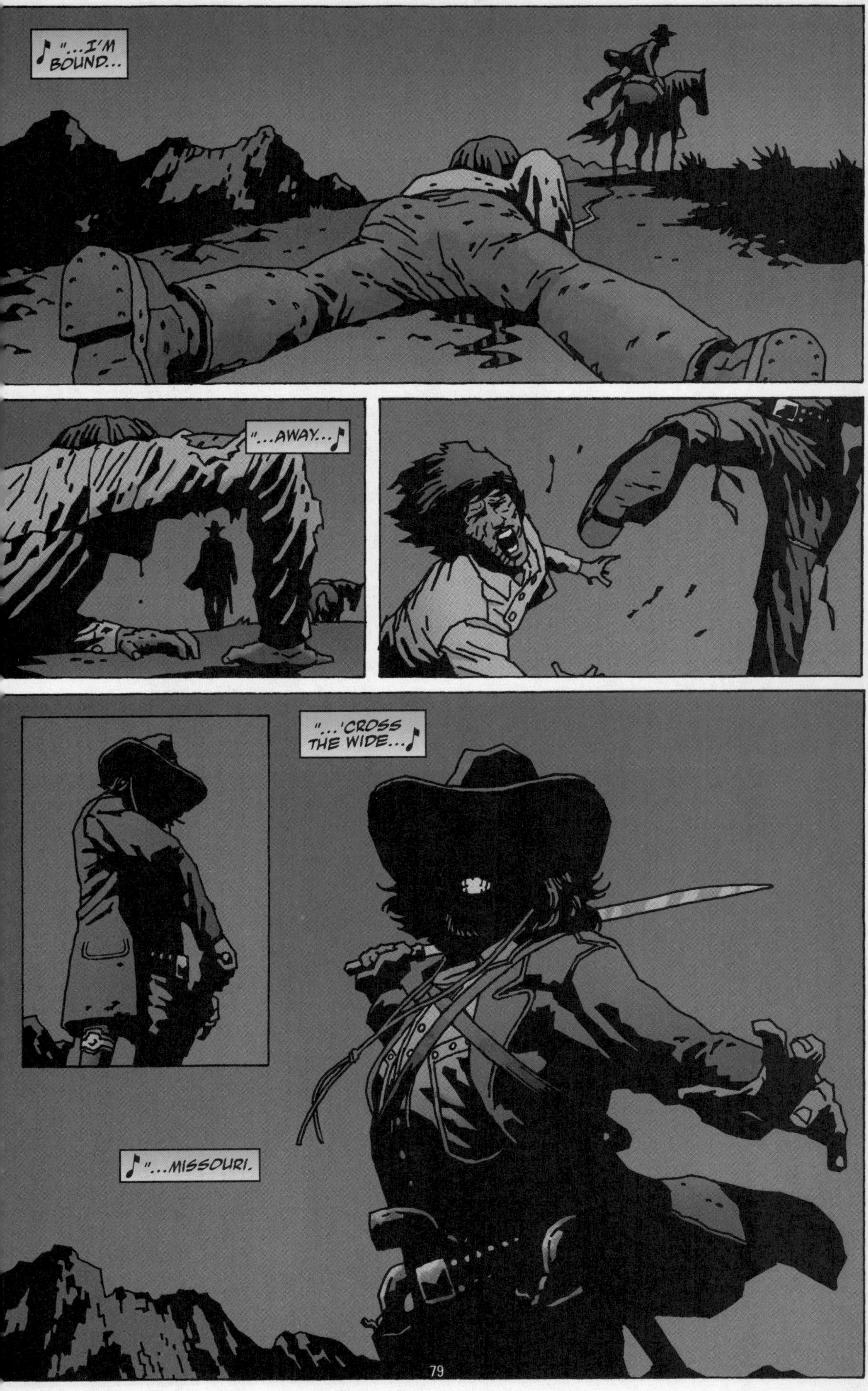
♪ "...I'M BOUND...
"...AWAY...♪
"...'CROSS THE WIDE...♪
♪ "...MISSOURI.

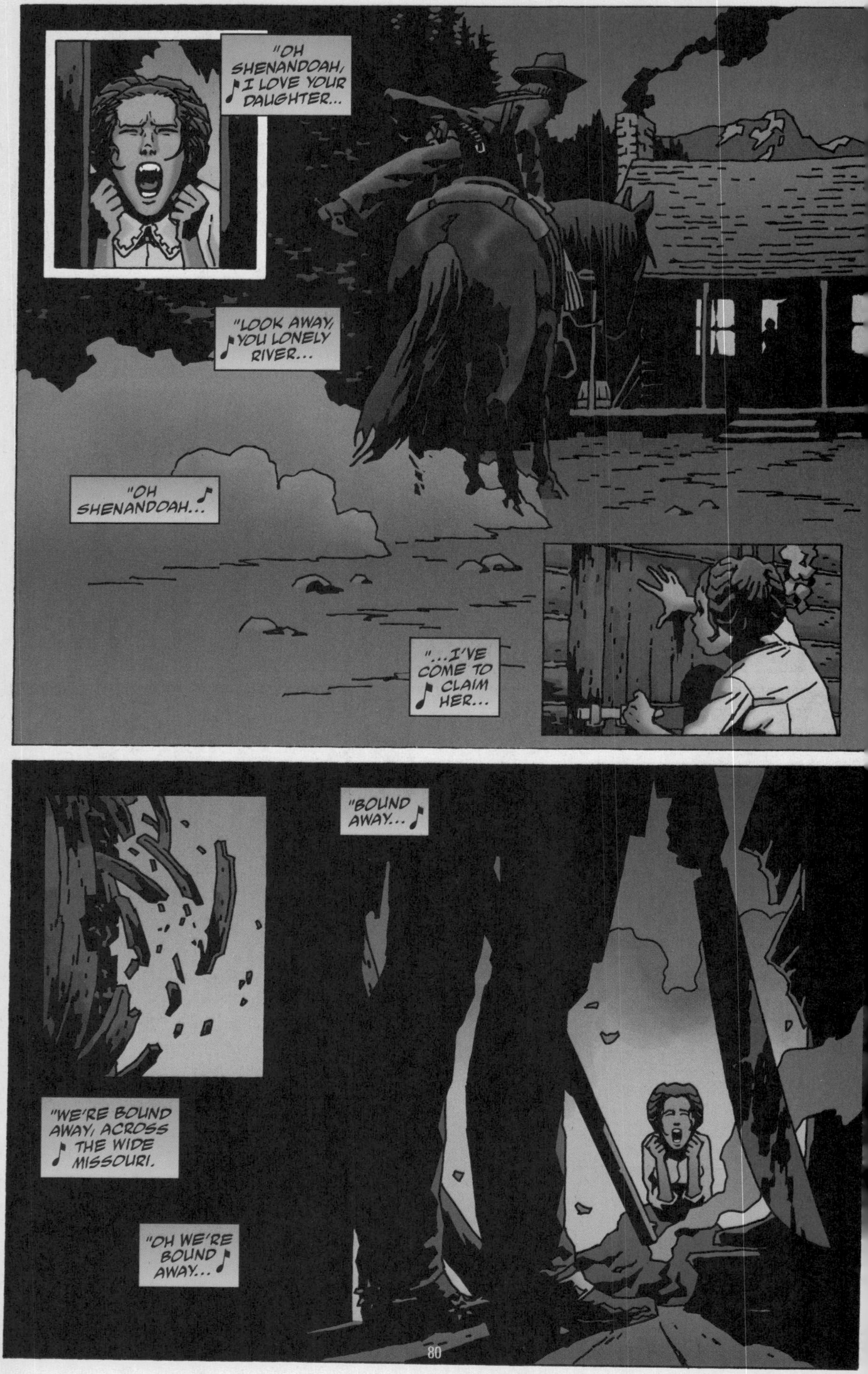
"OH SHENANDOAH, I LOVE YOUR DAUGHTER...
"LOOK AWAY, YOU LONELY RIVER...
"OH SHENANDOAH...
"...I'VE COME TO CLAIM HER...
"BOUND AWAY...
"WE'RE BOUND AWAY, ACROSS THE WIDE MISSOURI.
"OH WE'RE BOUND AWAY...

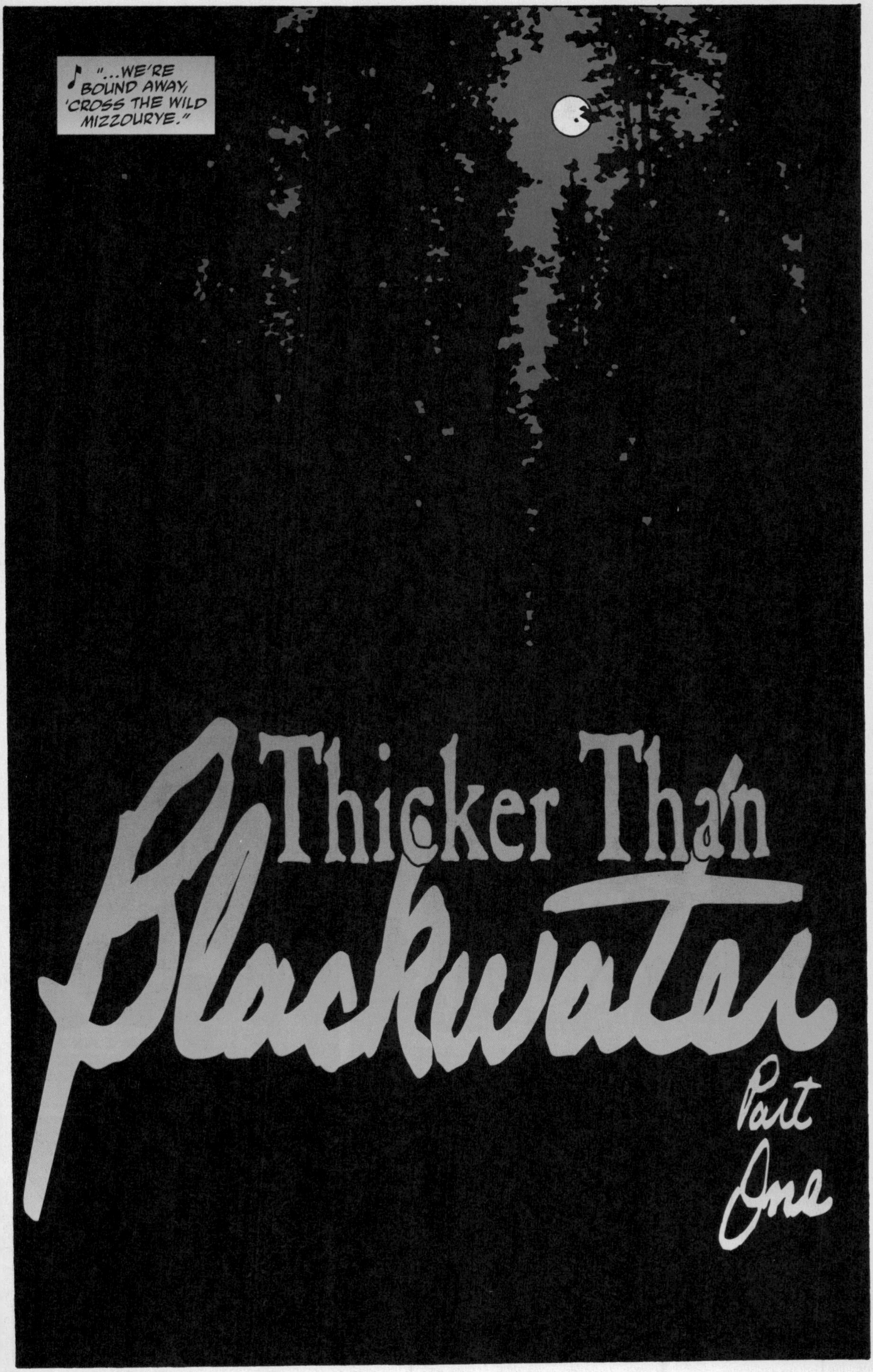
"...WE'RE BOUND AWAY, 'CROSS THE WILD MIZZOURYE."
Thicker Tha'n Blackwater
Part One

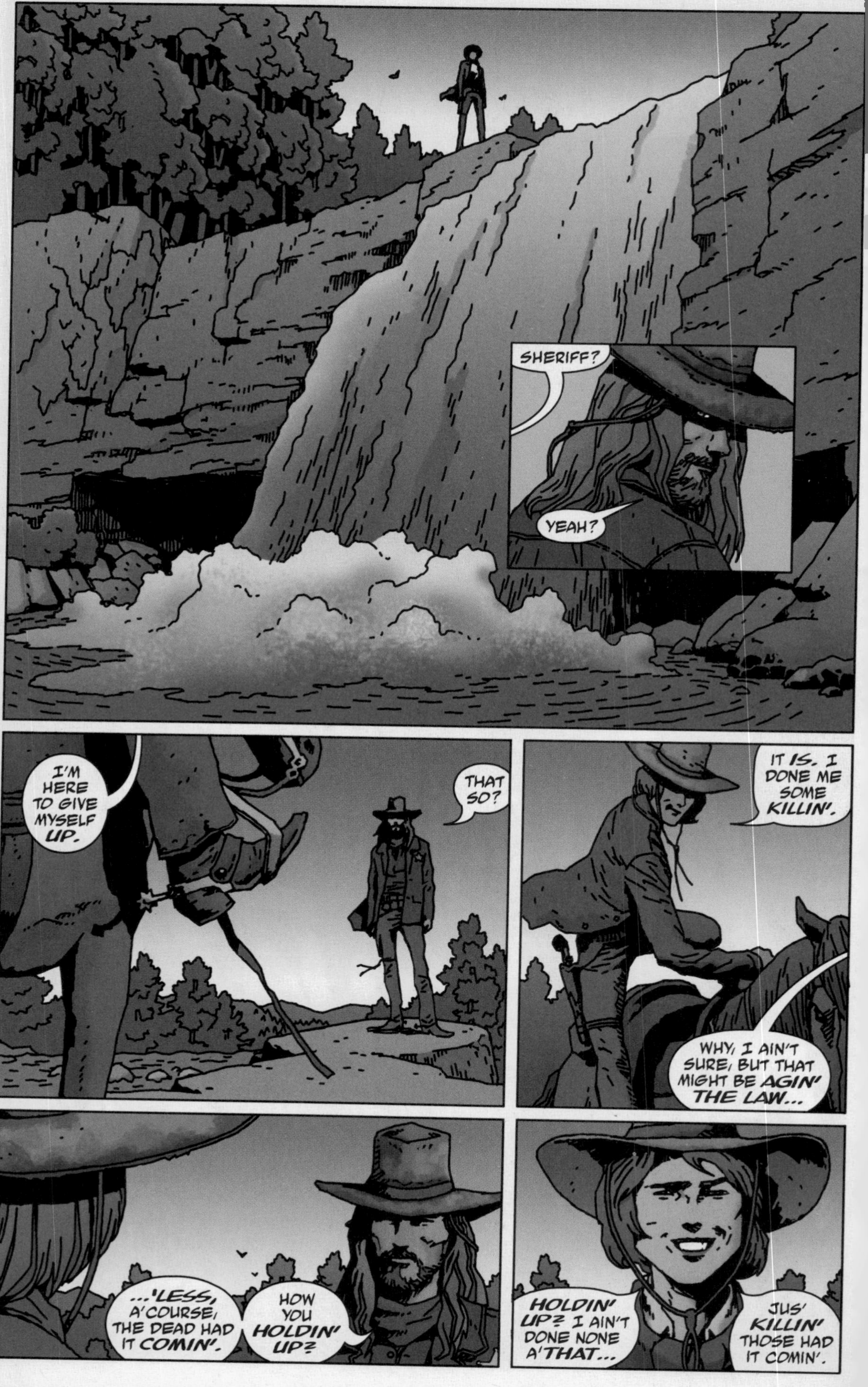
SHERIFF?
YEAH?
I'M HERE TO GIVE MYSELF UP.
THAT SO?
IT IS. I DONE ME SOME KILLIN'.
WHY, I AIN'T SURE, BUT THAT MIGHT BE AGIN' THE LAW...
...'LESS, A'COURSE, THE DEAD HAD IT COMIN'.
HOW YOU HOLDIN' UP?
HOLDIN' UP? I AIN'T DONE NONE A'THAT...
JUS' KILLIN' THOSE HAD IT COMIN'.

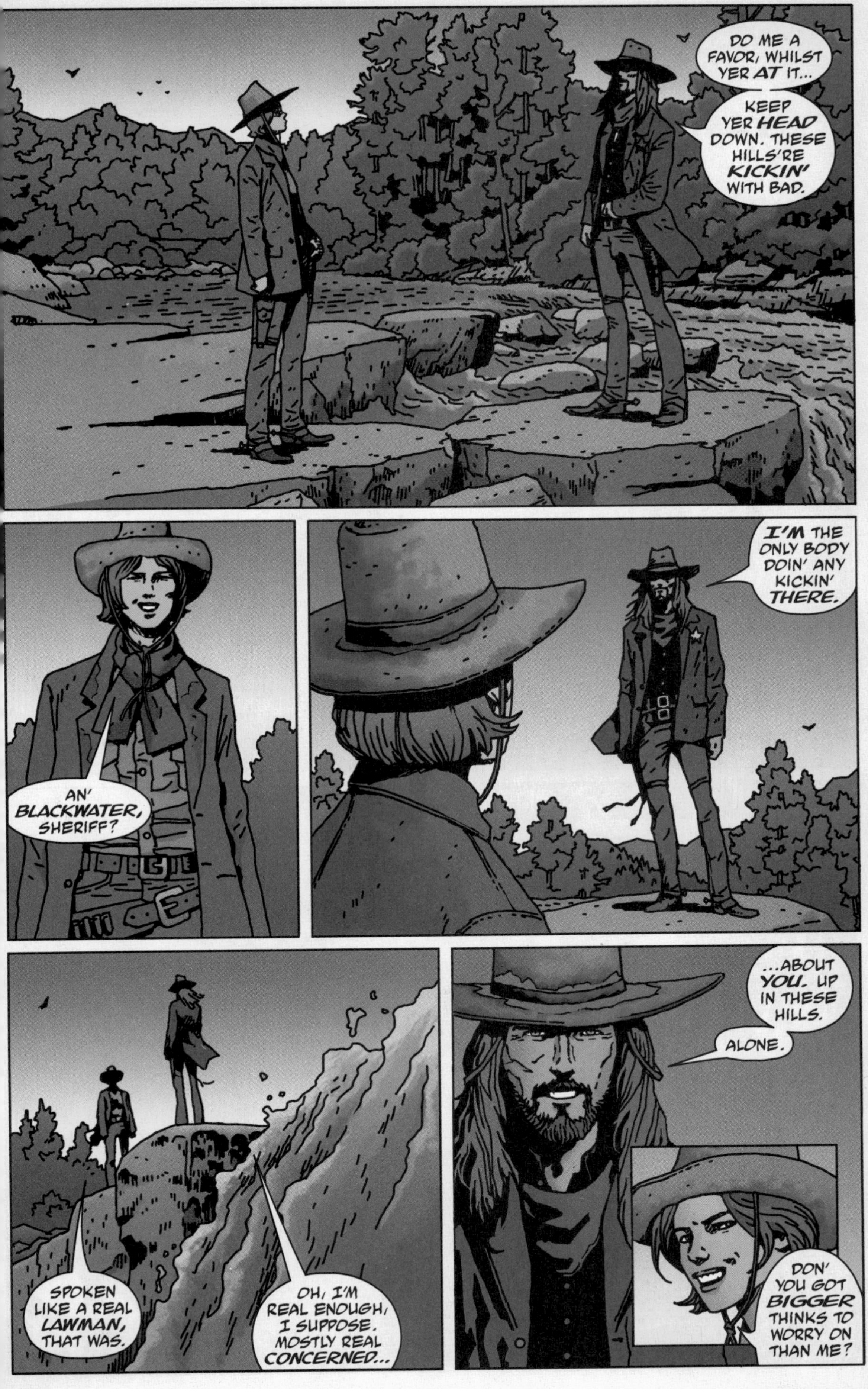
DO ME A FAVOR, WHILST YER AT IT...
KEEP YER HEAD DOWN. THESE HILLS'RE KICKIN' WITH BAD.
AN' BLACKWATER, SHERIFF?
I'M THE ONLY BODY DOIN' ANY KICKIN' THERE.
SPOKEN LIKE A REAL LAWMAN, THAT WAS.
OH, I'M REAL ENOUGH, I SUPPOSE. MOSTLY REAL CONCERNED...
...ABOUT YOU. UP IN THESE HILLS.
ALONE.
DON' YOU GOT BIGGER THINKS TO WORRY ON THAN ME?

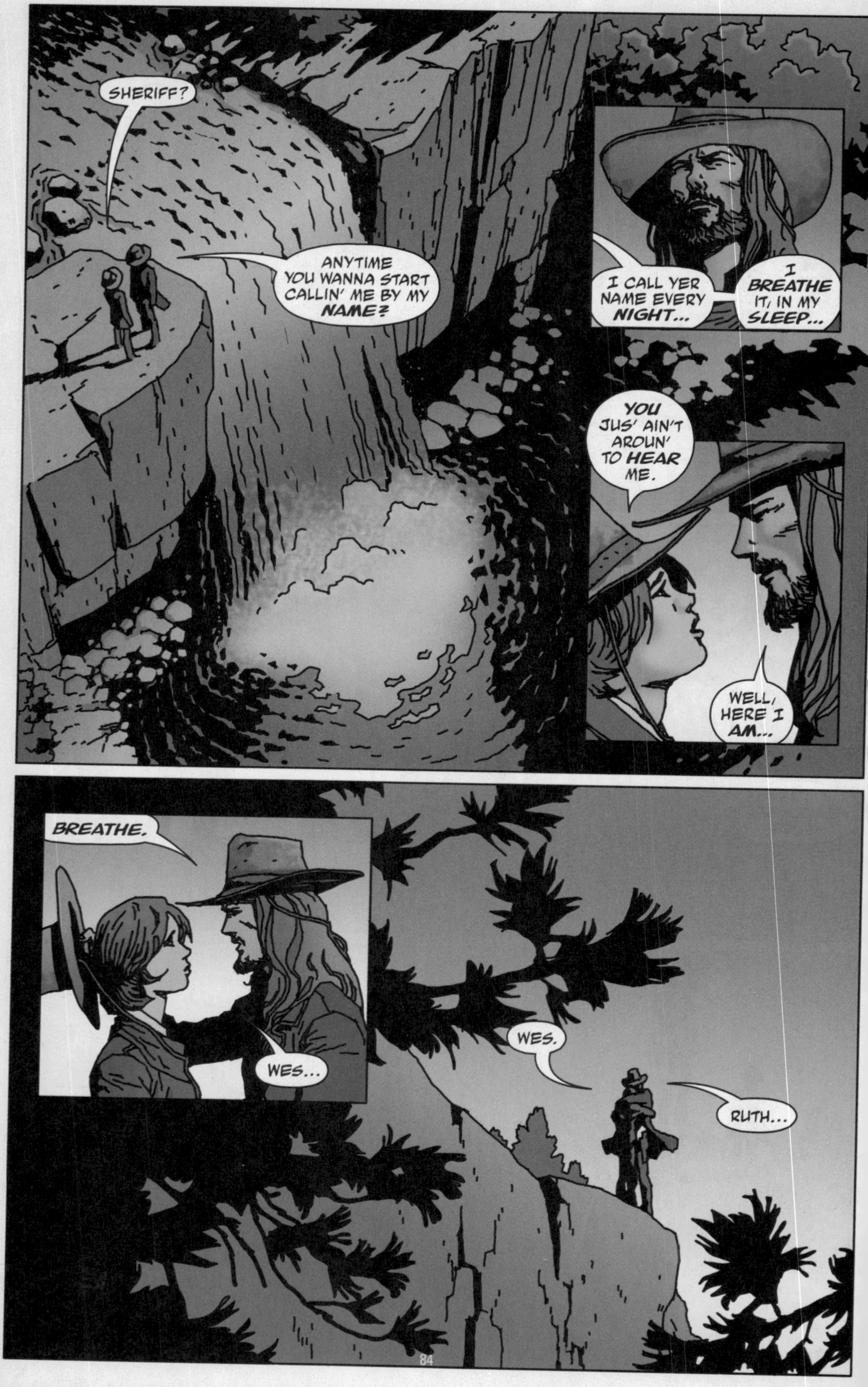
SHERIFF?
ANYTIME YOU WANNA START CALLIN' ME BY MY NAME?
I CALL YER NAME EVERY NIGHT...
I BREATHE IT, IN MY SLEEP...
YOU JUS' AIN'T AROUN' TO HEAR ME.
WELL, HERE I AM...
BREATHE.
WES...
WES.
RUTH...

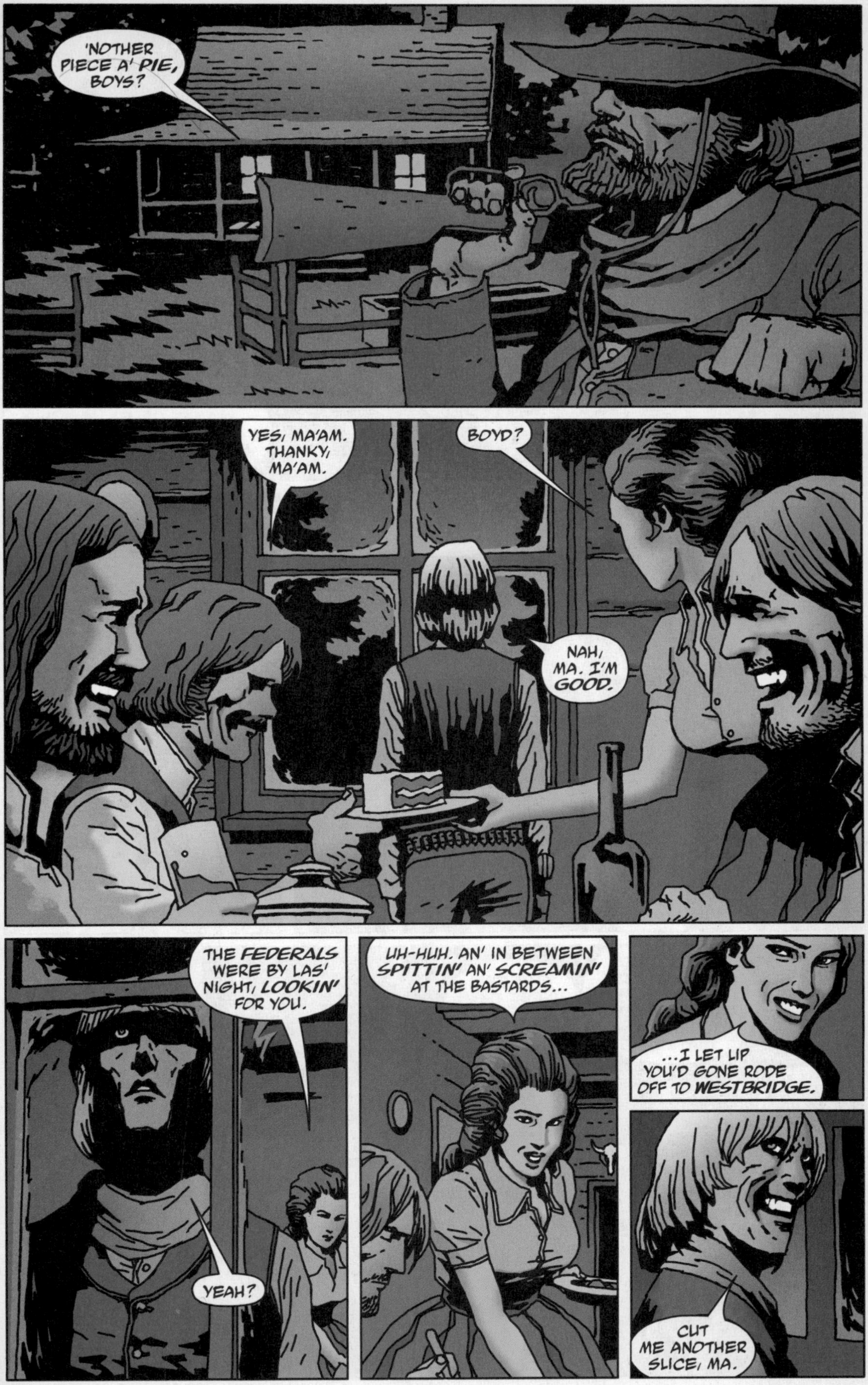
'NOTHER PIECE A' PIE, BOYS?
YES, MA'AM. THANKY, MA'AM.
BOYD?
NAH, MA. I'M GOOD.
THE FEDERALS WERE BY LAS' NIGHT, LOOKIN' FOR YOU.
YEAH?
UH-HUH. AN' IN BETWEEN SPITTIN' AN' SCREAMIN' AT THE BASTARDS...
...I LET LIP YOU'D GONE RODE OFF TO WESTBRIDGE.
CUT ME ANOTHER SLICE, MA.

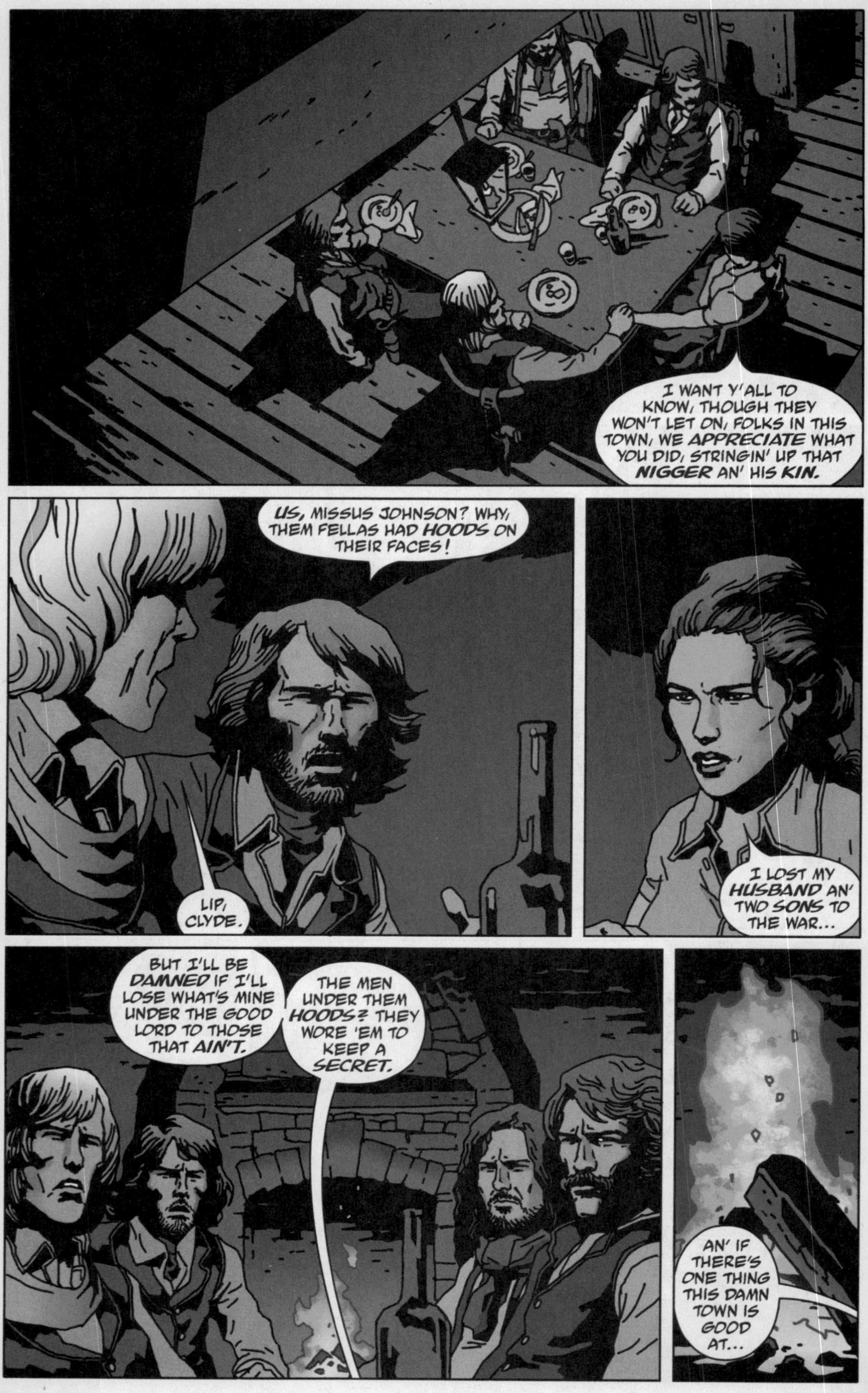
I WANT Y'ALL TO KNOW, THOUGH THEY WON'T LET ON, FOLKS IN THIS TOWN, WE *APPRECIATE* WHAT YOU DID, STRINGIN' UP THAT ***NIGGER*** AN' HIS ***KIN.***
US, MISSUS JOHNSON? WHY, THEM FELLAS HAD ***HOODS*** ON THEIR FACES!
LIP, CLYDE.
I LOST MY ***HUSBAND*** AN' TWO ***SONS*** TO THE WAR...
BUT I'LL BE ***DAMNED*** IF I'LL LOSE WHAT'S MINE UNDER THE GOOD LORD TO THOSE THAT ***AIN'T.***
THE MEN UNDER THEM ***HOODS?*** THEY WORE 'EM TO KEEP A ***SECRET.***
AN' IF THERE'S ONE THING THIS DAMN TOWN IS GOOD AT...

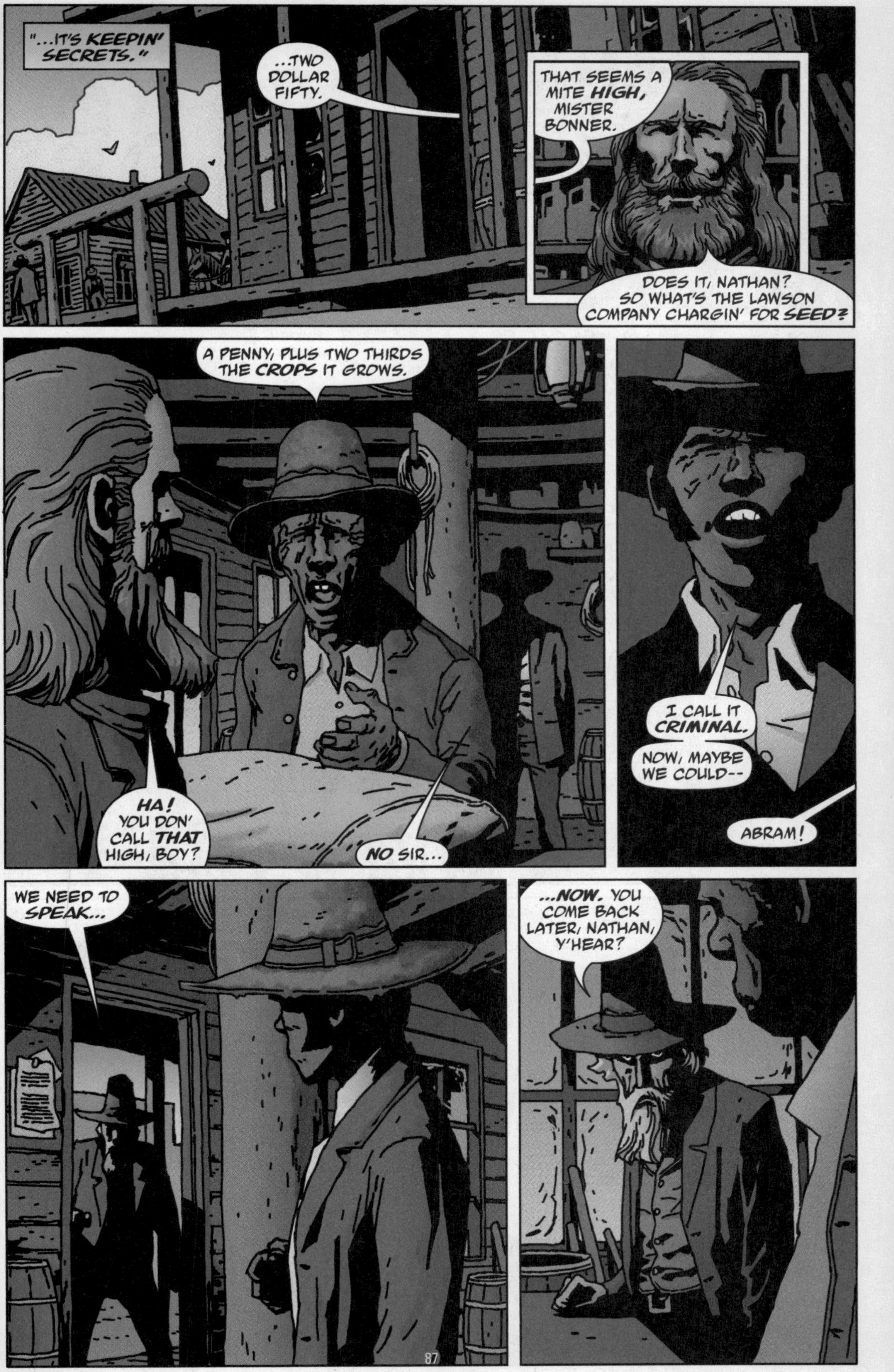
"...IT'S KEEPIN' SECRETS."
...TWO DOLLAR FIFTY.
THAT SEEMS A MITE HIGH, MISTER BONNER.
DOES IT, NATHAN? SO WHAT'S THE LAWSON COMPANY CHARGIN' FOR SEED?
A PENNY, PLUS TWO THIRDS THE CROPS IT GROWS.
HA! YOU DON' CALL THAT HIGH, BOY?
NO SIR...
I CALL IT CRIMINAL.
NOW, MAYBE WE COULD--
ABRAM!
WE NEED TO SPEAK...
...NOW. YOU COME BACK LATER, NATHAN, Y'HEAR?

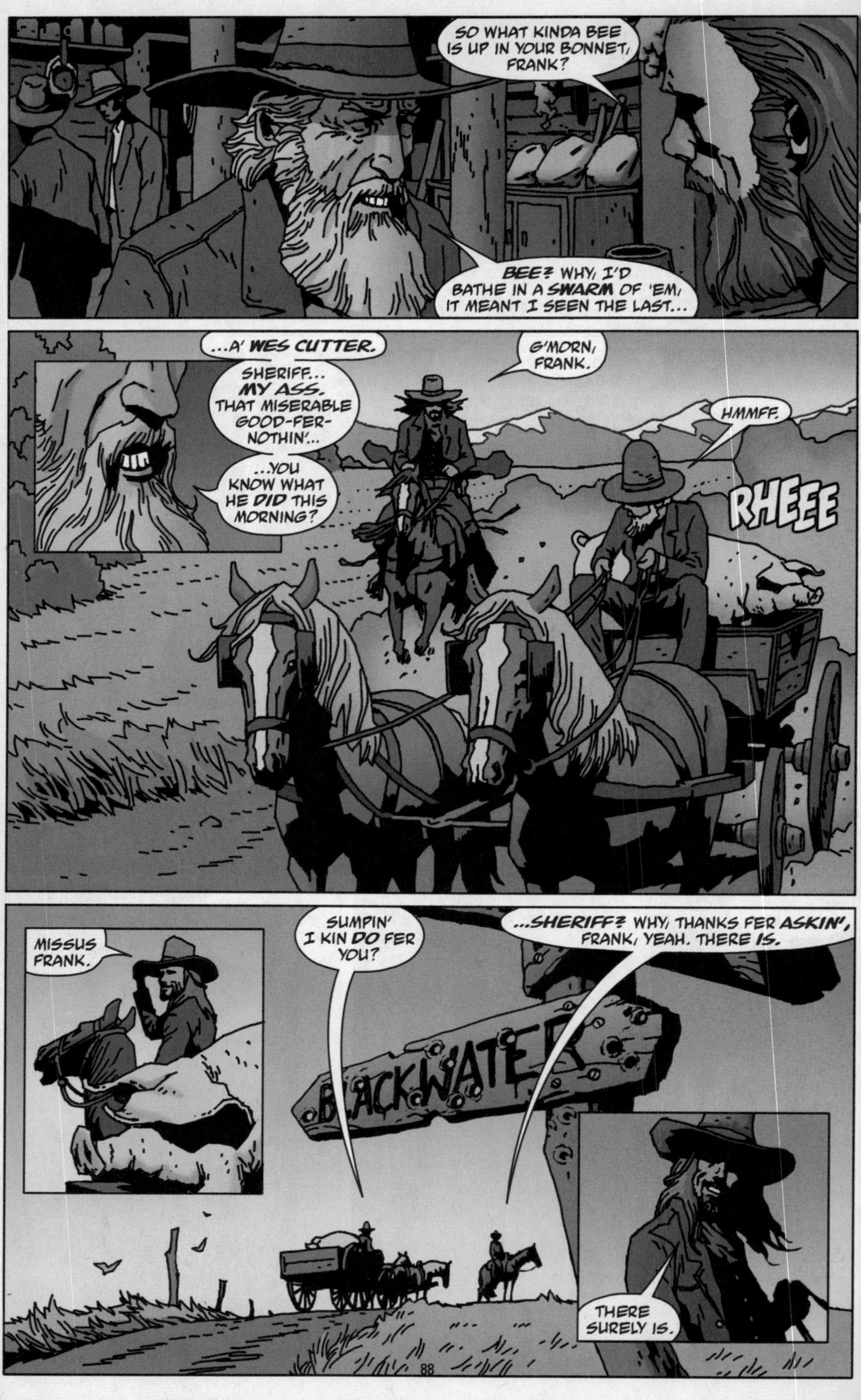
SO WHAT KINDA BEE IS UP IN YOUR BONNET, FRANK?
BEE? WHY, I'D BATHE IN A SWARM OF 'EM, IT MEANT I SEEN THE LAST...
...A' WES CUTTER.
SHERIFF... MY ASS. THAT MISERABLE GOOD-FER-NOTHIN'...
...YOU KNOW WHAT HE DID THIS MORNING?
G'MORN, FRANK.
HMMFF.
RHEEE
MISSUS FRANK.
SUMPIN' I KIN DO FER YOU?
...SHERIFF? WHY, THANKS FER ASKIN', FRANK, YEAH. THERE IS.
BLACKWATER
THERE SURELY IS.

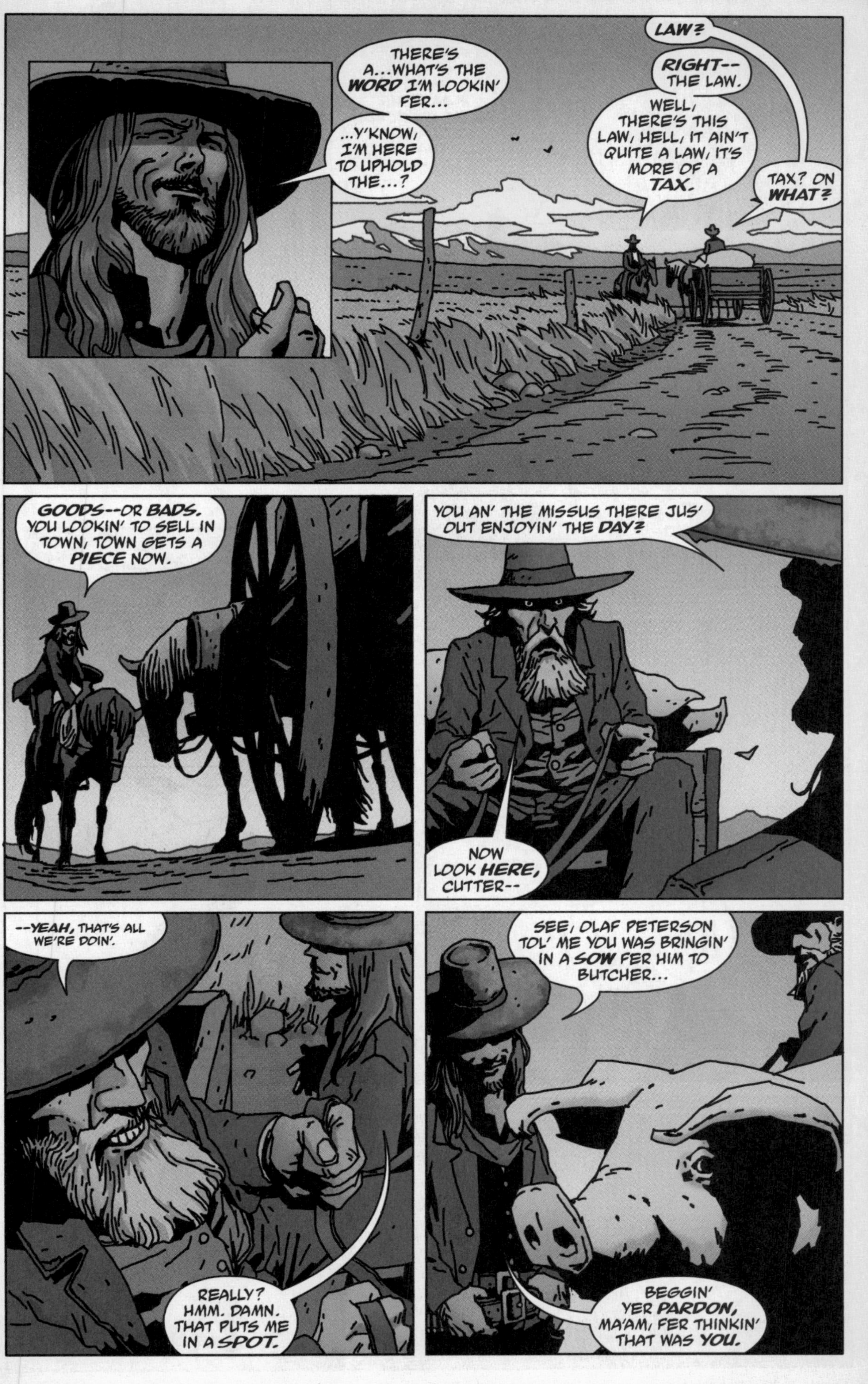
THERE'S A...WHAT'S THE WORD I'M LOOKIN' FER...
...Y'KNOW, I'M HERE TO UPHOLD THE...?
LAW?
RIGHT-- THE LAW.
WELL, THERE'S THIS LAW, HELL, IT AIN'T QUITE A LAW, IT'S MORE OF A TAX.
TAX? ON WHAT?
GOODS--OR BADS. YOU LOOKIN' TO SELL IN TOWN, TOWN GETS A PIECE NOW.
YOU AN' THE MISSUS THERE JUS' OUT ENJOYIN' THE DAY?
NOW LOOK HERE, CUTTER--
--YEAH, THAT'S ALL WE'RE DOIN'.
REALLY? HMM. DAMN. THAT PUTS ME IN A SPOT.
SEE, OLAF PETERSON TOL' ME YOU WAS BRINGIN' IN A SOW FER HIM TO BUTCHER...
BEGGIN' YER PARDON, MA'AM, FER THINKIN' THAT WAS YOU.

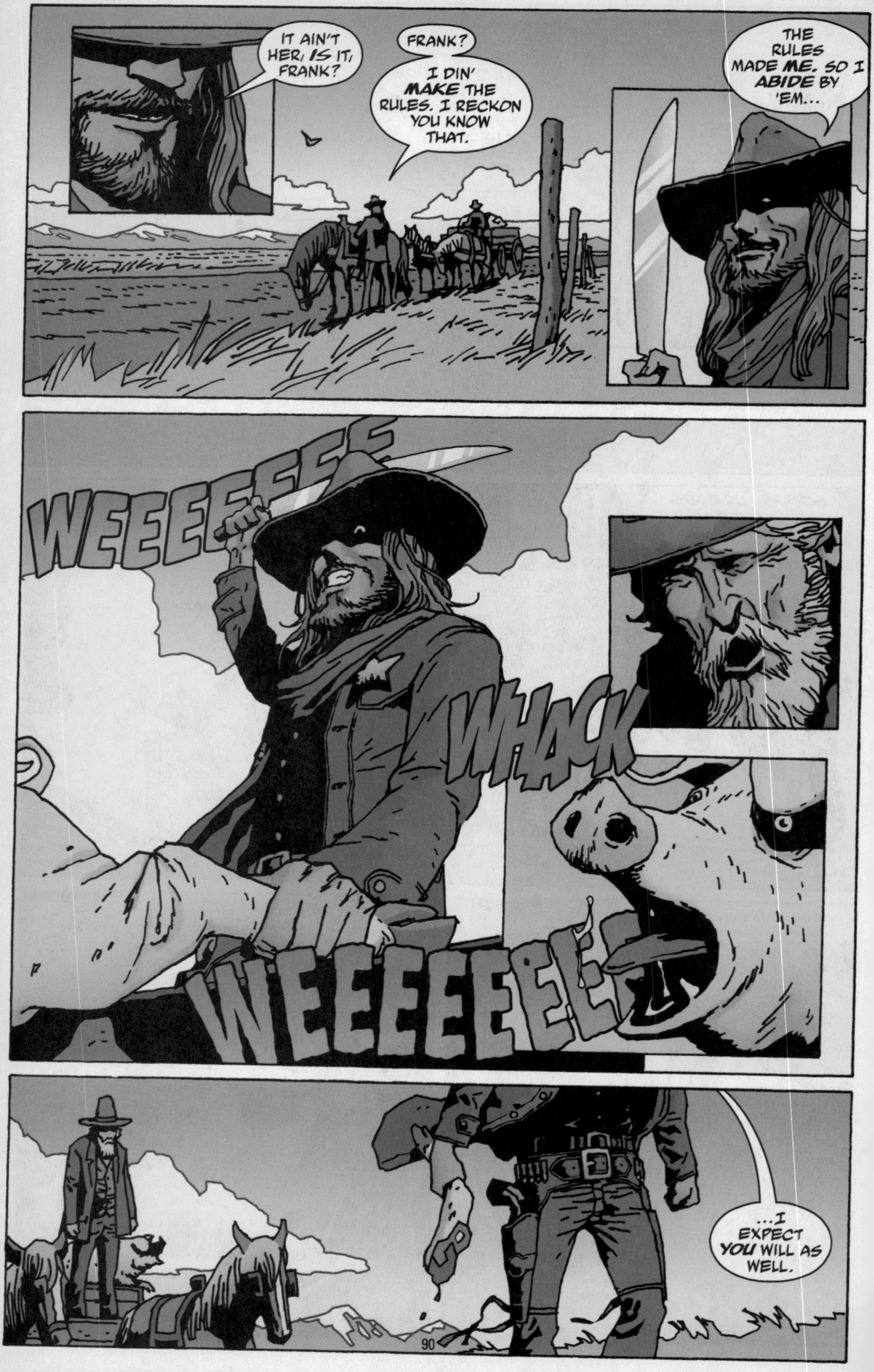
IT AIN'T HER, IS IT, FRANK?
FRANK?
I DIN' MAKE THE RULES. I RECKON YOU KNOW THAT.
THE RULES MADE ME. SO I ABIDE BY 'EM...
WEEEEEEE
WHACK
WEEEEEEEEE
...I EXPECT YOU WILL AS WELL.

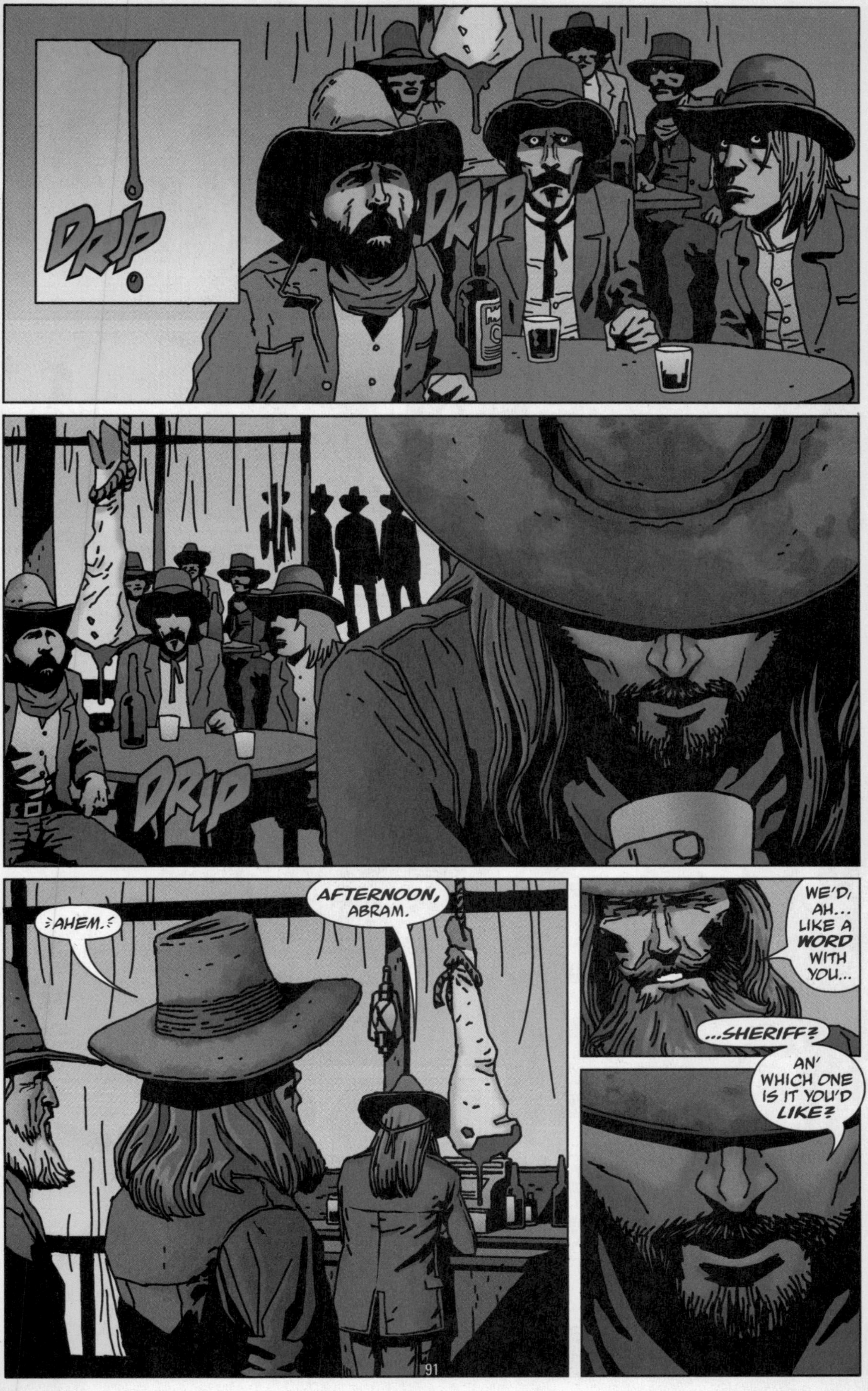
DRIP
DRIP
DRIP
AHEM.
AFTERNOON, ABRAM.
WE'D, AH... LIKE A WORD WITH YOU...
...SHERIFF?
AN' WHICH ONE IS IT YOU'D LIKE?

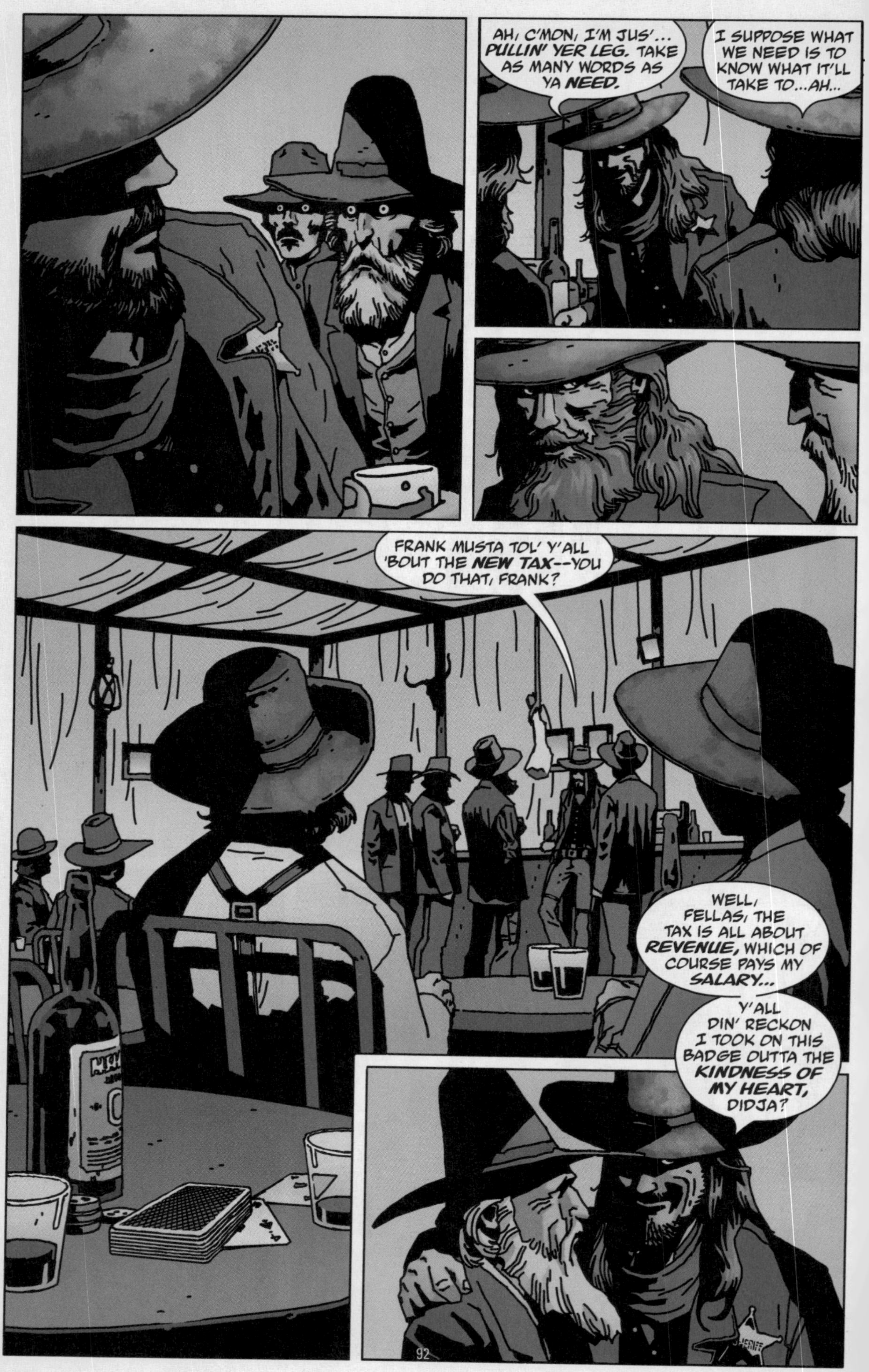
AH, C'MON, I'M JUS'... PULLIN' YER LEG. TAKE AS MANY WORDS AS YA NEED.
I SUPPOSE WHAT WE NEED IS TO KNOW WHAT IT'LL TAKE TO...AH...
FRANK MUSTA TOL' Y'ALL 'BOUT THE NEW TAX--YOU DO THAT, FRANK?
WELL, FELLAS, THE TAX IS ALL ABOUT REVENUE, WHICH OF COURSE PAYS MY SALARY...
Y'ALL DIN' RECKON I TOOK ON THIS BADGE OUTTA THE KINDNESS OF MY HEART, DIDJA?

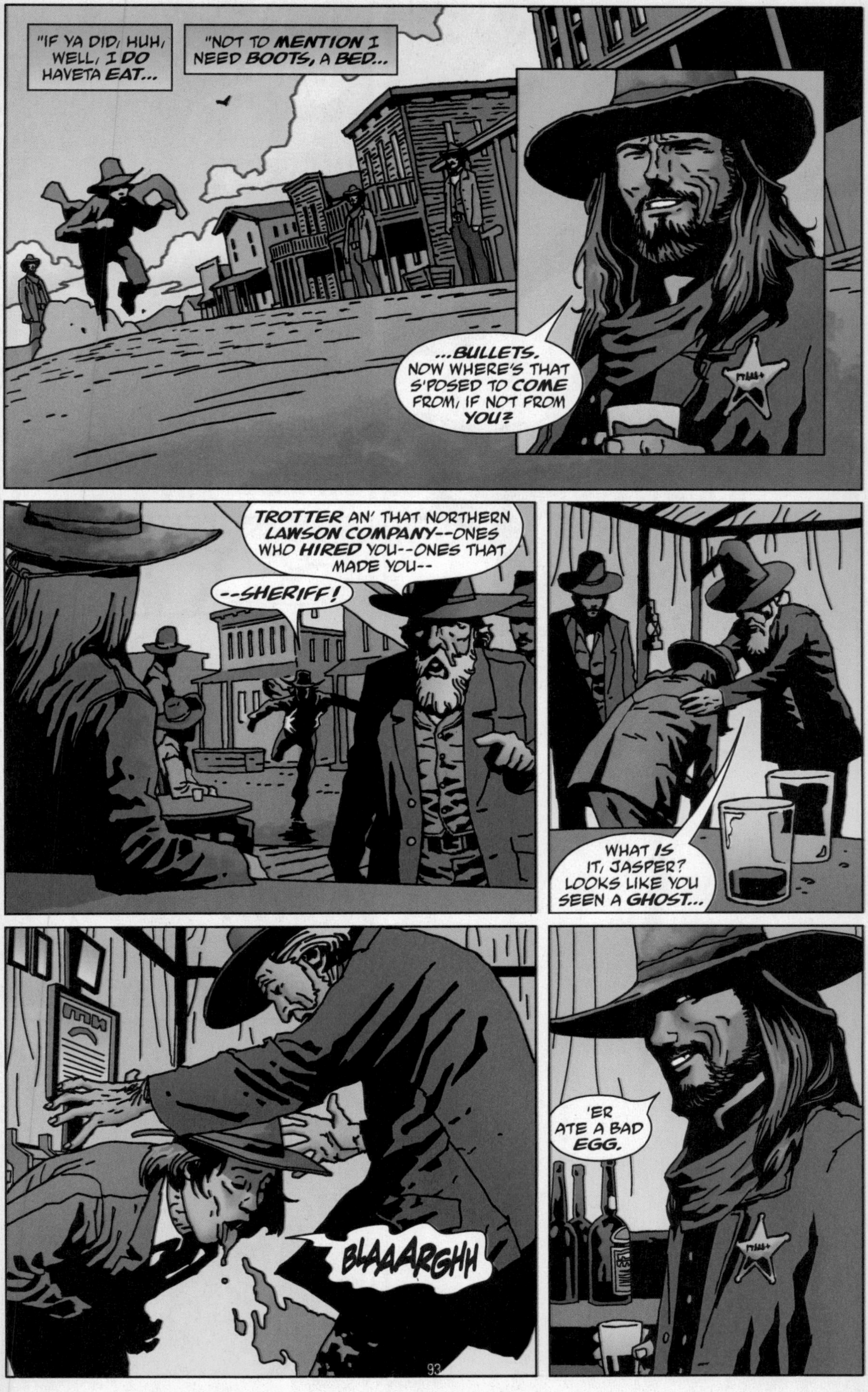
"IF YA DID, HUH, WELL, I DO HAVETA EAT...
"NOT TO MENTION I NEED BOOTS, A BED...
...BULLETS. NOW WHERE'S THAT S'POSED TO COME FROM, IF NOT FROM YOU?
TROTTER AN' THAT NORTHERN LAWSON COMPANY--ONES WHO HIRED YOU--ONES THAT MADE YOU--
--SHERIFF!
WHAT IS IT, JASPER? LOOKS LIKE YOU SEEN A GHOST...
BLAAARGHH
'ER ATE A BAD EGG.

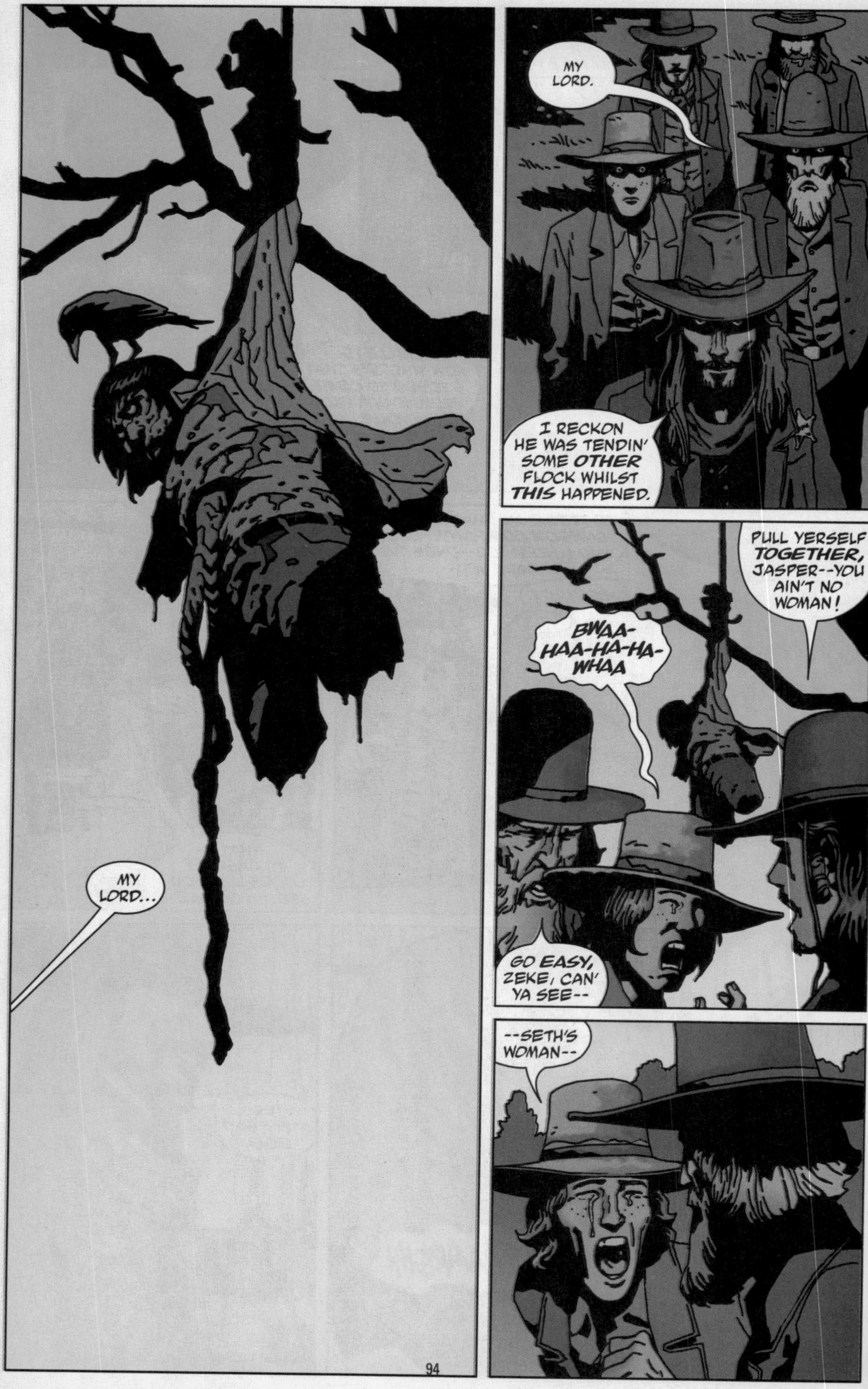
MY LORD...
MY LORD.
I RECKON HE WAS TENDIN' SOME OTHER FLOCK WHILST THIS HAPPENED.
PULL YERSELF TOGETHER, JASPER--YOU AIN'T NO WOMAN!
BWAA-HAA-HA-HA-WHAA
GO EASY, ZEKE, CAN'YA SEE--
--SETH'S WOMAN--

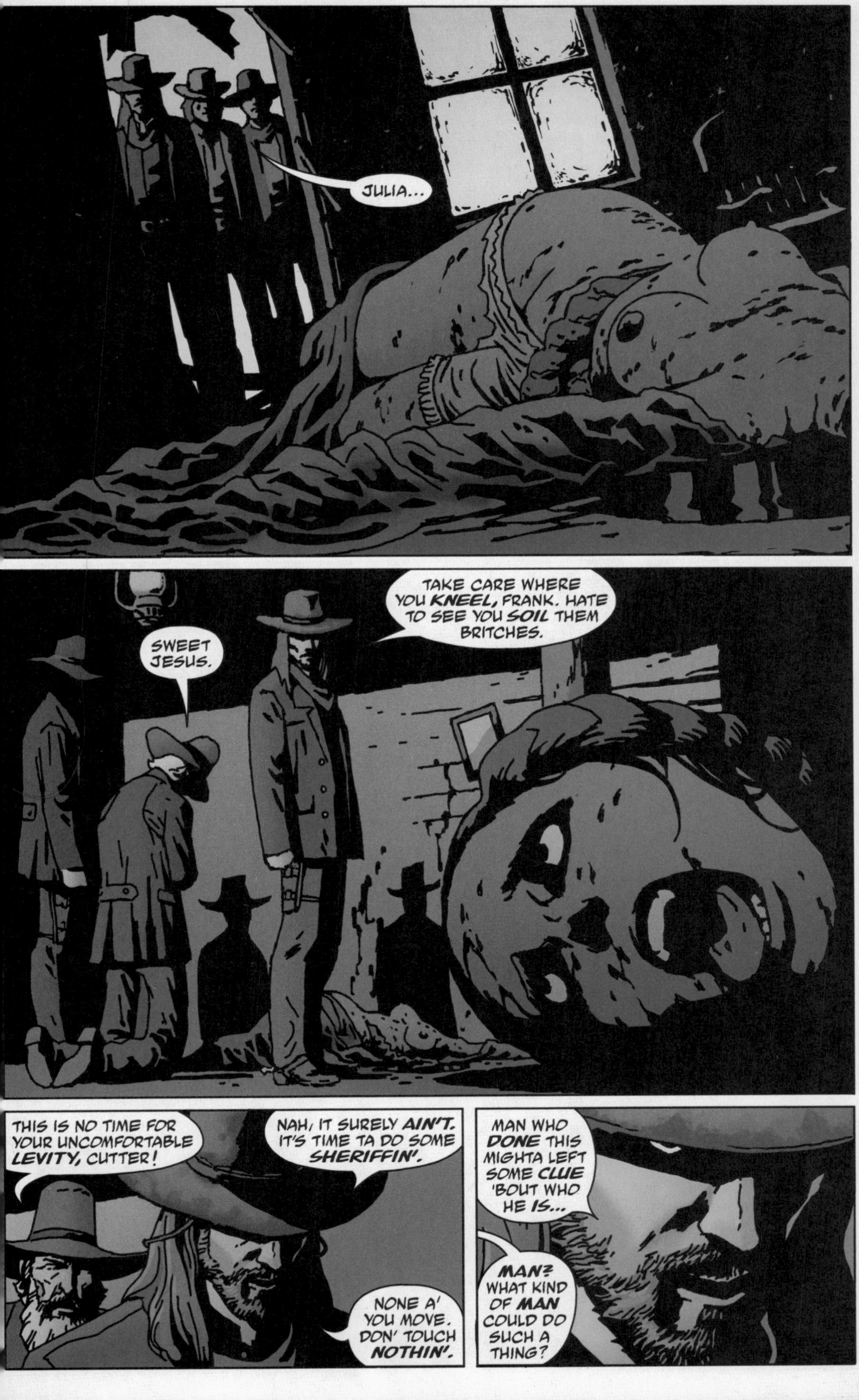
JULIA...
SWEET JESUS.
TAKE CARE WHERE YOU KNEEL, FRANK. HATE TO SEE YOU SOIL THEM BRITCHES.
THIS IS NO TIME FOR YOUR UNCOMFORTABLE LEVITY, CUTTER!
NAH, IT SURELY AIN'T. IT'S TIME TA DO SOME SHERIFFIN'.
NONE A' YOU MOVE. DON' TOUCH NOTHIN'.
MAN WHO DONE THIS MIGHTA LEFT SOME CLUE 'BOUT WHO HE IS...
MAN? WHAT KIND OF MAN COULD DO SUCH A THING?

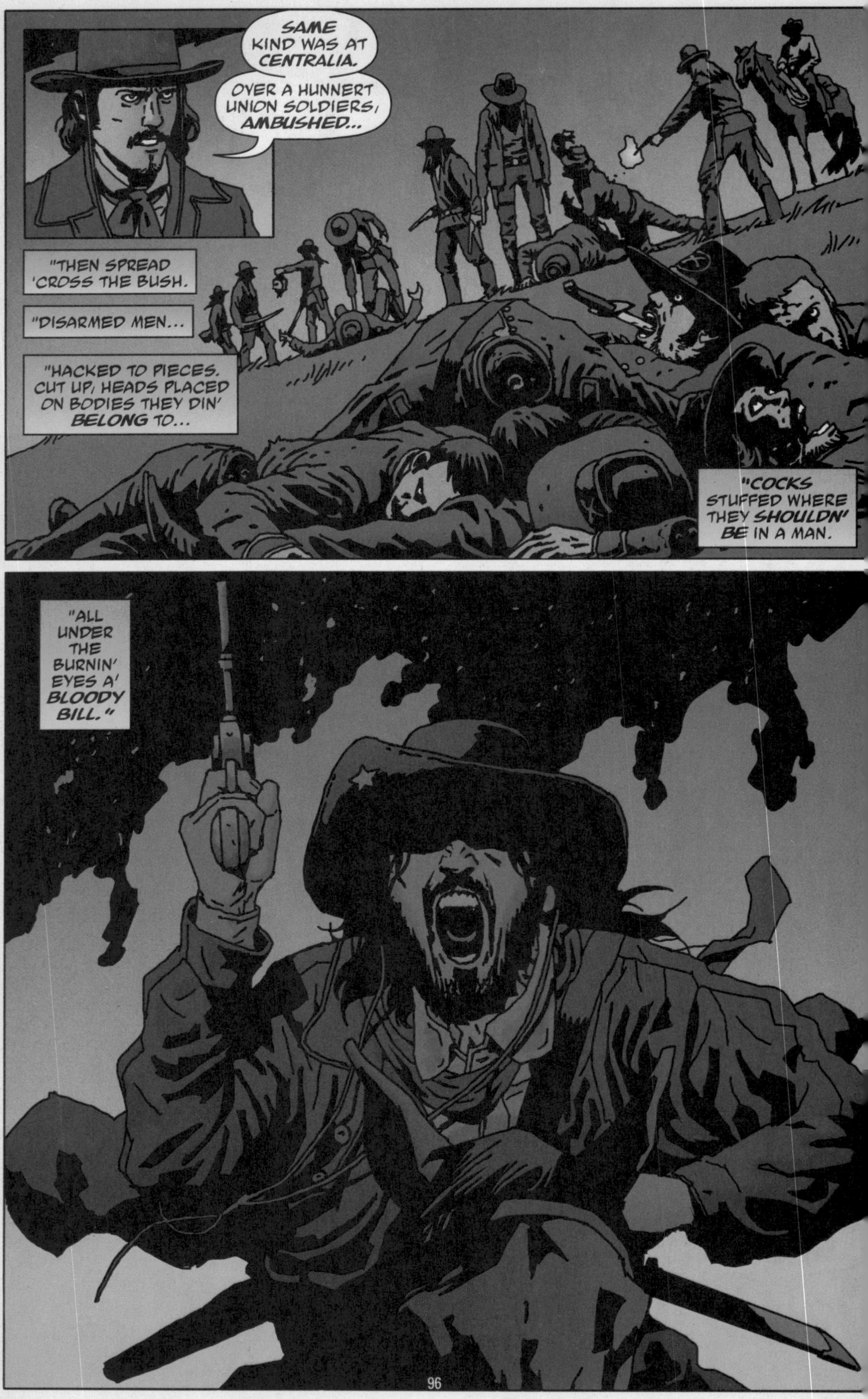
SAME KIND WAS AT CENTRALIA.
OVER A HUNNERT UNION SOLDIERS, AMBUSHED...
"THEN SPREAD 'CROSS THE BUSH.
"DISARMED MEN...
"HACKED TO PIECES. CUT UP, HEADS PLACED ON BODIES THEY DIN' BELONG TO...
"COCKS STUFFED WHERE THEY SHOULDN' BE IN A MAN.
"ALL UNDER THE BURNIN' EYES A' BLOODY BILL."

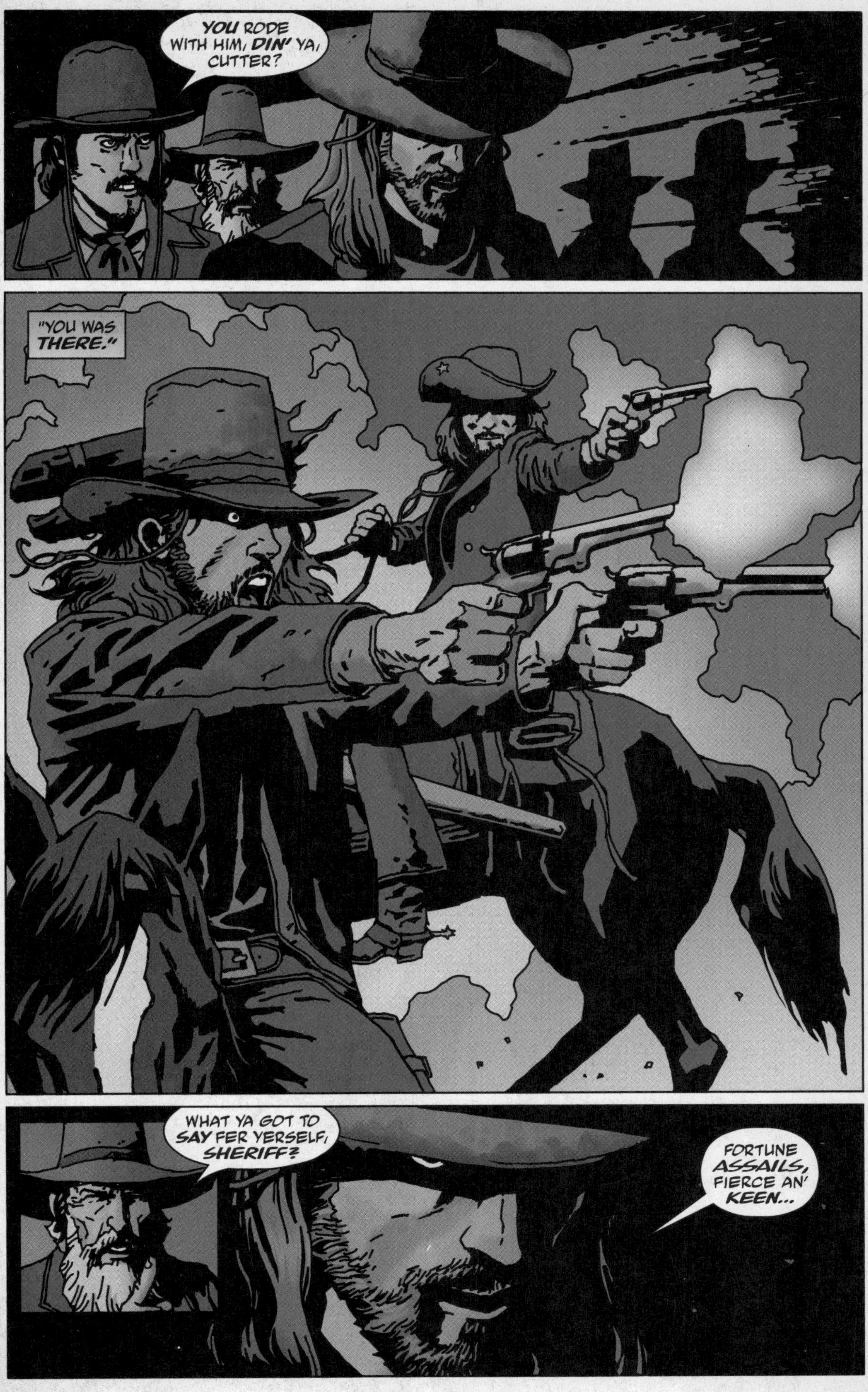
YOU RODE WITH HIM, DIN' YA, CUTTER?
"YOU WAS THERE."
WHAT YA GOT TO SAY FER YERSELF, SHERIFF?
FORTUNE ASSAILS, FIERCE AN' KEEN...

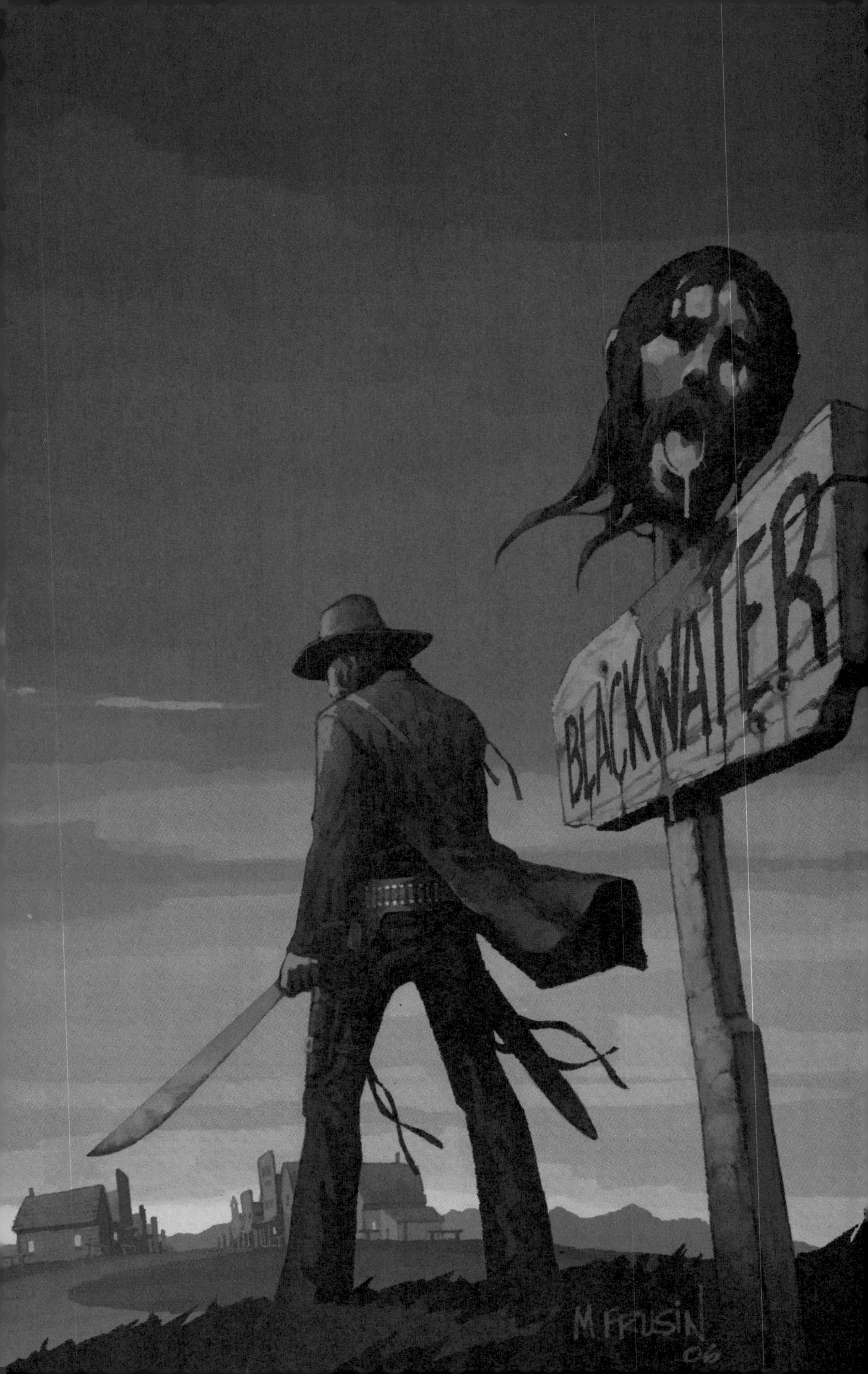
BLACKWATER
M FRUSIN
06

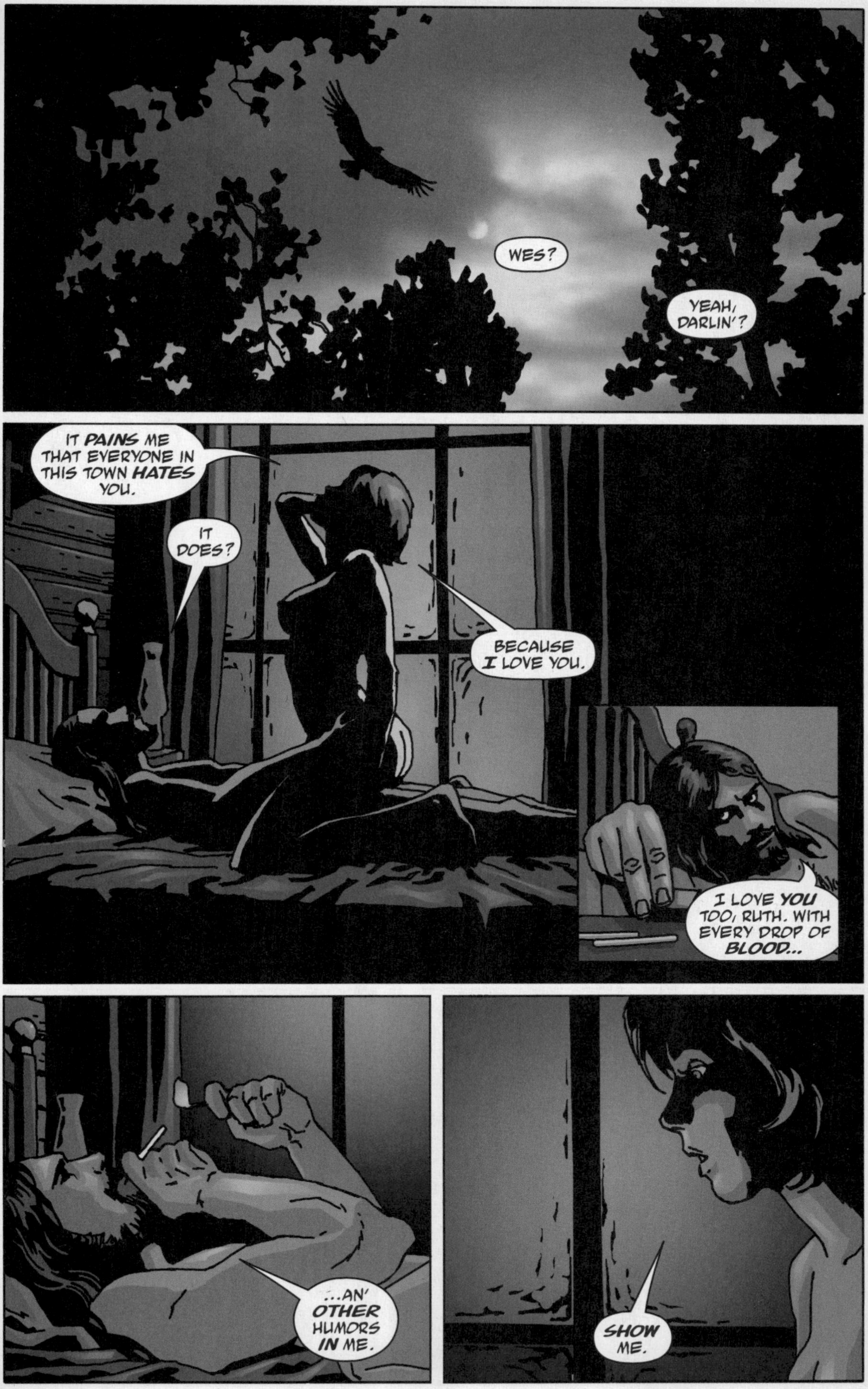
WES?
YEAH, DARLIN'?
IT PAINS ME THAT EVERYONE IN THIS TOWN HATES YOU.
IT DOES?
BECAUSE I LOVE YOU.
I LOVE YOU TOO, RUTH. WITH EVERY DROP OF BLOOD...
...AN' OTHER HUMORS IN ME.
SHOW ME.

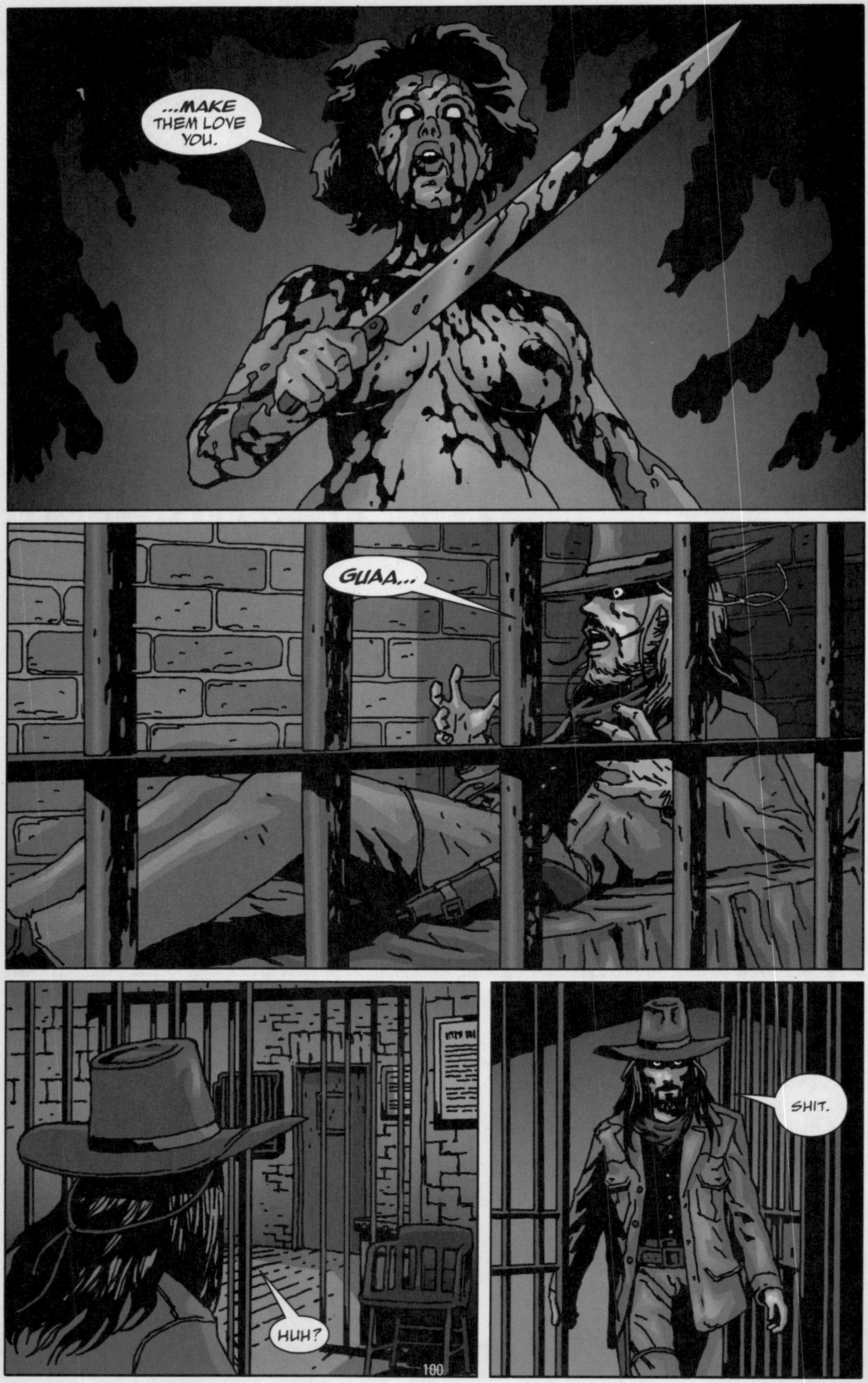
...MAKE THEM LOVE YOU.
GUAA...
HUH?
SHIT.

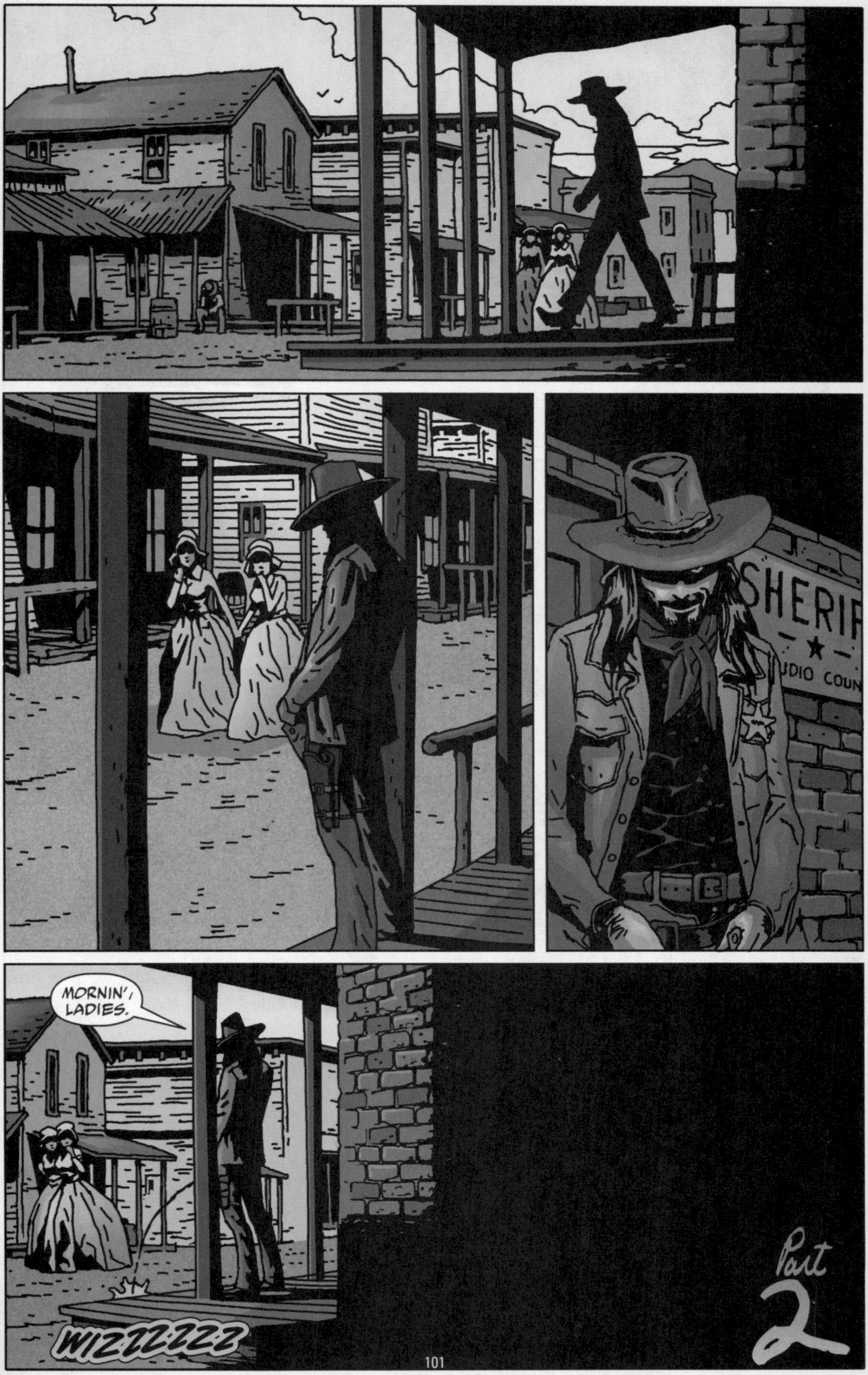
SHERIF
UDIO COUN
MORNIN', LADIES.
WIZZZZZZ
Part 2

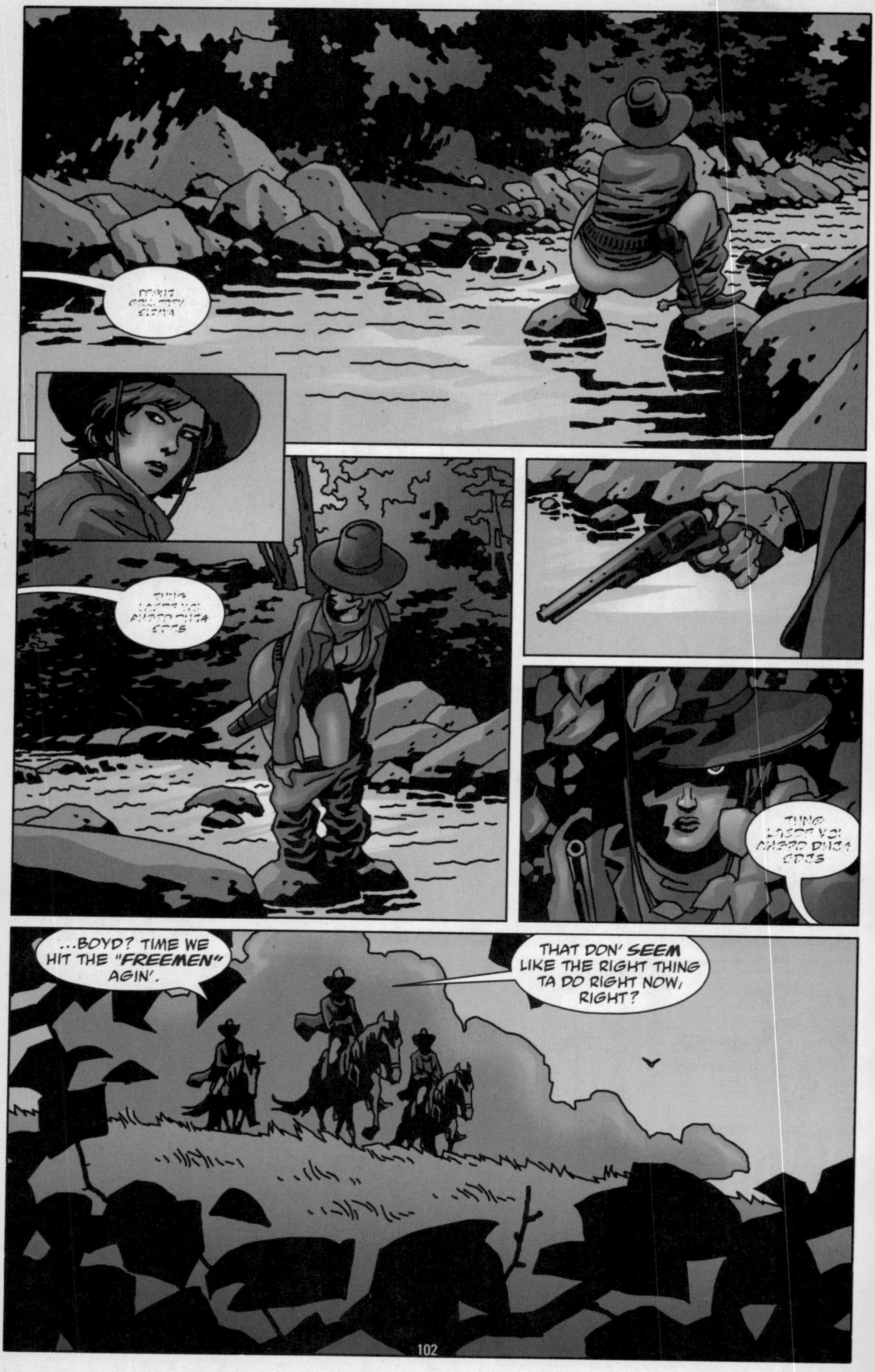
...BOYD? TIME WE HIT THE "FREEMEN" AGIN'.
THAT DON' SEEM LIKE THE RIGHT THING TA DO RIGHT NOW, RIGHT?

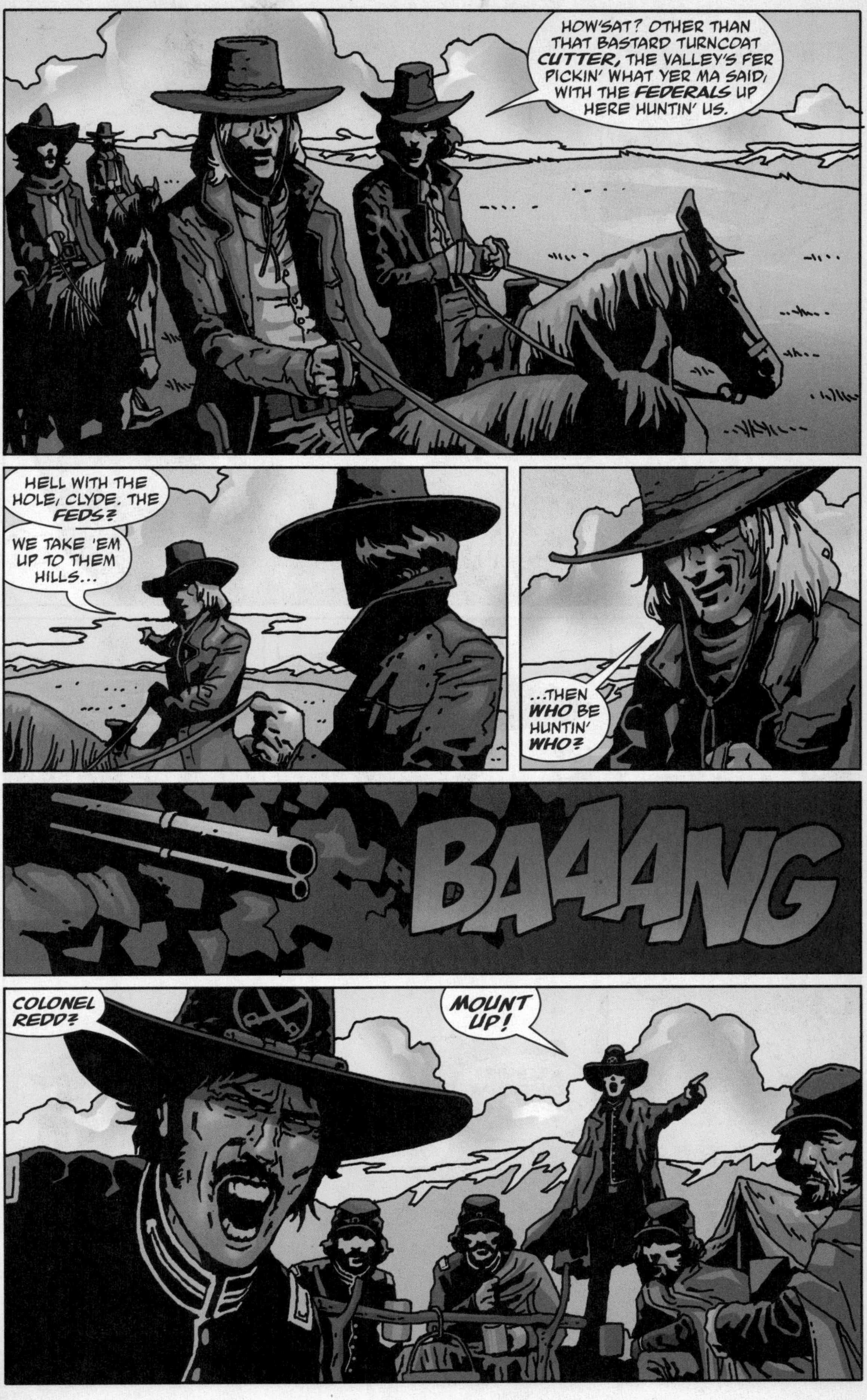
HOW'SAT? OTHER THAN THAT BASTARD TURNCOAT CUTTER, THE VALLEY'S FER PICKIN' WHAT YER MA SAID, WITH THE FEDERALS UP HERE HUNTIN' US.
HELL WITH THE HOLE, CLYDE. THE FEDS?
WE TAKE 'EM UP TO THEM HILLS...
...THEN WHO BE HUNTIN' WHO?
BAAANG
COLONEL REDD?
MOUNT UP!

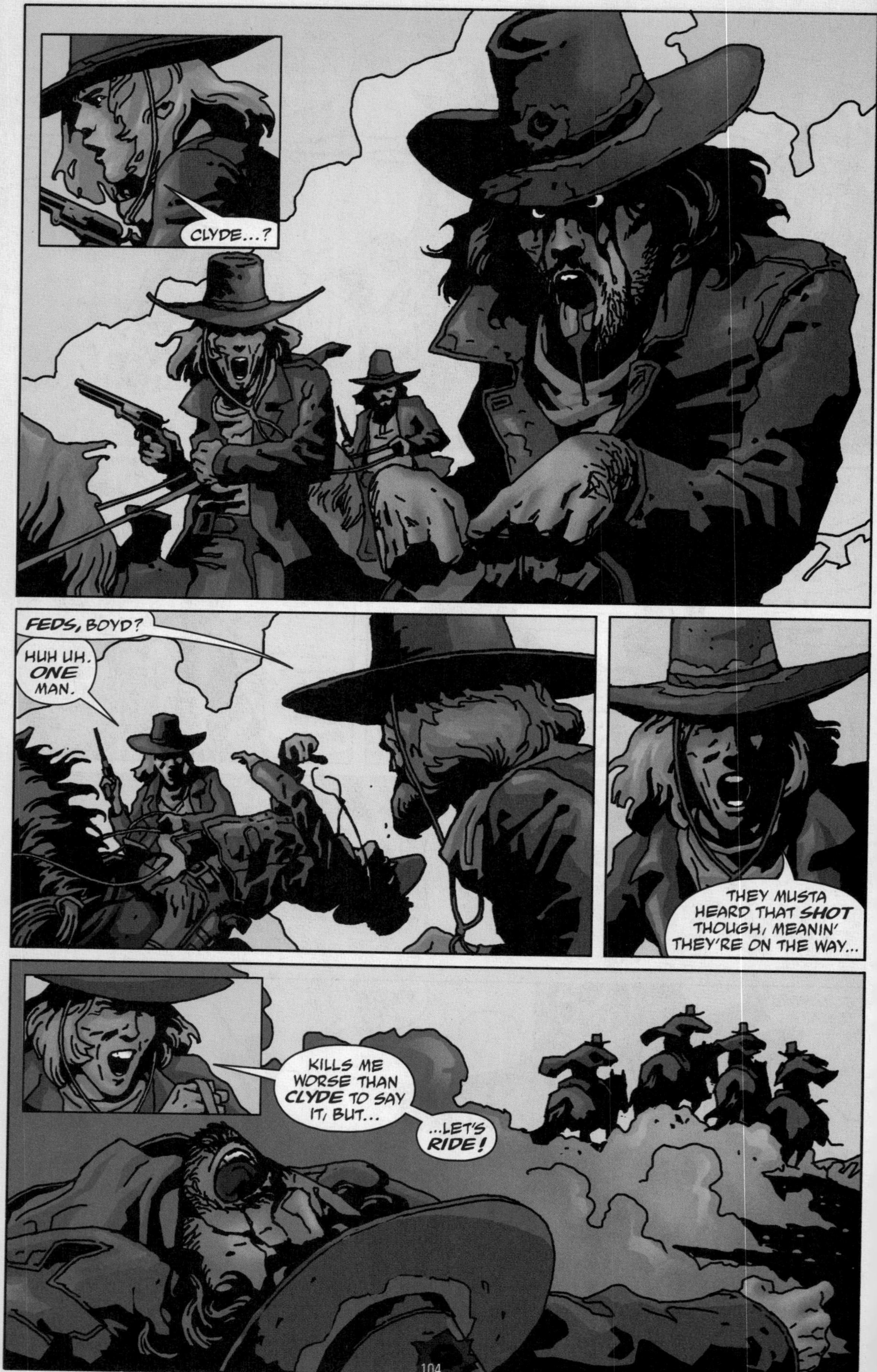
CLYDE...?
FEDS, BOYD?
HUH UH. ONE MAN.
THEY MUSTA HEARD THAT SHOT THOUGH, MEANIN' THEY'RE ON THE WAY...
KILLS ME WORSE THAN CLYDE TO SAY IT, BUT...
...LET'S RIDE!

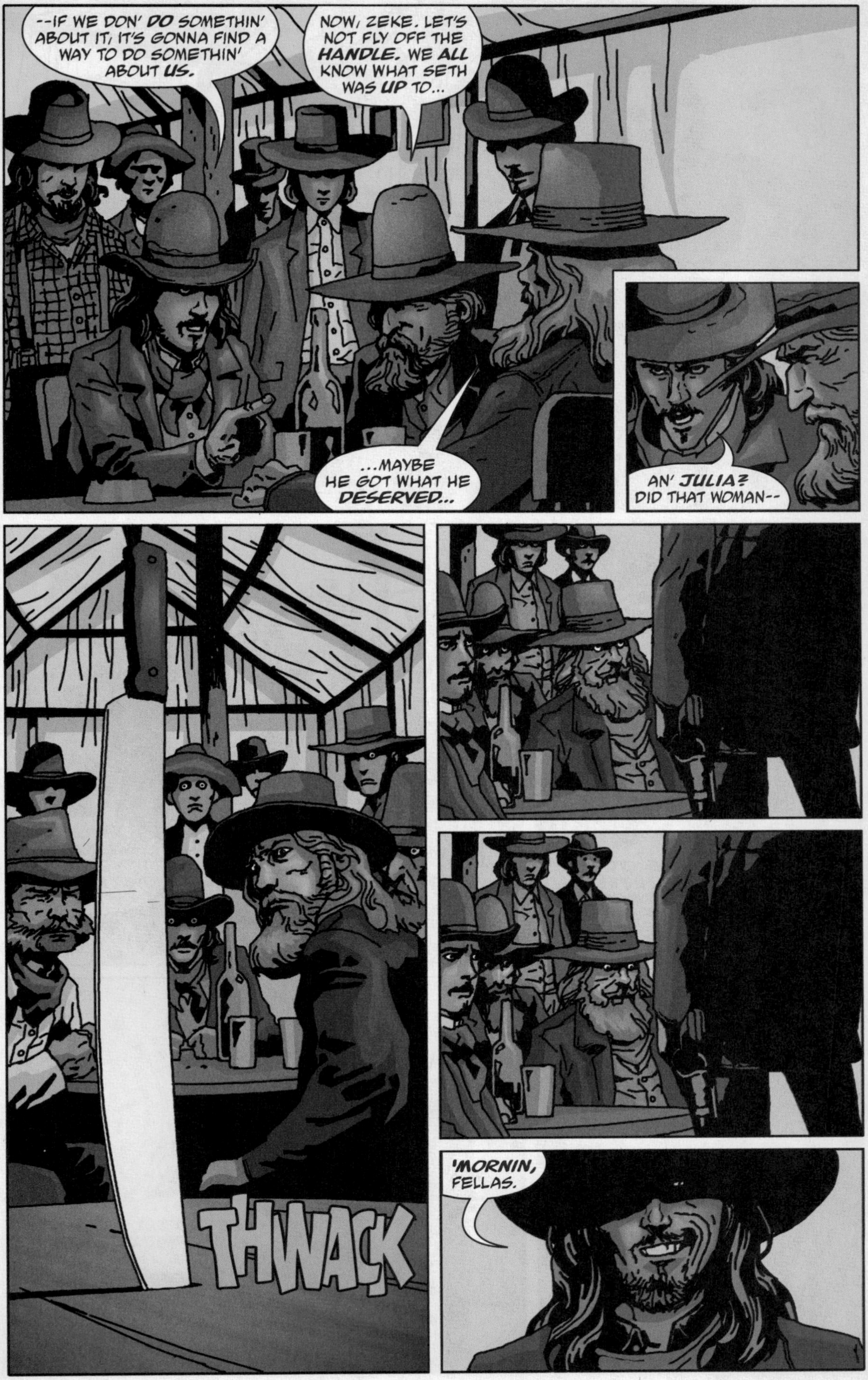
--IF WE DON' DO SOMETHIN' ABOUT IT, IT'S GONNA FIND A WAY TO DO SOMETHIN' ABOUT US.
NOW, ZEKE. LET'S NOT FLY OFF THE HANDLE. WE ALL KNOW WHAT SETH WAS UP TO...
...MAYBE HE GOT WHAT HE DESERVED...
AN' JULIA? DID THAT WOMAN--
THWACK
'MORNIN, FELLAS.

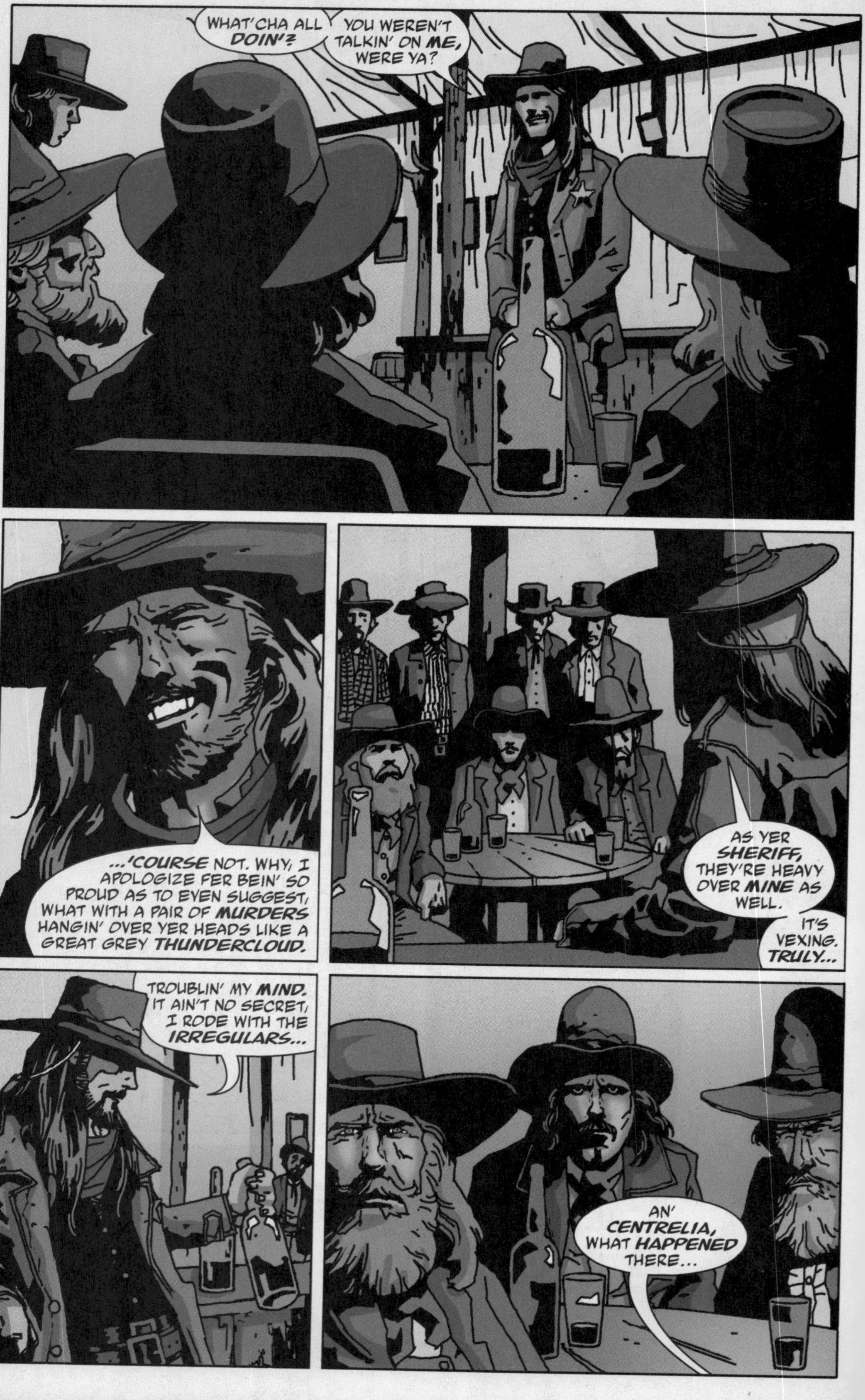
WHAT'CHA ALL DOIN'?
YOU WEREN'T TALKIN' ON ME, WERE YA?
...'COURSE NOT. WHY, I APOLOGIZE FER BEIN' SO PROUD AS TO EVEN SUGGEST, WHAT WITH A PAIR OF MURDERS HANGIN' OVER YER HEADS LIKE A GREAT GREY THUNDERCLOUD.
AS YER SHERIFF, THEY'RE HEAVY OVER MINE AS WELL.
IT'S VEXING. TRULY...
TROUBLIN' MY MIND. IT AIN'T NO SECRET, I RODE WITH THE IRREGULARS...
AN' CENTRELIA, WHAT HAPPENED THERE...

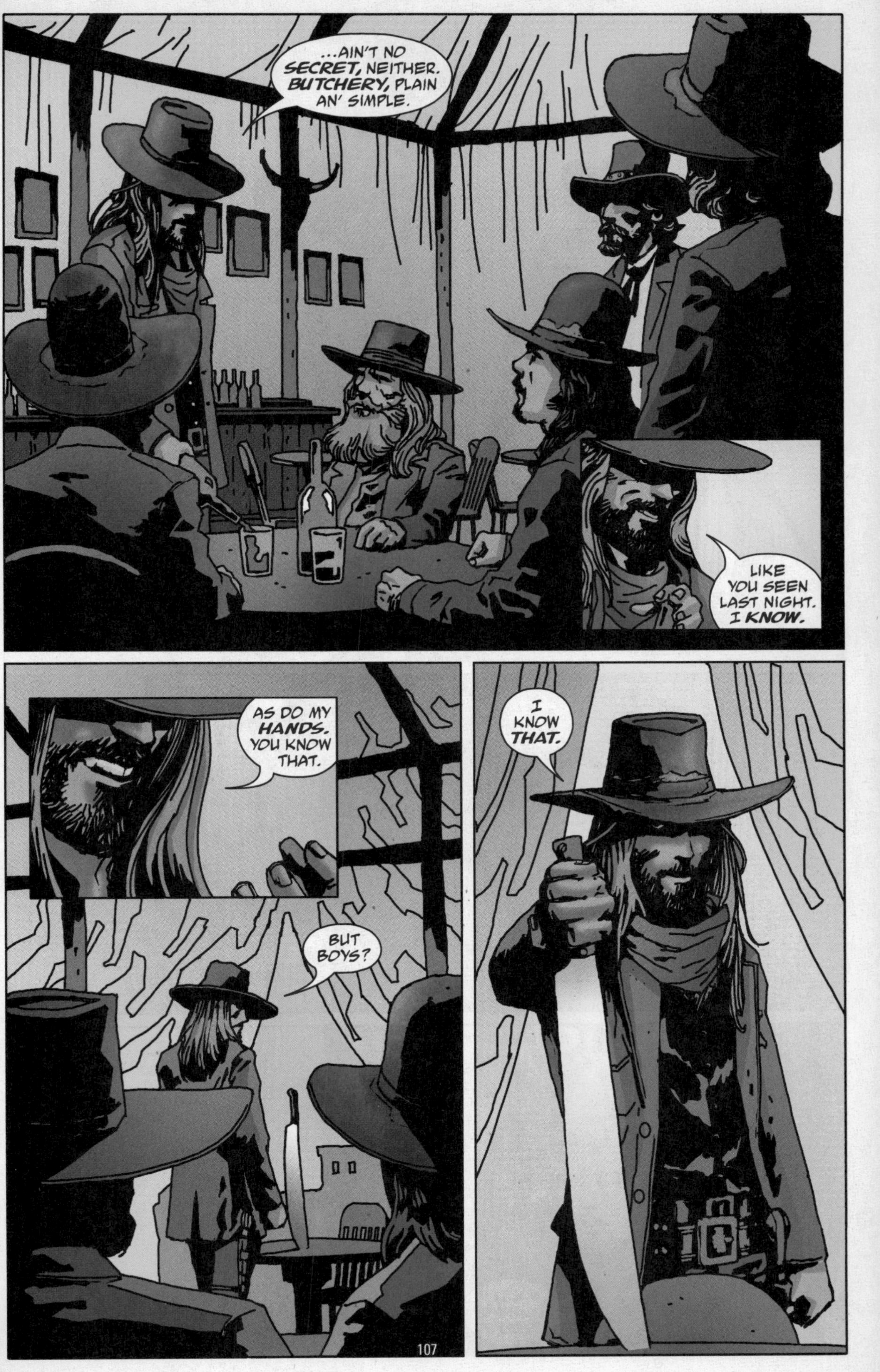
...AIN'T NO SECRET, NEITHER. BUTCHERY, PLAIN AN' SIMPLE.
LIKE YOU SEEN LAST NIGHT. I KNOW.
AS DO MY HANDS. YOU KNOW THAT.
BUT BOYS?
I KNOW THAT.

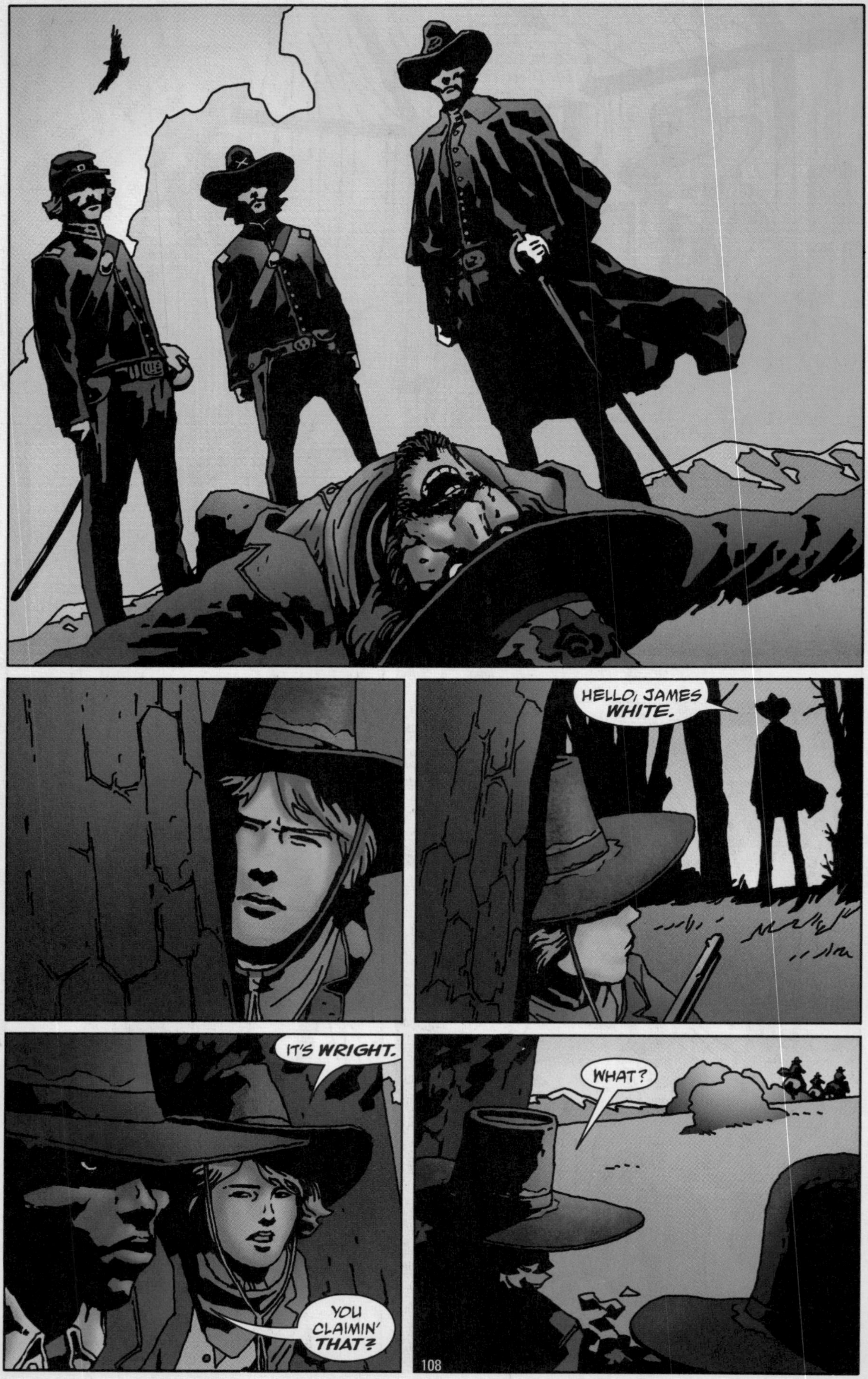
HELLO, JAMES WHITE.
IT'S WRIGHT.
YOU CLAIMIN' THAT?
WHAT?

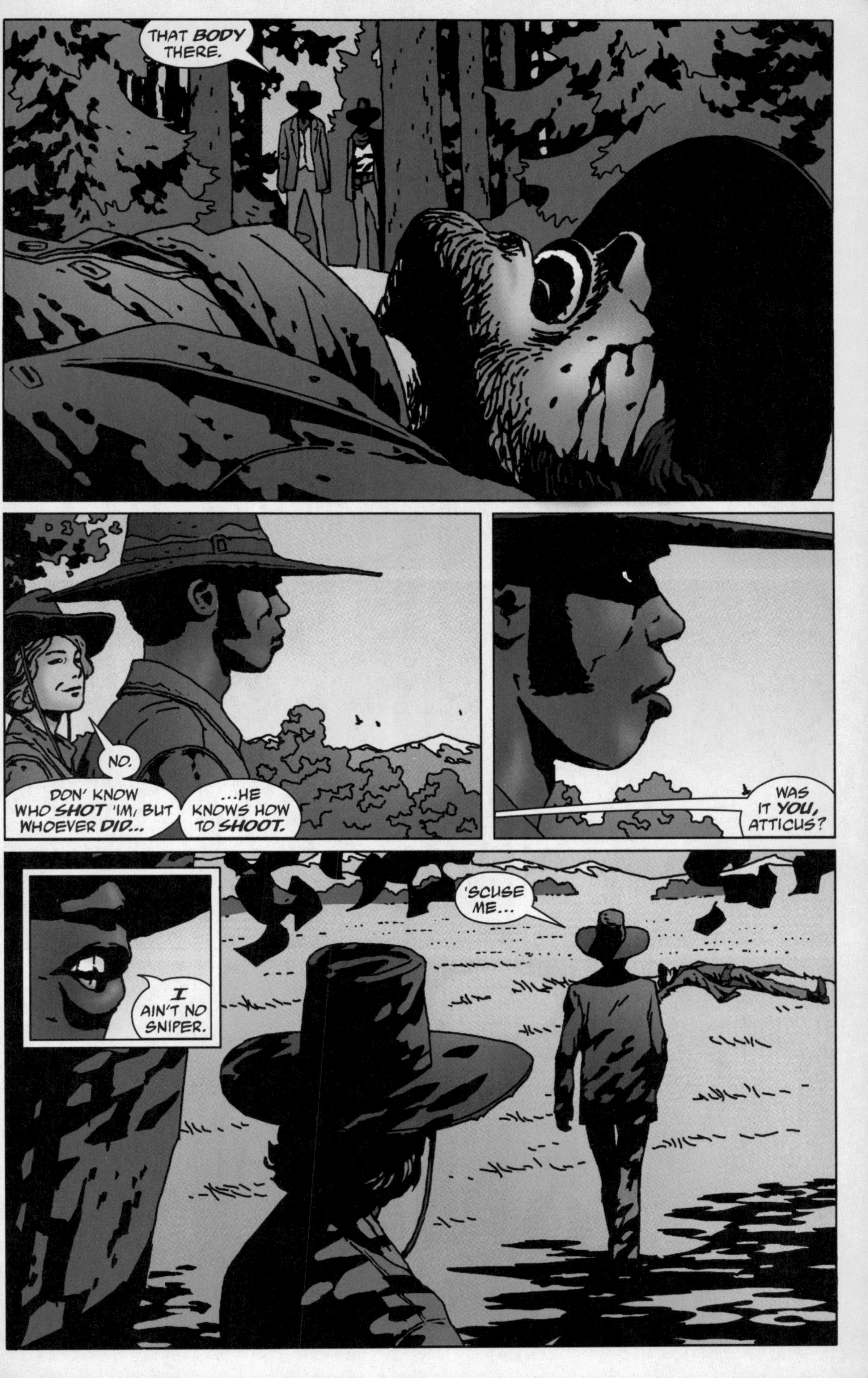
THAT BODY THERE.
NO.
DON' KNOW WHO SHOT 'IM, BUT WHOEVER DID...
...HE KNOWS HOW TO SHOOT.
WAS IT YOU, ATTICUS?
I AIN'T NO SNIPER.
'SCUSE ME...

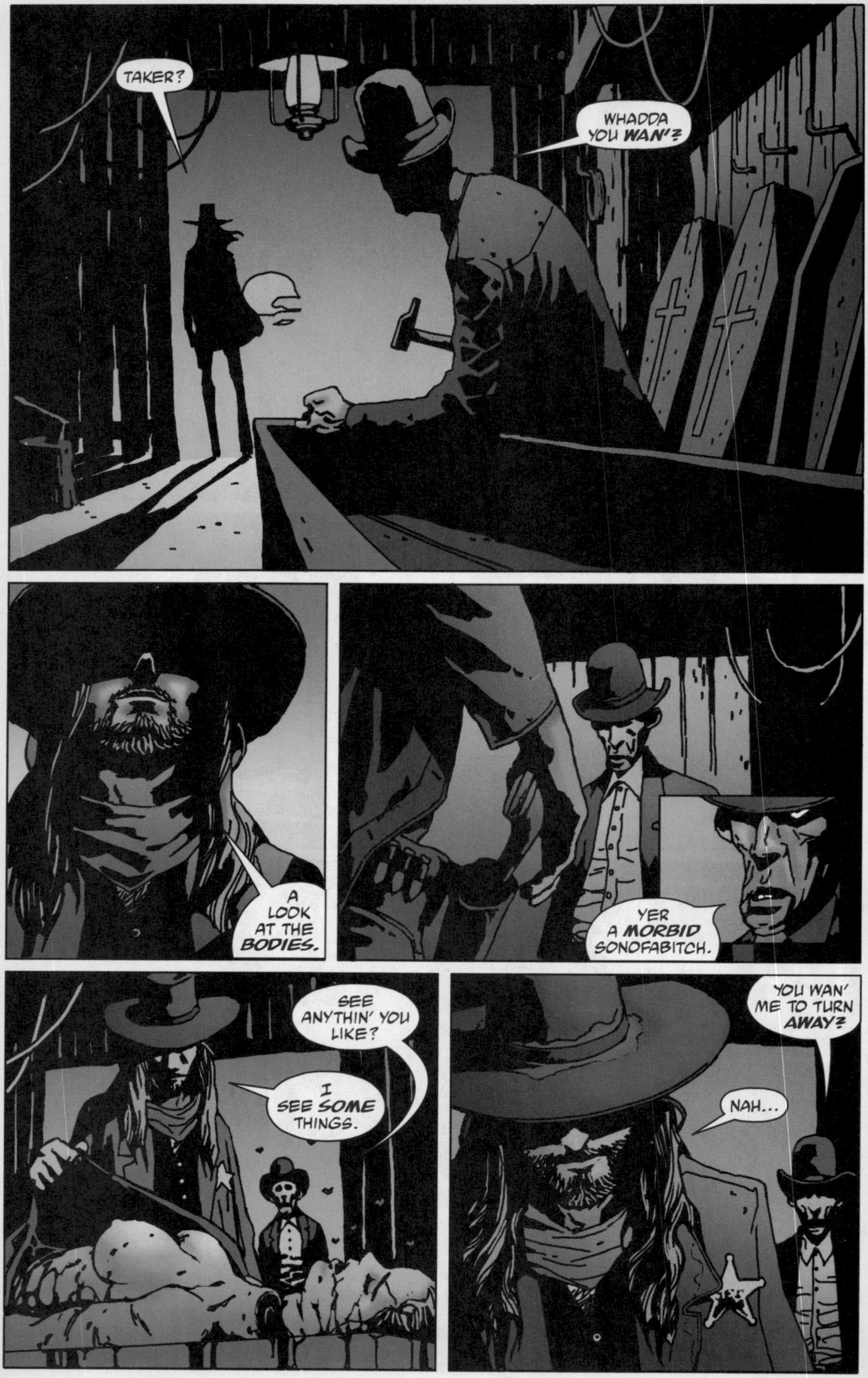
TAKER?
WHADDA YOU WAN'?
A LOOK AT THE BODIES.
YER A MORBID SONOFABITCH.
SEE ANYTHIN' YOU LIKE?
I SEE SOME THINGS.
YOU WAN' ME TO TURN AWAY?
NAH...

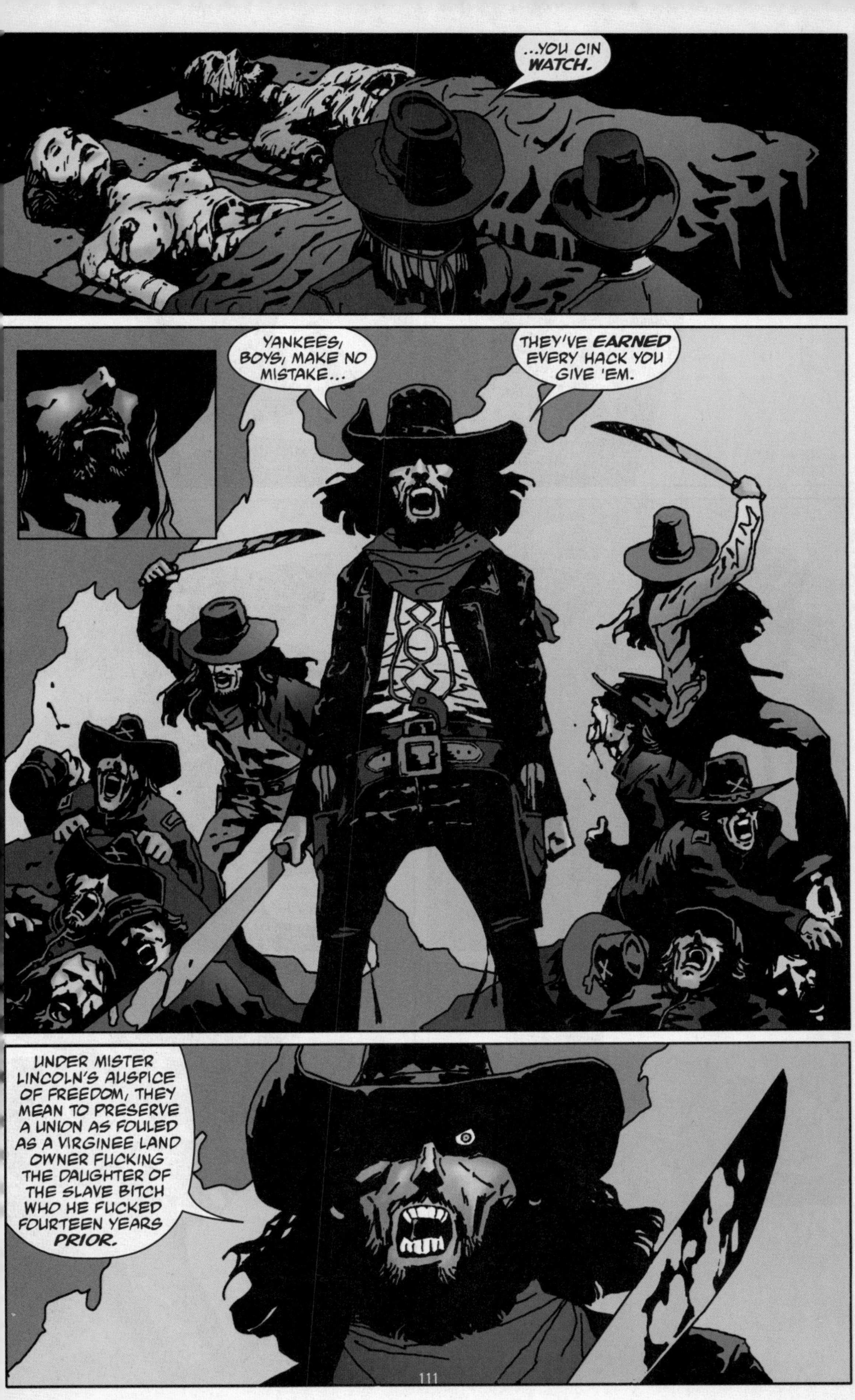
...YOU CIN **WATCH.**
YANKEES, BOYS, MAKE NO MISTAKE...
THEY'VE **EARNED** EVERY HACK YOU GIVE 'EM.
UNDER MISTER LINCOLN'S AUSPICE OF FREEDOM, THEY MEAN TO PRESERVE A UNION AS FOULED AS A VIRGINEE LAND OWNER FUCKING THE DAUGHTER OF THE SLAVE BITCH WHO HE FUCKED FOURTEEN YEARS **PRIOR.**

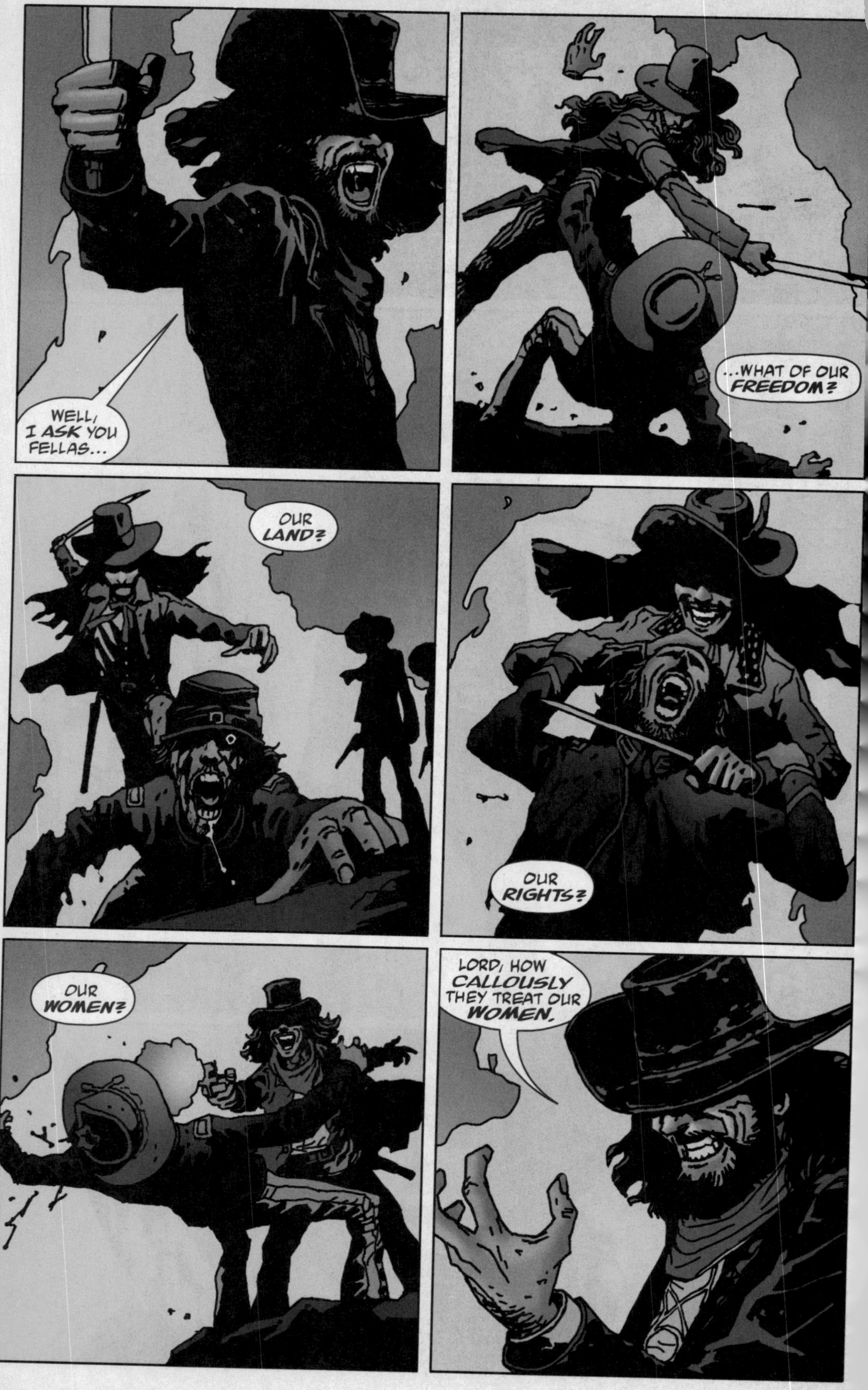
WELL, I ASK YOU FELLAS...
...WHAT OF OUR FREEDOM?
OUR LAND?
OUR RIGHTS?
OUR WOMEN?
LORD, HOW CALLOUSLY THEY TREAT OUR WOMEN.

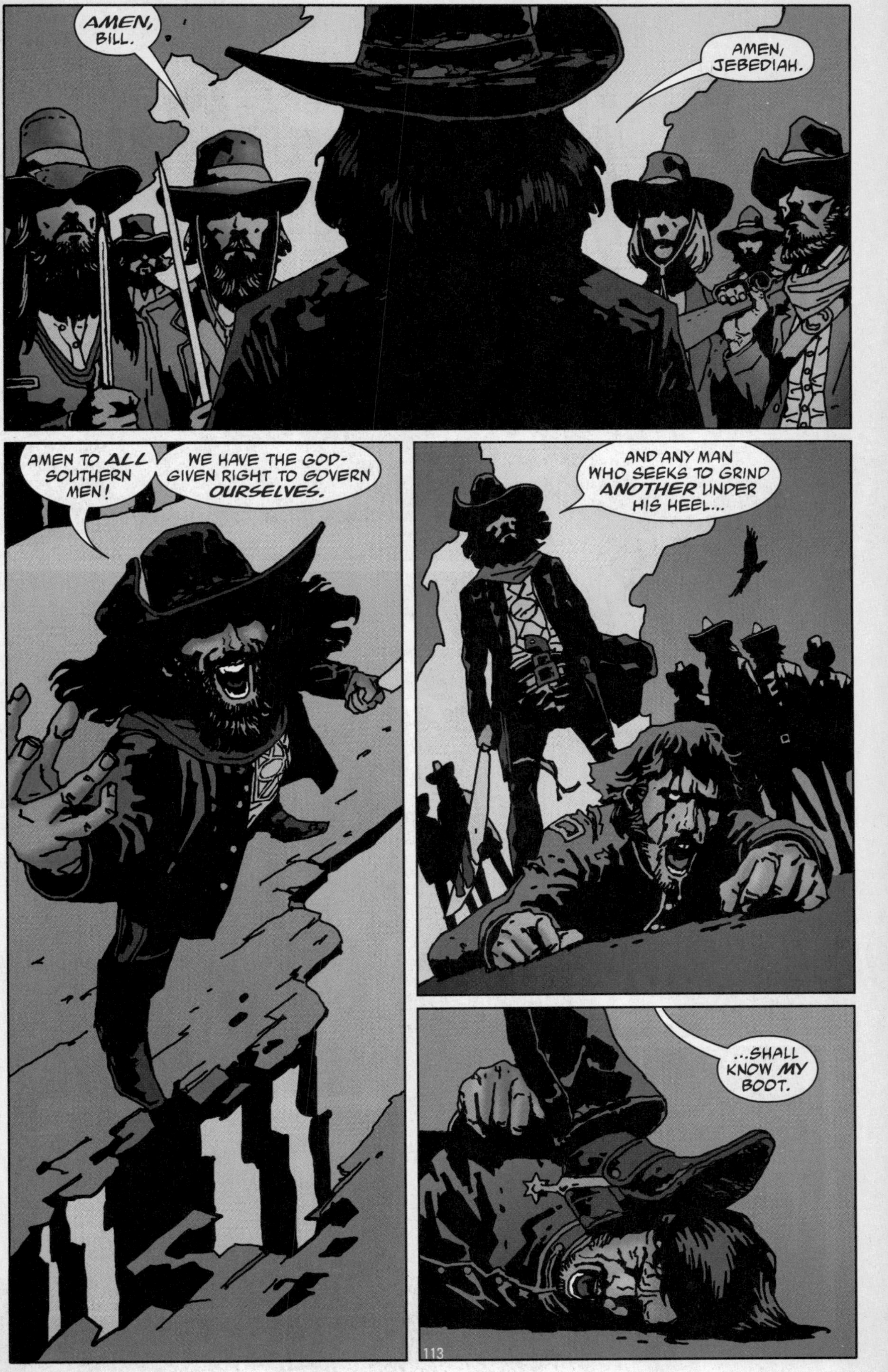
AMEN, BILL.
AMEN, JEBEDIAH.
AMEN TO ALL SOUTHERN MEN!
WE HAVE THE GOD-GIVEN RIGHT TO GOVERN OURSELVES.
AND ANY MAN WHO SEEKS TO GRIND ANOTHER UNDER HIS HEEL...
...SHALL KNOW MY BOOT.

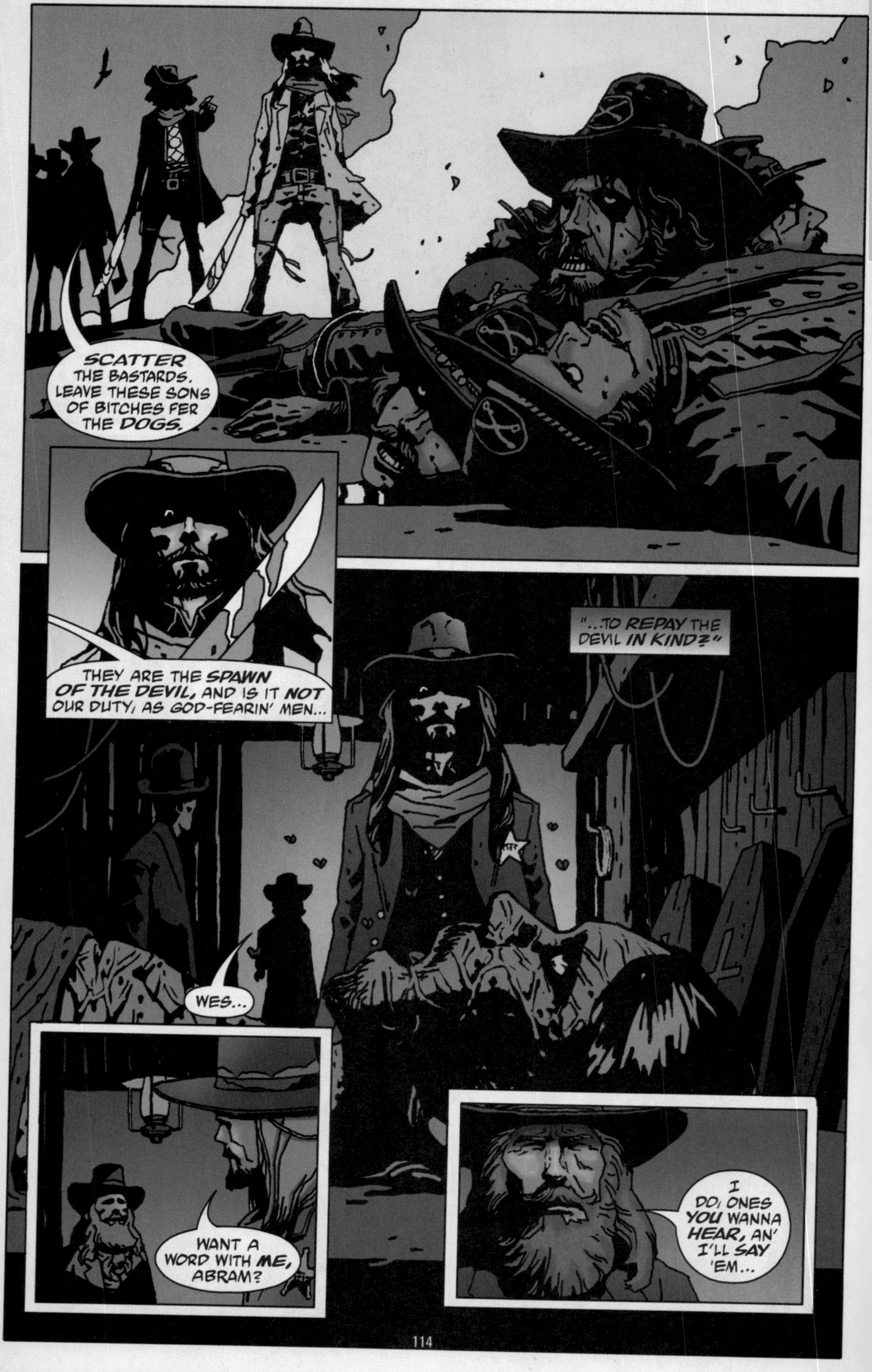
SCATTER THE BASTARDS. LEAVE THESE SONS OF BITCHES FER THE DOGS.
THEY ARE THE SPAWN OF THE DEVIL, AND IS IT NOT OUR DUTY, AS GOD-FEARIN' MEN...
"...TO REPAY THE DEVIL IN KIND?"
WES...
WANT A WORD WITH ME, ABRAM?
I DO, ONES YOU WANNA HEAR, AN' I'LL SAY 'EM...

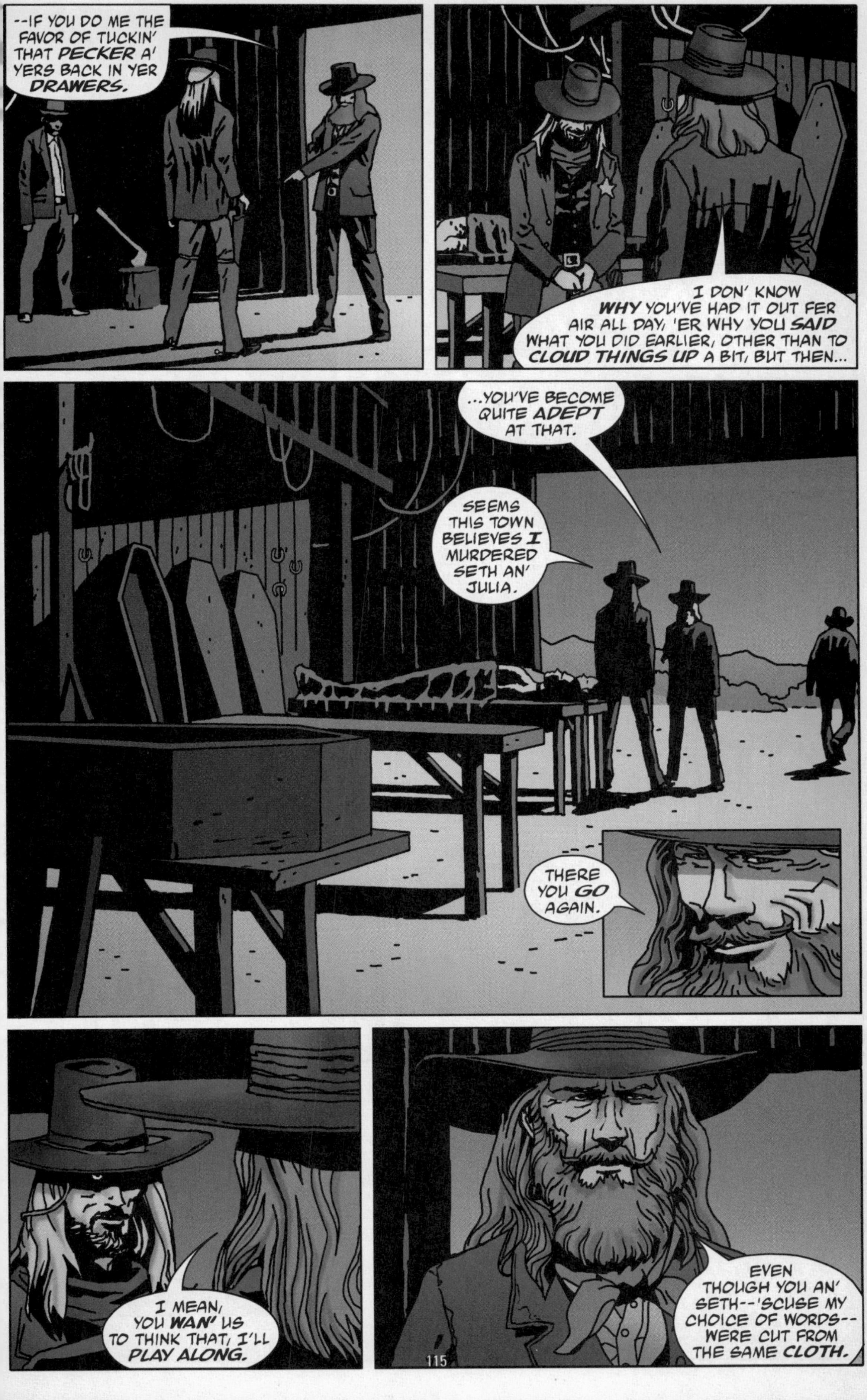

--IF YOU DO ME THE FAVOR OF TUCKIN' THAT PECKER A' YERS BACK IN YER DRAWERS.
I DON' KNOW WHY YOU'VE HAD IT OUT FER AIR ALL DAY, 'ER WHY YOU SAID WHAT YOU DID EARLIER, OTHER THAN TO CLOUD THINGS UP A BIT, BUT THEN...
...YOU'VE BECOME QUITE ADEPT AT THAT.
SEEMS THIS TOWN BELIEVES I MURDERED SETH AN' JULIA.
THERE YOU GO AGAIN.
I MEAN, YOU WAN' US TO THINK THAT, I'LL PLAY ALONG.
EVEN THOUGH YOU AN' SETH--'SCUSE MY CHOICE OF WORDS--WERE CUT FROM THE SAME CLOTH.

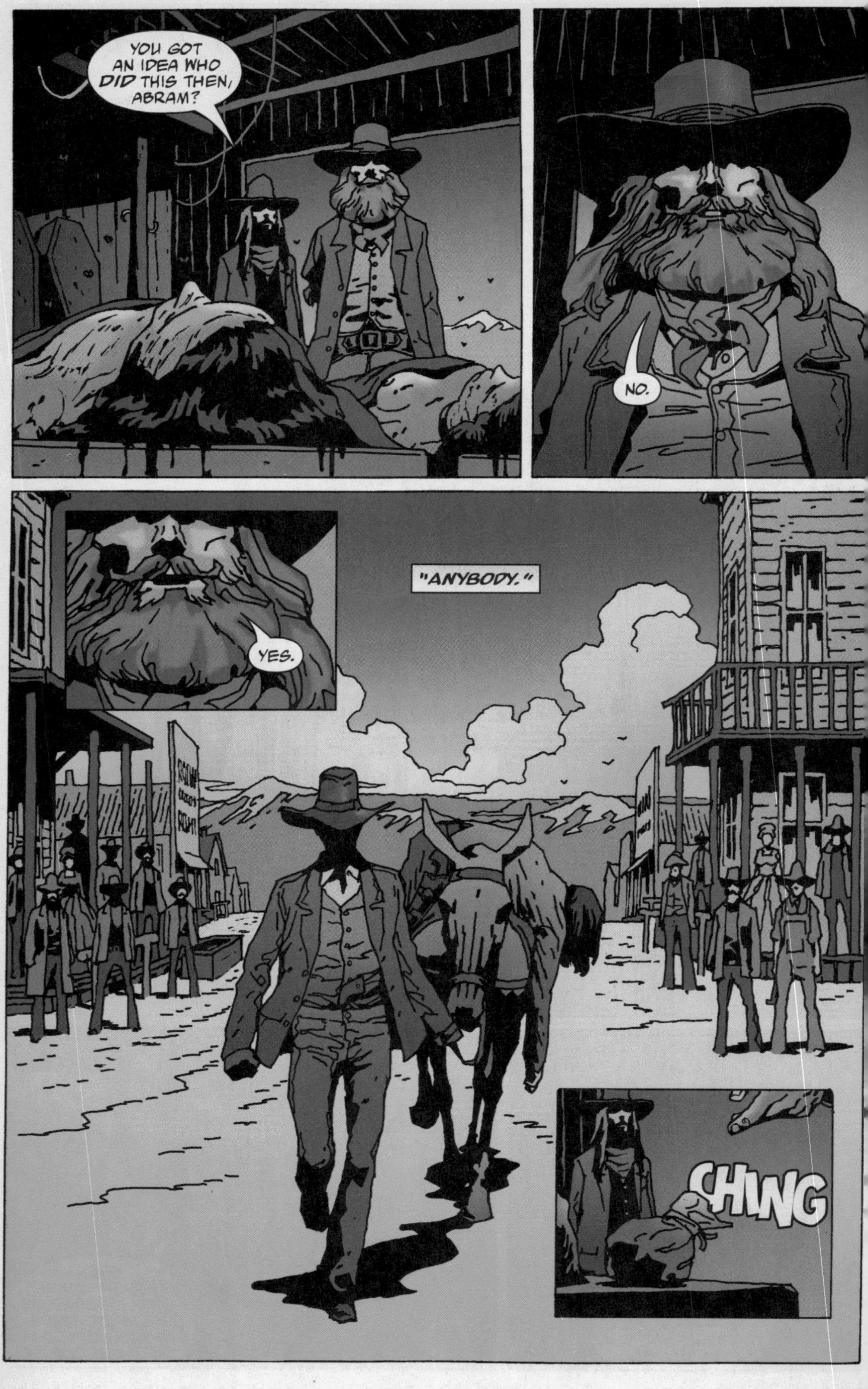
YOU GOT AN IDEA WHO DID THIS THEN, ABRAM?
NO.
YES.
"ANYBODY."
CHING

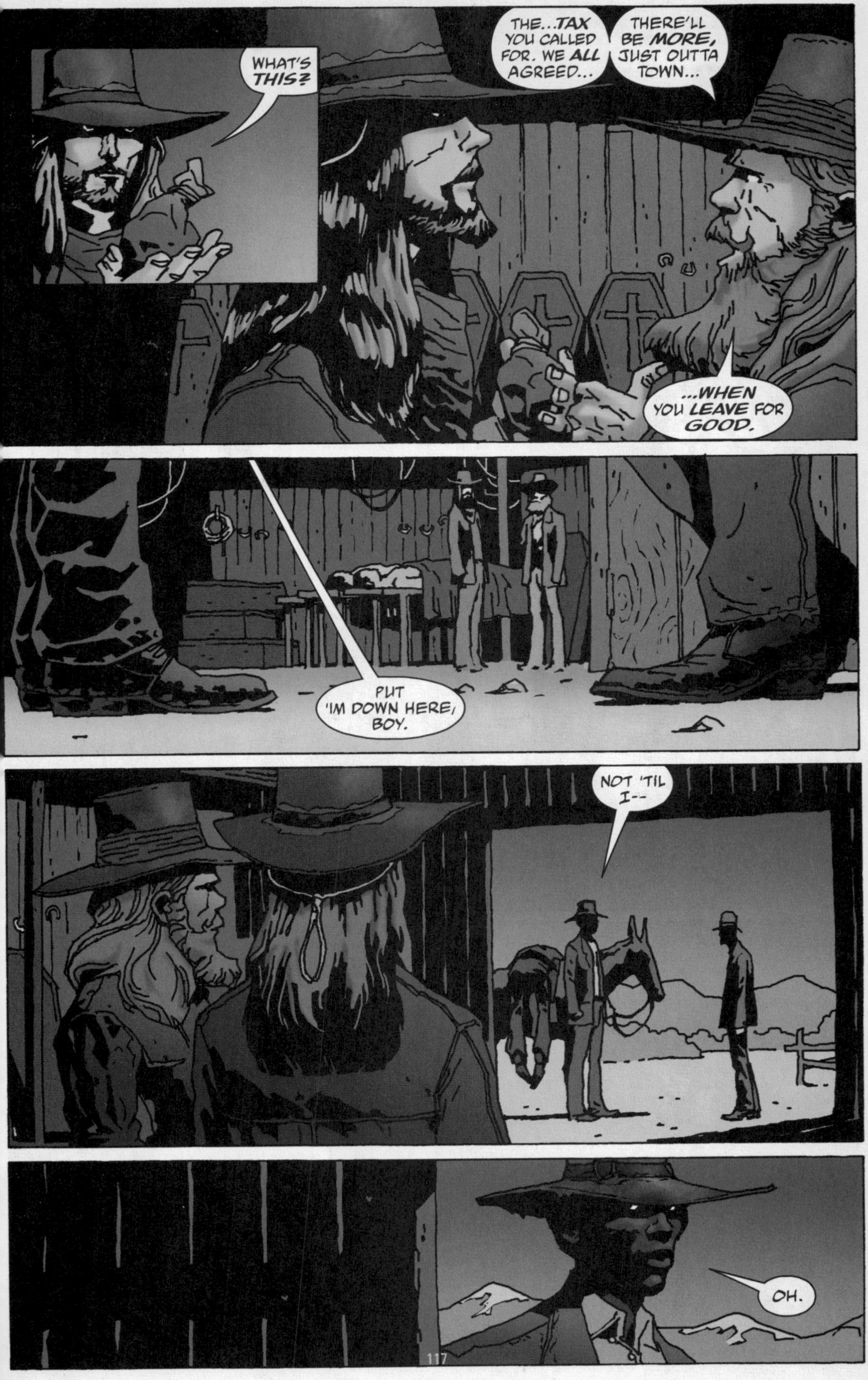
WHAT'S THIS?
THE...TAX YOU CALLED FOR. WE ALL AGREED...
THERE'LL BE MORE, JUST OUTTA TOWN...
...WHEN YOU LEAVE FOR GOOD.
PUT 'IM DOWN HERE, BOY.
NOT 'TIL I--
OH.

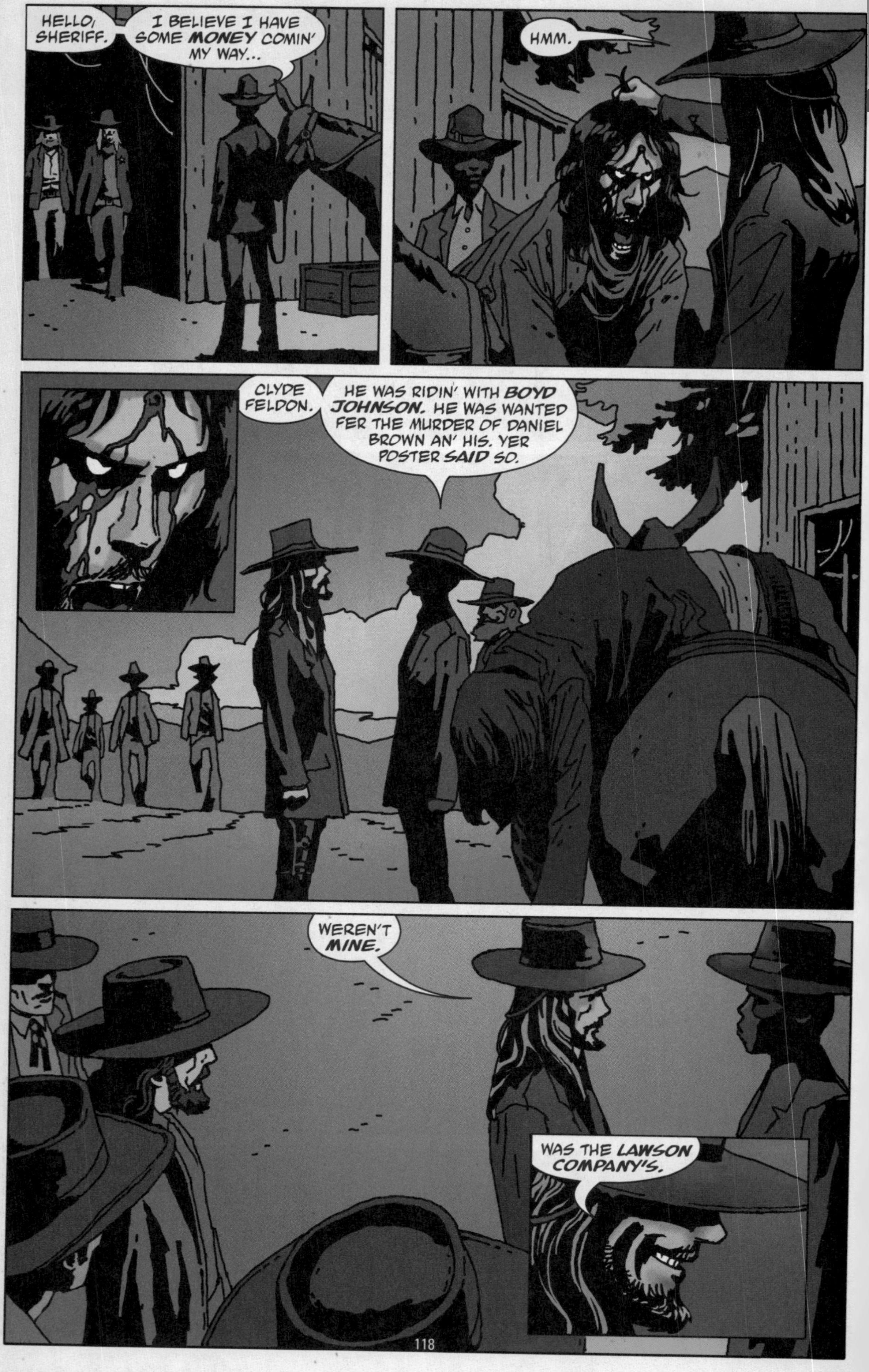
HELLO, SHERIFF.
I BELIEVE I HAVE SOME MONEY COMIN' MY WAY...
HMM.
CLYDE FELDON.
HE WAS RIDIN' WITH BOYD JOHNSON. HE WAS WANTED FER THE MURDER OF DANIEL BROWN AN' HIS. YER POSTER SAID SO.
WEREN'T MINE.
WAS THE LAWSON COMPANY'S.

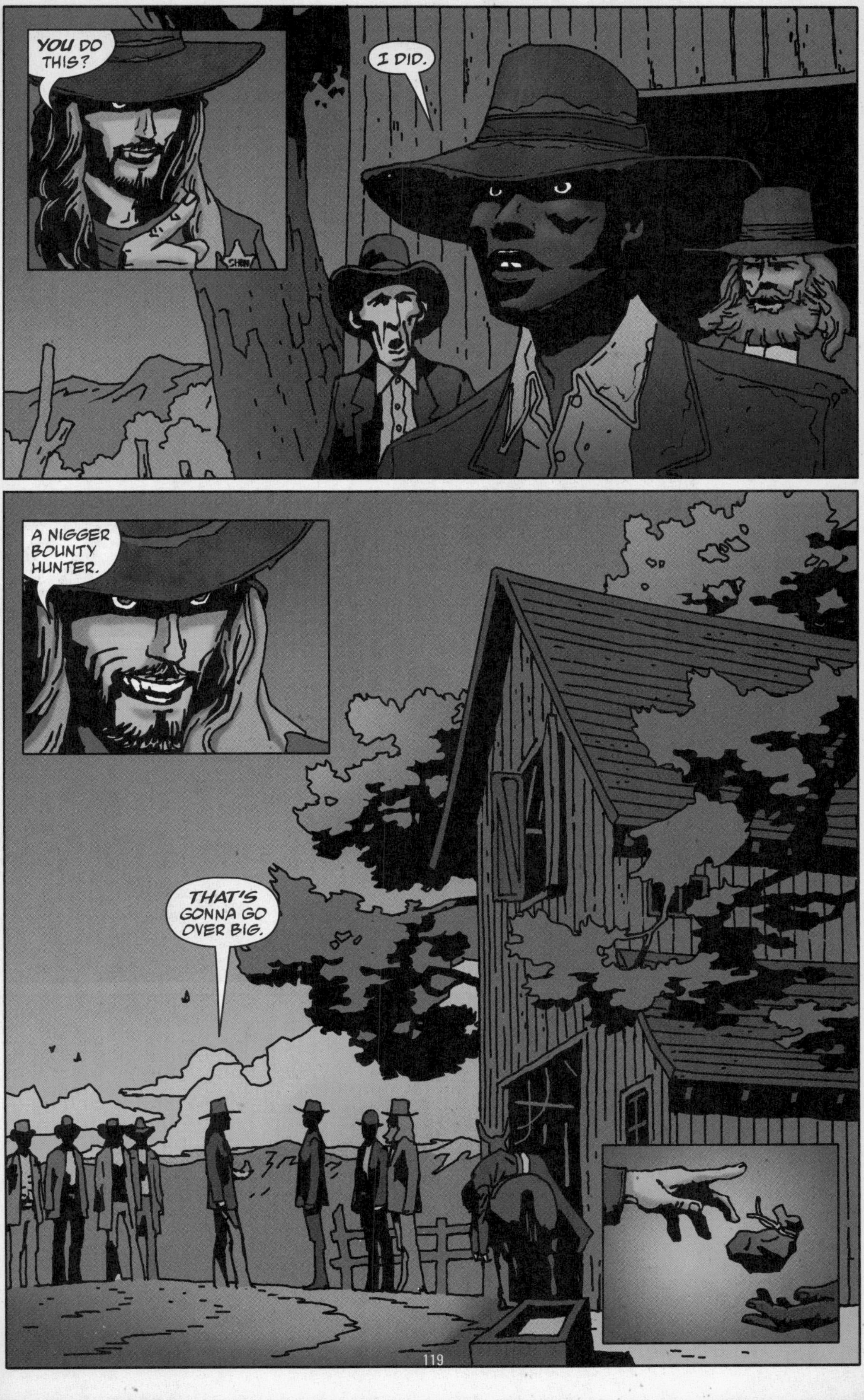
YOU DO THIS?
I DID.
A NIGGER BOUNTY HUNTER.
THAT'S GONNA GO OVER BIG.

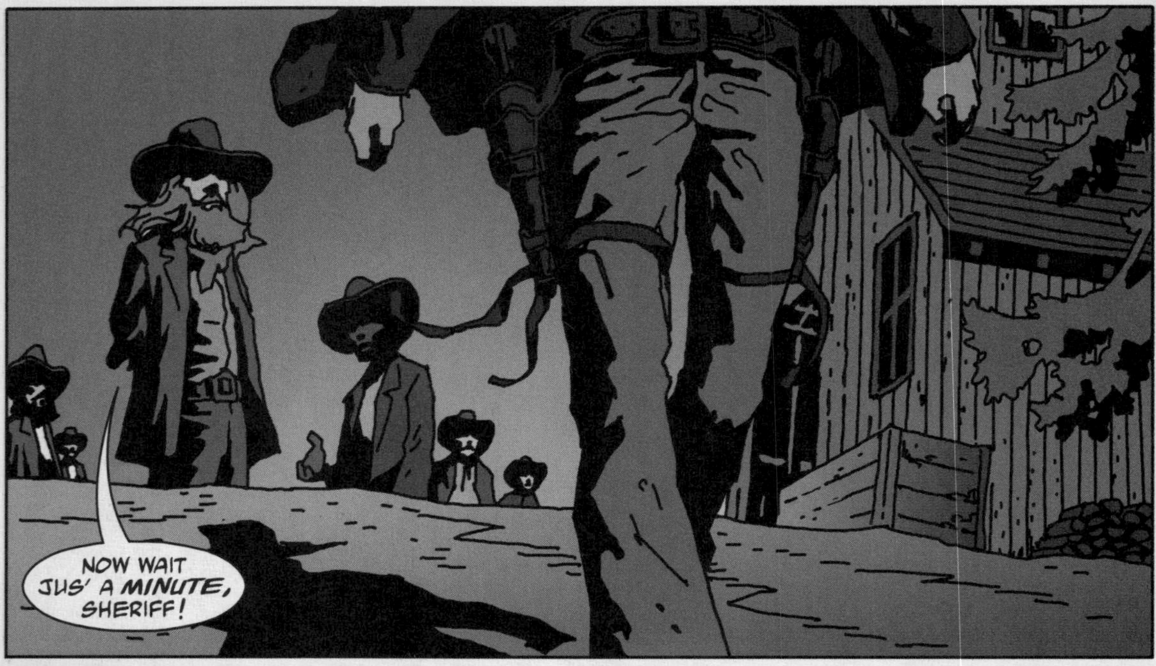
NOW WAIT JUS' A MINUTE, SHERIFF!

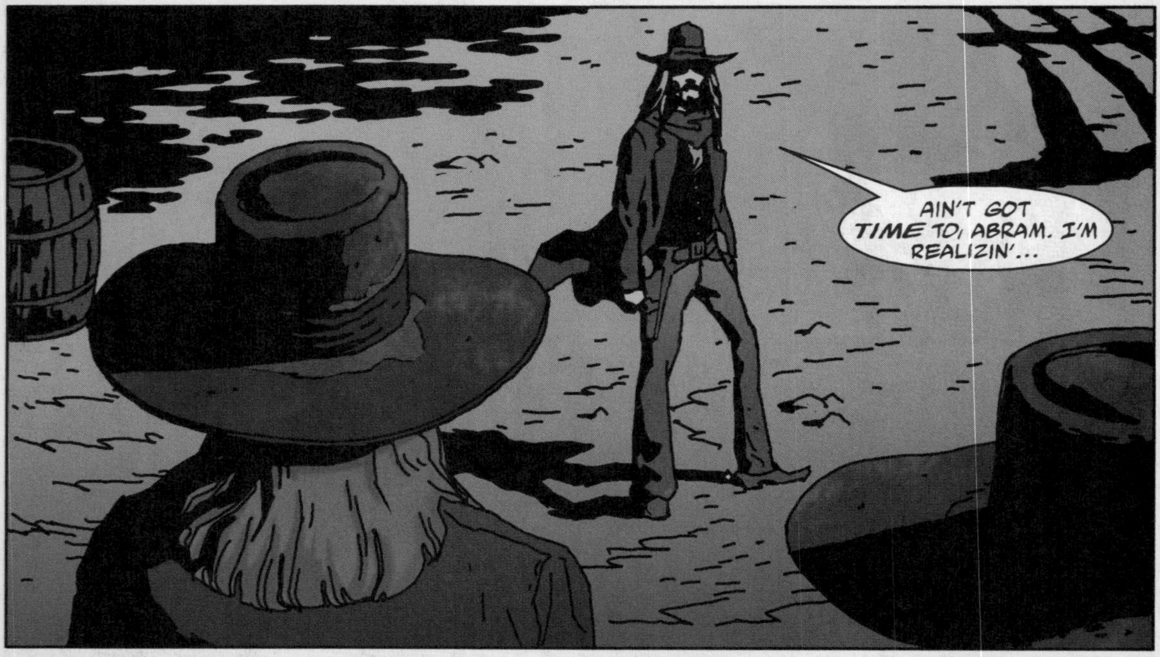
AIN'T GOT TIME TO, ABRAM. I'M REALIZIN'...

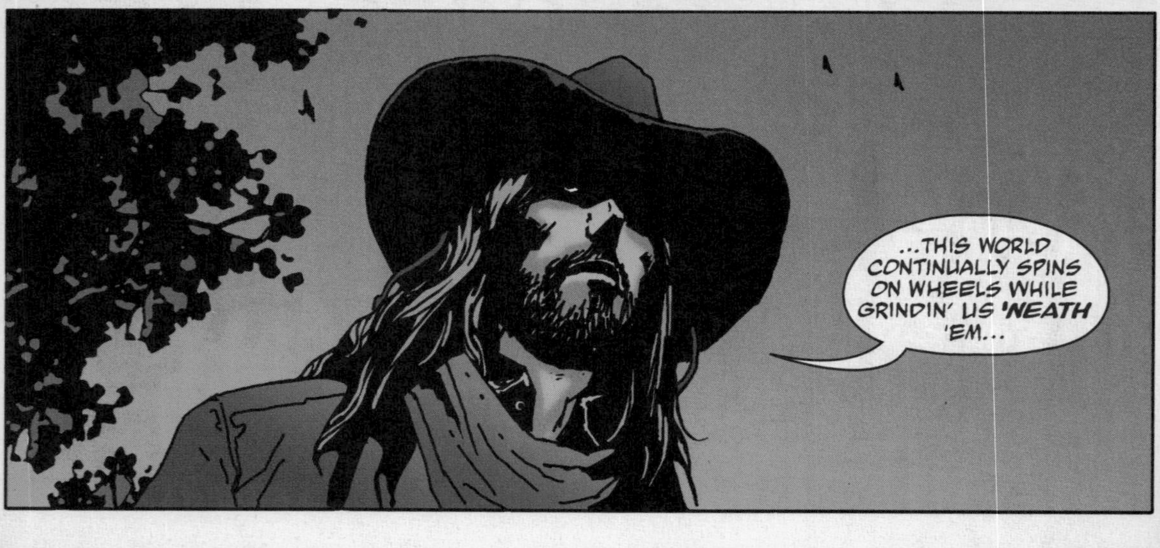
...THIS WORLD CONTINUALLY SPINS ON WHEELS WHILE GRINDIN' US 'NEATH 'EM...

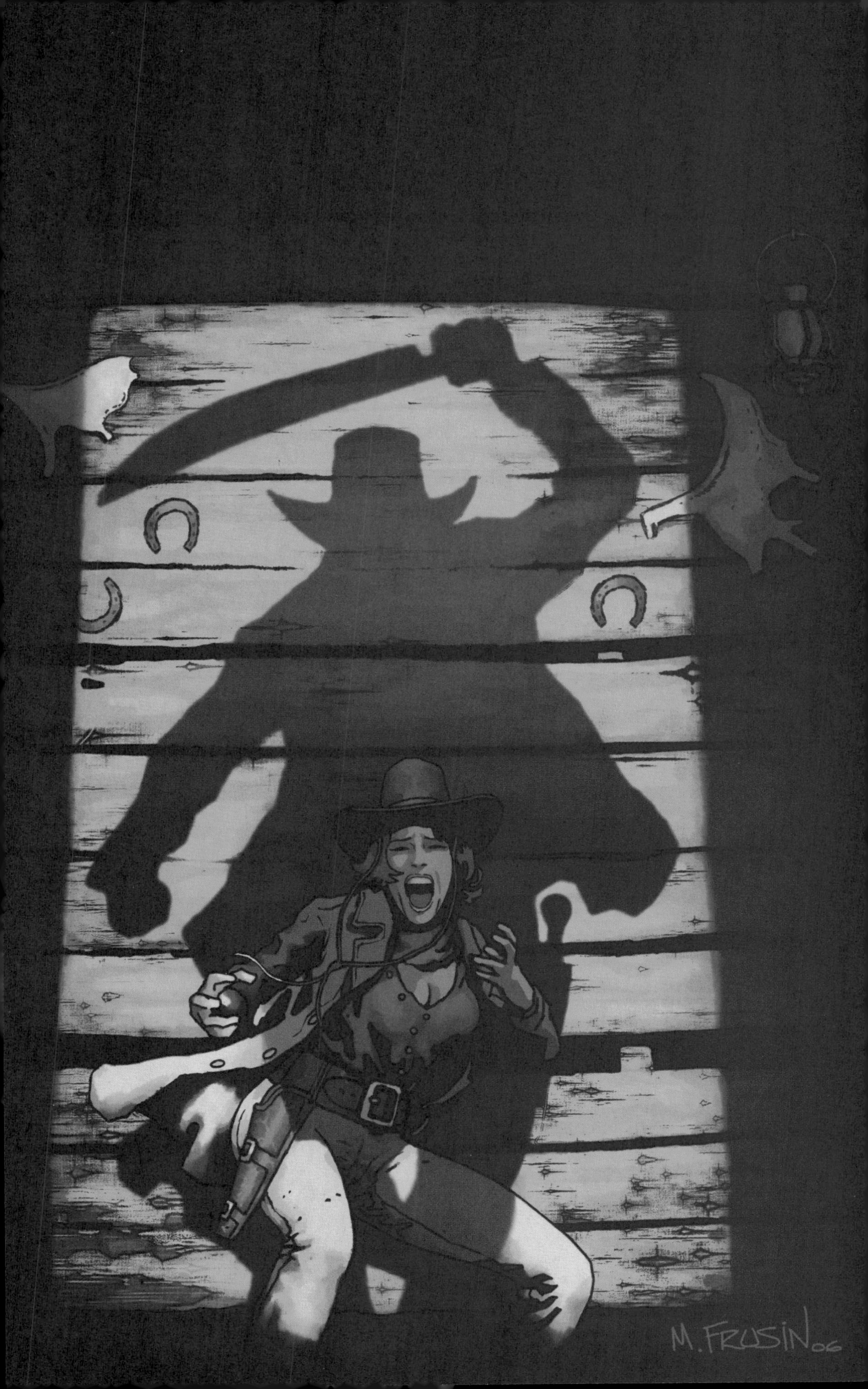
M. FRUSIN 06

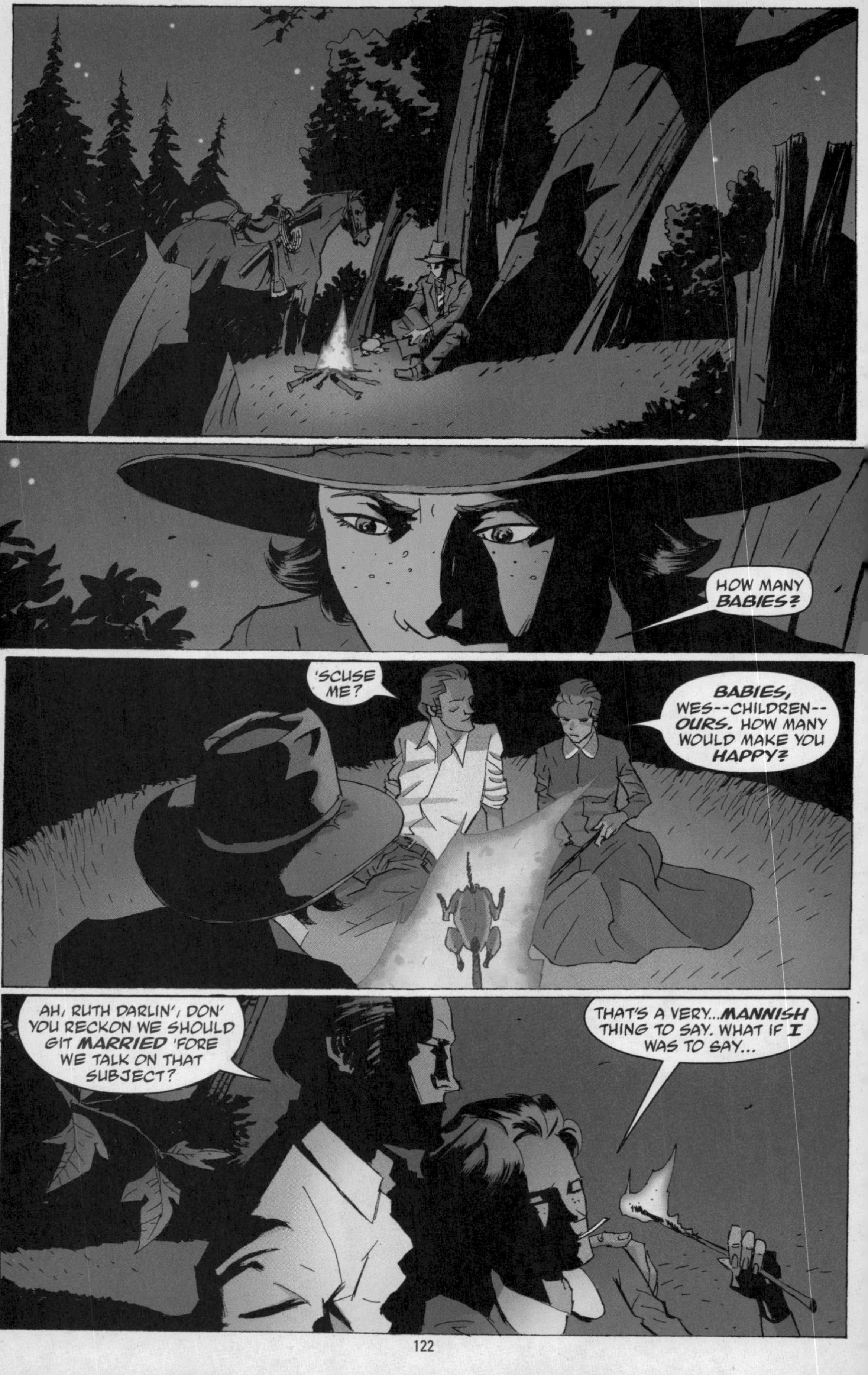
HOW MANY BABIES?
'SCUSE ME?
BABIES, WES--CHILDREN--OURS. HOW MANY WOULD MAKE YOU HAPPY?
AH, RUTH DARLIN', DON' YOU RECKON WE SHOULD GIT MARRIED 'FORE WE TALK ON THAT SUBJECT?
THAT'S A VERY...MANNISH THING TO SAY. WHAT IF I WAS TO SAY...

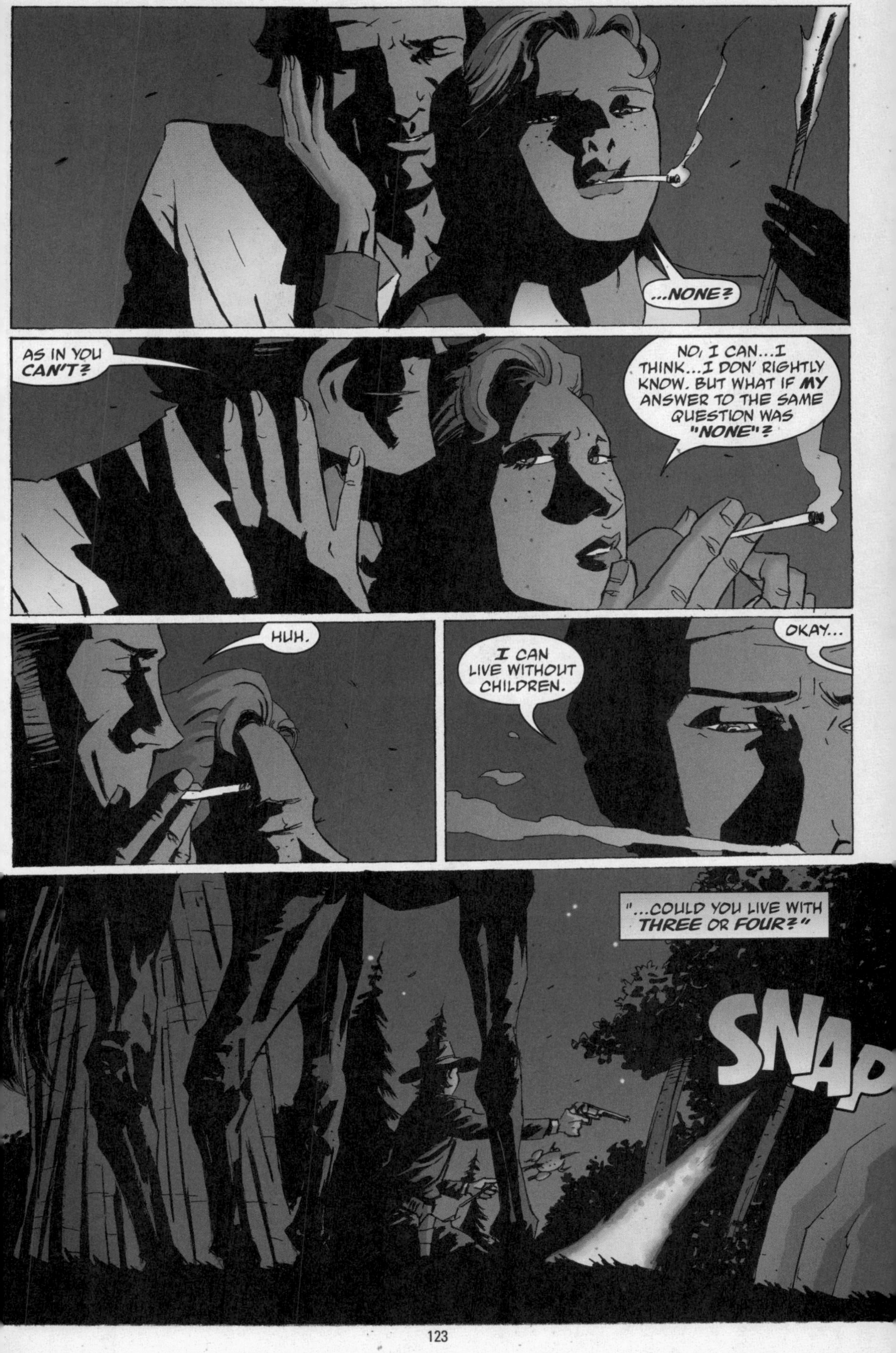
...NONE?
AS IN YOU CAN'T?
NO, I CAN...I THINK...I DON' RIGHTLY KNOW. BUT WHAT IF MY ANSWER TO THE SAME QUESTION WAS "NONE"?
HUH.
I CAN LIVE WITHOUT CHILDREN.
OKAY...
"...COULD YOU LIVE WITH THREE OR FOUR?"
SNAP

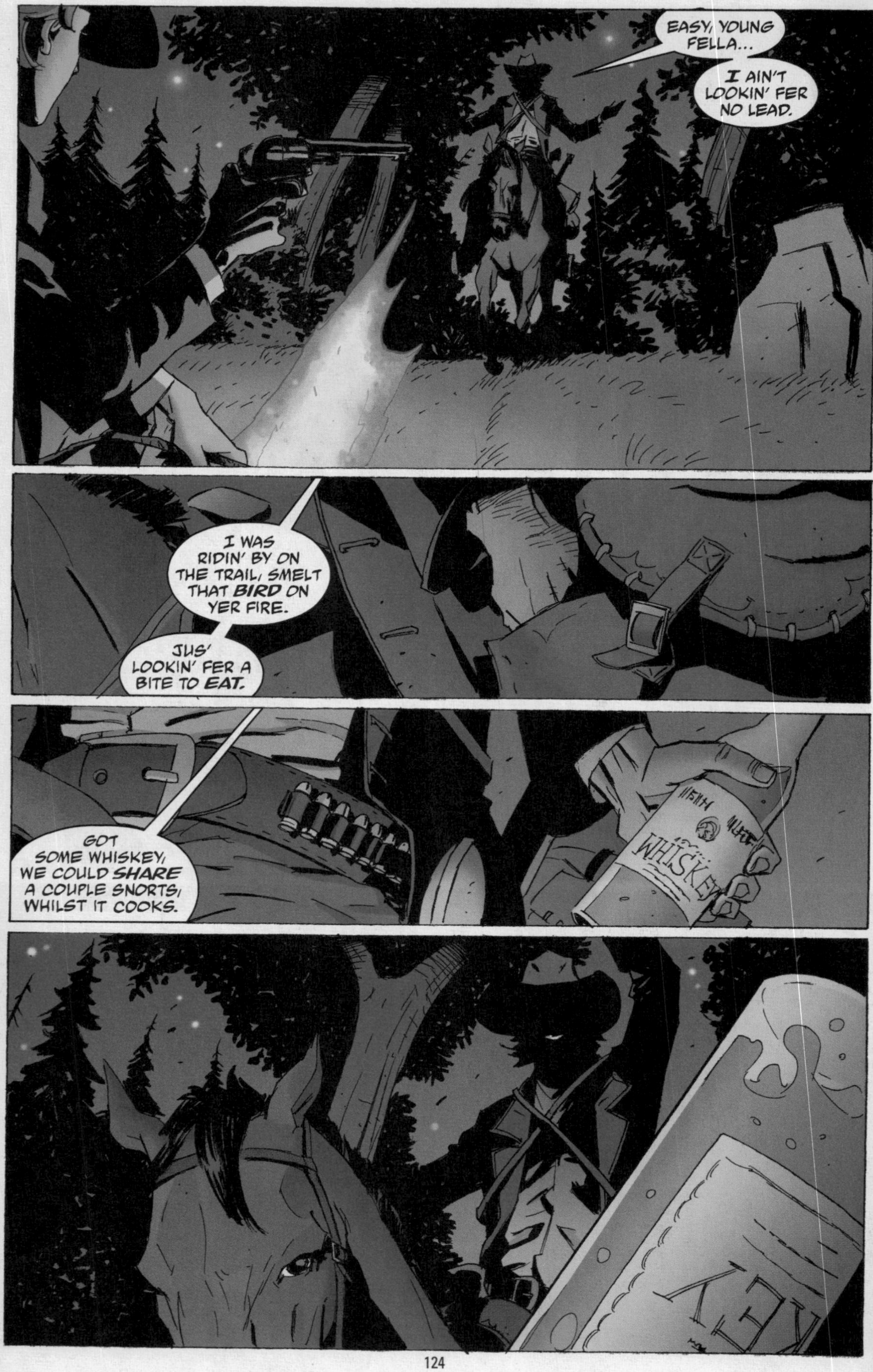

EASY, YOUNG FELLA...
I AIN'T LOOKIN' FER NO LEAD.
I WAS RIDIN' BY ON THE TRAIL, SMELT THAT BIRD ON YER FIRE.
JUS' LOOKIN' FER A BITE TO EAT.
GOT SOME WHISKEY, WE COULD SHARE A COUPLE SNORTS, WHILST IT COOKS.
WHISKEY
KEY

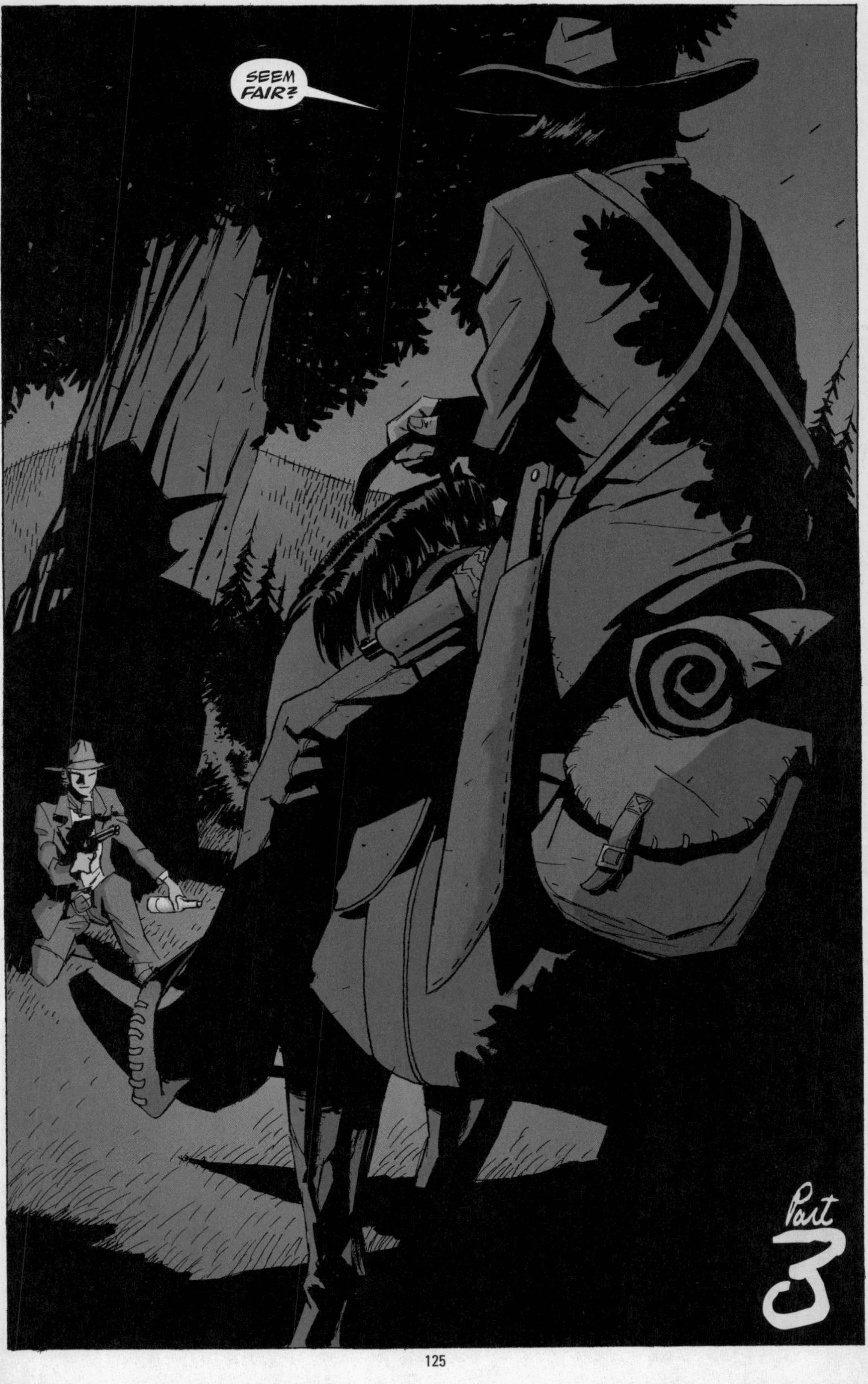
SEEM FAIR?
Part 3

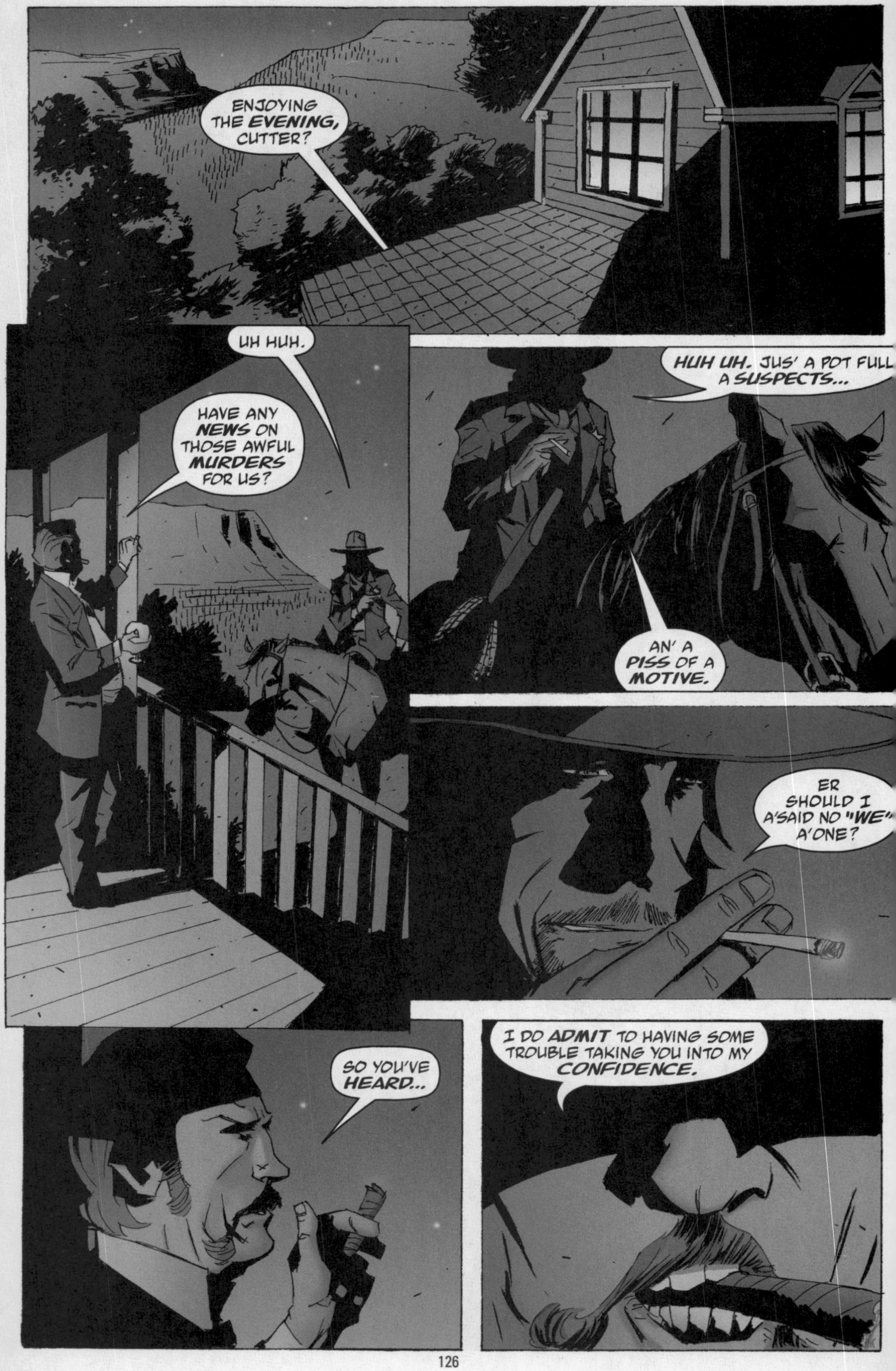
ENJOYING THE EVENING, CUTTER?
UH HUH.
HAVE ANY NEWS ON THOSE AWFUL MURDERS FOR US?
HUH UH. JUS' A POT FULL A SUSPECTS...
AN' A PISS OF A MOTIVE.
ER SHOULD I A'SAID NO "WE" A'ONE?
SO YOU'VE HEARD...
I DO ADMIT TO HAVING SOME TROUBLE TAKING YOU INTO MY CONFIDENCE.

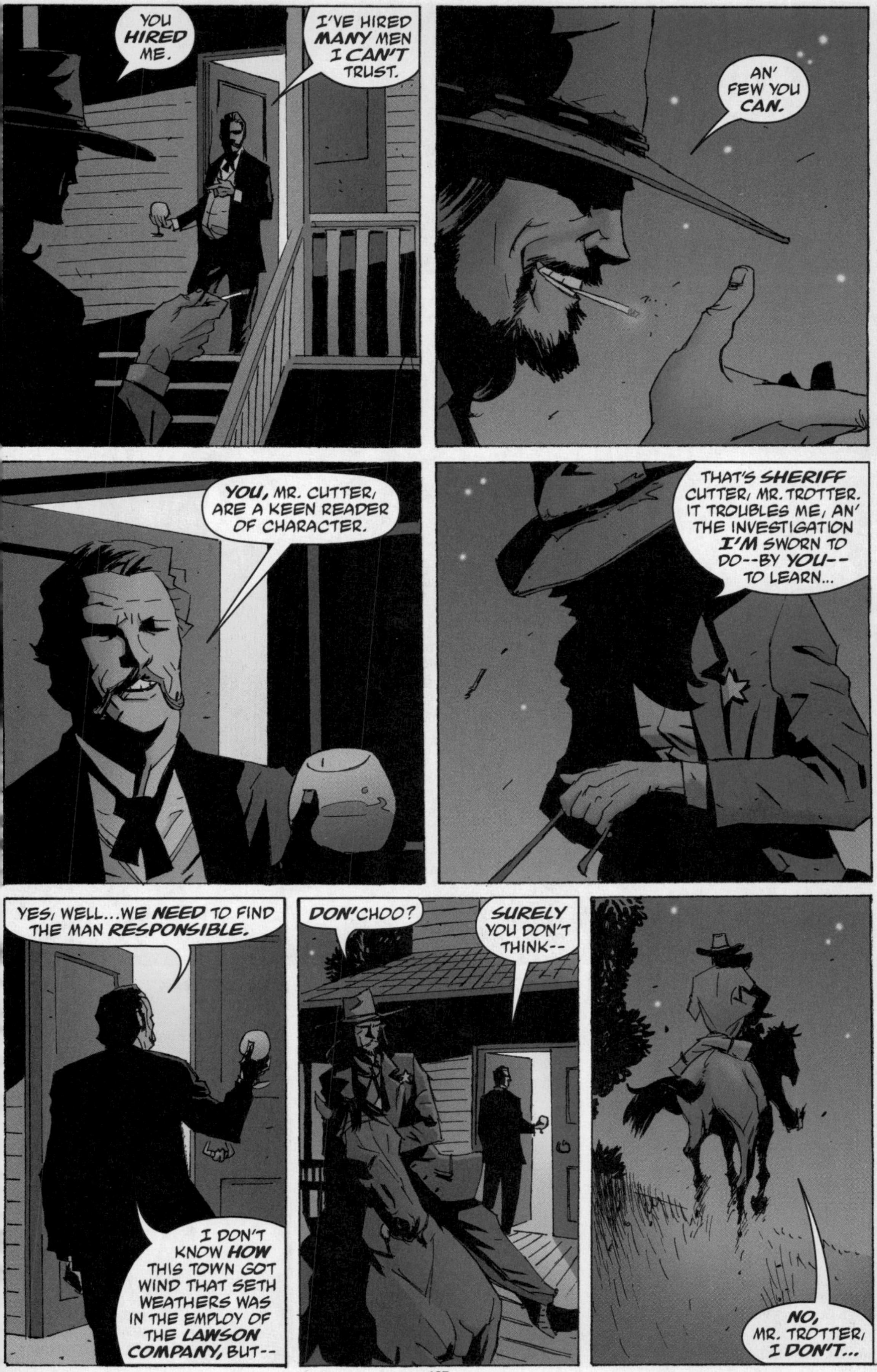
YOU HIRED ME.
I'VE HIRED MANY MEN I CAN'T TRUST.
AN' FEW YOU CAN.
YOU, MR. CUTTER, ARE A KEEN READER OF CHARACTER.
THAT'S SHERIFF CUTTER, MR. TROTTER. IT TROUBLES ME, AN' THE INVESTIGATION I'M SWORN TO DO--BY YOU--TO LEARN...
YES, WELL...WE NEED TO FIND THE MAN RESPONSIBLE.
I DON'T KNOW HOW THIS TOWN GOT WIND THAT SETH WEATHERS WAS IN THE EMPLOY OF THE LAWSON COMPANY, BUT--
DON'CHOO?
SURELY YOU DON'T THINK--
NO, MR. TROTTER, I DON'T...

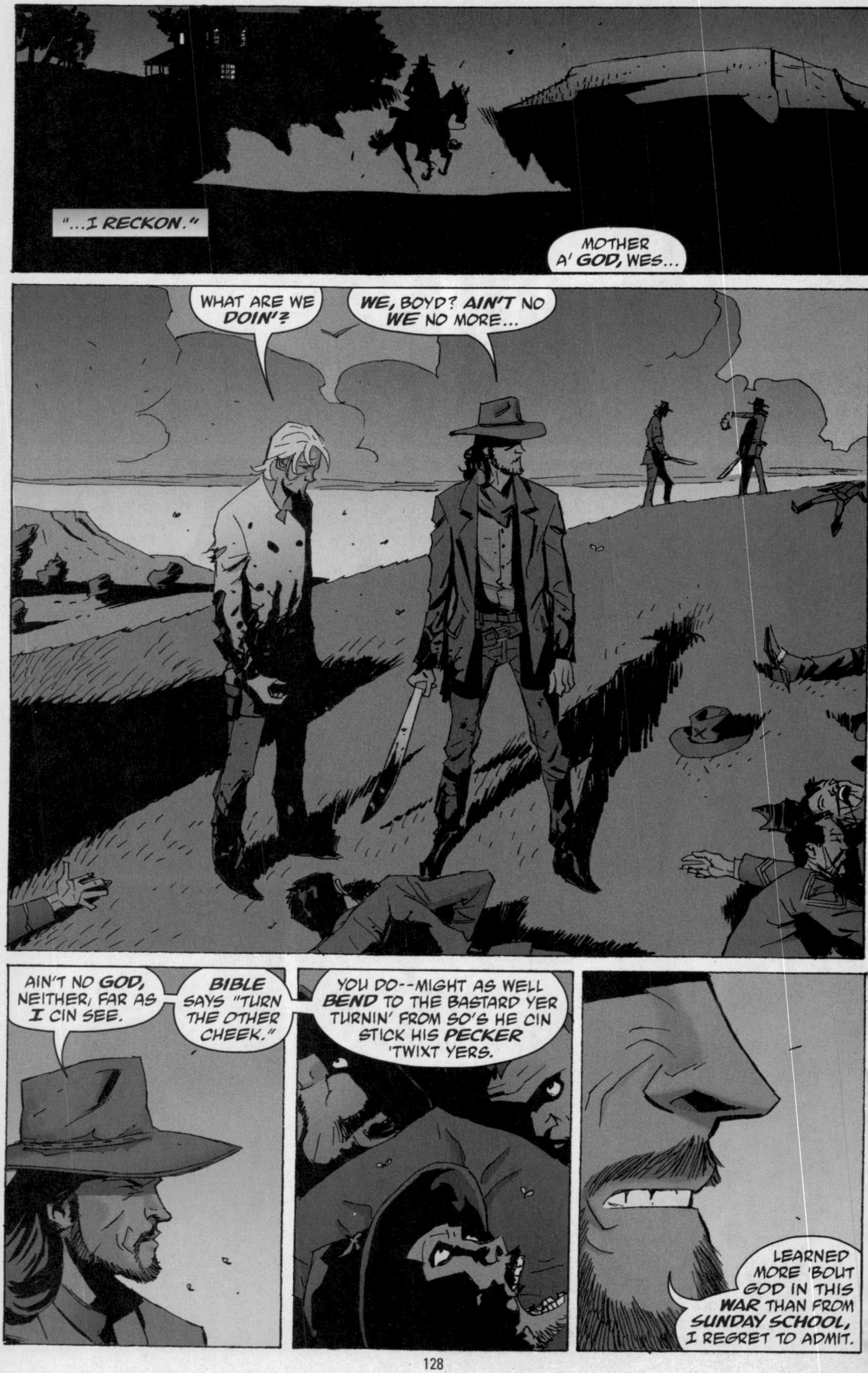
"...I RECKON."
MOTHER A' GOD, WES...
WHAT ARE WE DOIN'?
WE, BOYD? AIN'T NO WE NO MORE...
AIN'T NO GOD, NEITHER, FAR AS I CIN SEE.
BIBLE SAYS "TURN THE OTHER CHEEK."
YOU DO--MIGHT AS WELL BEND TO THE BASTARD YER TURNIN' FROM SO'S HE CIN STICK HIS PECKER 'TWIXT YERS.
LEARNED MORE 'BOUT GOD IN THIS WAR THAN FROM SUNDAY SCHOOL, I REGRET TO ADMIT.

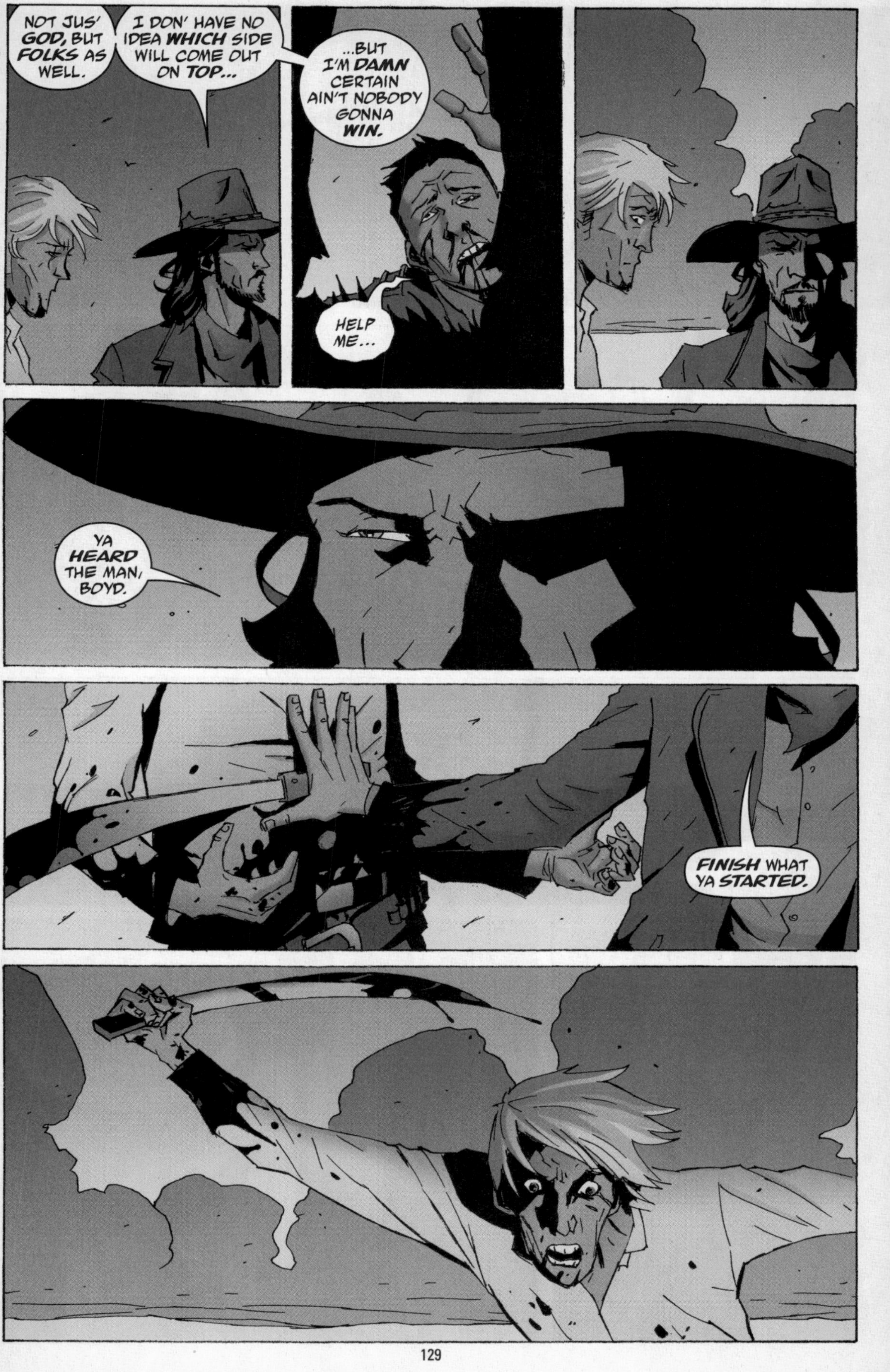
NOT JUS' GOD, BUT FOLKS AS WELL.
I DON' HAVE NO IDEA WHICH SIDE WILL COME OUT ON TOP...
...BUT I'M DAMN CERTAIN AIN'T NOBODY GONNA WIN.
HELP ME...
YA HEARD THE MAN, BOYD.
FINISH WHAT YA STARTED.

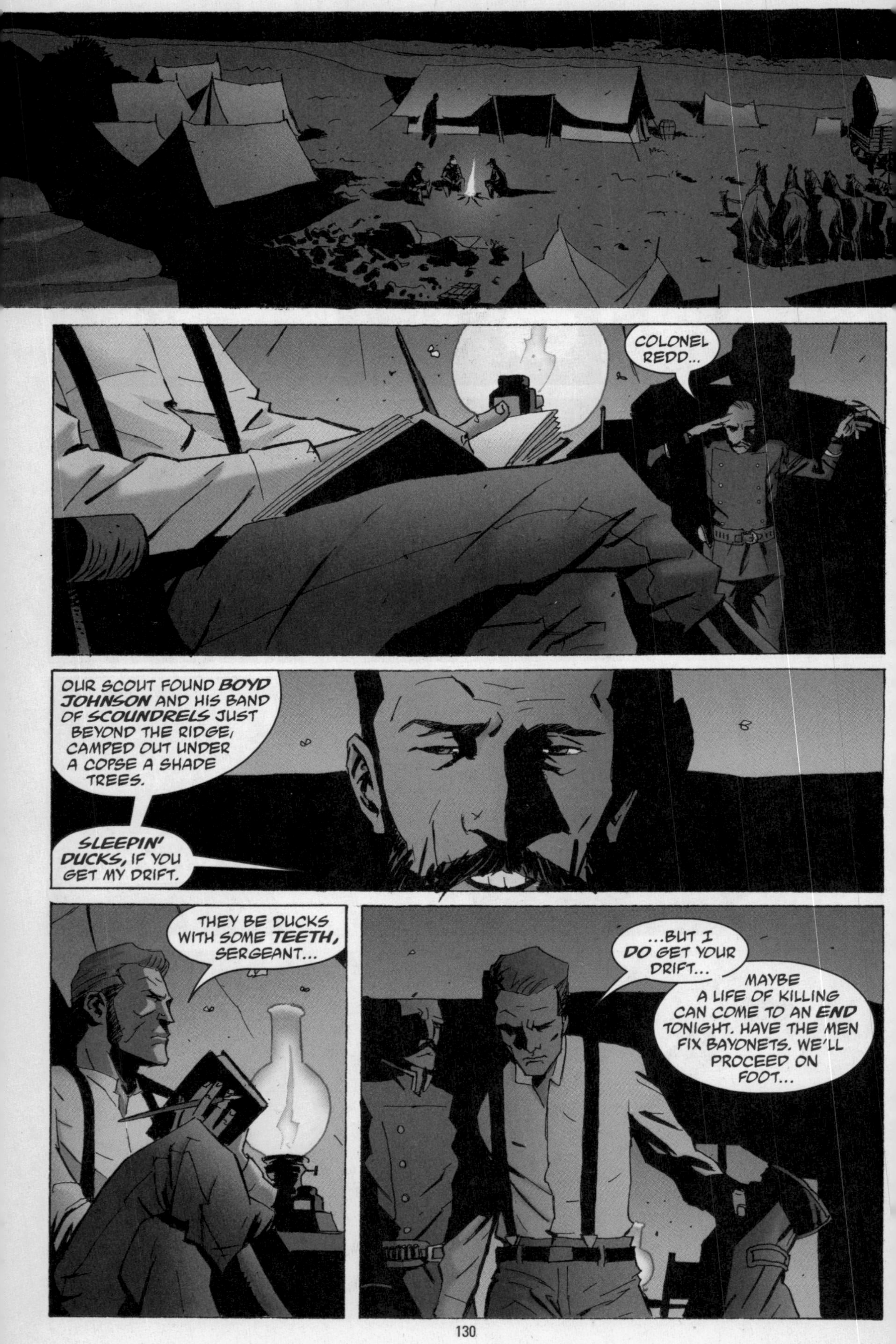

COLONEL REDD...
OUR SCOUT FOUND BOYD JOHNSON AND HIS BAND OF SCOUNDRELS JUST BEYOND THE RIDGE, CAMPED OUT UNDER A COPSE A SHADE TREES.
SLEEPIN' DUCKS, IF YOU GET MY DRIFT.
THEY BE DUCKS WITH SOME TEETH, SERGEANT...
...BUT I DO GET YOUR DRIFT...
MAYBE A LIFE OF KILLING CAN COME TO AN END TONIGHT. HAVE THE MEN FIX BAYONETS. WE'LL PROCEED ON FOOT...

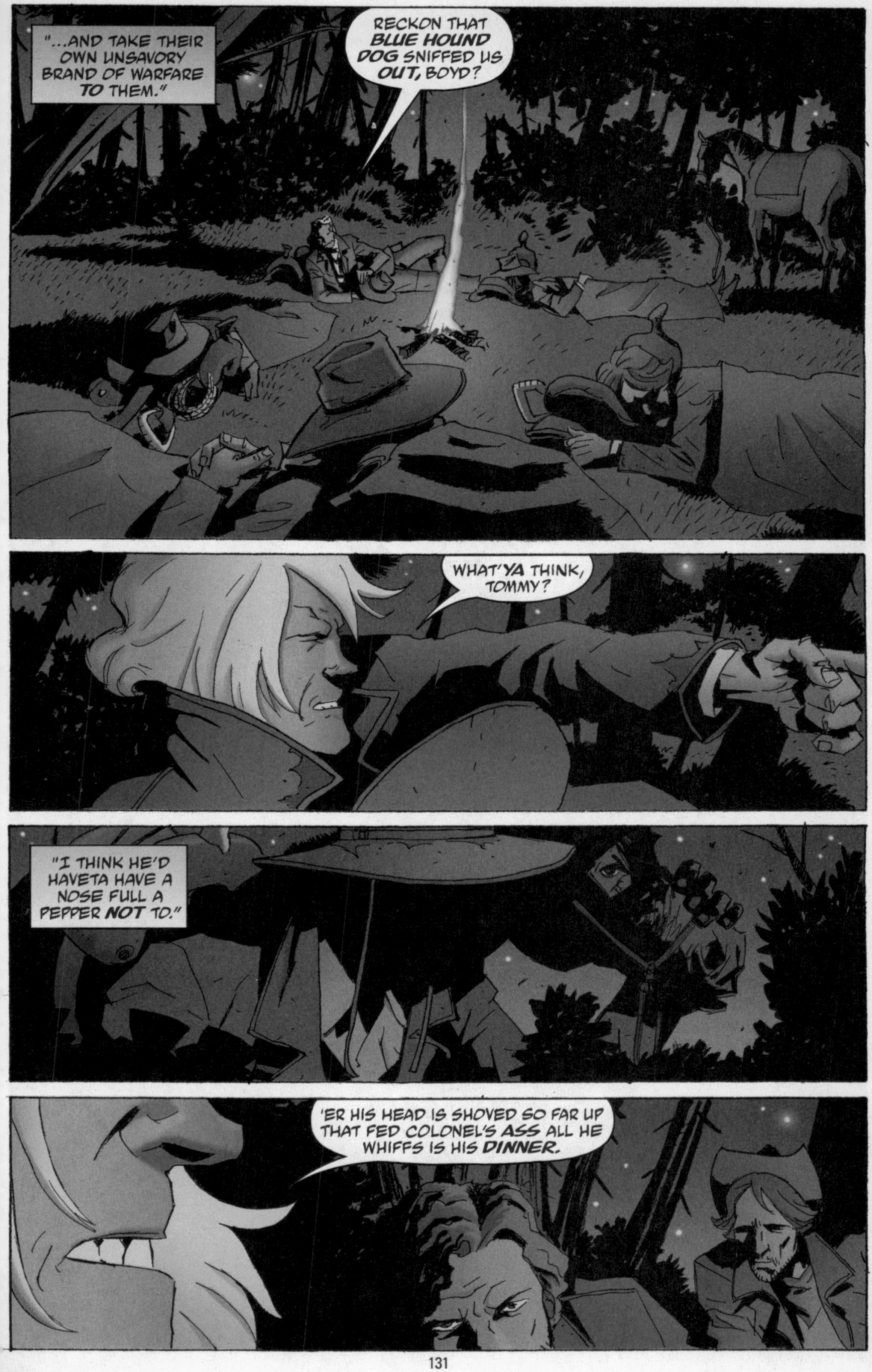
"...AND TAKE THEIR OWN UNSAVORY BRAND OF WARFARE TO THEM."
RECKON THAT BLUE HOUND DOG SNIFFED US OUT, BOYD?
WHAT'YA THINK, TOMMY?
"I THINK HE'D HAVETA HAVE A NOSE FULL A PEPPER NOT TO."
'ER HIS HEAD IS SHOVED SO FAR UP THAT FED COLONEL'S ASS ALL HE WHIFFS IS HIS DINNER.

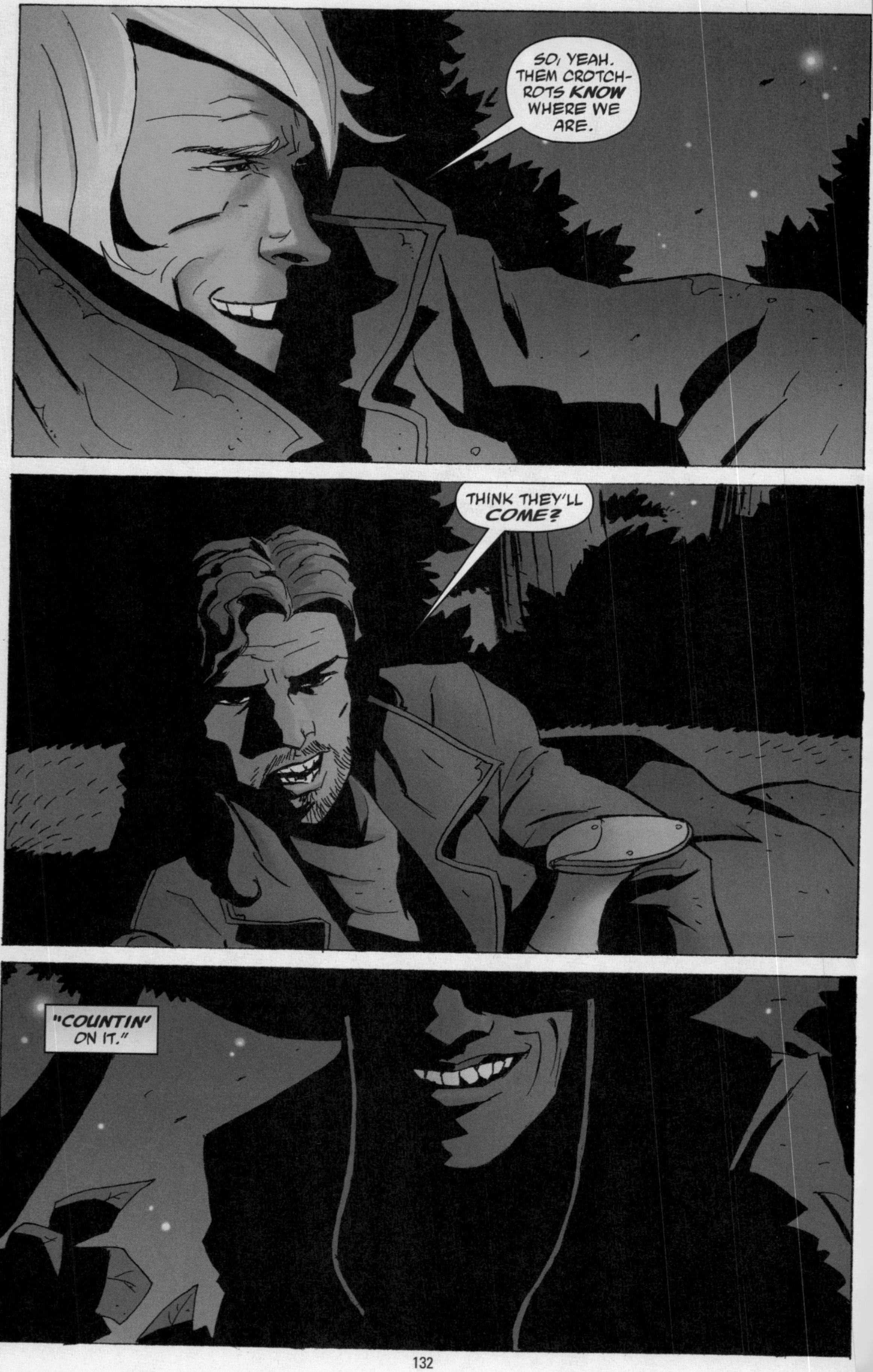
SO, YEAH. THEM CROTCH-ROTS **KNOW** WHERE WE ARE.
THINK THEY'LL **COME?**
"**COUNTIN'** ON IT."

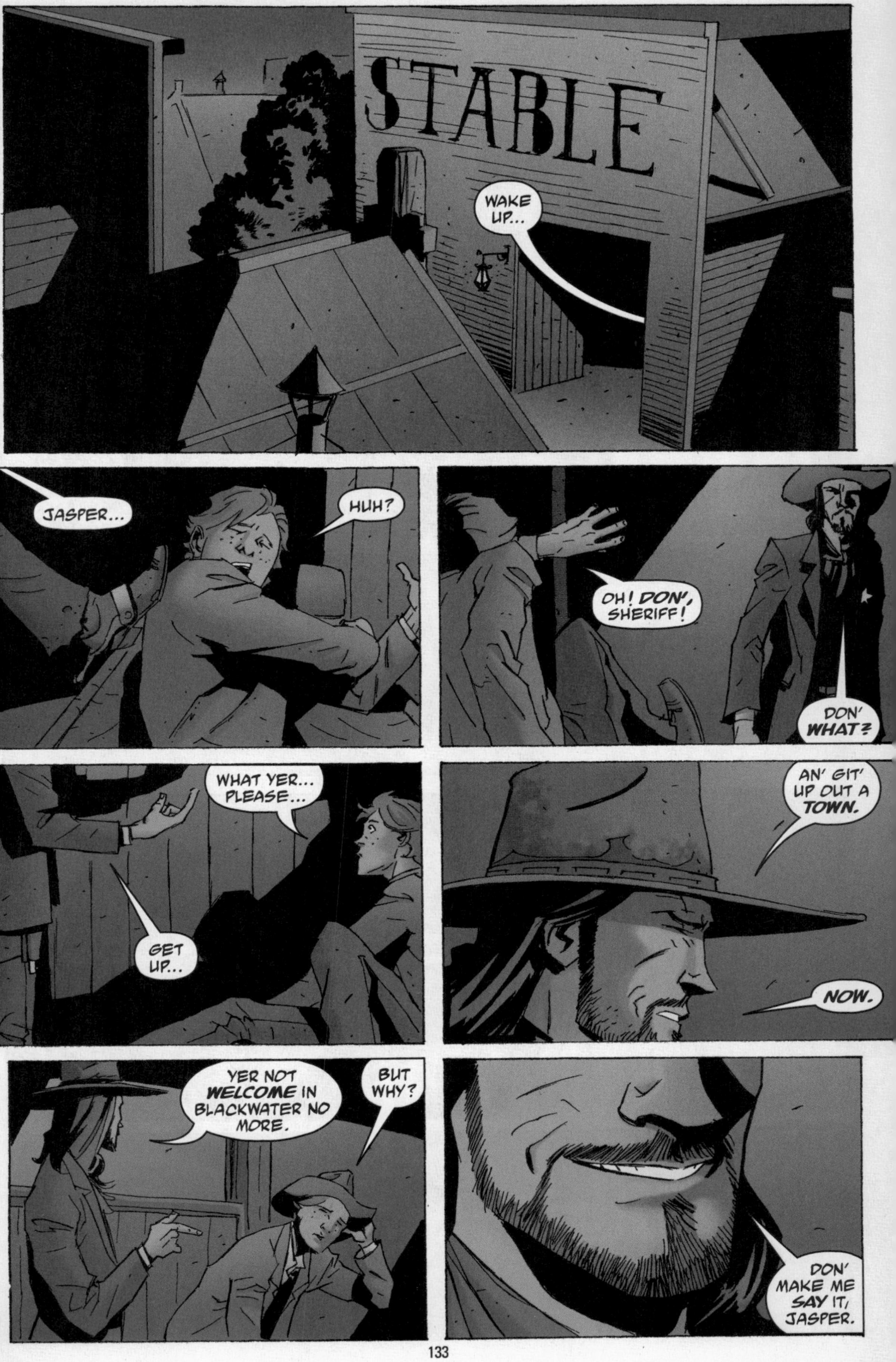
STABLE
WAKE UP...
JASPER...
HUH?
OH! DON', SHERIFF!
DON' WHAT?
WHAT YER... PLEASE...
GET UP...
AN' GIT' UP OUT A TOWN.
NOW.
YER NOT WELCOME IN BLACKWATER NO MORE.
BUT WHY?
DON' MAKE ME SAY IT, JASPER.

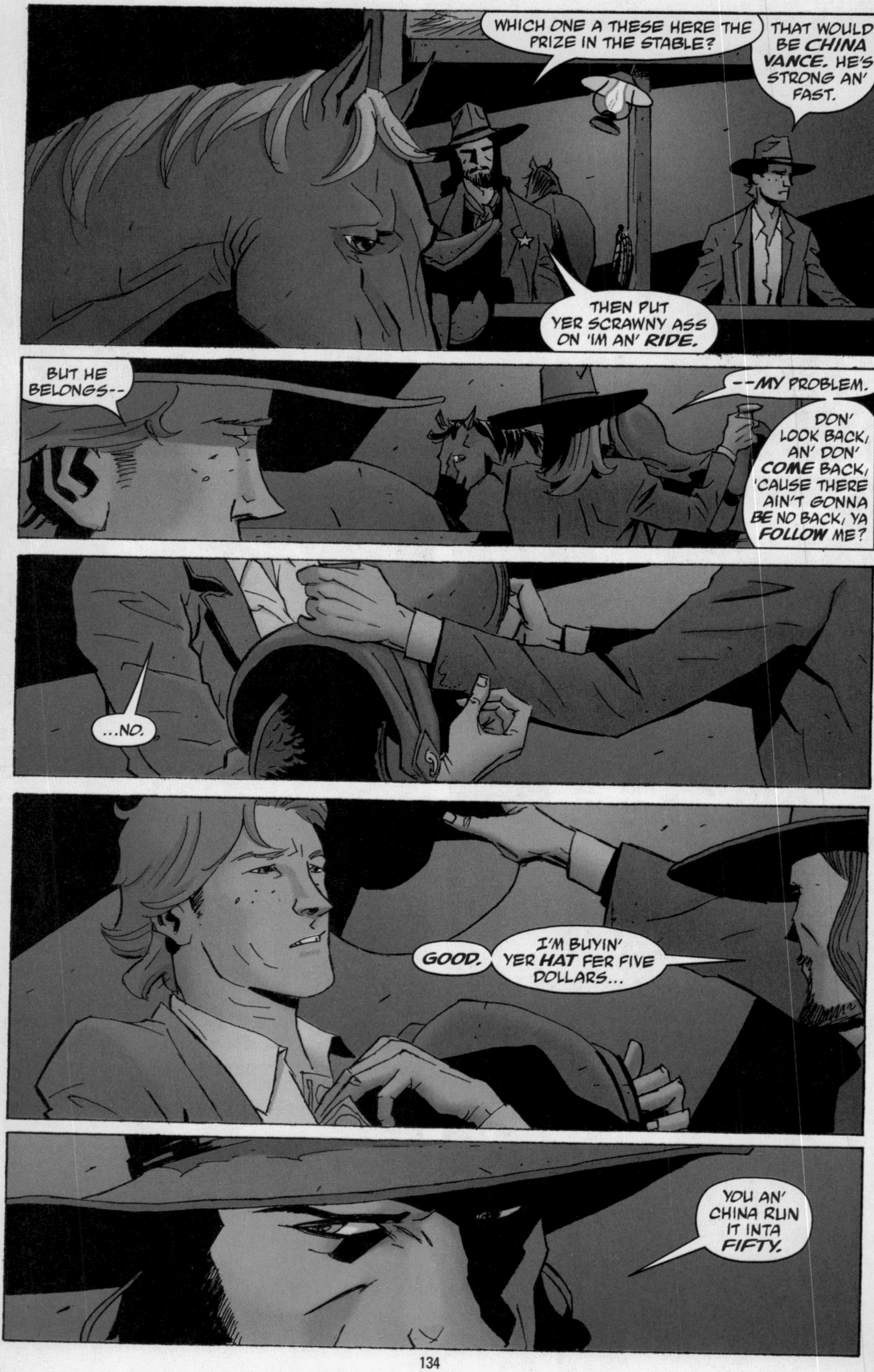
WHICH ONE A THESE HERE THE PRIZE IN THE STABLE?
THAT WOULD BE CHINA VANCE. HE'S STRONG AN' FAST.
THEN PUT YER SCRAWNY ASS ON 'IM AN' RIDE.
BUT HE BELONGS--
--MY PROBLEM.
DON' LOOK BACK, AN' DON' COME BACK, 'CAUSE THERE AIN'T GONNA BE NO BACK, YA FOLLOW ME?
...NO.
GOOD.
I'M BUYIN' YER HAT FER FIVE DOLLARS...
YOU AN' CHINA RUN IT INTA FIFTY.

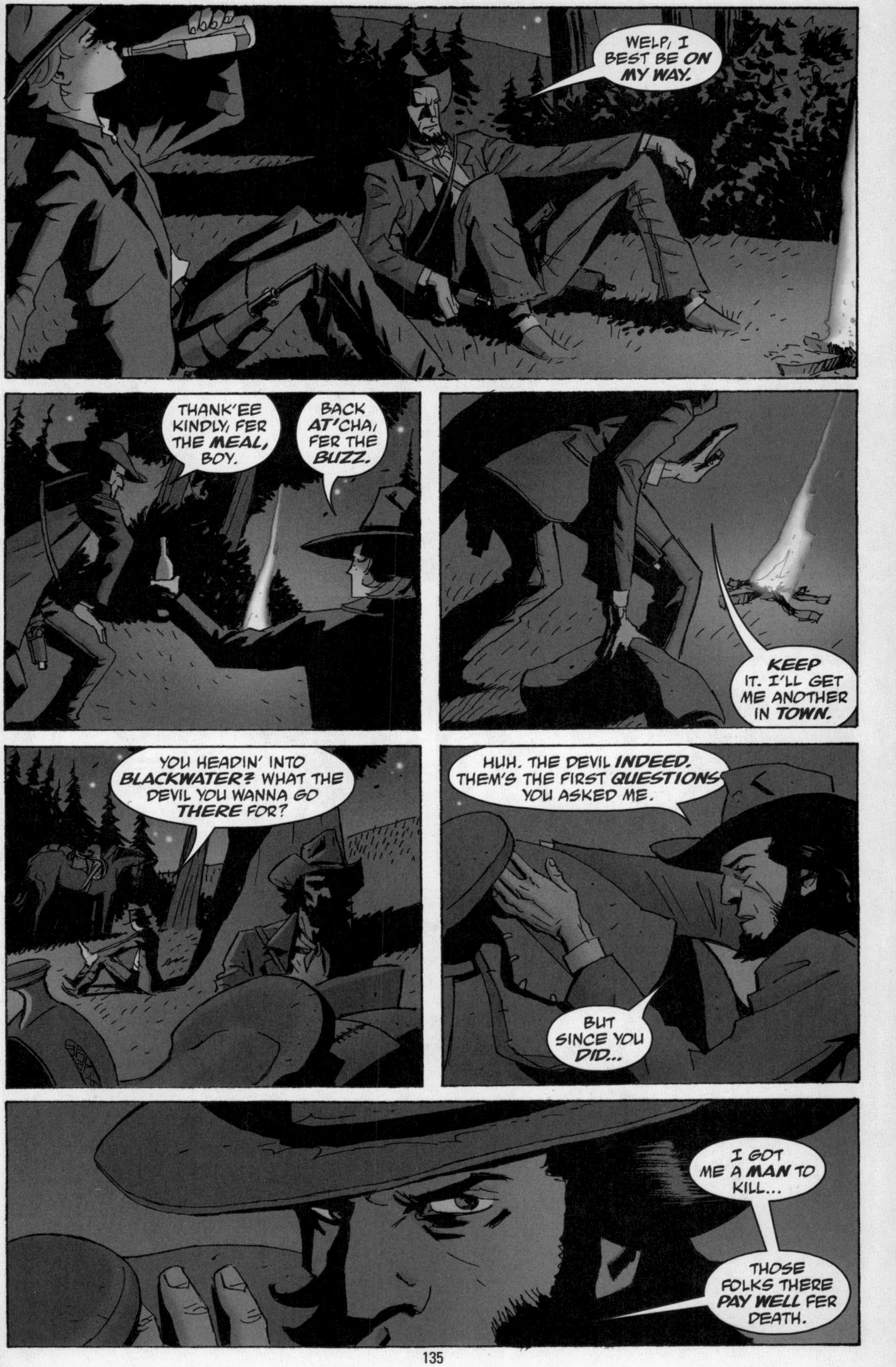
WELP, I BEST BE ON MY WAY.
THANK'EE KINDLY, FER THE MEAL, BOY.
BACK AT'CHA, FER THE BUZZ.
KEEP IT. I'LL GET ME ANOTHER IN TOWN.
YOU HEADIN' INTO BLACKWATER? WHAT THE DEVIL YOU WANNA GO THERE FOR?
HUH. THE DEVIL INDEED. THEM'S THE FIRST QUESTIONS YOU ASKED ME.
BUT SINCE YOU DID...
I GOT ME A MAN TO KILL...
THOSE FOLKS THERE PAY WELL FER DEATH.

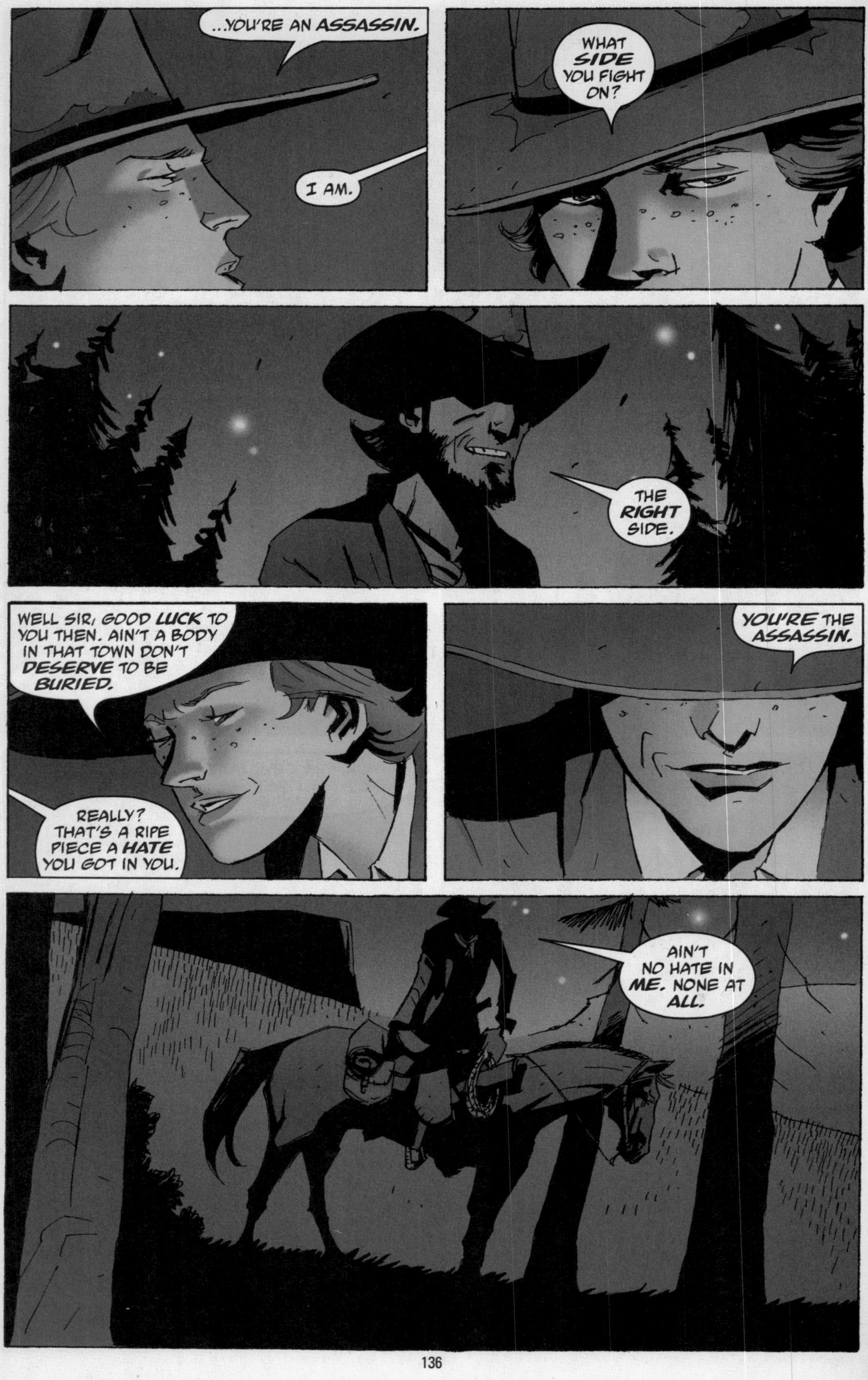
...YOU'RE AN ASSASSIN.
I AM.
WHAT SIDE YOU FIGHT ON?
THE RIGHT SIDE.
WELL SIR, GOOD LUCK TO YOU THEN. AIN'T A BODY IN THAT TOWN DON'T DESERVE TO BE BURIED.
REALLY? THAT'S A RIPE PIECE A HATE YOU GOT IN YOU.
YOU'RE THE ASSASSIN.
AIN'T NO HATE IN ME. NONE AT ALL.

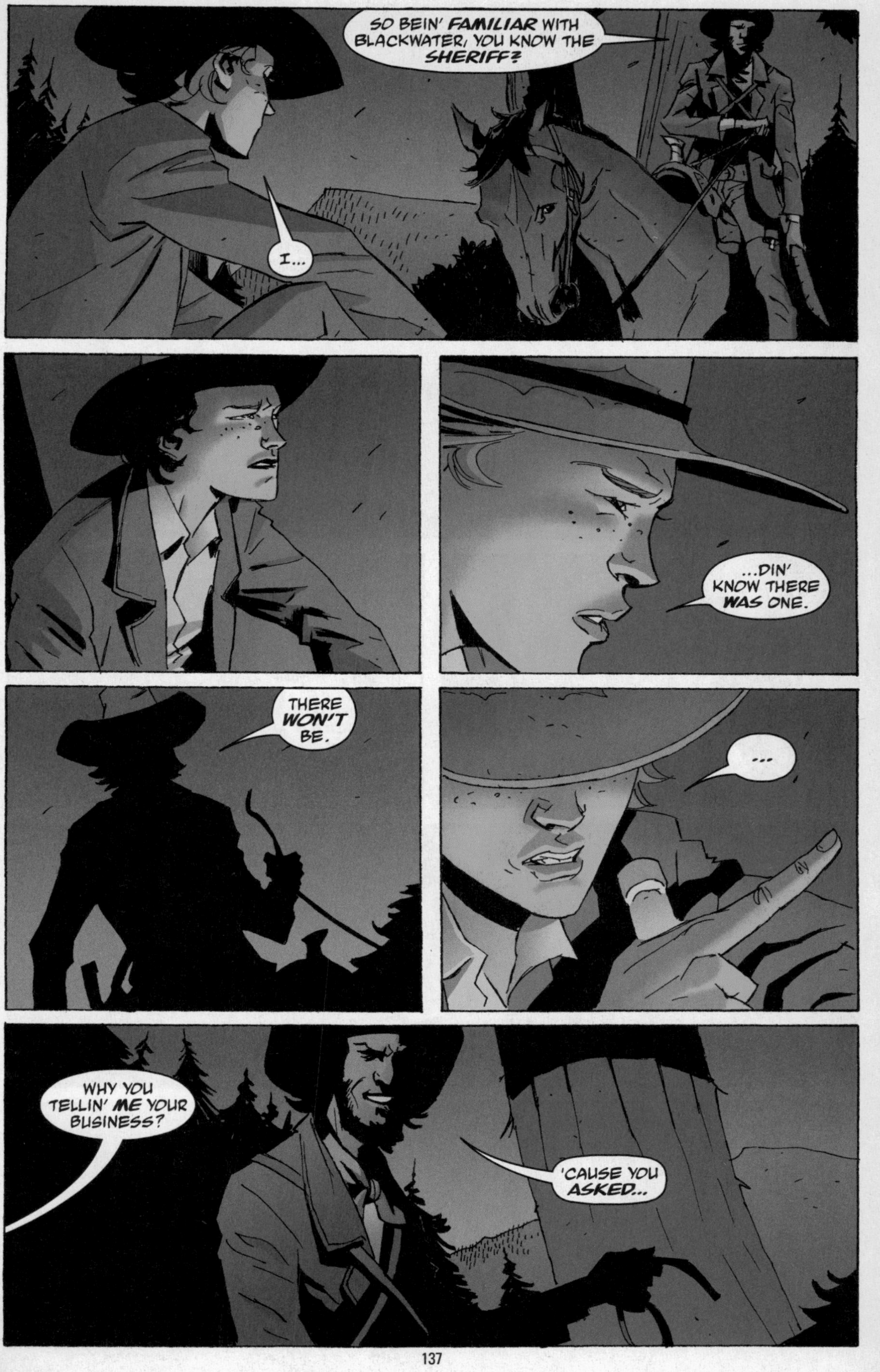
SO BEIN' FAMILIAR WITH BLACKWATER, YOU KNOW THE SHERIFF?
I...
...DIN' KNOW THERE WAS ONE.
THERE WON'T BE.
...
WHY YOU TELLIN' ME YOUR BUSINESS?
'CAUSE YOU ASKED...

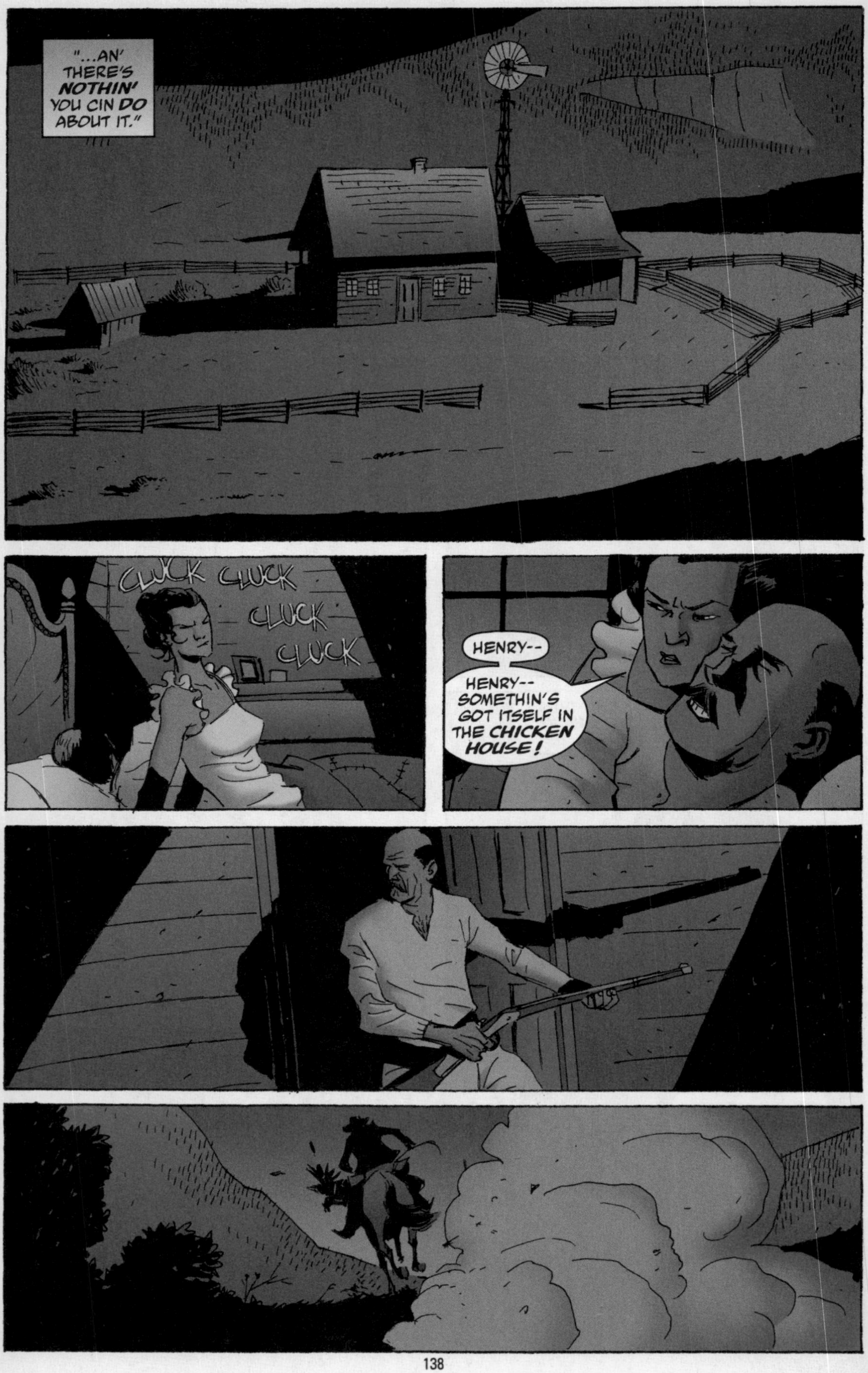
"...AN' THERE'S **NOTHIN'** YOU CIN **DO** ABOUT IT."
CLUCK CLUCK CLUCK CLUCK
HENRY--
HENRY-- SOMETHIN'S GOT ITSELF IN THE **CHICKEN HOUSE!**

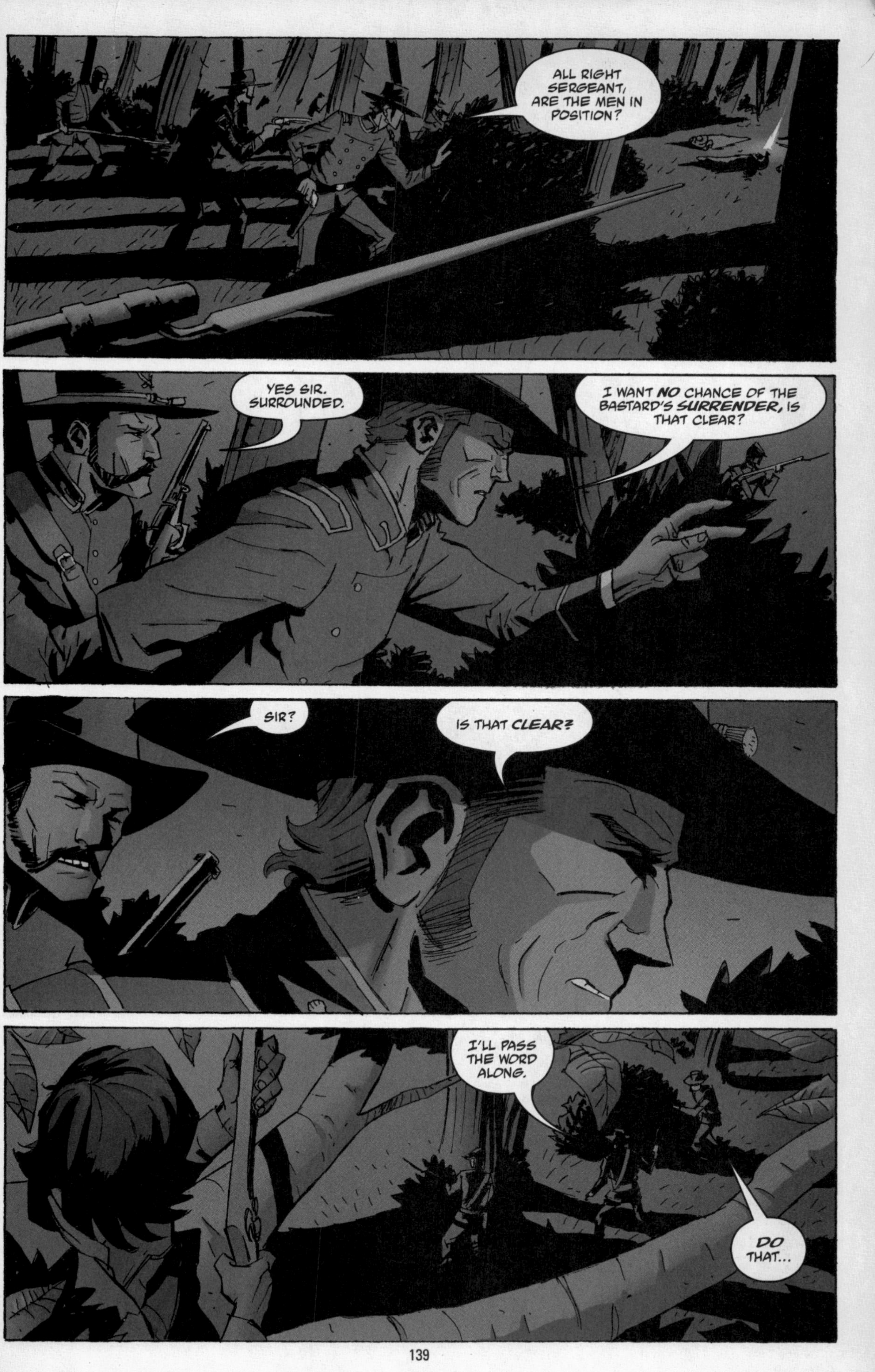
ALL RIGHT SERGEANT, ARE THE MEN IN POSITION?
YES SIR. SURROUNDED.
I WANT NO CHANCE OF THE BASTARD'S SURRENDER, IS THAT CLEAR?
SIR?
IS THAT CLEAR?
I'LL PASS THE WORD ALONG.
DO THAT...

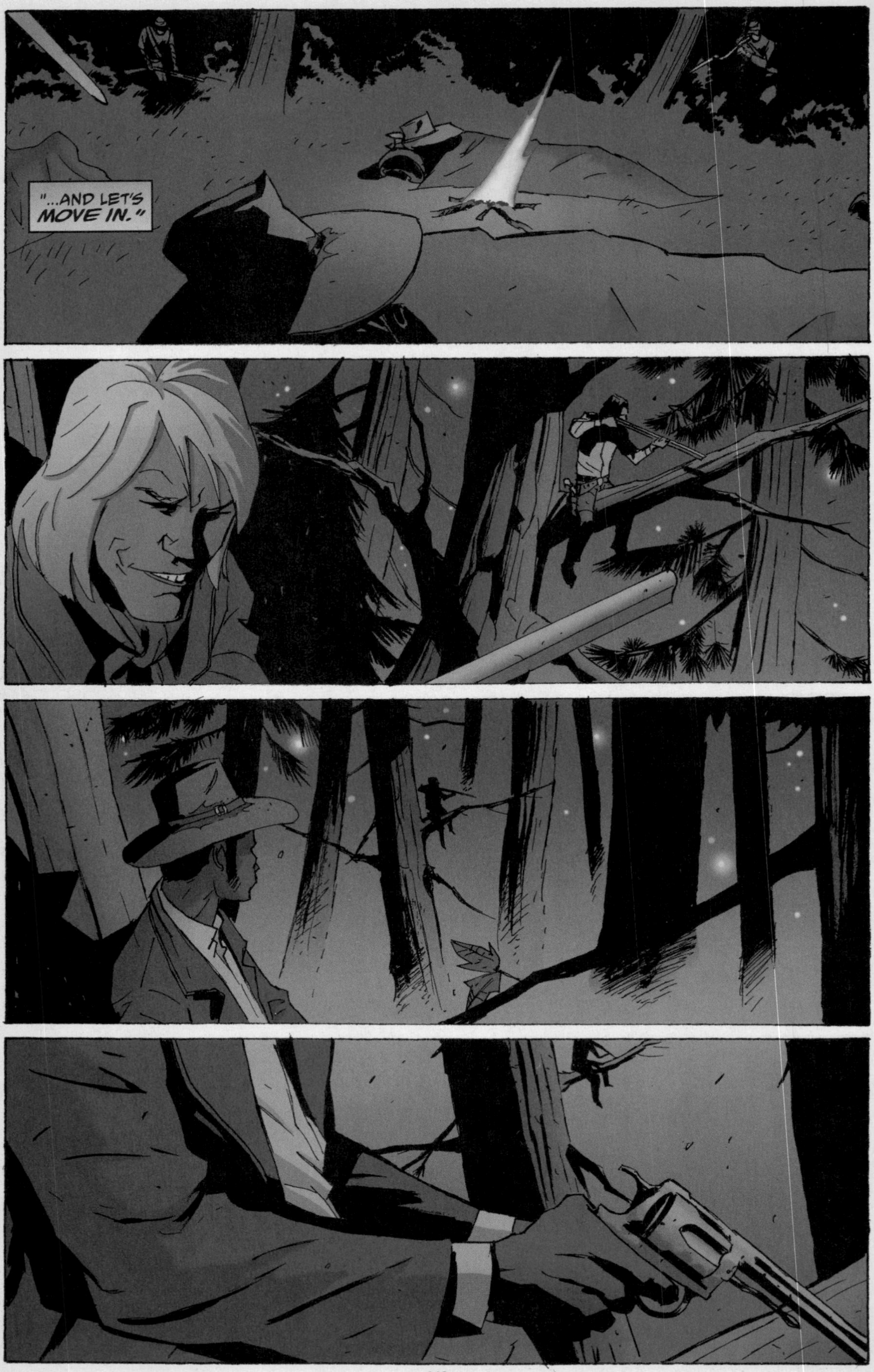
"...AND LET'S
MOVE IN."

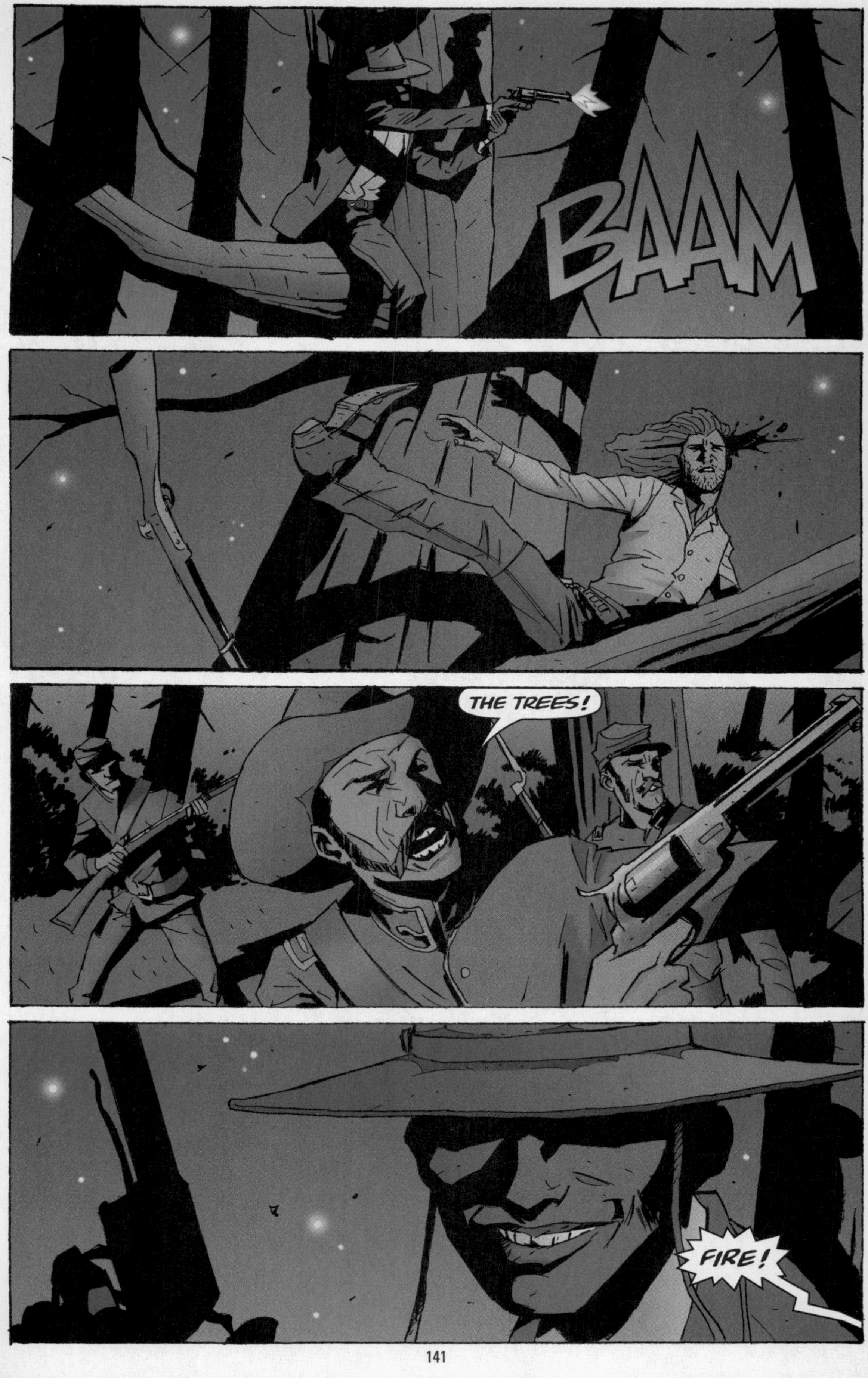
BAAM
THE TREES!
FIRE!

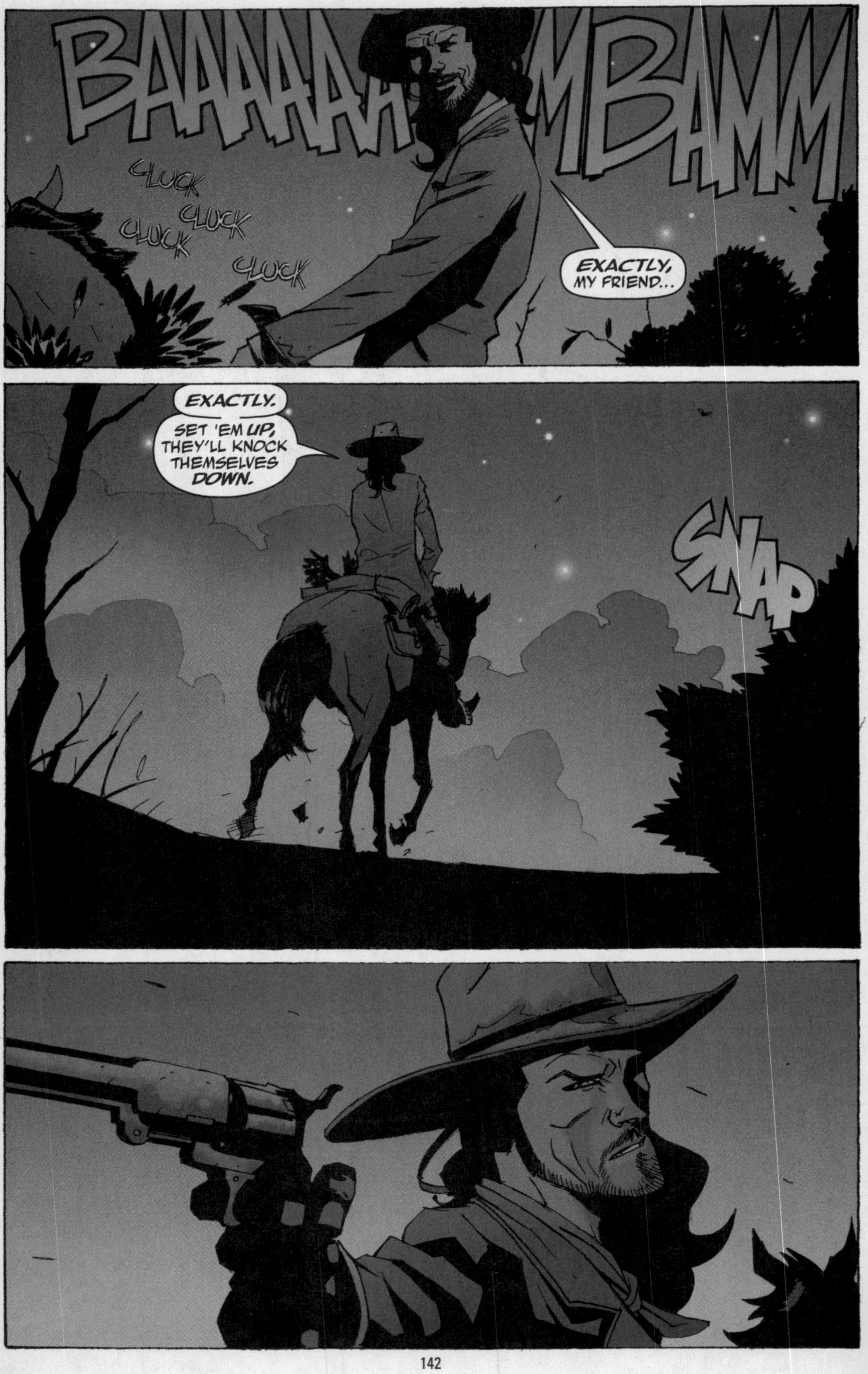
BAAAAAAMBAMM
CLUCK
CLUCK
CLUCK
CLUCK
EXACTLY, MY FRIEND...
EXACTLY.
SET 'EM UP, THEY'LL KNOCK THEMSELVES DOWN.
SNAP

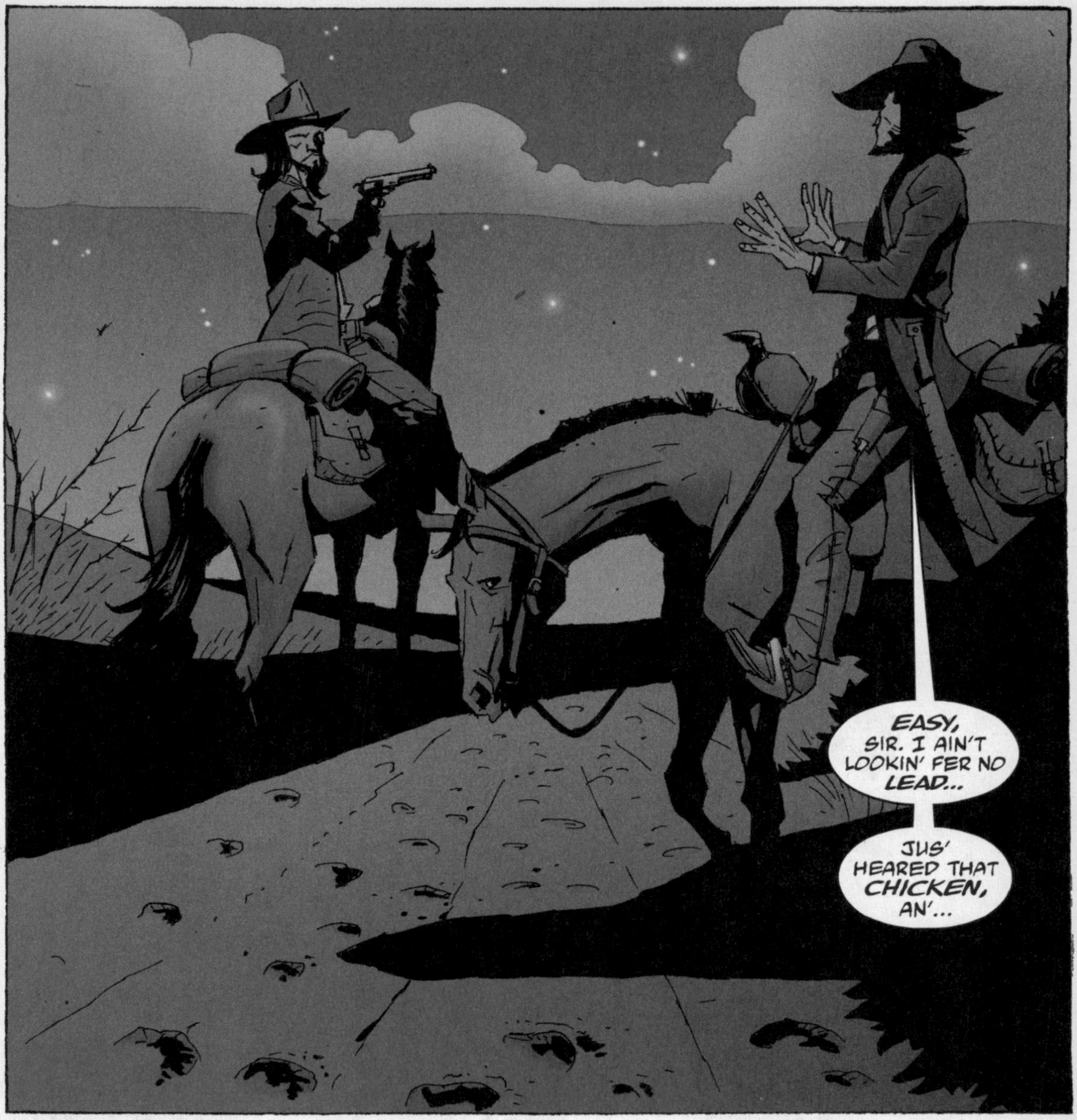
EASY, SIR. I AIN'T LOOKIN' FER NO LEAD...
JUS' HEARED THAT CHICKEN, AN'...

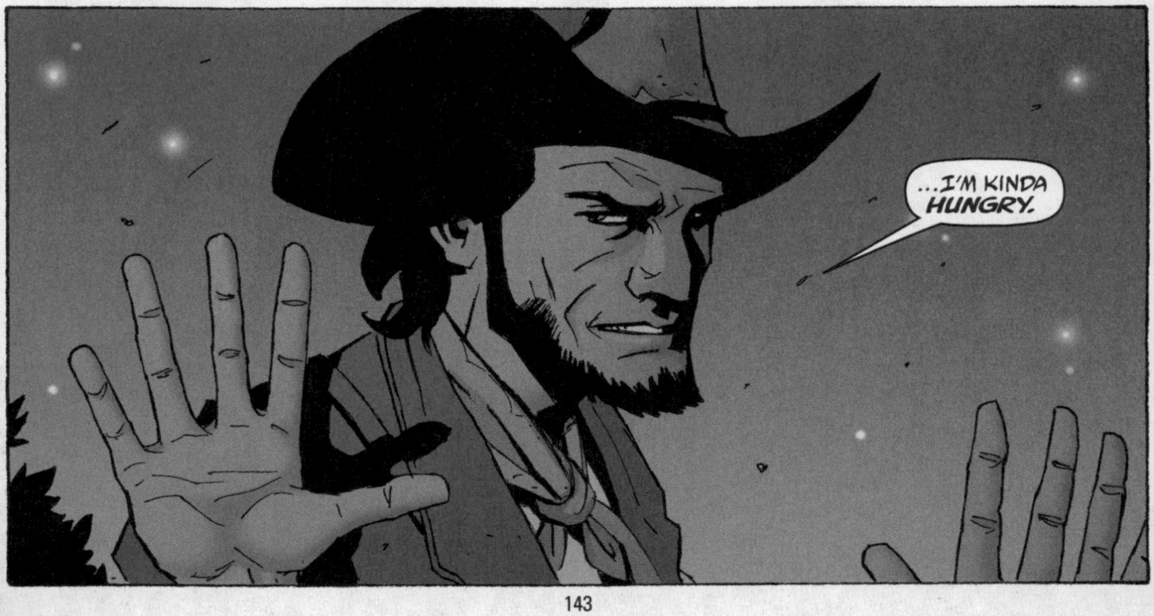
...I'M KINDA HUNGRY.

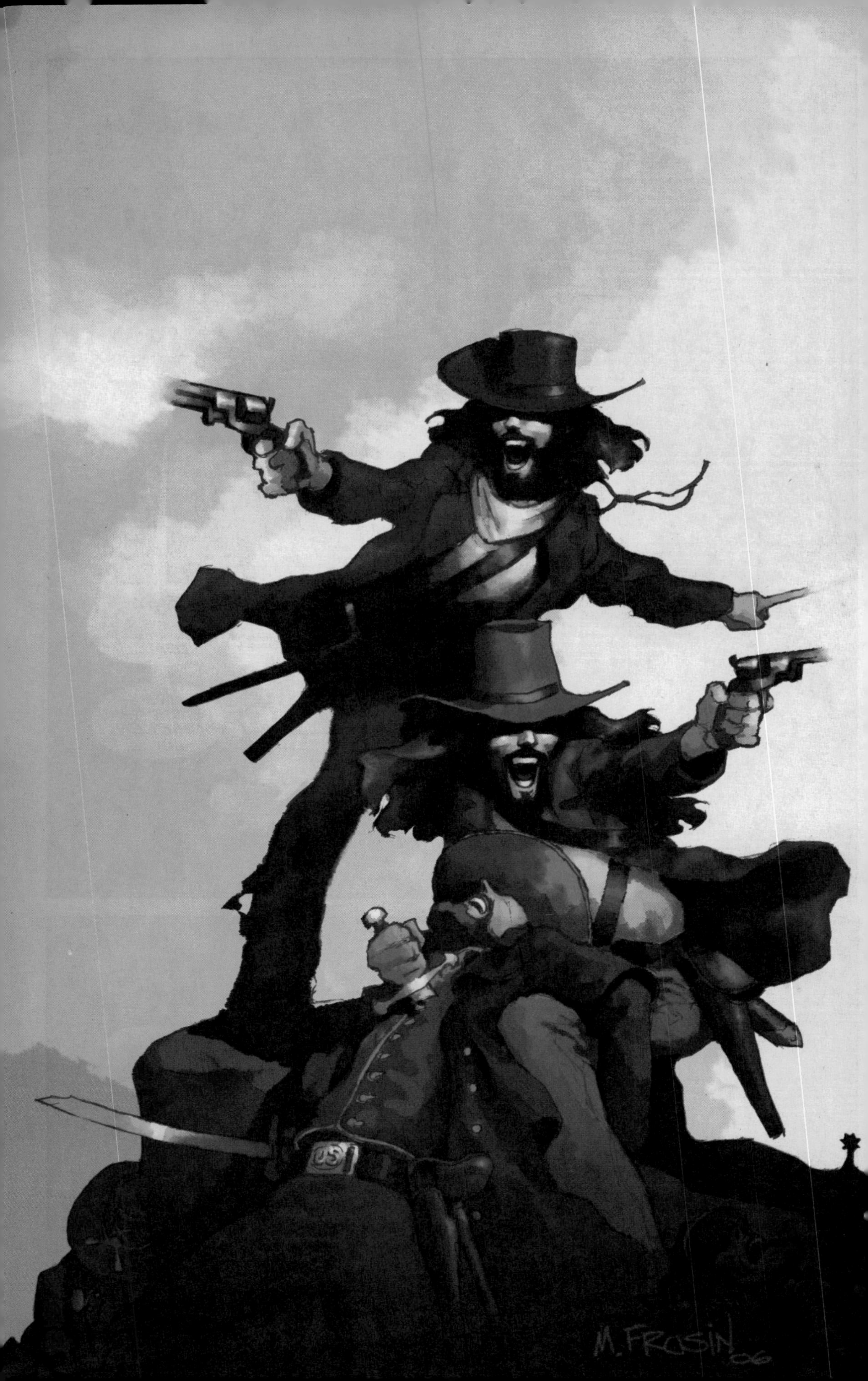
M. FRASIN '06

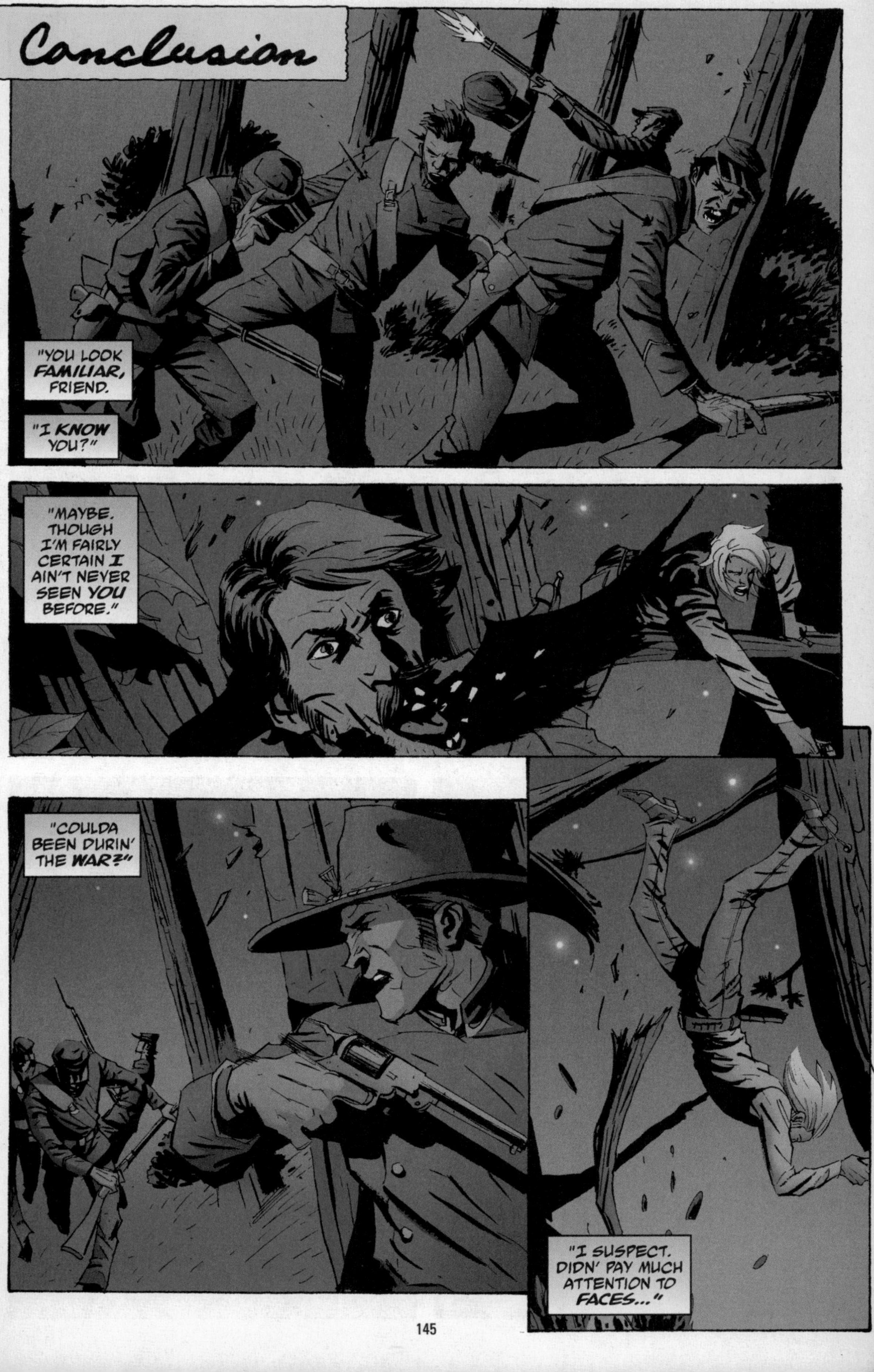
Conclusion
"YOU LOOK FAMILIAR, FRIEND.
"I KNOW YOU?"
"MAYBE. THOUGH I'M FAIRLY CERTAIN I AIN'T NEVER SEEN YOU BEFORE."
"COULDA BEEN DURIN' THE WAR?"
"I SUSPECT. DIDN' PAY MUCH ATTENTION TO FACES..."

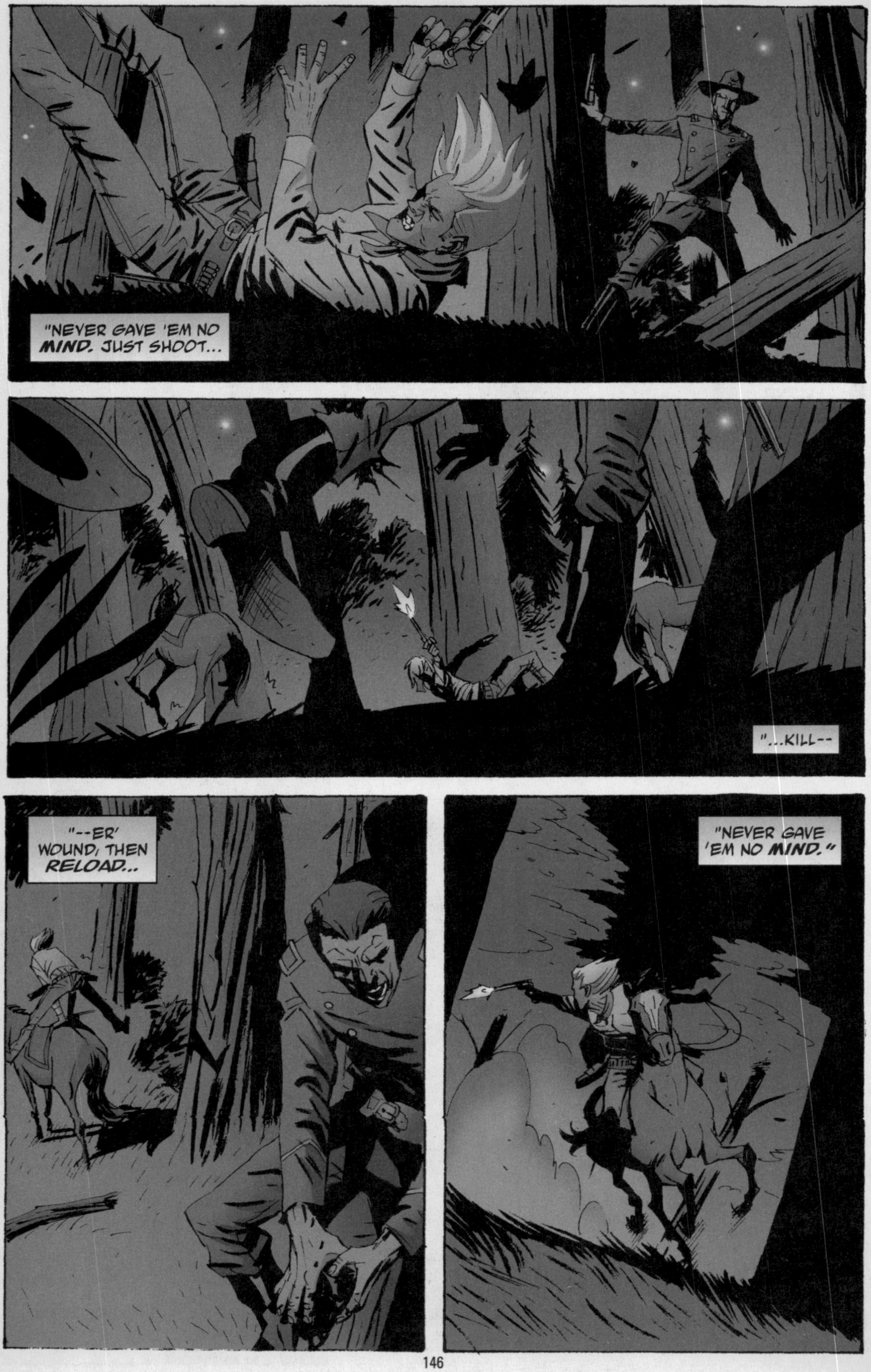
"NEVER GAVE 'EM NO MIND. JUST SHOOT...
"...KILL--
"--ER' WOUND, THEN RELOAD...
"NEVER GAVE 'EM NO MIND."

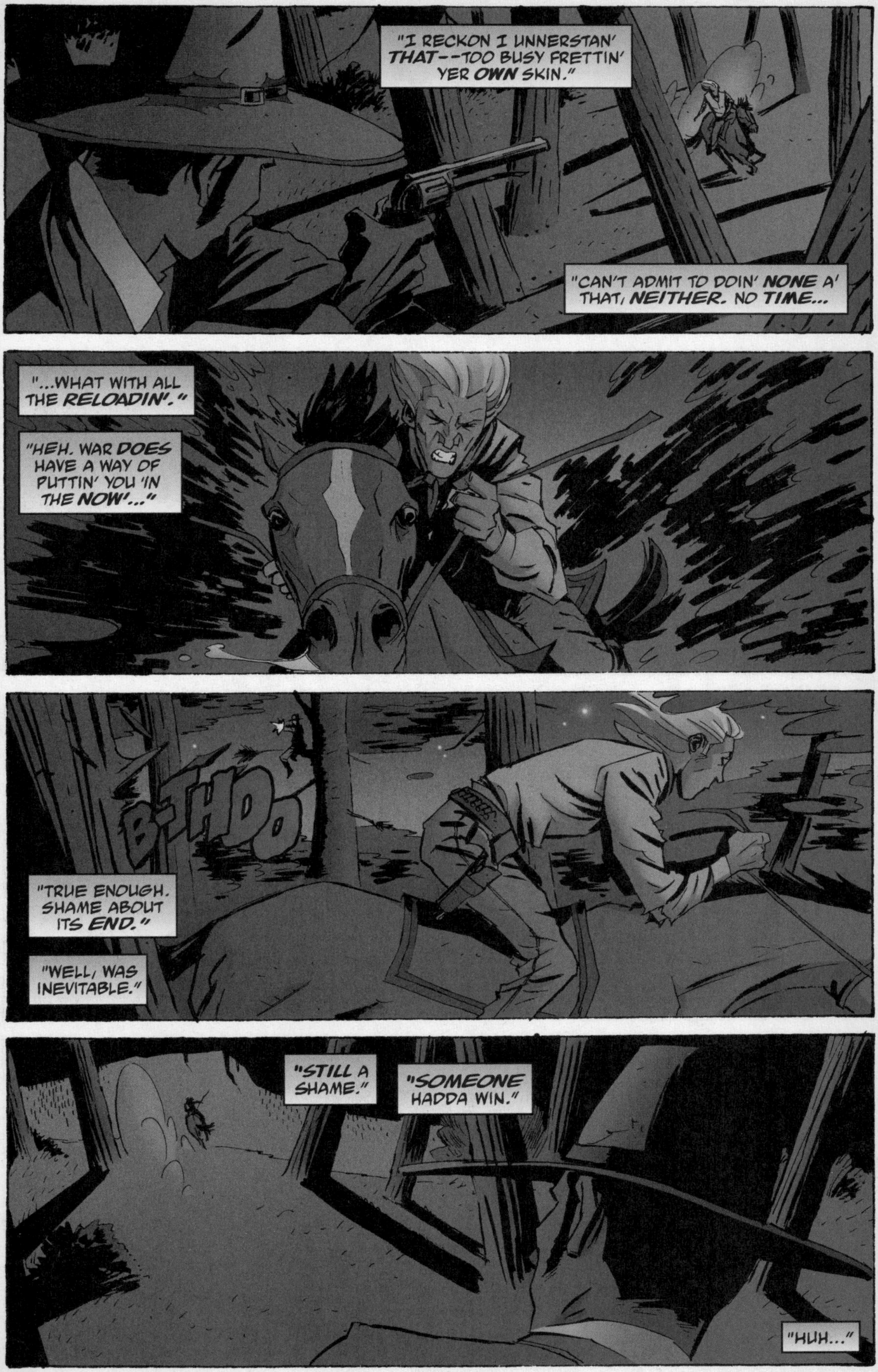
"I RECKON I UNNERSTAN' THAT--TOO BUSY FRETTIN' YER OWN SKIN."
"CAN'T ADMIT TO DOIN' NONE A' THAT, NEITHER. NO TIME...
"...WHAT WITH ALL THE RELOADIN'."
"HEH. WAR DOES HAVE A WAY OF PUTTIN' YOU 'IN THE NOW'..."
B-THDO
"TRUE ENOUGH. SHAME ABOUT ITS END."
"WELL, WAS INEVITABLE."
"STILL A SHAME."
"SOMEONE HADDA WIN."
"HUH..."

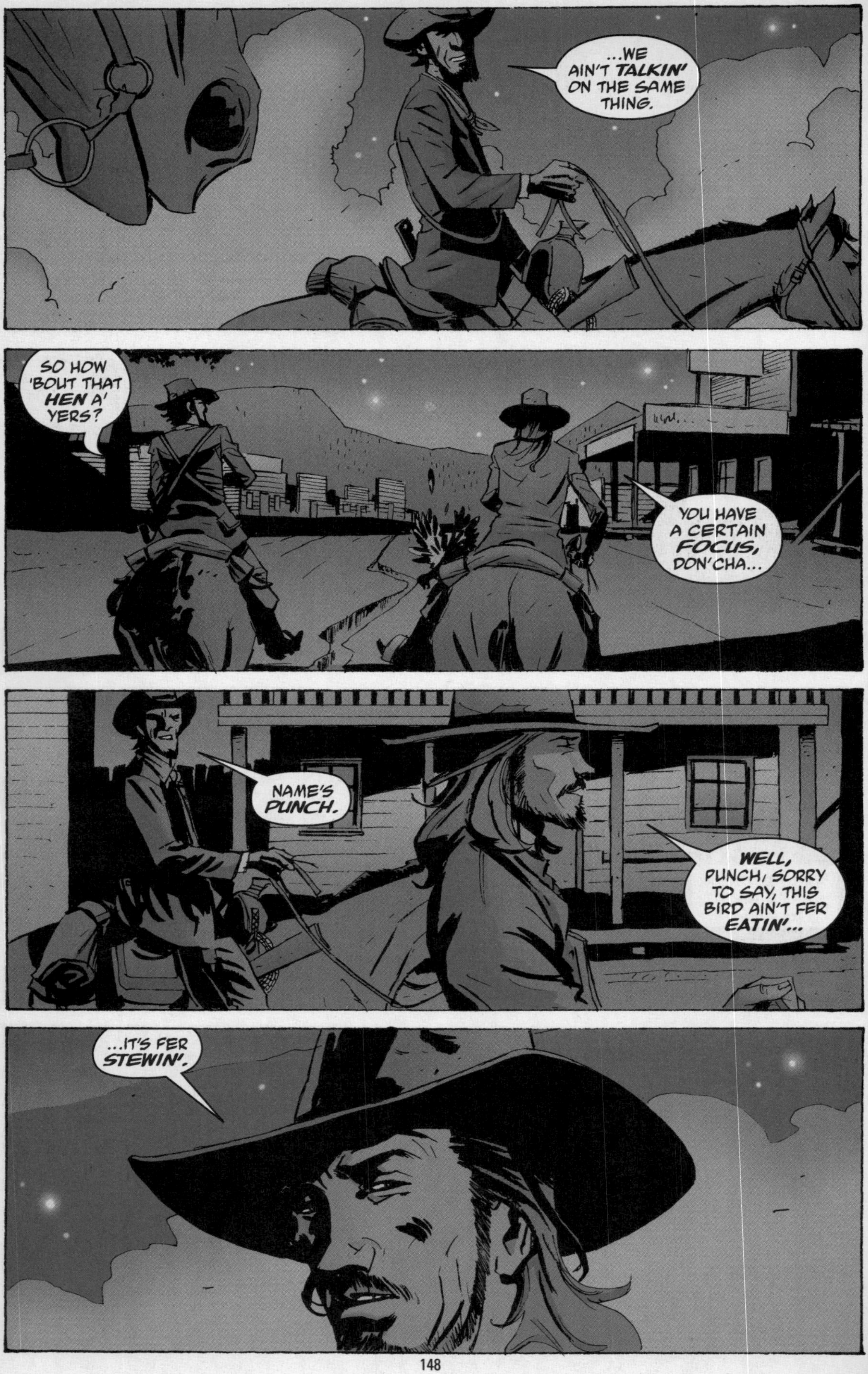
...WE AIN'T TALKIN' ON THE SAME THING.
SO HOW 'BOUT THAT HEN A' YERS?
YOU HAVE A CERTAIN FOCUS, DON'CHA...
NAME'S PUNCH.
WELL, PUNCH, SORRY TO SAY, THIS BIRD AIN'T FER EATIN'...
...IT'S FER STEWIN'.

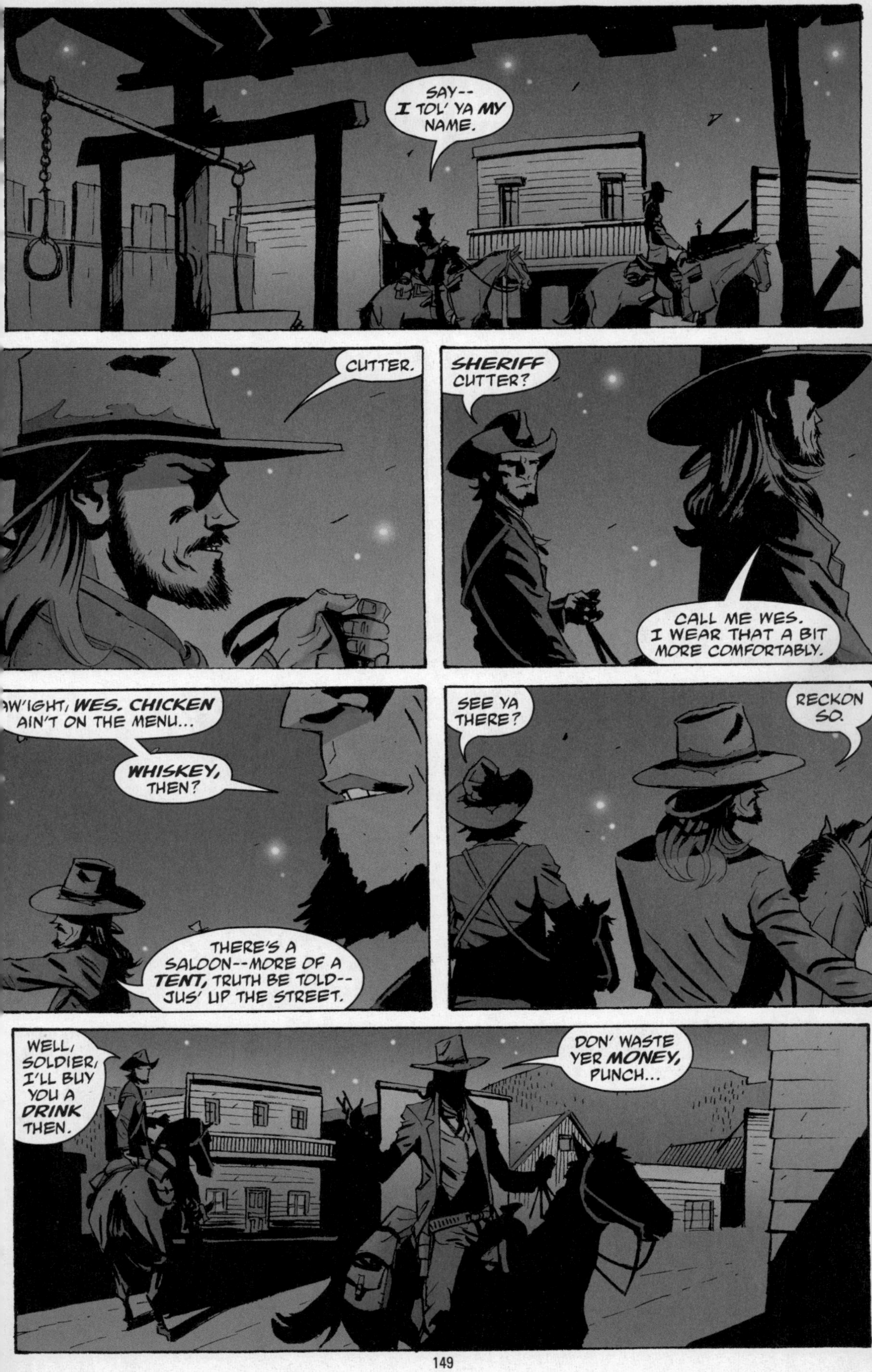
SAY-- I TOL' YA MY NAME.
CUTTER.
SHERIFF CUTTER?
CALL ME WES. I WEAR THAT A BIT MORE COMFORTABLY.
AW'IGHT, WES. CHICKEN AIN'T ON THE MENU...
WHISKEY, THEN?
THERE'S A SALOON--MORE OF A TENT, TRUTH BE TOLD-- JUS' UP THE STREET.
SEE YA THERE?
RECKON SO.
WELL, SOLDIER, I'LL BUY YOU A DRINK THEN.
DON' WASTE YER MONEY, PUNCH...

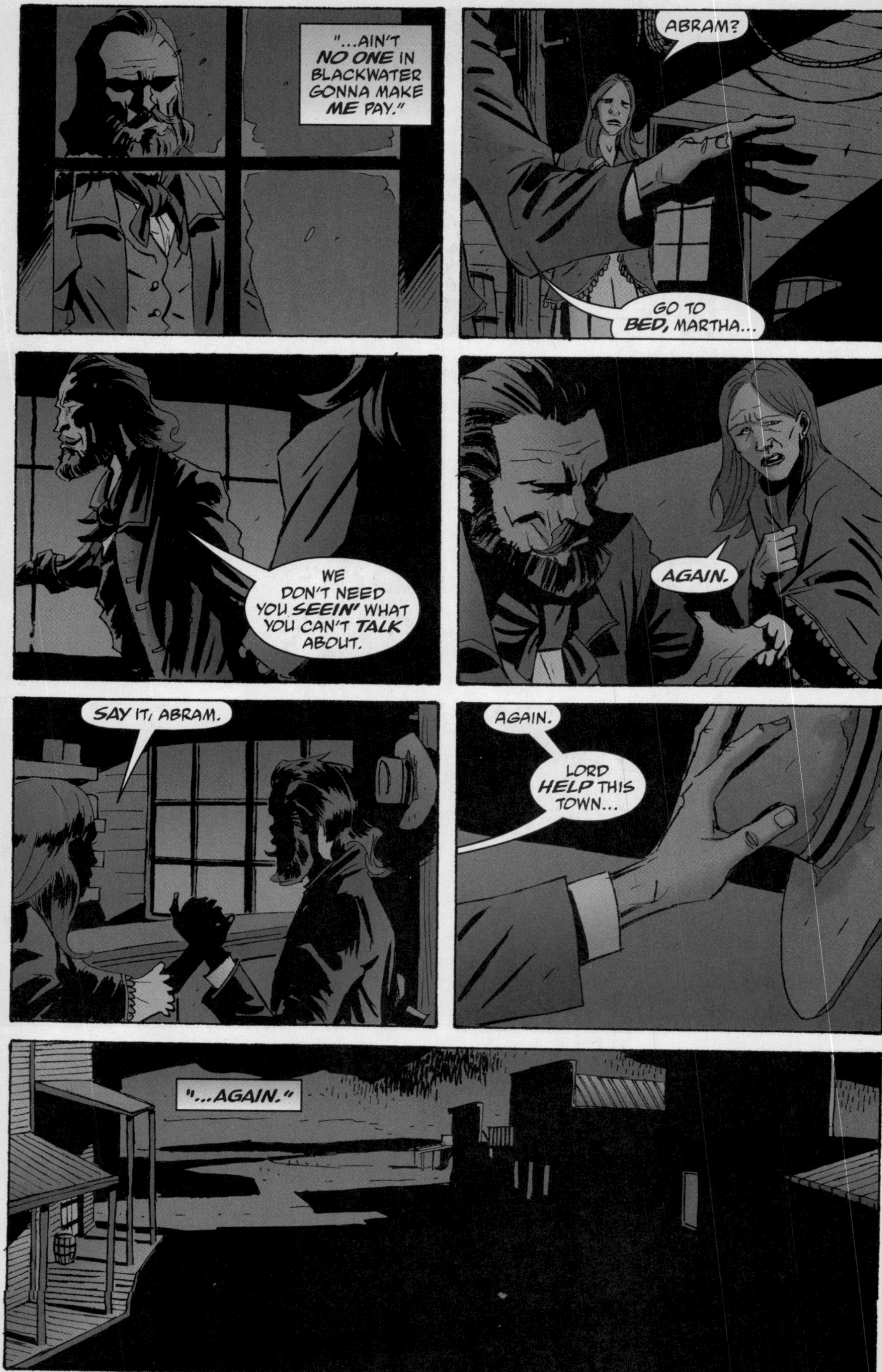
"...AIN'T NO ONE IN BLACKWATER GONNA MAKE ME PAY."
ABRAM?
GO TO BED, MARTHA...
WE DON'T NEED YOU SEEIN' WHAT YOU CAN'T TALK ABOUT.
AGAIN.
SAY IT, ABRAM.
AGAIN.
LORD HELP THIS TOWN...
"...AGAIN."

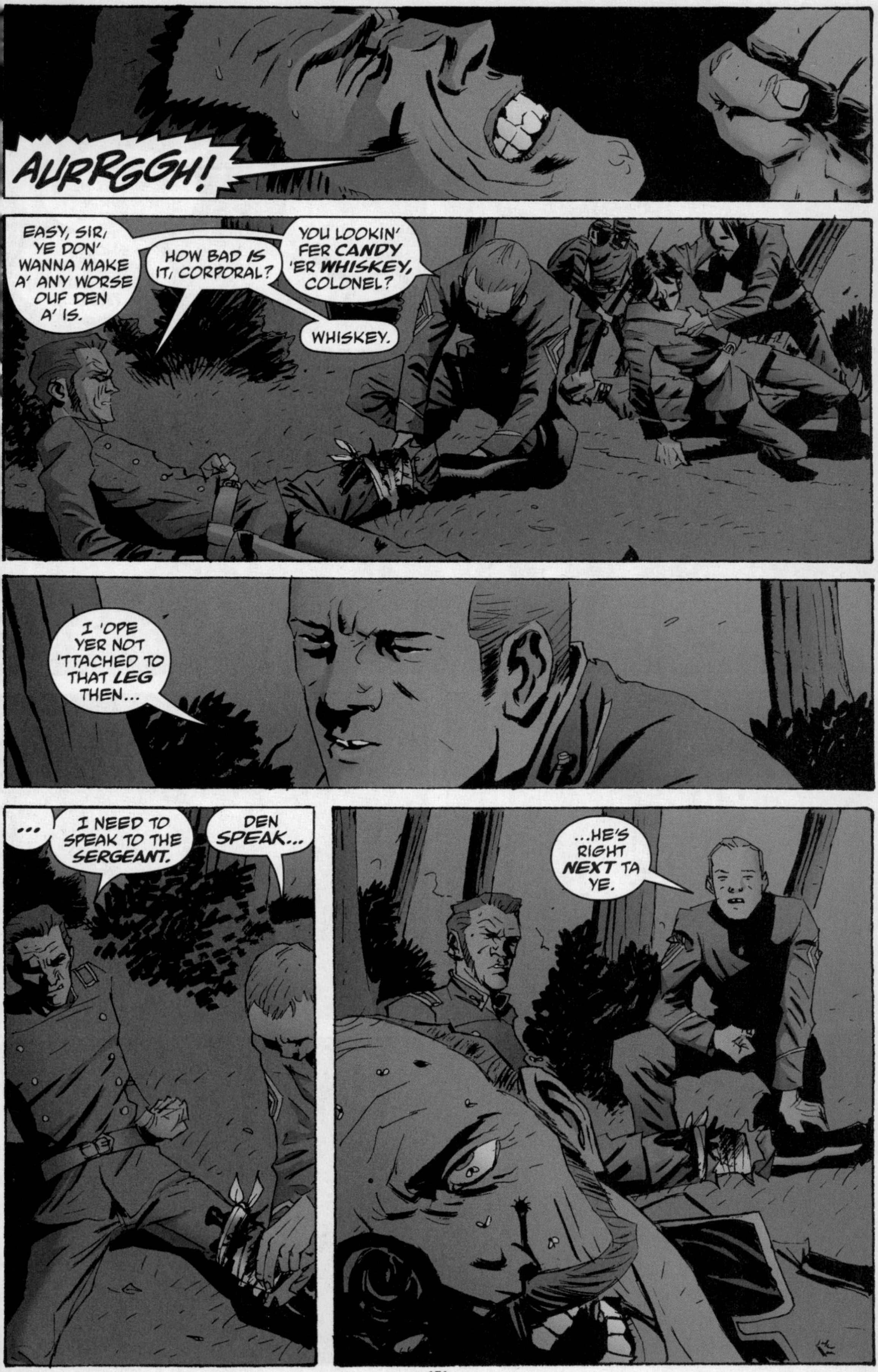
AURRGGH!
EASY, SIR, YE DON' WANNA MAKE A' ANY WORSE OUF DEN A' IS.
HOW BAD IS IT, CORPORAL?
YOU LOOKIN' FER CANDY 'ER WHISKEY, COLONEL?
WHISKEY.
I 'OPE YER NOT 'TTACHED TO THAT LEG THEN...
...
I NEED TO SPEAK TO THE SERGEANT.
DEN SPEAK...
...HE'S RIGHT NEXT TA YE.

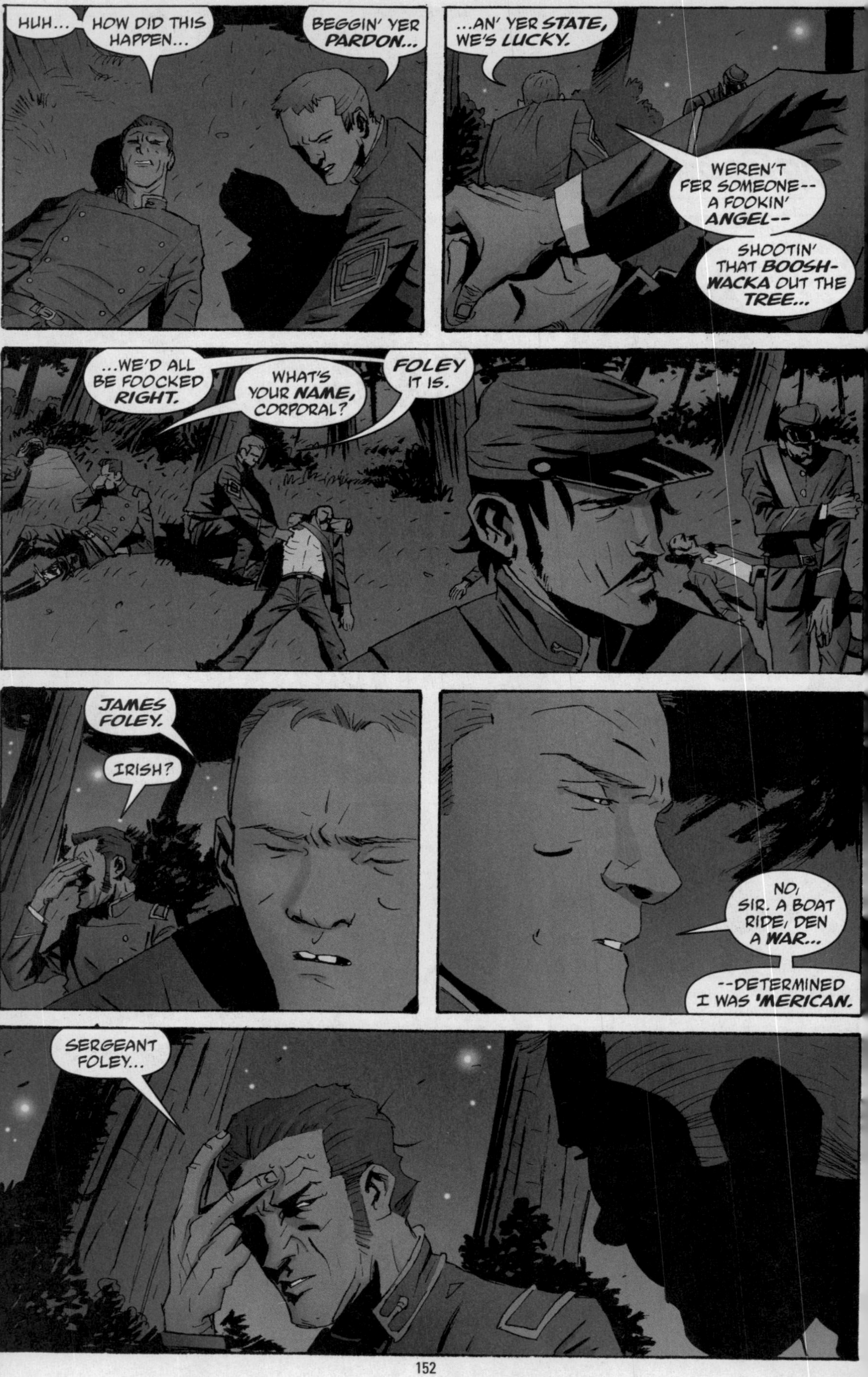
HUH...
HOW DID THIS HAPPEN...
BEGGIN' YER PARDON...
...AN' YER STATE, WE'S LUCKY.
WEREN'T FER SOMEONE-- A FOOKIN' ANGEL--
SHOOTIN' THAT BOOSH-WACKA OUT THE TREE...
...WE'D ALL BE FOOCKED RIGHT.
WHAT'S YOUR NAME, CORPORAL?
FOLEY IT IS.
JAMES FOLEY.
IRISH?
NO, SIR. A BOAT RIDE, DEN A WAR...
--DETERMINED I WAS 'MERICAN.
SERGEANT FOLEY...

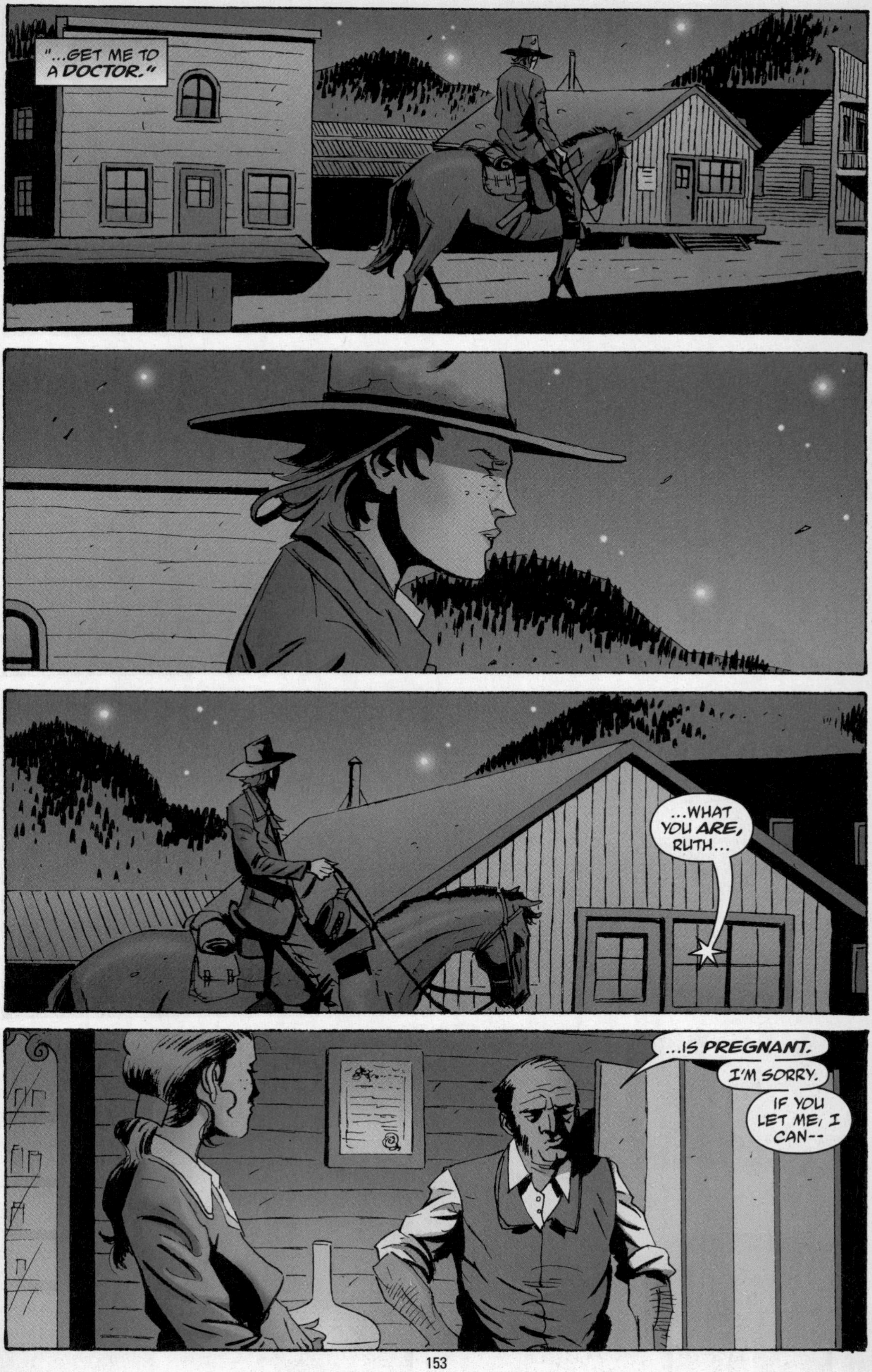
"...GET ME TO A DOCTOR."
...WHAT YOU ARE, RUTH...
...IS PREGNANT.
I'M SORRY.
IF YOU LET ME, I CAN--

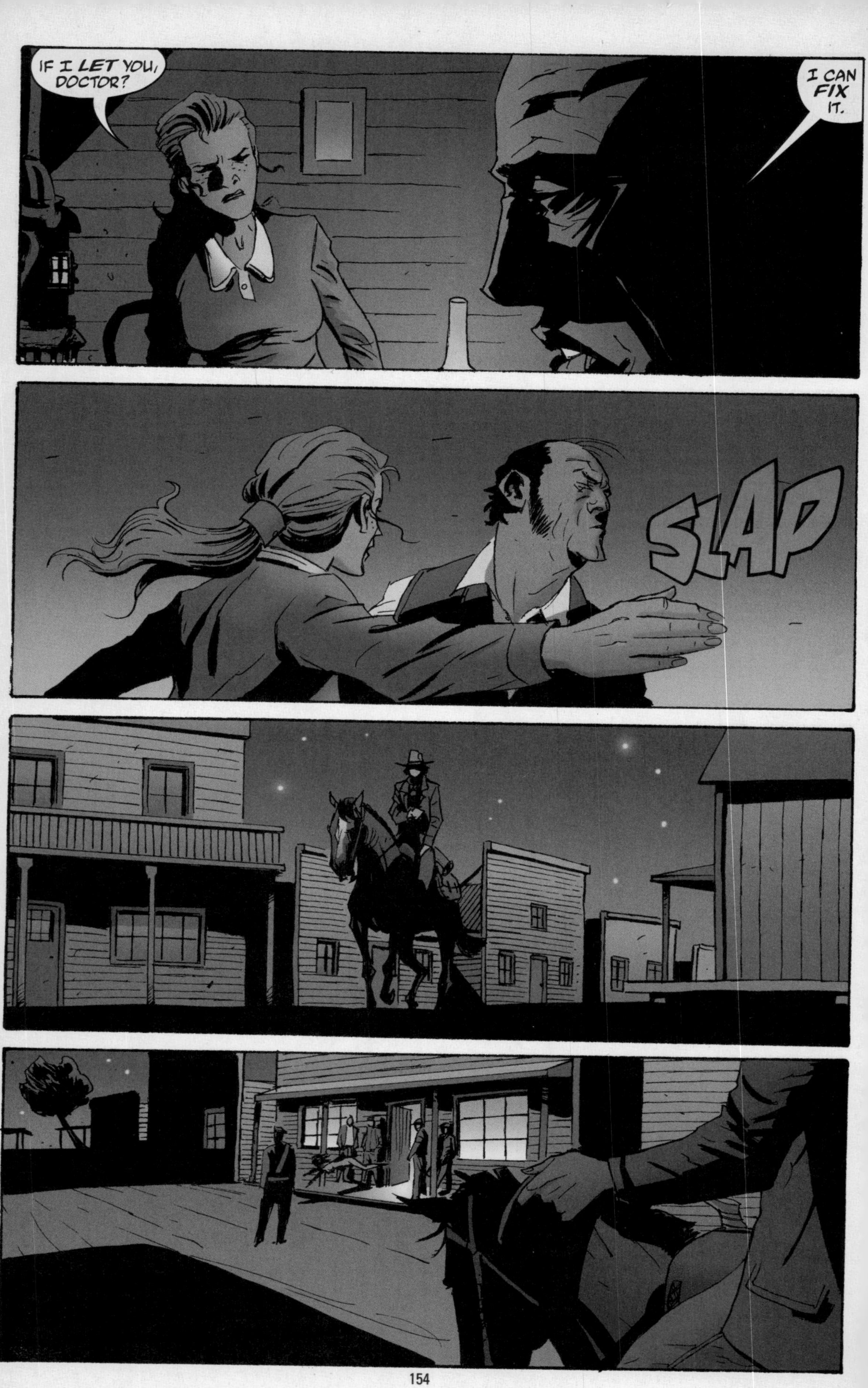
IF I LET YOU, DOCTOR?
I CAN FIX IT.
SLAP

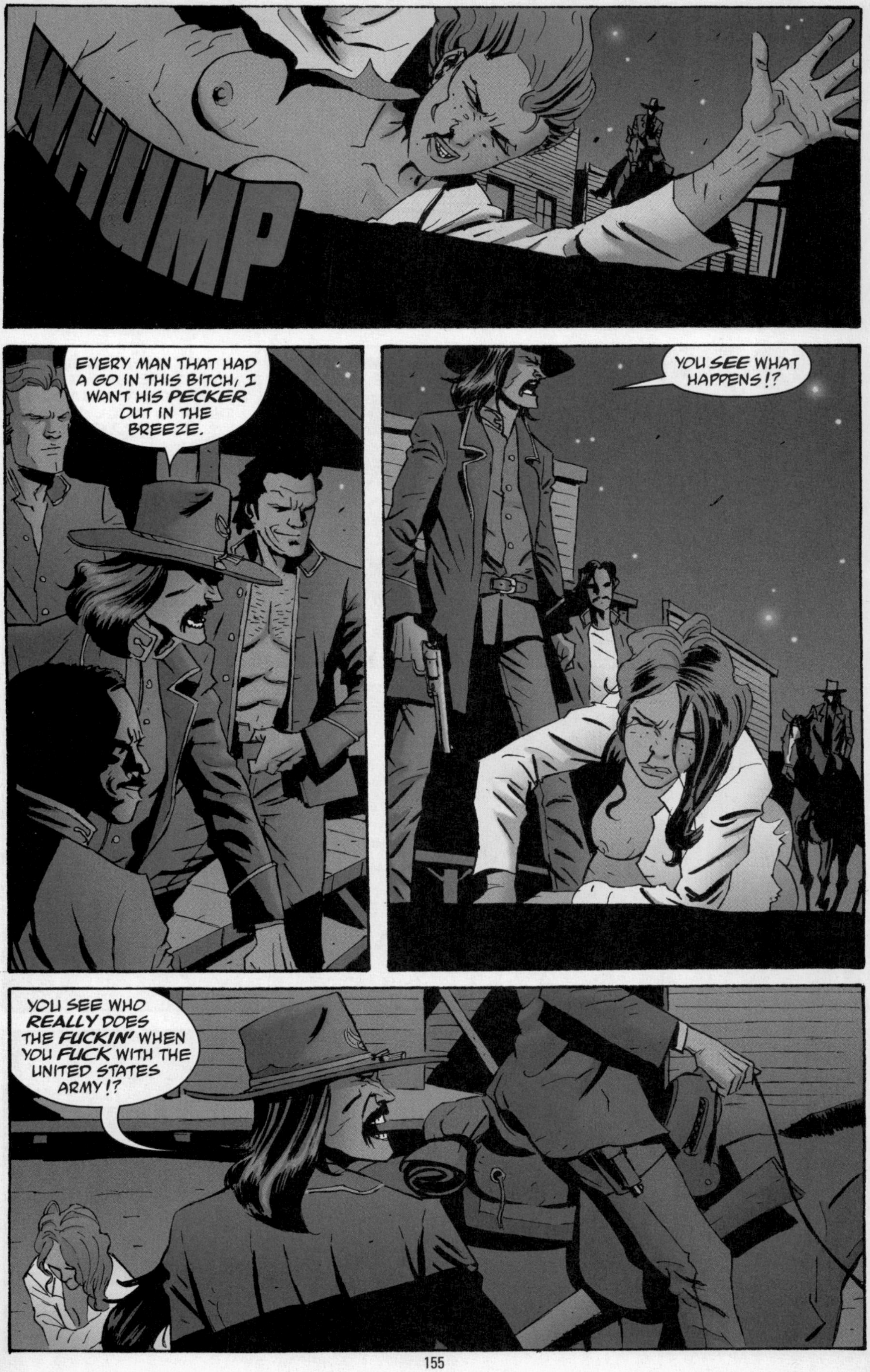
WHUMP
EVERY MAN THAT HAD A GO IN THIS BITCH, I WANT HIS PECKER OUT IN THE BREEZE.
YOU SEE WHAT HAPPENS!?
YOU SEE WHO REALLY DOES THE FUCKIN' WHEN YOU FUCK WITH THE UNITED STATES ARMY!?

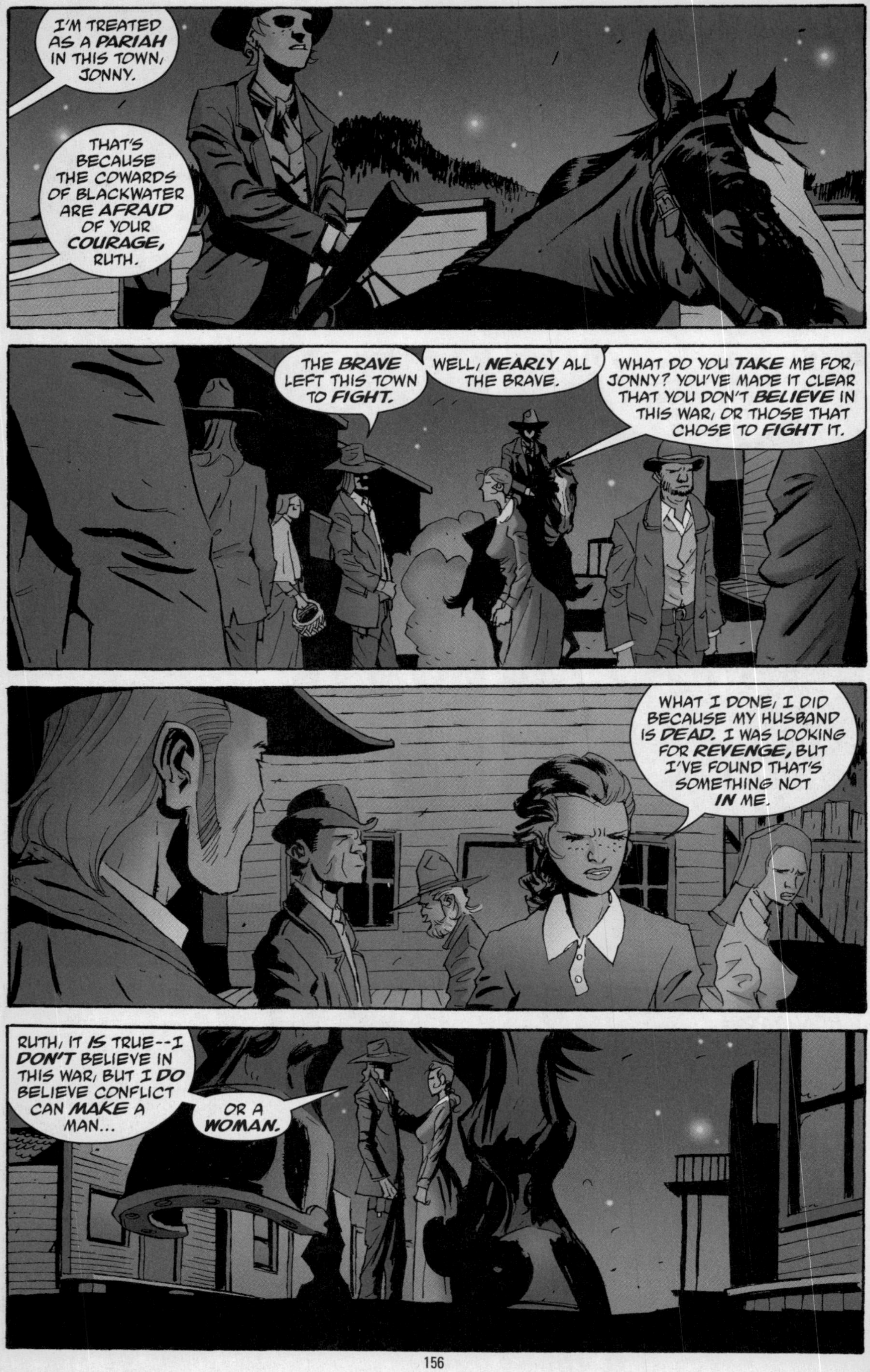
I'M TREATED AS A PARIAH IN THIS TOWN, JONNY.
THAT'S BECAUSE THE COWARDS OF BLACKWATER ARE AFRAID OF YOUR COURAGE, RUTH.
THE BRAVE LEFT THIS TOWN TO FIGHT.
WELL, NEARLY ALL THE BRAVE.
WHAT DO YOU TAKE ME FOR, JONNY? YOU'VE MADE IT CLEAR THAT YOU DON'T BELIEVE IN THIS WAR, OR THOSE THAT CHOSE TO FIGHT IT.
WHAT I DONE, I DID BECAUSE MY HUSBAND IS DEAD. I WAS LOOKING FOR REVENGE, BUT I'VE FOUND THAT'S SOMETHING NOT IN ME.
RUTH, IT IS TRUE--I DON'T BELIEVE IN THIS WAR, BUT I DO BELIEVE CONFLICT CAN MAKE A MAN...
OR A WOMAN.

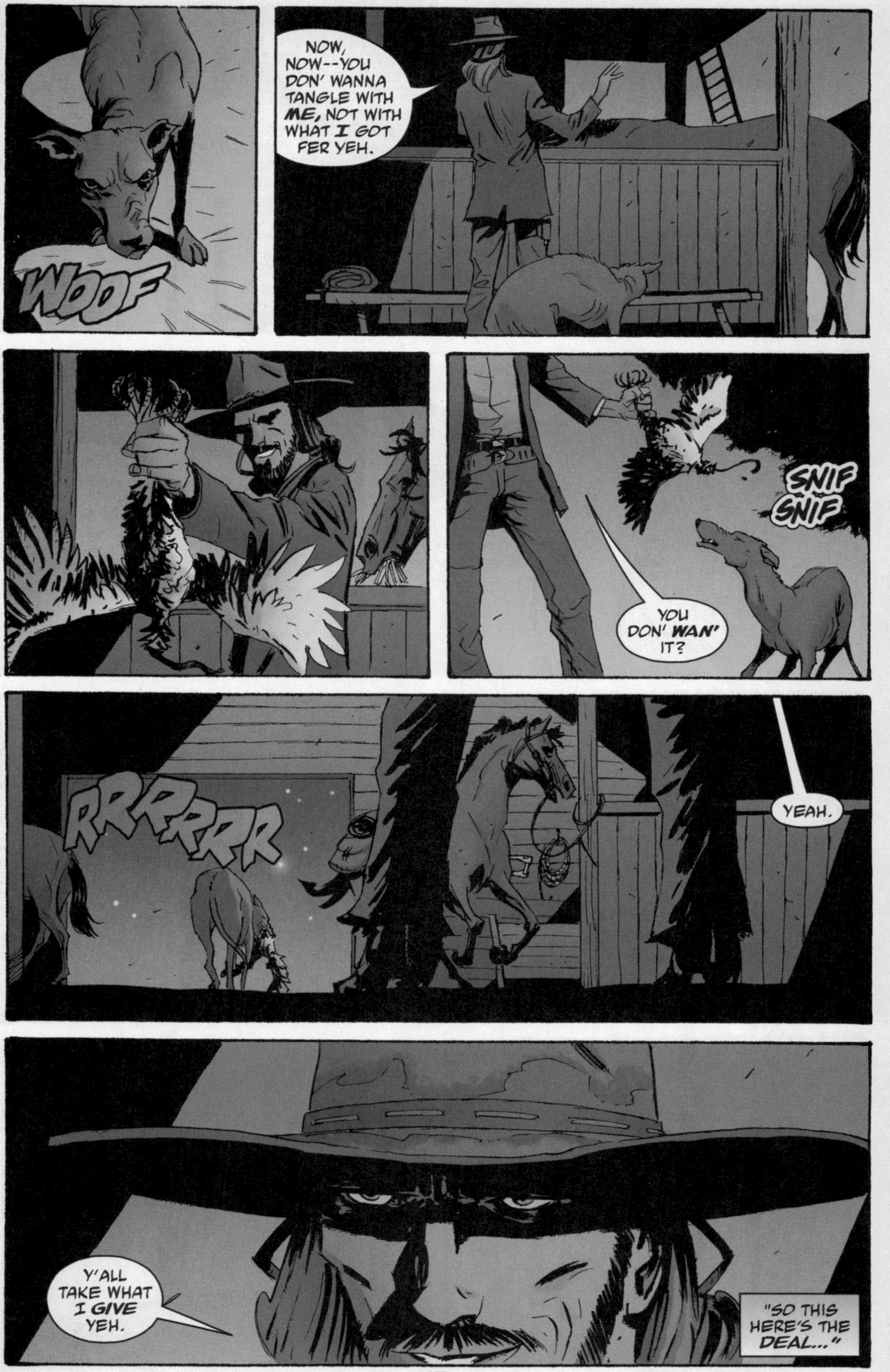
WOOF
NOW, NOW--YOU DON' WANNA TANGLE WITH ***ME***, NOT WITH WHAT ***I*** GOT FER YEH.
SNIF SNIF
YOU DON' ***WAN'*** IT?
RRRRRR
YEAH.
Y'ALL TAKE WHAT ***I GIVE*** YEH.
"SO THIS HERE'S THE ***DEAL...***"

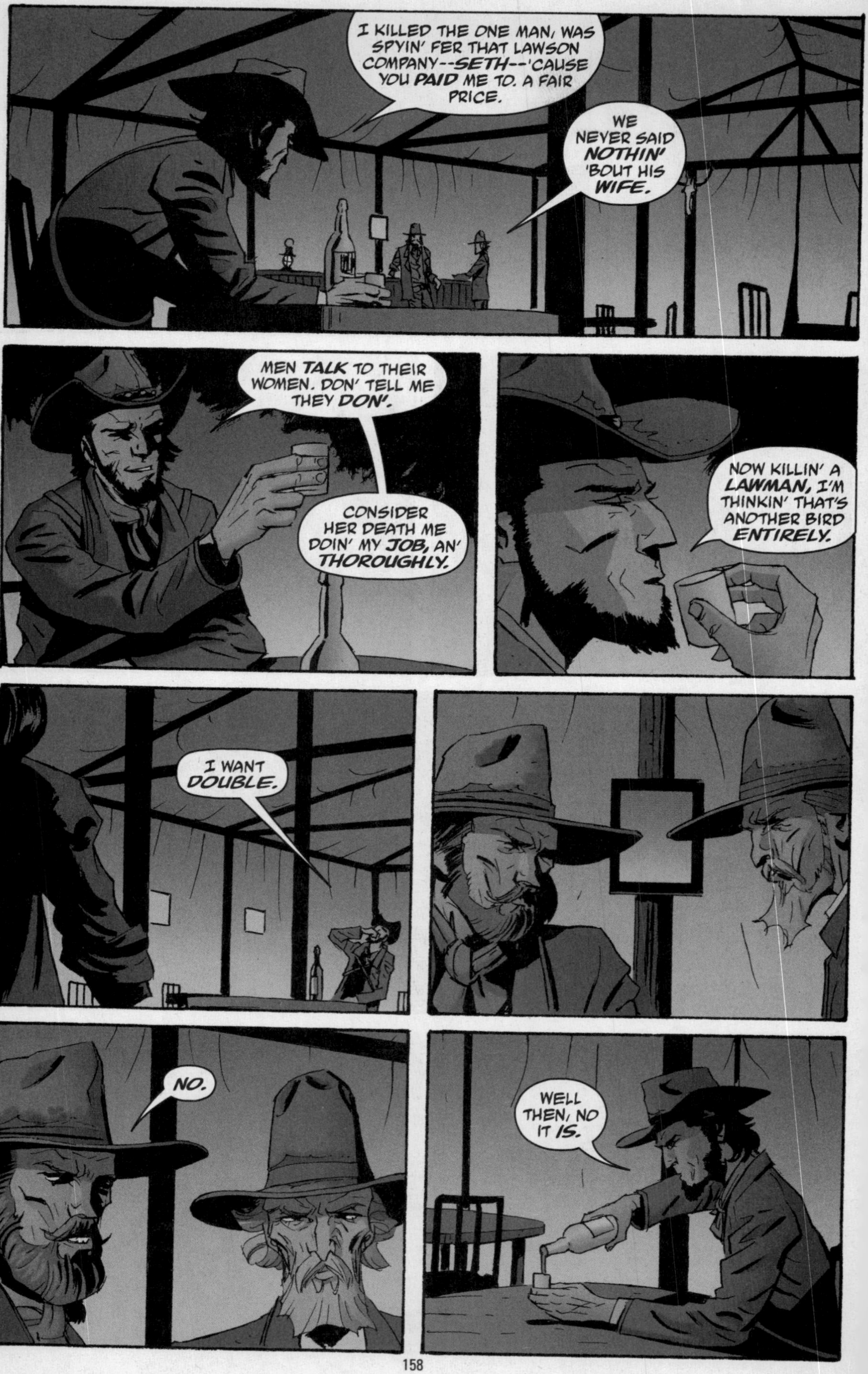
I KILLED THE ONE MAN, WAS SPYIN' FER THAT LAWSON COMPANY--SETH--'CAUSE YOU PAID ME TO. A FAIR PRICE.
WE NEVER SAID NOTHIN' 'BOUT HIS WIFE.
MEN TALK TO THEIR WOMEN. DON' TELL ME THEY DON'.
CONSIDER HER DEATH ME DOIN' MY JOB, AN' THOROUGHLY.
NOW KILLIN' A LAWMAN, I'M THINKIN' THAT'S ANOTHER BIRD ENTIRELY.
I WANT DOUBLE.
NO.
WELL THEN, NO IT IS.

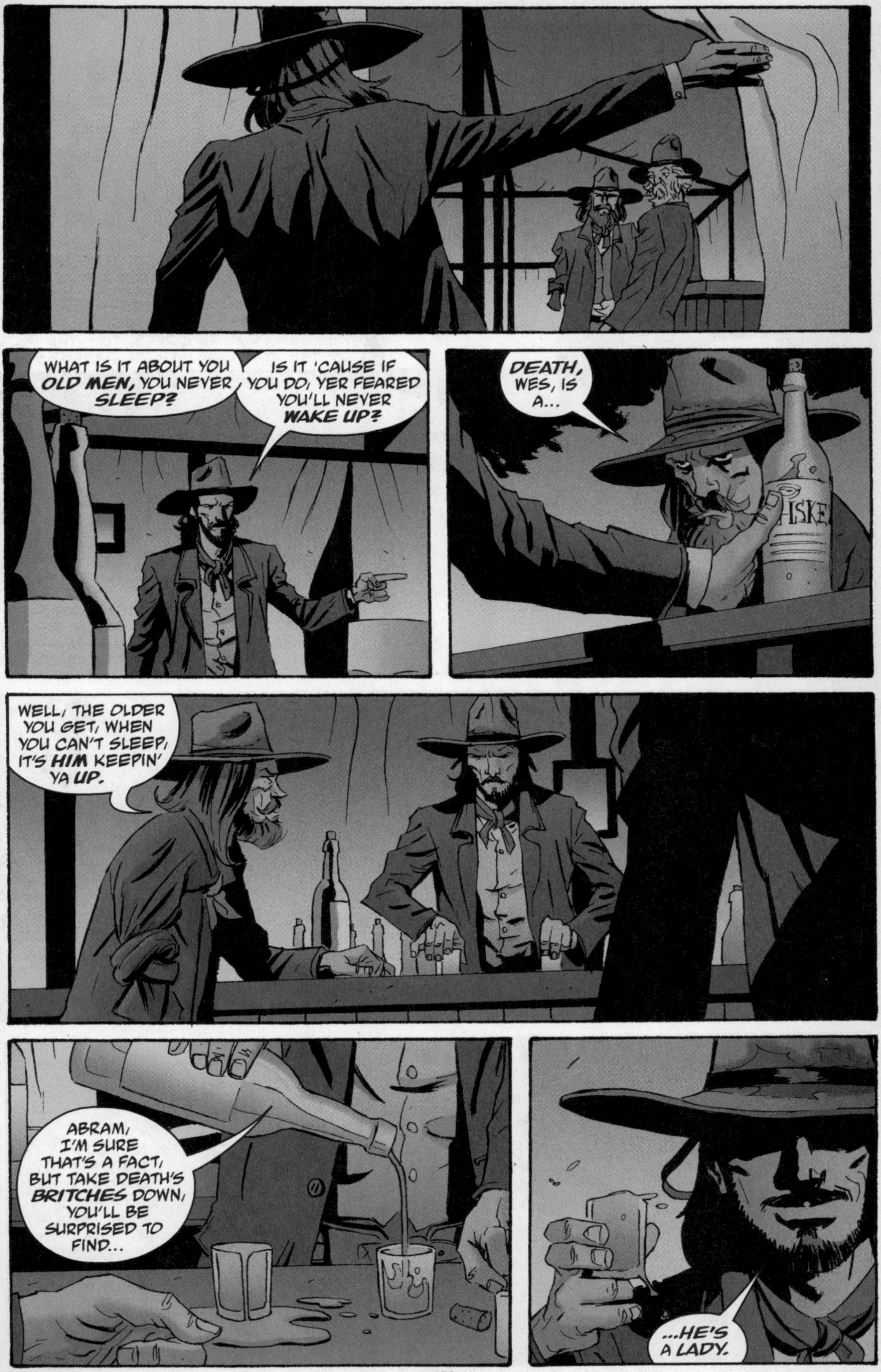
WHAT IS IT ABOUT YOU OLD MEN, YOU NEVER SLEEP?
IS IT 'CAUSE IF YOU DO, YER FEARED YOU'LL NEVER WAKE UP?
DEATH, WES, IS A...
WELL, THE OLDER YOU GET, WHEN YOU CAN'T SLEEP, IT'S HIM KEEPIN' YA UP.
ABRAM, I'M SURE THAT'S A FACT, BUT TAKE DEATH'S BRITCHES DOWN, YOU'LL BE SURPRISED TO FIND...
...HE'S A LADY.

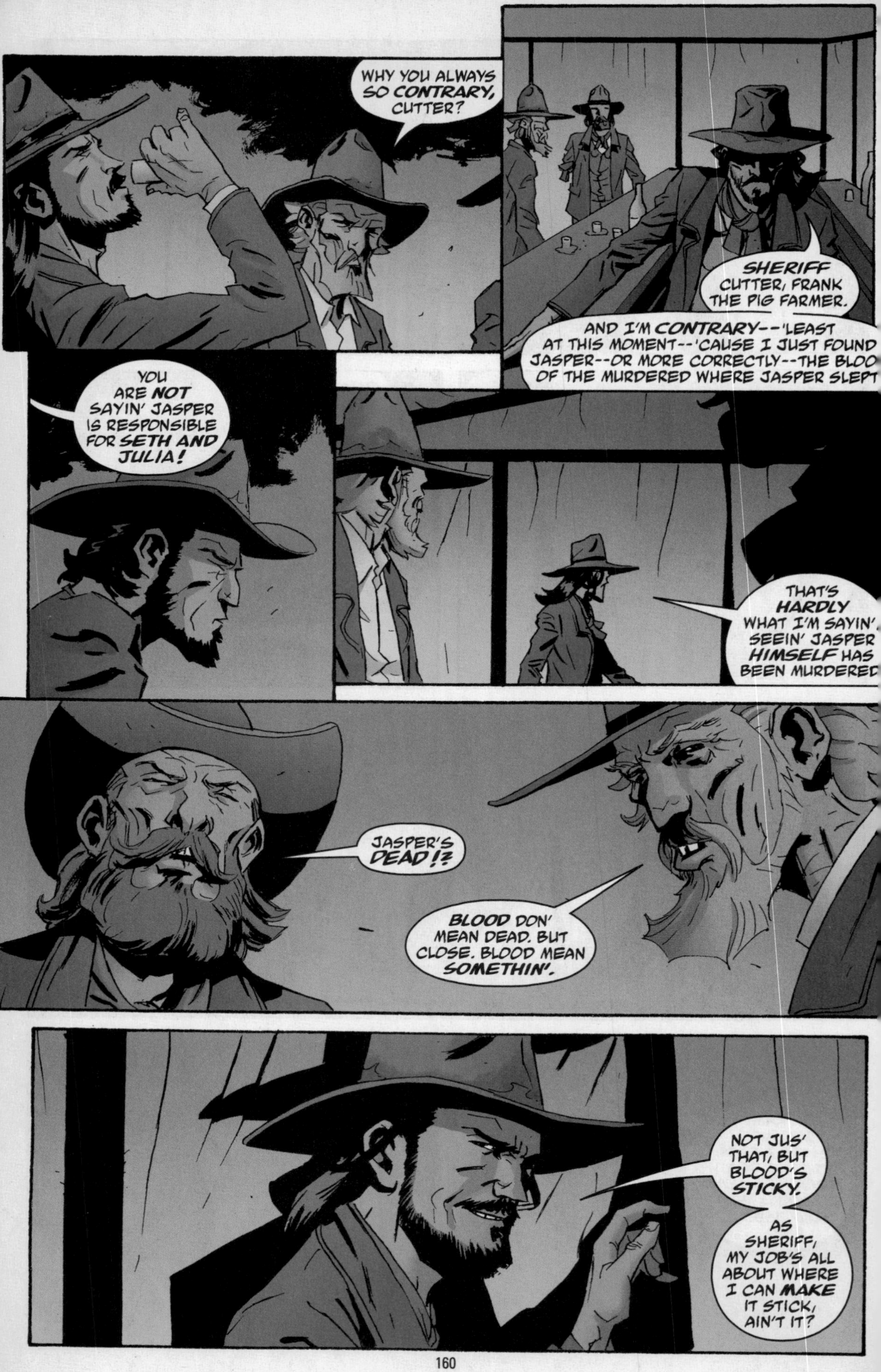
WHY YOU ALWAYS SO CONTRARY, CUTTER?
SHERIFF CUTTER, FRANK THE PIG FARMER.
AND I'M CONTRARY--'LEAST AT THIS MOMENT--'CAUSE I JUST FOUND JASPER--OR MORE CORRECTLY--THE BLOO OF THE MURDERED WHERE JASPER SLEPT
YOU ARE NOT SAYIN' JASPER IS RESPONSIBLE FOR SETH AND JULIA!
THAT'S HARDLY WHAT I'M SAYIN', SEEIN' JASPER HIMSELF HAS BEEN MURDERED
JASPER'S DEAD!?
BLOOD DON' MEAN DEAD. BUT CLOSE. BLOOD MEAN SOMETHIN'.
NOT JUS' THAT, BUT BLOOD'S STICKY.
AS SHERIFF, MY JOB'S ALL ABOUT WHERE I CAN MAKE IT STICK, AIN'T IT?

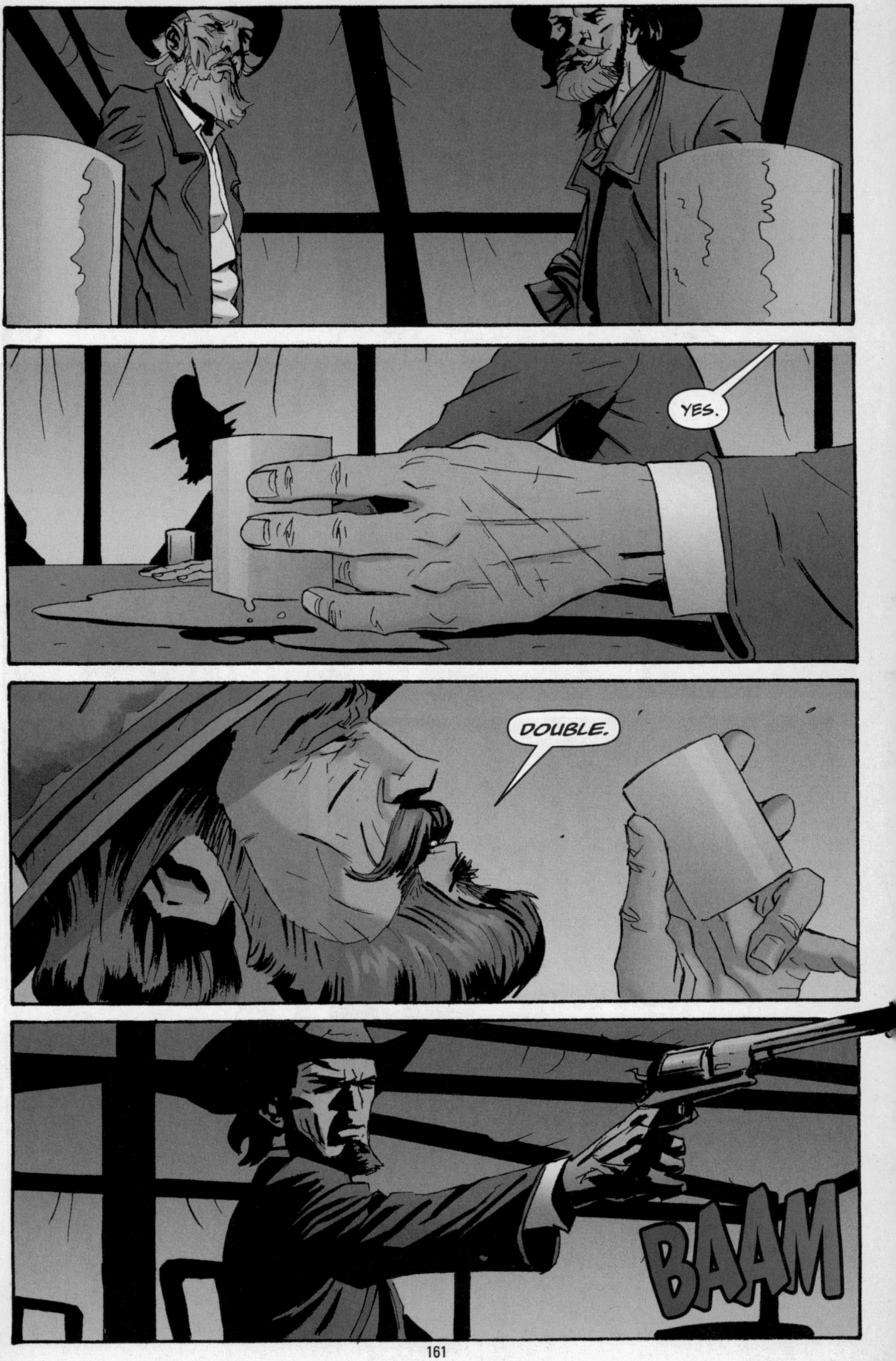
YES.
DOUBLE.
BAAM

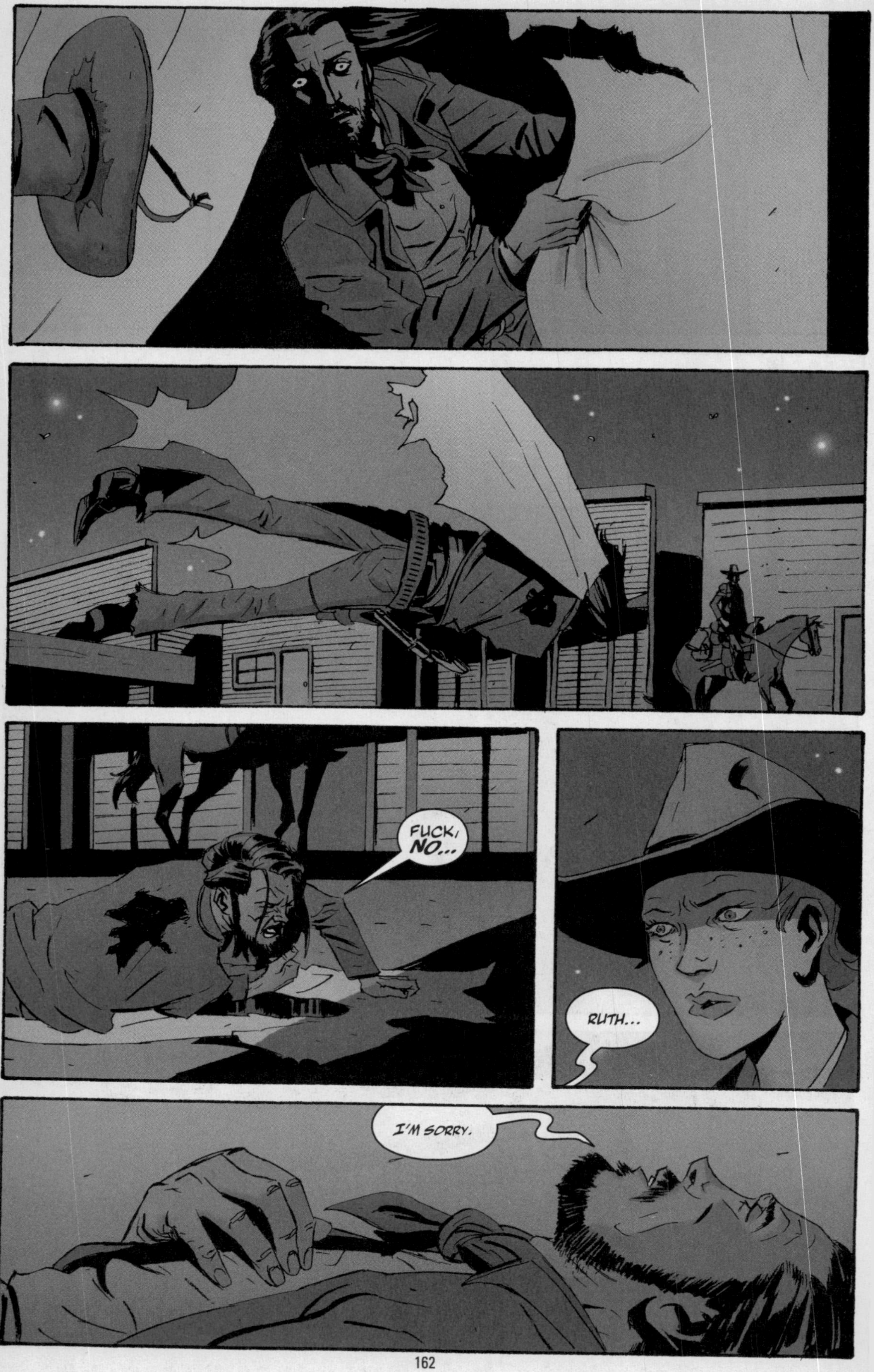
FUCK, NO...
RUTH...
I'M SORRY.

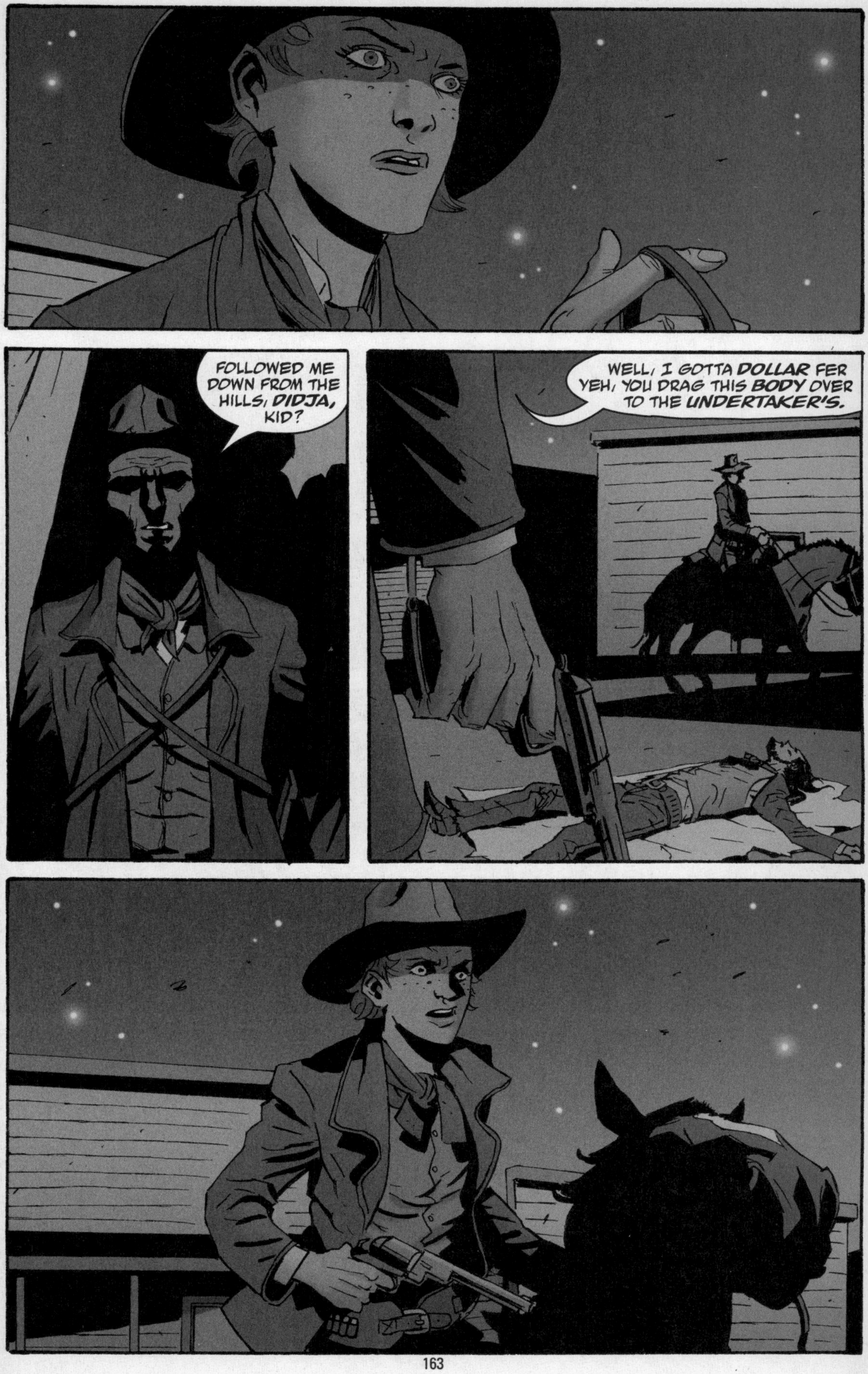

FOLLOWED ME DOWN FROM THE HILLS, DIDJA, KID?
WELL, I GOTTA DOLLAR FER YEH, YOU DRAG THIS BODY OVER TO THE UNDERTAKER'S.

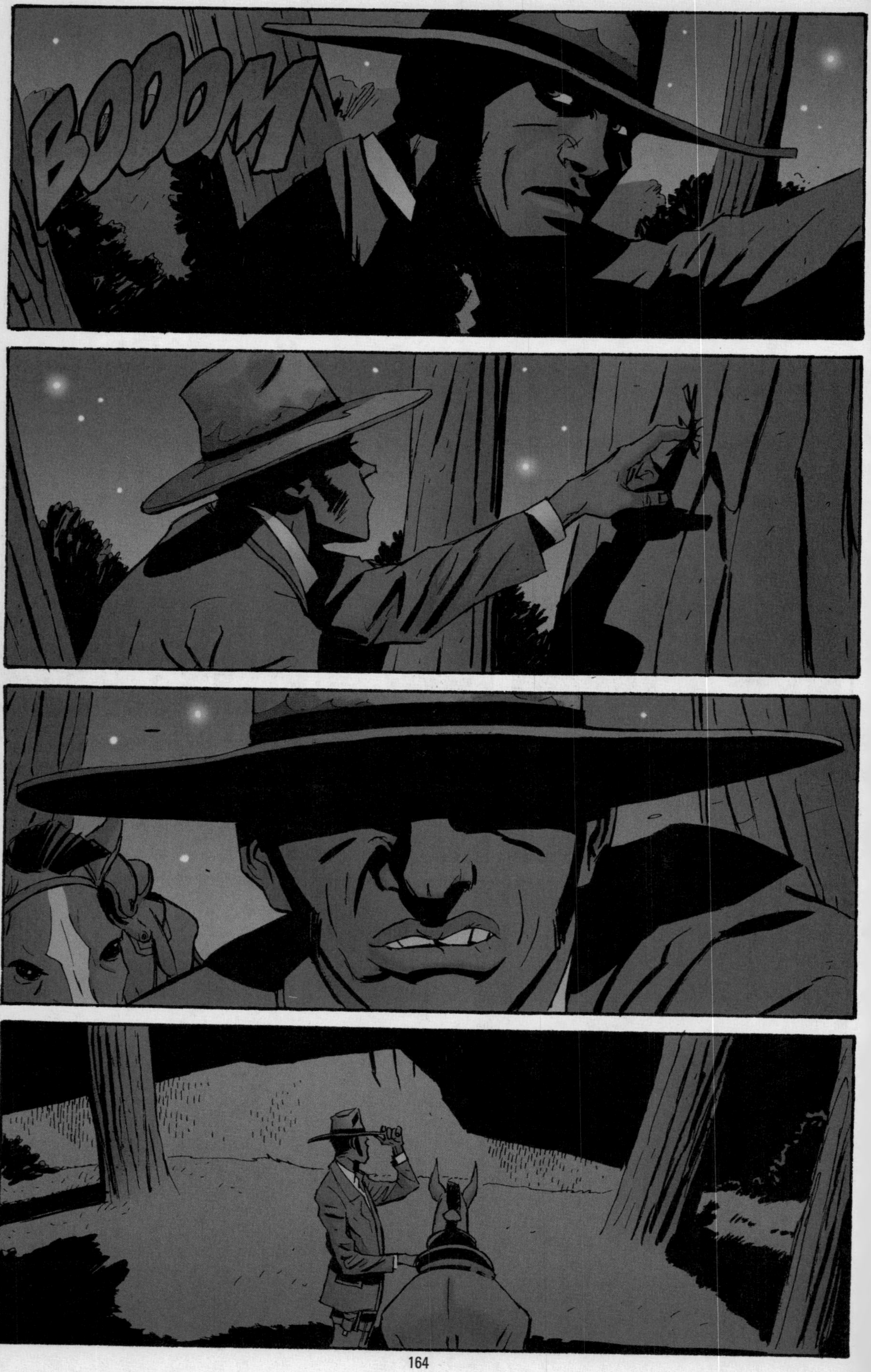
BOOOM

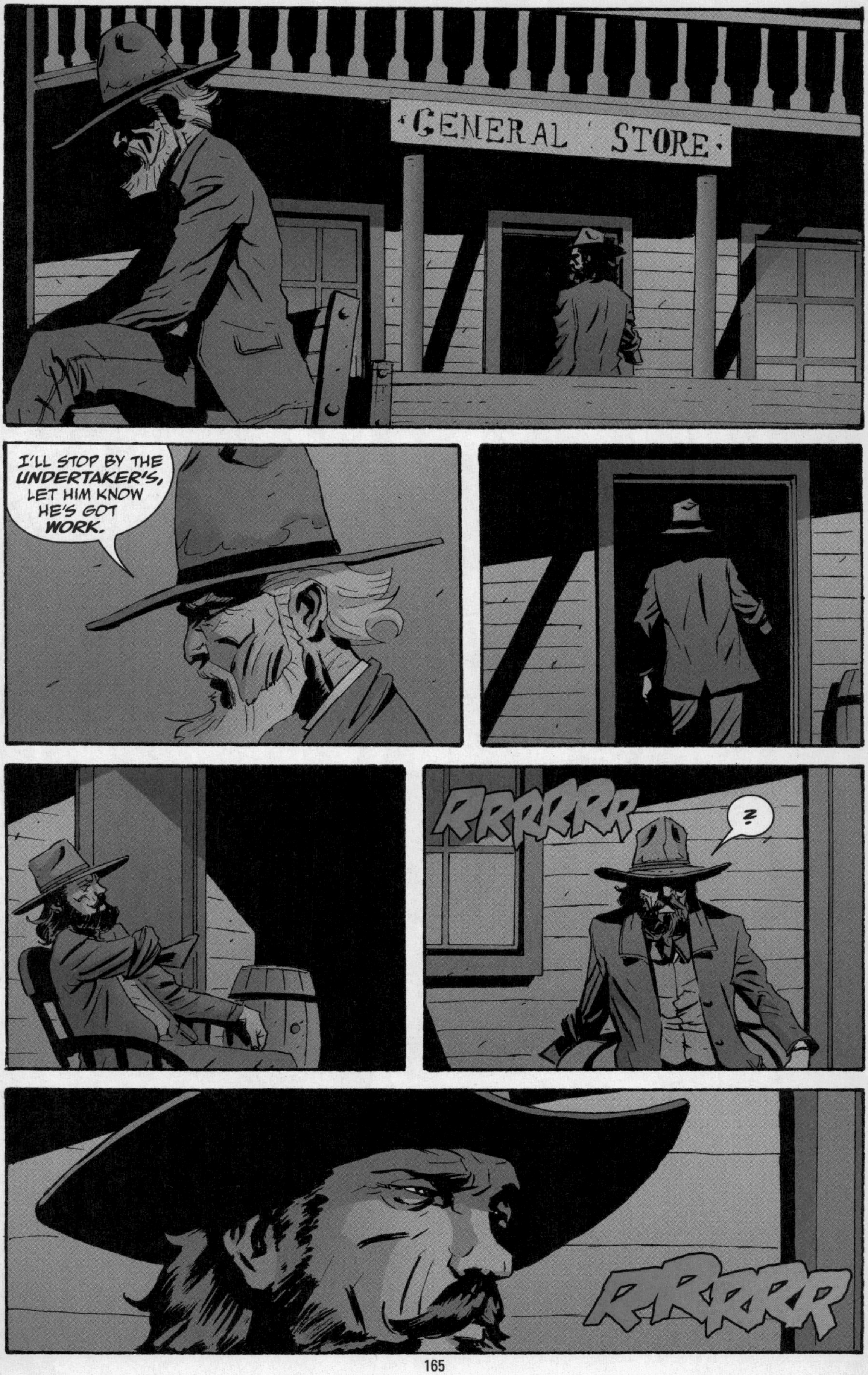
GENERAL STORE
I'LL STOP BY THE UNDERTAKER'S, LET HIM KNOW HE'S GOT WORK.
RRRRRR
?
RRRRR

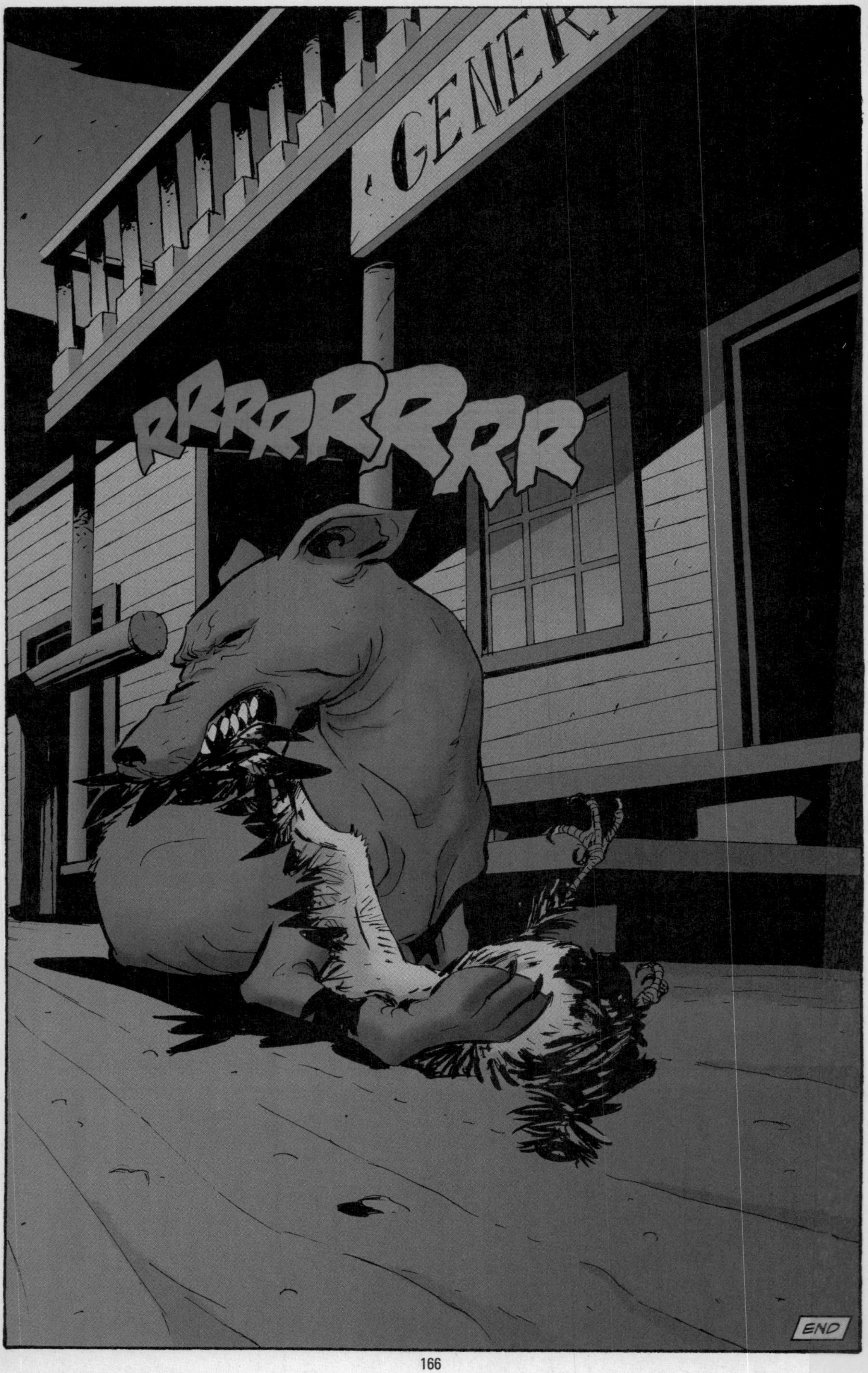
GENER
RRRRRRRRRR
END